To Samantha and Lillian

Accounting and F

Mana

Accounting and Financial Management

Developments in the International hospitality industry

Edited by

Peter Harris
and
Marco Mongiello

AMSTERDAM • BOSTON • HEIDELBERG • LONDON • NEW YORK • OXFORD
PARIS • SAN DIEGO • SAN FRANCISCO • SINGAPORE • SYDNEY • TOKYO
Butterworth-Heinemann is an imprint of Elsevier

Butterworth-Heinemann is an imprint of Elsevier
Linacre House, Jordan Hill, Oxford OX2 8DP
30 Corporate Drive, Suite 400, Burlington, MA 01803

First edition 2006

British Library Cataloguing in Publication Data
A catalogue record for this book is available from the British Library

Library of Congress Cataloguing in Publication Data
Control Number: 2005937837

ISBN–13: 978-0-7506-6729-6
ISBN–10: 0-7506-6729-X

For information on all Butterworth-Heinemann publications
visit our web site at http://books.elsevier.com

Typeset by Macmillan India, Bangalore
Printed and bound in Great Britain by MPG Books Ltd, Cornwall

06 07 08 09 10 11   10 9 8 7 6 5 4 3 2 1

Working together to grow
libraries in developing countries

www.elsevier.com | www.bookaid.org | www.sabre.org

ELSEVIER   BOOK AID
            International   Sabre Foundation

Contents

Contents

Foreword

As a senior executive of a fast growing hotel company in Europe, Middle East and Africa, with hotel operations in some fifty countries, I know how difficult it is to find the time to keep track of new research and development in the areas of accounting and financial management within our industry.

Accounting and Financial Management: Developments in the International Hospitality Industry edited by Peter Harris and Marco Mongiello is an effective and indispensable reference that helps me and others like me keep abreast of research and development in our industry. In addition, I believe this book is of invaluable importance to those studying at different levels of education, accountants in the hospitality business and advisors to the hospitality industry.

This book is not only made attractive by the range of international authors and the combination of well-written chapters, but also by the demonstration of how accounting and financial management interrelates and contributes to the broad spectrum of business activities. Written by industry mavens who have drawn on their practical experience from different areas of the hospitality industry and academic researchers, these chapters are recommended reading for anyone interested in the hospitality industry.

Part One of the book deals with performance measurement and includes six interesting chapters about various aspects of performance measurement in the hospitality industry. This section is loaded with useful information including benchmarking and measuring productivity in the restaurant industry. In my view, the hospitality business is well structured for benchmarking and for measuring financial success at all levels of operation. Part One of the book is a true goldmine of knowledge for those seeking advice on performance management and plenty of references for those wanting more information.

The focus of Part Two of the book is information management, a highly relevant subject for all of us. Most of us struggle with the Uniform System of Accounts and have been doing so for a very long time. This section of the book offers several solutions to overcome some of the fundamental weaknesses in the Uniform System and complements the accounting standard/chart of accounts in a meaningful and manageable way. Implementing some of these solutions in our operations is a must if we want to manage our organizations efficiently and effectively. For instance, drawing on the expertise of Peter Harris, we ourselves at Rezidor SAS Hospitality have engaged with marginal analysis and implemented *The Profit Planning Framework* in our organization, an indispensable tool that helps us understand the behaviour of fixed and variable costs in operations.

Asset Management is the theme of Part Three of the book which emphasizes a number of longer-term issues and techniques. The chapters in this section vary from sale and leaseback transactions, to investment appraisals and to career development for finance professionals in the industry. This information is highly pertinent and important to our business and for our professional growth.

The insight of the editors, Professor Peter Harris and Dr Marco Mongiello, together with the other contributors, makes this book a significant contribution that will influence the way we develop accounting and financial management in the hospitality industry in the future.

Knut Kleiven
Deputy President & Chief Financial Officer
Rezidor SAS Hospitality

Preface

The main purpose of this book is to present new and interesting research and developments in the field of accounting and financial management as they relate to the work of managing enterprises and organizations in the international hospitality industry. Although the focus is on hotels, the content can readily be interpreted in a broader context. Many hospitality organizations contain hotel services components such as the provision of rooms, food and beverage facilities and, therefore, the examples and illustrations can be related to restaurants, licensed house management, hospital and university services, clubs and so on.

The content comprises state-of-the-art contributions from a wide range of academics and practitioners engaged in hospitality activities around the globe including researchers, university lecturers, practising accountants, professional consultants and senior managers and executives associated with the international hospitality industry in the UK and abroad. The material is drawn from their work and experience and relates directly to the management of hospitality undertakings.

Most books written for the hospitality industry tend to concentrate on accounting and financial management techniques in a theoretical context. In contrast, this work presents new findings and developments drawn from a combination of live fieldwork, practical experience and academic research. In this context it is anticipated the readership will include: practising managers and financial controllers in hospitality organizations, professional accountants and consultants, postgraduate candidates researching for PhDs and studying for master's degrees in hospitality and tourism management, and final year undergraduate students of hospitality management who elect to take an accounting and finance option.

Notwithstanding the classification or grouping of the material presented here, the range of topics brings together a rich fund of knowledge and experience from contributors who operate internationally throughout the world, including Europe, North America and Australasia. Without their generosity and commitment to the sharing and dissemination of information a book of this kind would not be possible; a debt of gratitude is owed to them all. We are so proud to have them associated with this publication.

Acknowledgement is also due to a number of our colleagues for their support and tolerance throughout the preparation of the manuscript. Finally, thanks go to Sally North, Tim Goodfellow and Francesca Ford of Elsevier/Butterworth-Heinemann who, as usual, have been patient, considerate and supportive throughout.

Our single wish is that the reader finds this book to be of practical use.

Peter Harris and Marco Mongiello
August, 2005

Editors

Peter Harris is professor of accounting and financial management at Oxford Brookes University. He graduated from the University of Strathclyde and holds the HCIMA professional qualification and the Certified Diploma in Accounting and Finance. He trained and held managerial positions in the hospitality industry. Professor Harris is the author of numerous books and articles on applied accounting and is past Visiting Professor at the Institut de Management Hotelier International (Cornell University-ESSEC) Paris. Through his research into cost behaviour, profit planning techniques and performance measurement he undertakes consultancy assignments and conducts seminars in the UK and abroad for a number of leading national and international hotel organizations. He was recently presented with the British Association of Hospitality Accountants' Lifetime Achievement Award for his contribution to hospitality accounting education.

Dr Marco Mongiello is principal lecturer in financial and management accounting at the University of Westminster. He is a member of the Italian Institute of Chartered Accountants and obtained a PhD at Venice Ca' Foscari University with a thesis on performance measurement in the service sector. He has been teaching and researching at Venice Ca' Foscari and Oxford Brookes Universities and is currently leading the finance subject area at the Harrow Business School, University of Westminster; his research domain being 'management accounting' and 'management accounting applied to the hospitality and tourism fields'. Dr Mongiello also carries out editorial activities and consultancy assignments internationally.

Contributors

Tommy Andersson is professor of tourism management at Gothenburg University. He previously served as programme director at the European Tourism Research Institute in Sweden for 4 years and before that as professor in management accounting at Bodo Graduate School of Business in Norway. Dr Andersson's interest in tourism economics started in 1995. He then undertook an economic impact analysis of a Bruce Springsteen rock event. At the same time Dr Andersson started to teach hospitality accounting. Today he is programme director of a master programme in tourism and hospitality management taught at the School of Business, Economics and Law at Gothenburg University and is also responsible for a module in managerial economics. His main research interests are economic impact analysis, event management, management accounting in restaurants, and cost-benefit analysis. He has published books and journal articles and is on the editorial board for academic journals in tourism and hospitality.

Helen Atkinson is a principal lecturer at the school of service management in the University of Brighton. She has a background in hospitality management and is a qualified management accountant with CIMA. She has lectured, researched and published in the area of hospitality accounting since 1989 and is currently on the education committee of BAHA (the British Association of Hospitality Accountants). Her research interests include: strategic management accounting, performance management, strategy implementation in the hospitality and service industries, and approaches to budgeting in hotels. Journal publications include: Atkinson H and Brander Brown J (2001) Rethinking Performance Measures: Assessing Progress in UK Hotels, *International Journal of Contemporary Hospitality Management*, **13**(3): 128–135, Brander Brown J and Atkinson H (2001) Budgeting in the information age: a fresh approach, *International Journal of Contemporary Hospitality Management*, **13**(3): 136–143.

Paul Beals, PhD, is visiting professor at France's IMHI-ESSEC Business School, where he is responsible for MBA courses in finance and hotel real estate. For more than 25 years, Beals's academic research and consulting have been concentrated in hotel industry development and financing, asset management, and management contracts. He has taught hospitality financial management and real estate finance at Cornell University, Boston University, University of Denver, and Switzerland's Glion Hotel School. Beals's writings, primarily in the area of hotel finance and investments, have appeared in *The Cornell Quarterly, Journal of Real Estate Finance, Real Estate Review, Journal of Hospitality Financial Management, Journal of Retail and Leisure Property, L'Hôtel Revue,* and *Le Monde*. Beals is the lead editor of *Hotel Asset Management: Principles and Practices*. A member of Phi Beta Kappa and the Cornell Hotel Society, Beals earned master's and doctorate degrees from Cornell University.

Cathy Burgess qualified in hospitality management at Leeds Polytechnic (now Leeds Metropolitan University) and then spent thirteen years in various operational and financial management positions within the hotel and catering industry. Her later appointments were as a financial controller with Marriott Corporation and Thistle Hotels. In 1989 she was appointed senior lecturer in accounting at Oxford Brookes University, teaching financial management to degree and master's level students, and gained her MPhil in 1993. She maintains close links with industry through research and consultancy and as a council member and membership officer of the British Association of Hospitality Accountants, for which she has been elected an honorary fellow. Her current research interests include the role and professional development of the hospitality financial manager.

Paolo Collini is full professor of management accounting and strategic management at the University of Trento (Italy). From 1993 to 1998 he was assistant professor in management at the University of Venezia (Italy). He holds an MBA from Boston University and a PhD in management and economics from University of Venezia. He is a certified public accountant. Professor Collini's main research interests focus on cost management and control with a strong attention to the relationship between decision-making and cost information in complex organizations. He is the author of books and articles in the field of management control and accounting. He is associate dean of the Faculty of Economics at the University of Trento and member of the scientific committee of CUOA Business School.

Professor **Agnes Lee DeFranco** began her teaching career in 1988, specializing in hospitality accounting, finance, cost control, and purchasing courses. Her formal education includes a Bachelor of Science in hotel and restaurant management, a Master in Business Administration with a concentration in finance, and a Doctorate in education in higher education administration. She has been a recipient of both teaching and research awards and is active in a number of local, state, national and international organizations. She currently serves as the vice president of the 'Hospitality Financial and Technology Professionals'. She is active with I-CHRIE in their finance committee and future fund committee and was their treasurer from 1999 to 2002. From 1999 to 2003, she also carried an administrative role as the associate dean and subsequently the interim dean of the Conrad N. Hilton College. Her research areas are hospitality finance, cost control, accounting, and cultural and diversity issues.

Howard Field, chartered accountant, fellow of Hotel & Catering International Management Association, honorary fellow of British Association of Hospitality Accountants (founder member and served on the council and on various committees), honorary Fellow of Hotel Controllers Association (Hong Kong), visiting fellow at Oxford Brookes University, founded FM Recruitment in 1985, specializing in financial, IT and purchasing management, and professional consultancy appointments within the hospitality sector. He is non-executive director of Airport Hotels General Partner, Arena4Finance, and Hotel Investment Advisors. Prior career spans unit, divisional and corporate financial management positions with UK and international hotel groups and in professional consultancy.

Ian Graham is managing director of The Hotel Solutions Partnership Ltd, a consultancy that works with international hotel companies to unlock strategic advantage. Ian was formerly a director in the travel, tourism and leisure practice of Andersen/Deloitte & Touche. Prior to joining Andersen/Deloitte & Touche in 1999, Ian held a variety of senior executive positions in the hotel industry in the Europe, Middle East and Africa region, principally with Bass Hotels & Resorts and prior to that with ITT Sheraton. Ian is a graduate of the University of Surrey's department of hotel and catering management. He is a fellow of the Institute of Chartered Accountants of England and Wales, and a member of the International Society of Hospitality Consultants. He has been a visiting fellow at Oxford Brookes University for eight years and is a non-executive director of the leading hospitality charity Springboard UK Ltd.

Professor **Zheng Gu** holds a BS degree in economics, an MA in applied economics and a PhD in finance. He teaches hospitality finance and quantitative methods at both graduate and undergraduate levels. His research and consultancy focus on financial management and operations analysis for the hospitality and tourism industries. Professor Gu was the president of the Association of Hospitality Financial Education (AHFME) in the USA from 1999 to 2000. He is the editor of *UNLV Journal* of *Hospitality, Tourism and Leisure Science (HTL Science)* and guest editor, associate editor, consulting editor or editorial board member of six other hospitality/tourism research journals. Professor Gu has more than 100 articles published in academic and professional journals. He has served as editor, section editor, author, co-author, or chapter author of many books. Dr Gu has received numerous awards for his research achievements in hospitality management.

Professor **Chris Guilding** works with Griffith University's department of tourism, leisure, hotel and sport management and is also director of Griffith's Service Industry Research Centre. He is a member of the Chartered Institute of Management Accountants and has taught accounting and finance in universities in Australia, Canada, England and New Zealand. Chris has more than 30 publications and papers in refereed journals that include: *Journal of Hospitality & Tourism Research; Tourism Management; Accounting, Organizations and Society; Business Horizons; British Journal of Management and Journal of Marketing Management*. In recent years, he has developed a specific interest in accounting for tourism and hospitality issues. In 2002 his book *Financial Management for Hospitality Decision Makers* was published by Butterworth-Heinemann. In 2005 he acted as chairperson for the 'Strata and Community title in Australia for the 21st Century' conference.

Mine Haktanir is a lecturer in accounting and financial management in the School of tourism and hospitality management at Eastern Mediterranean University, Turkish Republic of Northern Cyprus. She completed her PhD in performance measurement in independent hotels at Oxford Brookes University. She teaches management accounting and financial management courses both at undergraduate and postgraduate levels within the school. She is the programme coordinator of the Master's degree in tourism management and has responsibilities in coordinating the curricular activities of the school. She was the assistant director of the school and has experience in managing the university restaurant for a number of years. Her research interests include understanding the performance measurement practices in small service businesses and in independent hotels. She has attended both local and international conferences and published articles on hospitality performance measurement.

Dr **Rebecca Hawkins** is a freelance consultant offering specialist tourism and consultancy services to the tourism sector. She is also currently the research and consultancy fellow within the department of hospitality, leisure and tourism management at Oxford Brookes University. During her career, Rebecca has written many of the reports that have formed the response of the tourism sector to sustainable development issues. These include the WTTC, WTO and Earth Council interpretation of Agenda 21 into an action plan for the sector, the analysis by WWF of the effectiveness of tourism certification schemes, an assessment of the data required to benchmark the sustainable development credentials of hotels and higher education institutions and the development of tourism strategies for a range of international organizations. Rebecca is currently a principal of the 'hospitable climates energy management programme', and advisor to the Considerate Hoteliers Association, a key consultant on a programme to improve the amount of glass recycled from hospitality businesses in the UK. She is also working with TravelWatch on a project funded by the Travel Foundation to assess the relative local economic benefits of different types of accommodation in the Eastern Caribbean.

Pekka Heikkilä has been lecturer in business accounting at Haaga Institute Polytechnic for 12 years. He was recognized as Certified HTM-Auditor (Finland) in 1993 and has completed Certification in managerial accounting and finance in the School of hotel administration in Cornell University, New York (1997). Before the position in Haaga Institute he has worked permanently in Ernst & Young auditing in northern Finland where most of the customers were local tourism operators. Currently he performs consulting and auditing in addition to teaching work. He is also writing (with Timo Saranpää) a guide book of business accounting for the Finnish Hotel and Restaurant Association.

Tracy Jones is principal lecturer in accounting in the Department of Hospitality, Leisure and Sports Management at Cheltenham and Gloucestershire University, UK. She worked in various sectors of the hospitality industry before joining Oxford Polytechnic (now Oxford Brookes University) to complete the HCIMA professional qualification, being awarded the Greene Belfield-Smith Award for achieving the highest marks nationally in the financial management examination. She remained at Oxford, completing a BSc (Hons) in hotel and catering management and an MPhil for her research into the financial and operating needs of managers in hotel companies. Her main teaching areas are finance and accounting within the hospitality programmes and she is currently in the process of researching hotel budgeting practices in the UK for a PhD. She has published her work in a number of journals and books.

Vira Krakhmal obtained a Bachelor's degree in business and economics from Kiev State University, Ukraine and a Master's degree in international hotel and tourism management at Oxford Brookes University. Since graduating, she has gained wide experience working as a research analyst at HVS International, a hotel valuation consultancy. Vira is currently completing her PhD research project in the area of customer profitability analysis in hotels, the findings of which are planned to be disseminated to the industry in the form of a *BAHA Recommended Practice Guide*. The project involved her working closely with a number of major international hotel groups that participated in, and sponsored, the project.

Dawne Lamminmaki is a lecturer in accounting at the Graduate School of Management at Griffith University. Dawne is a member of the Certified Management Accountants of Canada and has worked and studied in Canada, England, New Zealand and Australia. She has been in academia for over ten years, seven of which were with the school of accounting and finance at Griffith University. Dawne's research interests are in the area of management accounting, and she has conducted research in the areas of capital budgeting, trade credit management, management accounting systems, and outsourcing. More recently, her research interests have been in the area of hospitality. In September 2003 she graduated with her PhD which looked at outsourcing in the hotel industry. Publications in refereed journals include: *International Journal of Contemporary Hospitality Management, Journal of Business Finance & Accounting, Australian Accounting Review, International Journal of Accounting and Pacific Accounting Review.*

For over 30 years, **Geoff Parkinson** has specialized in the international hotel markets of the UK, Europe and the Middle East. Prior to establishing HiA, he was the managing director of a number of international hospitality consulting firms including Horwath UK,

BDO, Christie Consulting and Hospitality Consulting International. Working for and with many of the world's leading hotel operating groups, investors and financial institutions, he has advised on acquisitions and disposals, formulated and implemented expansion and repositioning strategies, researched, benchmarked and implemented profit improvement plans, carried out operational reviews, competitive market assessments, feasibility and investment viability studies. He has a particular expertise in the negotiation of key commercial clauses within operational leases and management agreements. HiA works as the owner's representative and hotel asset managers for major investors providing hotel sector experience and knowledge and ensuring their relationship with hotel operators is equitable and to the owners advantage.

Timo Saranpää has worked in the restaurant business as an entrepreneur and a manager for 15 years. He has built up a catering chain based on an idea of a partial entrepreneurship and ownership. He sold the company to ISS Finland (part of the ISS Group, Denmark) at the beginning of 2004. While working as a restaurant entrepreneur he has also been conducting lecturing and consulting business in the hospitality industry and in the municipal sector. He has also participated in writing two books in accounting for the restaurant business, one being an official guide book of business accounting for the Finnish hotel and restaurant industry – currently under preparation with Pekka Heikkilä. Mr Saranpää is preparing his doctoral thesis on the subject of entrepreneurship in municipal services.

Jean-Pierre van der Rest is lecturer in business economics and strategic marketing at Leiden University, The Netherlands. He received his Bachelor in Business Administration in hotel administration from the Maastricht hotel management school, and his MA in managerial economics from the University of Durham. Prior to joining Leiden University in 2002, he was lecturer in business administration at The Hague University of professional education. He has been a visiting lecturer in finance at the International Hotel Management Institute Switzerland, and the Maastricht hotel management school. He has written two book chapters on pricing, a number of entries for the Elsevier Butterworth-Heinemann International Encyclopedia of Hospitality Management, and contributed several articles to professional journals. He specializes in theoretical and applied pricing theory. His teaching interests include management accounting, strategic marketing and business methodology.

Charles Whittaker began his career in the hospitality industry as Controller of the 400-room Lisbon Sheraton in Portugal and then was promoted to vice-president and divisional controller for Europe, Africa and Middle East, based in Brussels. He later held the post of director of finance and development with Scott's Hospitality, a major franchisee of Holiday Inn and Marriott. Charles subsequently worked for Hilton International as finance director for 40 hotels in Europe. In the above roles his responsibilities included accounting, finance, IT and legal matters and the negotiation, acquisition, disposal and construction of major hotels in the UK and overseas. Academically, Charles is a fellow of the Institute of Chartered Accountants, holds an honours degree in economics from Sheffield University, a first class honours degree in Arts from the Open University, and an MA in English Studies with distinction at Oxford Brookes University.

Performance Management

This part of the book opens with two reviews of performance measurement literature and practices in the hospitality industry; the first refers to the independent hotels, chapter 1, and the second embraces the broader range of productivity measures, chapter 2. The first two chapters serve as an introduction to the core topic of performance management, which is subsequently addressed in a strategic perspective and with reference to traditional and more innovative performance management techniques. The strategic perspective is presented in chapter 3, where an extensive literature review comprises contributions from the generic and the hospitality industry literature. Evidence of the use of budgeting as a traditional technique of performance management is then provided in chapter 4, while the last two chapters introduce theoretical reflections on benchmarking in the hospitality industry, chapter 5, and propose an innovative performance management methodology, corroborated by first evidence of application, chapter 6.

1 Performance measurement in independent hotels

2 Productivity in the restaurant industry: how to measure productivity and improve process management

3 Performance management in the international hospitality industry

4 Budgetary practice within hospitality

5 Benchmarking: measuring financial success in the hotel industry

6 Developing a benchmarking methodology for the hotel industry

Performance measurement in independent hotels

Mine Haktanir

Introduction

Performance measurement is an important component of decision-making processes. As the overall objective of all forms of organization is to provide satisfaction for their stakeholders, developing appropriate performance measures and interpreting the outcomes are vital issues. With the growth in international travel and therefore, increasing demand in hospitality businesses, performance measurement in the hospitality industry has gained particular importance as a tool for effective decision-making.

Accounting information systems provide formal means of gathering data to support and coordinate the decision-making of businesses in light of overall organizational goals. Although profitability is the most commonly used basis for defining success, other measures, including cost, revenue and asset and liability accounts, are utilized. The comparison of budgeted and actual results is recognized as forming the basis for evaluating overall performance and helping to monitor and control operations. In hospitality businesses, ratios, which facilitate benchmarking, are commonly used.

However, these traditional performance measures have been heavily criticized for encouraging short termism, lacking strategic focus, discouraging continuous improvement and for not being externally focused. In an attempt to overcome these criticisms, performance measurement frameworks have been developed, primarily to encourage a more balanced view. For example, Lynch and Cross (1991) described a pyramid of measures which integrates performance through the hierarchy of the organization. Fitzgerald et al. (1991) distinguished between the results and their determinants. Kaplan and Norton (1992) use the four perspectives of the balanced scorecard (BSC).

Although a number of studies (see Bolton, 1971; Stanworth and Gray, 1991; Jarvis et al., 2000; Marriott and Marriott, 2000) have explored the way performance measurement is perceived and employed in independently owned businesses, there appears to be insufficient detailed research into actual performance measurement practices of such organizations. When hotel businesses are considered, independently owned and managed hotels are considered as the traditional model of hotel operations and understanding the operational characteristics of hotel provision begins with them (Jones and Lockwood, 1989). They are a dominant feature of the hotel industry in many countries and the majority of establishments are independently owned and operated (Morrison, 1998). In contrast to this, they have received limited attention from researchers (Shaw and Willams, 1994; Main, 1995) where group hotels have been the core of research in the management control and performance measurement literature. With increasing pressure from customer expectations and growing competition, independent hotels must start to develop effective performance measurement systems in a strategic context. In particular, they require accurate information in terms of sales and costs for an effective decision-making mechanism (Adams, 1997). Objective financial data are not publicly available and access to performance data is severely restricted for independent, privately held companies (Jogaratnam et al., 1999). Therefore, this chapter largely focuses on the research that has been carried out on performance measurement in independent hotels.

Defining performance measurement

The term 'performance measurement' has been in existence for a long time as an important component of the decision-making process, yet it only gained popularity in 1990s, particularly in the development of new management accounting techniques.

Among the many definitions, one suggests performance measurement is '... the process of quantifying actions, where measurement is the process of quantification and action leads to performance' (Neely et al., 1995:80). There is a range of reasons for utilizing performance measures, including:

- to indicate where more or less effort is required

- to monitor activities in units and/or divisions and through time for diagnosing problems and taking corrective actions

- to carry out planning, monitoring and control functions. Performance measures provide a realistic basis from which to construct plans

- to facilitate continuous improvement in key areas and to promote behaviour in ways that would help sustain competitive advantage

- to support improvements in resource allocation and better decision-making

- to specify responsibilities and to reinforce the accountability of employees and managers and, in particular, to detect inefficiencies with the help of management accounting information

- to provide regular information for staff appraisal, motivation and rewarding. Performance measurement is perceived as one means of motivating people towards achieving organizational goals.

Although there are several reasons for utilization of performance measures, overall it is considered to be an integral part of the management processes, to identify areas of poor performance or opportunities so that better plans can be developed.

Financial measures of performance

Information regarding end results of operations is provided by financial performance measures and there is evidence that, in many countries, financial performance measures are of primary importance. Accounting information systems provide a formal means of gathering data to support and coordinate the decision-making of businesses in light of overall organizational goals. They 'provide quantitative and common yardsticks to evaluate achievement relative to a plan or to compare parts of the company' (Emmanuel et al., 1990:222).

Profitability is the most commonly used basis for defining success, such that it is used in the lead tables of performances in *Business Week*, *Management Today* and similar journals. Profit sometimes is an absolute measure but more often is a ratio, such as earning per share, return on investment or return on shareholders' funds, and is presented as a comparison with other companies over a period of time. Traditionally, businesses have relied upon accounting information, such as cost, revenue and asset and liability accounts, in order to explain the cause and effect relationship that determines the financial outcome of the operations. In recent years, responsibility accounting that provides financial information and forms the basis for the performance measurement and management control system in many organizations is recognized as a key to management control systems.

Budgets have consistently proved to be an important financial tool to represent a standard for effectiveness and efficiency measures. Performance reports are a common means of providing the key financial budgeted and actual information for each responsibility centre in order to control the organizations' operations effectively. This comparison of budgeted and actual results is recognized as forming the basis for evaluating overall performance, helping control future operations and providing incentives for motivating the staff. The roles of budgets in organizations are diverse:

1 a system of authorization

2 a forecasting and planning tool

3 a means of communication and coordination

4 a motivational device

5 a means of performance evaluation and control

6 a basis for decision-making (Emmanuel et al., 1990).

Although financial performance measures provide objective results and are mainly utilized as a rewarding and motivational tool, there has been increasing recognition that the implementation of financial performance measures on their own were seen to provide a limited perspective on the performance of a company. The main shortcomings are:

- Short termism, in particular of profitability measures, is determined as a handicap for businesses. Measures of share/equity, asset return, bottom line profit and residual income emphasize a 'short-termist' approach. However, marketing/sales ratio and profit sales margin would emphasize a longer-term approach.

- The past information provided relative to ongoing operations is inappropriate in the dynamic business environment. Measures that are flexible and that can assist managers to make decisions for the current operations are highly important. It also encourages managers to keep minimum variance from the standard rather than continual motivation for improvement.

- Results, rather than ongoing managerial efforts, are reflected with financial measures. Better performance measures are required to cope with the emerging managerial techniques such as total quality management.

- Lack of strategic focus and failure to provide data on quality, responsiveness and flexibility.

- Failure to provide information on the external factors, such as what customers want and how the competitors are performing.

Operational measures of performance

Although financial measures of performance are of primary importance for the success of businesses, they can produce better performance information when used in conjunction with non-financial measures. They are valuable supplements to financial measures as they are expected to supply information that would improve the financial outcome and support and monitor the strategic initiatives.

New, non-financial measures are needed in order to cope with the changing operational environment, which primarily includes quality, just-in-time delivery and increase in product ranges. These new measures must be flexible, directly related to the strategy, non-financial, easily understood and highly responsive to the daily production situation. In addition, performance measurement systems require non-financial measures at operational levels, particularly to be used as a tool for motivating employees. It is also noted that '. . . day to day control of the manufacturing and distribution operations are better handled with non-financial measures' (Maskell, 1989:33).

The financial systems were normally used as a feedback mechanism to report the outcomes and their variance with the planned – once the financial goals were met, some other criteria became important. Other systems that dealt with more critical or uncertain areas of performance, for instance customer satisfaction, cycle time improvement and quality, were used in a more interactive fashion by management.

Operational measures were used in service businesses to a large extent, such that the service quality, flexibility, resource utilization and innovation were the operational determinants of the competitiveness and financial performance outcomes in Fitzgerald et al.'s (1991) performance measurement framework for service businesses. Empirical work in certain businesses has resulted in either dominance of financial outcome measures rather than the means of achieving these outcomes, or more interest in operational measures, resulting in an imbalance between the two dimensions.

Performance measurement in the hospitality industry

The Uniform Systems of Accounts for the Lodging Industry (1996) is the commonly practised method of recording and analysing accounting data in hospitality businesses. The characteristics of the industry play an important role in utilizing an appropriate approach to accounting and performance measurement. For this reason, the key features of hospitality businesses are reviewed by Harris (1999) to include fixed capacity, perishability, erratic demand, product range, real-time activity, labour intensity, location, size, production and consumption, capital intensity and cost structure. It is suggested that the business orientation and the industry context of the business is a key determinant of developing effective accounting, control and performance measurement methods (Kotas, 1975).

The results of financial statements have significance if they are compared with some form of yardstick. The main source of information for comparison comes from two sources: internal performance, which is past results and budget performance, and external performance, which is inter-company results and industry studies. There is a considerable degree of consensus among managers in hospitality organizations and academic writers alike that the budgetary control process is a valuable control and management tool in hospitality businesses. Ratios, which facilitate benchmarking, are the most commonly used measures in hospitality businesses in order to monitor and control operations. This information is compared and measured against goals to indicate where problems and successes are. Andrew and Schmidgall (1993:58) state that 'by tracking a selected set of ratios, hospitality managers are able to maintain a fairly accurate perception of the effectiveness and efficiency of their operations'.

The monthly occupancy percentage, the cost of labour percentage and the cost of food sold percentage were the three most commonly used measures in hospitality businesses, however, different groups of users assign different values to the ratios. The main users of ratios are the management, the owners and the creditors. They all rate different measures to be important such that the management uses operating ratios more than others, the owners consider profitability ratios extensively and the creditors utilize solvency ratios for making decisions. It is believed that the results reflected their natural interest in the business. In another study, it was identified that guest satisfaction measures are the key indicators used at operational levels of hotels and financial measures are utilized at the senior management levels (Haktanir and Harris, 2005). In addition to the above common measures, cash flow analysis is important, in particular, its relationship to three major activities of the business: operations, investment and finance.

A Chartered Institute of Management Accountants' (CIMA) study, carried out by Collier and Gregory (1995), exhibited interesting findings for both financial and non-financial measures of performance. Return on investment, which is believed to be the favourite measure in manufacturing businesses, is used only when new investments are undertaken. The most common way of measuring performance is through a comparison of actual with budgeted figures. From the six hotel companies studied, the common performance measures used can be listed as room yield, hotel profit contribution, occupancy rates and labour costs to turnover. Although the importance of measures of quality was well understood, a number of different ways of measuring it were captured, such as guest questionnaires, mystery guests and quality standard forms. Rewarding, referred to as a bonus system, is used in two-thirds of the cases studied where the budgeted versus actual results were the basis of the entire system. Overall, hotel performance measurement is not only criticized for its high reliance on quantitative measures, but also for its short-termist approach, its focus on efficiency rather than effectiveness measures and its high consideration of internal rather than external analysis.

Although both operational and financial measures are considered in hospitality businesses, in parallel to the developments in generic management accounting, it is stressed that there is high dependence on financial measures, which can lead to lack of balance and strategic focus. Geller (1985a) provided a list of the most commonly used performance measures by US hotel companies, which indicates the majority to be operational measures. A similar study carried out in the UK by Brander Brown et al. (1996) revealed that the users of performance measures consider both financial and operational measures to a high extent but, in contrast to Geller (1985a,b), they found a high reliance on financial measures, which may imply an unbalanced managerial focus. Further to this, Brander Brown and McDonnell (1995) reported the results of a pilot study designed to apply the BSC approach to the hotel sector. They suggest that the specific nature and value of any BSC would be contingent upon its level (unit or corporate level), context of application (department or functional area) and the time period/prevailing circumstances during which it is to be used. In addition, the empirical research of Brander Brown and Harris (1998) yielded evidence that achieving a balance of performance information, in terms of type, financial-operation dimensions and the links between key performance areas are necessary for the design of appropriate performance management systems in full-service hotels. It was also emphasized that effective communication of performance information at all levels, therefore producing and communicating clear and understandable performance information, is a core element of the performance management system.

Performance measurement in independent hotels

A recently completed research project (Haktanir, 2004) provides interesting insights into the complex nature of performance measurement in independent hotels. It investigates performance measurement practices in the real-life context of independent hotels in order to develop a framework for use in these businesses.

A grounded theory approach was undertaken and a multiple case study approach was adopted. This research strategy facilitated the development of a rich understanding of the performance measurement practices, through in-depth study of the issue in its own context. The following aspects were developed regarding the case selection of the research:

- The hotels were selected from the population 'independent hotels in Northern Cyprus'. Statistically, individually owned and managed hotels are some 45 per cent of the total hotel businesses. In addition, a large part of the partnerships, which are 48 per cent of the overall figure, are believed to be independently owned and managed properties. (The figures are obtained from the Ministry of State and Deputy Prime Ministry of the Turkish Republic of Northern Cyprus. The information was a tabular listing of properties rather than statistical presentations. The researcher processed the obtained data to come up with the percentage share of each ownership type.) An examination of the hotel industry indicates that independent hotels dominate the hotel industry in Northern Cyprus and, therefore, this research into the performance measurement practices of independent hotels covers a relevant group within the industry.

- The selected cases represent two groups within the independent hotel category: remotely owned (where the owner is not involved in the management of the business) and owner-managed (where the owner and the manager is the same person) hotels.

- The property features that are believed to be important for the research are listed below:
  - the size of the hotel needs to be above 100 room capacity so that the appropriate information and reservation systems would be available
  - the four or five star hotels were decided upon to be in the sampling group so that there is a certain level of service and different facilities available to study
  - almost all hotels in Northern Cyprus are holiday and resort type, therefore, studying the 'resort' hotel group is both easily accessible and more representative.

Eventually, six cases were selected for this research. They are listed in chronological order in Table 1.1.

Table 1.1
Information about the participant cases

Case	Stars	Ownership type	Room type	Room & bed no.	Catering type	Main contact
Case I: Mediterranean Hotel	5	Remotely owned	Hotel & bungalow	392 rooms 912 bed	BB, half, full	GM
Case II: Palm Hotel	4	Remotely owned	Hotel	108 rooms 216 bed	BB, half, full	GM
Case III: Hotel Aqua	4	Owner managed	Hotel & bungalow	133 room 72 bungalow 515 bed	BB, half, full, Self-catering	F&B manager
Case IV: Beach Hotel	4	Owner managed	Hotel	110 room 222 bed	BB, half, full	F&B manager
Case V: River Hotel	4	Owner managed	Bungalow	105 bungalow 290 bed	BB, half, full, Self-catering	Mother of GM
Case VI: Chance Hotel	5	Remotely owned	Hotel	192 room 392 bed	BB, half, full	FO manager

BB: Bed and breakfast, GM: general manager, F&B: food and beverage, FO: front office.

Data were collected from owners, general managers, department managers and employees by using an in-depth semi-structured interviewing method. In addition, observation and documentation methods of data collection were utilized in order to triangulate the findings and to gain a deeper insight into the real-life processes of the case studies. The informants from each case and the data collection method utilized are shown in Table 1.2.

Table 1.2
The informants and the data collection methods

Informant	Case I	Case II	Case III	Case IV	Case V	Case VI
Staff – front office	I, D, O	I, D, O (2)	I, D, O (2)	I, D, O	I, D, O (2)	I, D, O (2)
Staff – cost accounting	I		I, O	I		I
Staff – F&B service		I (2)	I			
Staff – administrative	I, D (2)					
Front office manager	I	I, D	I, O	I, D	I, D, O	I
Housekeeping manager	I, D	I	I, O	I	I	I
Personnel manager	I	I, D		I		
Accounting manager	I, D	I, D	I, D	I, D	I, D	I, D
Guest relations manager	I, D, O	I, D, O				I, D
Food & beverage manager	I	I, D, O	I, D, O	I (2)[1]	I, O	I, D
Assistant GM	I, D[2]					
GM		I, D, O				I, D
GM/owner			I, D, O	I	I	
Regional executive/owner	I	I				I

Source: Adapted from individual case reports. I: interview, D: documentation, O: observation (2): two informants from the same unit.
[1] The organizational structure of Case IV did not have one food and beverage manager, instead, two separate units of kitchen and food and beverage service. Both of these persons were informants.
[2] Assistant GM was the acting GM at the time of the case study. The researcher was also informed that the assistant GM has been with the hotel for very many years and he would give better information about the inquired issues.

An inductive data analysis approach was employed in order to allow the theory to emerge from the data. Primarily, within case analysis of each case was carried out. In the second level of analysis, owner-managed independent hotels and the remotely-owned independent hotels are compared in separate groups. Each of the two groups had three case hotels, where, in the next level of analysis, all the six cases were compared and contrasted.

The analysis process resulted in the development of a number of categories:

- Business dynamics (explores the decision-making mechanism, core elements of the business, and the information flow). This category has emerged as the central category
- Overall performance aspects (explores the kind of performance measures used, the reasons for utilizing them, the way they are conducted for the hotel in general, and for the departments specifically)
- Employee measures of performance (incorporates all employee related issues with employee performance measurement)
- Customer satisfaction measures (explores the type of performance measures utilized and explains how they are incorporated to overall activities and decision-making)
- Financial measures (reflects on the type, form and the way financial measures are utilized in relation to performance measurement practices)
- Innovation activities (explores and identifies the new activities and their importance for the business's performance measurement).

Findings

When the owner-managed case hotels (three hotels) were analysed, the following key issues emerged:

- There is a strong family involvement in all three hotels. This has several key consequences on management; one of them is family privacy concerning the use of financial information, this limits the sharing of such information. The other is the formation of an accounting system that satisfies the requirements of the owners. The accounting system is primarily based on cash information, which is one of the most important concerns of general managers and founders. In addition, sales information of revenue generating points and the profit figures are other important elements of the accounting systems. Therefore, the financial information and the accounting system are designed to satisfy the requirements of the owners and this information is not shared with non-family members. In addition to limitations of the receipt of financial information, there are also limitations involving access to computerized systems – once again, the family member department managers generally have more chances of accessing the system and reaching information. The family members, together with the founder and the general manager, are the final decision-makers, particularly for more strategic issues like investments.

- Family involvement has consequences in terms of management and operational control as well. The personal presence of managers and the general manager is a key type of performance measurement used for different purposes, including employee performance, guest satisfaction and operational success measurement. The control through personal presence is felt more in one of the hotels where the management team comprises of siblings. The efficacy of their 'we are always present' (food and beverage manager, River Hotel) personal control system is demonstrated by the fact that they use the least amount of figures for cost control of the three case study hotels.

- Additionally, the families' other businesses and occupations are effective in determining their management styles and control. Family members are influenced by their founder and other family members in establishing their management style. It was noted in the River Hotel that 'rent-a-car' is a department of the hotel – this is due to the fact that the family's original occupation was car rentals and they still have a reasonable size of business operating alongside the hotel business. In order for the family to control and combine the two businesses, they operate the rent-a-car business under the same roof. Similarly, the Beach Hotel has established their cost system according to the other businesses of the owner. The two restaurants the family owns specialize in 'kebabs' which use beef and lamb, and it was recognized that the cost report of the hotel is named as the 'meat usage report'. This indicates that systems and information used from them are affected by the other occupations of the family.

- Another significant point is the extended role of front office departments – it is more than the front office notion of hoteliers. It acts as a guest information and relations point in order to reach the widely accepted aim of guest satisfaction in all hotels. Further to this, in the River Hotel, the housekeeping department also reports to front office, which extends the responsibilities of the department even more. One reason for doing this is for the better understanding of the guests requirements from the rooms and thus to provide better service in return.

As a result of an overall analysis of the remotely-owned case hotels, the following key issues are concluded:

- All the owners of the remotely-owned case hotels live in Turkey. Owners of the Mediterranean and Chance Hotels are

Turkish and have no relationship in Northern Cyprus. In contrast, the owner of the Palm Hotel is a Turkish Cypriot. The two Turkish owners are involved in businesses in tourism, transportation and leisure industry and their key reason for having such investments in Northern Cyprus is to develop their already existing businesses outside the boundaries of Turkey. However, the Palm Hotel owner has a metal plant in Turkey and has no other hospitality or tourism involvement. His primary aim was to invest in his home country. As a result of this, the owner of the Palm Hotel visits the hotel more frequently, whereas the others are mostly remote to the property. This has a further implication such that the owner of the Palm Hotel has more informal means of measuring the hotel performance. He receives information from the family in Northern Cyprus who visits his hotel and has personal observation of the business during his visits to Northern Cyprus.

The key people in these hotels are the general managers. Financial information is supplied and decisions made by the owners and the general managers. The financial information dissemination is limited and the monthly performance reports are supplied to the owners and the general managers only. The department managers can reach the information they need, however, this depends on the capability of the computerized system and the access they have. For instance, the access is wider in the Chance Hotel as each department is responsible for reaching its own budget targets. However, in the Palm Hotel, only the food and beverage department manager receives some financial information in the form of cost reports.

The accounting system is primarily based on the principles of generally accepted uniform systems of accounts for hotels. The key information comes from the monthly and annual financial performance reports that include profit and loss statement, food and beverage cost statement, itemized sales statement and occupancy statement. The computerized information systems enable managers to reach primarily the revenue and occupancy figures.

- One of the consequences of owners being remote to the business is the formality regarding information flow. The general manager and owner base their communication and performance measurement on reporting. In addition, the department managers and the general manager have scheduled meetings and formal decision-making. They also have daily one-to-one communication for operational follow up. When examining the departments, it is noted that they are generally informal, having large reliance on personal observations and guest communications.

The guest relations departments also play important liaison roles in order to facilitate simultaneous decision-making.

- Other businesses of the owner are effective in determining the management styles and the control in the hotels. For instance, the accounting department of the Chance Hotel was one of the largest departments in the hotel, and the largest accounting department compared to the other case hotels. The reason for this is the presence of a sizable casino operation as part of routine hotel operations. Further to this, some of the managers of the Mediterranean Hotel were transferred from the owner's other hotel property in Turkey. Additionally, the hotel is used to support the operations of the airline company, therefore, it is not surprising that good pricing and selling strategies were the primary concern of the managers.

- The guest relations department plays an important role in terms of performance measurement of the hotels. They supply guest-related information both in verbal and written forms so that employee and departmental performances can be determined. For instance, the guest comment card results are the key indicators of employee performances and the 'employee of the month' rewards are given as a result of their evaluations. However, it is important to note that the front office departments also have guest relation roles besides their front office functions.

Evaluation

As a result of the comparison between all case hotels in the form of owner-managed to remotely-owned hotels, four key assertions are made. First, the management of these hotels should recognize the importance of the owner's involvement in the management of the hotel. The four main aspects developed are:

1 the quality of life, provision of job opportunities to family members and good status aims of owner-managers as opposed to the profit maximization aim of remotely-owned businesses

2 the owner-centred structure of owner-managed hotels in opposition to the formal structure of remotely-owned ones

3 the verbal and face-to-face management style of owner-managers as opposed to the more formal, report-based, management style of remotely-owned businesses

4 owner-managers' reliance on basic computerized systems with limited access, in contrast to generally accepted computerized systems with wider access and use in the remotely-owned ones.

Secondly, independent hotels relate their management and operations to other significant external and internal factors including:

1 proximity to the seaside influences the atmosphere, formality and kind of activities

2 high seasonal demand variations have significant influence on employee policies resulting in short-term perspectives for the independent hotels

3 the front office department is the centre of communication, coordination of functions and guest requests, where it plays a crucial role in building the desired hotel image

4 operational alternatives and investments for better operational results are commonly practiced in independent hotels; their measurement generally occurring in their results, primarily in the form of revenue generation of such activities.

Thirdly, it is suggested that the management of independent hotels should understand and recognize the importance of guest satisfaction and its measurement for their businesses. This would require them to identify the elements of the service industry, including primarily the simultancity feature that consequently leads to high guest interface and high reliance on measurement through guest feedback. In addition, the organizational culture – primarily communicated through the owner – is a powerful determinant of the extent of one-to-one guest relations at all levels of management and the resulting repeat business.

Lastly, independent hotels develop a range of performance measures in three categories:

1 'overall measures of performance' – due to the totality of processes (thus service-production-facility), non-financial measures for handling day-to-day operations, primarily occupancy and occupancy related information, and on-the-spot service measurement are utilized

2 'employee measures of performance' – due to the service feature of independent hotels, service quality measures interact with employee performance measures, simultaneous measurement of inputs and outputs is required and dependence on qualitative measures (verbal feedback and observation) is identified. In addition, the seasonal demand changes of the hotel industry in general and in Cyprus, in particular, cause difficulty in formalizing staff policies and lead to a high reliance on on-the-job training

3 'financial measures of performance' – although there is more reliance and more tendency to use financial measures in hospitality businesses, the extent of access and communication of financial information at different levels is limited; this is mainly due to the owners' perception of such information as being confidential to family members. Monitoring cash flow indicators at owner and general manager level, and measuring financial success of operations by sales and occupancy information is the accepted practice.

Conclusion

The findings indicated that performance measurement in the context of independent hotels is influenced by various organizational factors. For instance, the degree of owner's involvement in the operations and management of business is determined to be an important factor affecting the way management operates and performance measurement takes place. It is identified that when owners are involved in the management of businesses they restrict the flow of information and, in so doing, limit the involvement of managers and employees. In the case of an owner's direct involvement in management, the kind of information and information dissemination is limited by the owner. The extent of acceptance and usage of uniform accounting systems is largely influenced by the involvement of the owner. In addition, information to decision-makers is limited by cash flow and revenue related information. It is also apparent that owners require more flexible control systems as they establish business structures around themselves and their family members. This leads to the development of measures based on personal observation and, therefore, greater reliance on informal business processes.

The kind of business and the kind of services/products the business provides is another significant determinant of the performance measurement methods. For instance, utilization of 'overall measures of performance' in order to acquire an overview of the hotel performance is a common practice in independent hotels. The issue of the 'total hotel product' has been discussed by Harris (1999) who highlighted the complex nature of operating a hotel in terms of the total experience customers receive. Therefore, although the hotel information and accounting systems rely on a number of revenue and support centre departments (see *Uniform System of Accounts for the Lodging Industry*, 1996), designing the control systems of hotels with the use of such accounting information may prove insufficient. The 'total guest experience' implies that the consequences of any mistake at any point during a guest stay in the hotel can become a substantial overall issue and thus, the control and measurement of discrete parts (i.e. departments) of the business can only assist management to a limited degree. In effect, the financial information from the accounting systems of hotels requires to be supplemented by qualitative operational measures, such as on the spot (simultaneous) service and guest satisfaction measurement, in order to present a more comprehensive view of the hotel performance.

Department managers utilize employee measures and guest-related measures to a larger extent in their evaluation of departmental success. It is identified in the same research that one-to-one guest satisfaction feedback and repeat business figures are of prime importance to decision-makers. The simultaneity feature of service encounter at the hotels is the key reason for having such a reliance on one-to-one guest information. Management by personal presence facilitates direct interaction of managers both with staff and guests at every level of the business. This brings information through observation and verbal communication and therefore, action can be taken in real-time. In addition, having a guest relations department can also support the management by passing timely guest-related information.

References

Adam, D. (1997) *Management Accounting for the Hospitality Industry: A Strategic Approach*. Cassell, London.

Andrew, W.P. and Schmidgall, R.S. (1993) *Financial Management for the Hospitality Industry*. Educational Institute of American Hotel and Motel Association, East Lansing.

Bolton, J.E. (1971) *Report of the Committee of Inquiry on Small Firms (Bolton Report)*, Cmnd 4811. HMSO, London.

Brander Brown, J. and Harris, P. (1998) Performance management in the Hotel Industry: an Application of Eisenhardt's 'Roadmap'. *Paper presented at the Management Accounting Group Conference*, University of Aston, Birmingham.

Brander Brown, J. and McDonnell, B. (1995) The balanced scorecard: short term guest or long term resident? *International Journal of Contemporary Hospitality Management*, 7 (2/3), 7–11.

Brander Brown, J., McDonnell, B. and Lang, L. (1996) Performance measurement in UK hotel organisations: towards a balanced scorecard? *Paper presented at the Council on Hotel, Restaurant and Institutional Education 50th Annual Conference*, Washington, DC.

Collier, P. and Gregory, A. (1995) *Management Accounting in Hotel Groups*. CIMA, London.

Emmanuel, C., Otley, D. and Merchant, K. (1990) *Accounting for Management Control*. Chapman and Hall, London.

Fitzgerald, L., Johnston, R., Brignall, S., Silvestro, R. and Voss, C. (1991) *Performance Measurement in Service Businesses*. CIMA, London.

Geller, A.N. (1985a) Tracing the critical success factors for hotel companies. *The Cornell HRA Quarterly*, February, 76–81.

Geller, A.N. (1985b) The current state of hotel information system. *The Cornell HRA Quarterly*, May, 14–17.

Haktanir, M. (2004) Performance measurement in small service businesses: an investigation of independent hotels. *Unpublished PhD Thesis*, Oxford Brookes University.

Haktanir, M. and Harris, P.J. (2005) Performance measurement practice in an independent hotel context: a case study approach. *International Journal of Contemporary Hospitality Management*, **17** (1), 39–50.

Harris, P.J. (1999) *Profit Planning*, 2nd edn. Butterworth-Heinemann, Oxford.

Jarvis, R., Curran, J., Kitching, J. and Lightfoot, G. (2000) The use of quantitative and qualitative criteria in the measurement of performance in small firms. *Journal of Small Business and Enterprise Development*, **7** (2), 123–134.

Jogaratnam, G., Tse, E.C. and Olsen, M.D. (1999) Matching strategy with performance. *Cornell Hotel and Restaurant Administrative Quarterly*, August, 91–95.

Jones, P. and Lockwood, A. (1989) *The Management of Hotel Operations: An Innovative Approach to the Study of Hotel Management*. Cassell, London.

Kaplan, R.S. and Norton, D.P. (1992) The balanced scorecard: measures that drive performance. *Harvard Business Review*, January–February, 71–79.

Kotas, R. (1975) *Market Orientation in Hotel and Catering Industry*. Surrey University Press, London.

Lynch, R.L. and Cross, K.F. (1991) *Measure Up! Yardsticks for Continuous Improvement*. Basil Blackwell, Oxford.

Main, H. (1995) Information technology and the independent hotel – failing to make the connection? *International Journal of Contemporary Hospitality Management*, **7** (6), 30–32.

Marriott, N. and Marriott, P. (2000) Professional accountants and the development of a management accounting service for the small firm: barriers and possibilities. *Management Accounting Research*, **11** (4), 475–492.

Maskell, B. (1989) Performance measurement for world class manufacturing: Part 1. *Management Accounting*, May, 32–33.

Morrison, A. (1998) Small firm statistics: a hotel sector focus. *The Service Industry Journal*, **18** (1), 132–142.

Neely, A., Gregory, M. and Platts, K. (1995) Performance measurement system design: a literature review and research agenda.

International Journal of Operations and Production Management, **15** (4), 80–116.

Shaw, G. and Willams, A.M. (1994) *Critical Issues in Tourism: A Critical Perspective*. Blackwell Publishers, Oxford.

Stanworth, J. and Gray, C. (1991) *Bolton 20 years on: the small firm in the 1990s*. Paul Chapman Publishing, London.

Uniform System of Accounts for the Lodging Industry (1996) 9th revised edition. Educational Institute of the American Hotel and Motel Association, New York.

CHAPTER 2

Productivity in the restaurant industry: how to measure productivity and improve process management

Pekka Heikkilä and
Timo Saranpää

Introduction

Profitability as a precondition of management work

A restaurant business is as much an economic unit as any other enterprise. In managing the operations of a business, its various units and/or departments, information on the profitability of the operations is needed. The most important elements in profitability are economy and productivity. The results of these factors are monitored with the help of various key figures. Calculating the key figures requires numerical information on the operations.

The systematic processing of the information cannot succeed without knowledge of the most important concepts and methods in accountancy. Besides the basics in accountancy, a functional control system is needed so that the key figure information can be easily, punctually and correctly delivered to those who need it for decision-making. Information thus produced is best suited to serve the planning, supervision and management needs of business operations.

Reliable gathering, registering and processing of information are all essential for successful information use. In the background there needs to be a strong knowledge of the field, through which it is possible to form a sufficient understanding of the revenues and costs that should be taken into account. While planning the operations, it is important to be aware of all the various costs and revenues that are involved and what is the relationship between them in successful business operations. In other words, familiarity with the types of income and costs and also with the income statement and balance sheet structure is essential in order to be able to assess the various aspects of productivity. Deficiency in these skills makes it difficult, if not impossible, to plan and run profitable operations. As a result, learning is achieved through trial and error, with potentially severe consequences to the business.

Control of the productivity of a restaurant business requires knowledge of the laws of business in the field. Cause-and-effect relationships must be grasped between the decisions, actual business events and result reports. It is also important to understand the economic nature of all decisions, since all of them have their own impact on the results of the business operations.

Special characteristics of the restaurant industry from the point of view of productive and profitable operations

In order to achieve economically successful operations management must be fully familiar with all the factors that influence the profitability of their business. Regarding profitability goals, the significance of management cannot be neglected. Very often management skills are the deciding factor in whether or not the set goals are achieved. In part, management skills are about an ability to understand the special characteristics of practical business operations and profit logic in the field. This understanding helps in keeping the elements of profitability in check. This implies that it is very difficult to manage a business with no knowledge of the field in question. General management skills are also necessary, but there are many practical examples to support the view that a sound knowledge of the field furthers the achievement of goals significantly.

From the point of view of management (and profitability control), the following special characteristics of the restaurant business emerge as the most important.

Intensive competition

As a result of easy access to the market, competition is harsh in the restaurant industry. There are a large number of companies of various sizes and the significance of price competition is emphasized. However, price competition by itself rarely guarantees economic success. Long-term success is better guaranteed by the careful creation of a quality image. Through a quality image of a suitable level, a business can price its products more profitably than can the competitors.

Low net profit percentage

Because of tight price competition, the net profit percentage (net profit/turnover × 100) is low. Compared to many other industries, the net profit percentage is extremely low regardless of a high gross profit percentage. Therefore the control of profitability requires very precise cost control.

According to statistical work done on financial statements, the average net profit percentage of restaurant businesses in Finland in 2002 was about 4 per cent. This means that for each 10 euros product (including the 22 per cent value added tax), the company is left with a 33 cents 'pure' profit. The average net profit percentage in food restaurants is even lower – about 1.2 per cent of the turnover. Because of the low average profit margin, even the smallest error in, for example, catering for a single event might cost the company all the profit from the function. Extra costs may arise from careless processing of raw materials or the man-hours of the event being incorrectly planned. To eliminate these mistakes, service businesses must make their processes as efficient as they possibly can. The challenge for management of identifying low average profit margins is best grasped if the separately defined expenses are compared to the separate average profit of a single function and not to total turnover. This proves that there are simply no insignificant costs.

Long opening hours, seasonal variations in levels of sales

In service industry companies the work force is a major factor in both profitability and quality control. In the cost structure of a restaurant business this is visible in the large share of labour costs in the turnover. The control of labour costs requires strict control of the relationship between sales and man-hours, in other words efficiency in the use of labour. In addition, salary levels must remain within set limits. Long opening hours create pressure for growth in staff expenses and in order to succeed in controlling its cost structure a business must succeed in focusing the hours worked as carefully as possible in accordance with the high and low seasons in sales.

Many services in the restaurant industry are on offer virtually all day, every day of the year. In the companies' operations there are periods of both low and high sales. Staffing expenses must be focused so that during high season there is a sufficient amount of staff to satisfy demand and during low season there is only the amount of staff necessary to maintain a basic level of services.

The structure and variety in product group-related sales creates its own pressure on staffing expenses. The larger the share of food sales of total sales, the larger the labour costs (both in preparation and serving).

Because labour costs play such a significant role in restaurant management, making the shift schedule is one of the most important factors in profitability control. How and when a given task is done must be considered very carefully. Costs planning can be made more efficient by calculating the 'price' of each shift schedule in advance. This is achieved by the simple operation of multiplying the number of the hours in the shift schedule by the average work hour costs (the hourly wages plus additional expenses).

The problem in achieving the correct use of staff is significant when the product (i.e. service) cannot be kept on the shelf. Stocking can, however, in some situations, help in optimizing the use of the work force. It is for example possible to prepare for the activities and sales of the following day during less busy hours. It is also not necessarily cheaper to buy pre-processed raw materials if there is staff on duty in any case and can thus make use of the work hours by doing preparatory work. Besides all the above mentioned management tasks, the significance of staff know-how and satisfaction at work must always be borne in mind, all of which does not make the disposition of labour any easier to manage.

Customers' on-going interest in the quality of the product

Customers have an on-going interest in how the representatives of the business behave and this creates pressure for quality control, product development and marketing and thus on staff, management and leadership. Customers expect the company to consider health, hygiene, nutrition and environmental issues in their operations. This will inevitably show in the costs and create additional pressure for cost control. It is imperative to establish a balance between quality and costs and to remember that neither too high nor too low quality will bring the best economic results.

Continuous need for investment

Access to the restaurant business is in many cases easy, since the necessary investments are relatively low. Sometimes a business invests in preparation and serving facilities (in addition to equipment, machinery and other expenses) and must also take care of these investments. In addition to depreciation, annual maintenance costs consume their own share of the profits. In order to control these costs it is necessary to optimize the timing of investments and maintenance. If, for example, maintenance is always simply postponed, costs will end up being much higher.

Imagined purchase benefit and the importance of controlling the use of raw materials

'How can this possibly cost so much? You buy your materials and equipment wholesale for much cheaper than we ordinary consumers.' Does this customer comment on the price of raw materials strike a familiar chord? It is not, however, the truth in all cases. On the shelves of the retail shop the same raw materials are often much less expensive than when bought from the wholesaler. This is due to, for example, special offers and large purchasing volume in the shops. In order to counter this, the restaurant must be able to make the best possible use of the raw materials and to have as little waste as possible.

For many products, the level of raw material costs is small in relation to the labour costs. Fetching or ordering the raw materials from the wholesaler, preparing the product, serving and other tasks in the operation of a restaurant amount to the largest share of the price that the customer pays for the product. As the second largest cost element, the use of raw materials must be taken seriously.

Constant need for renewal

The fast changes in society constantly create potential new experiences for customers. Products and trends change quickly. Expectations grow and in a restaurant business, this creates pressure. Customers expect new products and services all the time. To keep up with new developments, a restaurant must constantly present fresh ideas. From the point of view of profitability control the aim is contrary: the fewer the products, the easier it is to operate efficiently. The balance exists somewhere in between these two extremes. On the one hand, there must be a sufficient number of products and they must be renewed sufficiently quickly in order to keep the customers interested but, on the other hand, the pace must not be too quick and there must not be too many products if profitable operation is to be sustained. By using internal accounting, the profitability of various products and product groups must be carefully followed so that the situation can be controlled.

The importance of cost centre management

All the above presented aspects of management have an impact on how much managerial input is needed in hospitality service production. Naturally, a low level of organization and low work and business management costs are the goal. This area of business management requires balanced planning. The amount of management input must be in correct relation to the number of staff and the quality and profit goals set for the produced service.

A low net profit percentage implies that reaching the budgeted costs and profits requires a very precise control of the various costs and the whole process. Anyone who has worked in restaurant management knows that a single operational unit cannot succeed without a good manager. Not underestimating the importance of the principles of teamwork in creating a motivating work atmosphere, it is not enough without strong (not authoritarian!) leadership to reach economic goals.

Productivity planning, monitoring and control

The elements of profitability

Business must always be efficient, economical and profitable. The profitability of a business must be planned at separate levels of operation as well as for the whole financial year. With the help of financial reports, the achievement of the objectives must be evaluated. Possible deviations between the plans and reality must be defined and analysed.

The goals of any economic activity – productivity and economy – can also be called elements of profitability. Through these goals the business aims at profit, which is the most important economic goal. The control of the above mentioned elements require the calculation of key figures relating to the economic success of the business. A good key figure fills the same criteria as a good financial report: it is simple, correctly timed and has the necessary content. The gathering of unnecessary information is always to be avoided. Accounting should be a means to an end, not the end itself.

Productivity

Productivity is the measure of production efficiency in business. Productivity refers to the level of output in relation to a given level of input. Productivity reflects the relationship between input and output in the operations. Productivity can also be called efficiency, which therefore refers to the relationship between production input and output. Productivity is not a concept based on amounts of money used:

$$productivity = production\ output/production\ input = output/input$$

production output means the total number of produced output units. Production input means, for example, the man-hours used in production.

The principle of productivity is to:

- achieve an output as large as possible for a certain amount of input

- achieve a certain output with as little input as possible

- achieve the best possible output with the least possible input.

The most important production inputs in a restaurant business are the raw materials, work force and capital invested in the form of various assets, such as premises, machinery and other fixed assets. Productivity can be calculated either as total productivity for the whole business or as the partial productivity of various production inputs, if the denominator is only one production factor at a time. Thus it is possible to define:

- total productivity

- productivity of labour

- productivity in the use of raw materials

- productivity of invested capital.

If total productivity improves, the reason might be one or more of the following:

- the production output has increased without an increase in the input

- the level of refinement has risen or better quality products have been produced

- less input has been used per product unit than previously.

In addition to the above mentioned classical production inputs, the inputs can also consist of the following:

- energy

- knowledge

- entrepreneurship.

It is difficult to measure and present knowledge and entrepreneurship numerically and therefore it is challenging to attempt a calculation of key figures for these inputs. In business operations in the restaurant industry, productivity most often means efficiency in the use of the work force. From the point of view of productivity, the aim is to achieve the maximum amount of revenue (e.g. turnover) for the given input (e.g. man-hours).

Economy as an element of productivity

Economy as a goal in business operations refers to the amount of economic input necessary for a certain amount of output. The aim is, of course, that the output is achieved with as little financial input as possible. Economy can be defined as the kind of productivity in which the input and output are expressed in terms of money. Thus, economy is in fact the same concept as productivity. The principle of economy is identical to the principle of productivity presented above.

In the hospitality industry, economy generally refers to economy in the use of raw materials, but also the amount in euros of other costs (e.g. labour costs) in relation to production quantities of single products and product groups must be controlled.

Perhaps the most commonly used key figures in business operations in the industry are:

- cost of sales, €/product unit (e.g. one portion)

- the same in reverse: the gross profit, €/product unit

- waste percentage of the cost of sales (in relation to the total cost of sales).

Profitability

In order to be able to maintain long-term operations, a company must be able to cover all costs involved in the business from sales and also to produce interest on the capital invested in the company. Operational profitability refers simply to the deduction of costs from revenue:

$$operational\ profitability = revenue - costs.$$

Key figures for profitability are all profit margins in the income statement. Profitability is evaluated by both absolute figures (in euros) and by relative percentage figures. These profitability key figures include for example:

- Profit before interests and taxes percentage = (the profit for the financial year before interests and taxes/turnover) × 100

- Return on capital employed = (profit before interests and taxes/invested capital) × 100.

Return on capital employed depends on the profit before interests and taxes percentage as well as on the efficiency of the use of capital, which refers to the invested capital in relation to the turnover achieved by using the invested capital. This is measured by the turnover of capital:

$$turnover\ of\ capital = turnover/invested\ capital.$$

The profit before interests and taxes percentage and the turnover of capital define the return on capital employed:

$$the\ return\ on\ capital\ employed = turnover\ of\ capital \times profit$$
$$before\ interests\ and\ taxes\ percentage.$$

Another defining factor in profitability is thus efficiency in the use of invested capital.

Productivity, economy and profitability are different aspects of the same phenomenon

In practice it should be noted that a company can operate productively and economically even if the operations dimension are not profitable. The production achieved by a certain work input may be productive for a certain period of time due to successful planning of the use of labour. Likewise, the use of raw materials may be very economical as a result of good product development and control systems. Still, the profitability of a business may weaken within the very same period of time if a decrease in the total revenue makes it impossible to cover total expenses. However, one of the basic prerequisites of profitable operation is that production processes have been organized productively and economically.

The goal in controlling productivity figures is improved profitability. In practice, improvement of productivity and profitability are usually achieved in the hospitality industry by taking the following measures:

1 Reducing costs without reducing output

- reducing raw material costs, labour costs and other operating costs

- rationalizing production

- work methods and staff development

- improving motivation, developing the organization and methods of remuneration

- discontinuing unessential operations

- rationalizing operations by investments and by purchasing more efficient machinery

- improving logistics

- finding new and more efficient channels of sales and distribution

2 Increasing unit output without changes in the costs per unit

- increasing sales prices and sales volume

- more efficient marketing and product development

3 By optimizing the invested capital in relation to the operation

- optimizing the value and turnover of inventory

- optimizing the value and turnover of fixed assets

- disposing of unnecessary property

- optimizing the amounts and terms of payment of receivables

- efficient collection of receivables.

Productivity control

Key figures in operational productivity and profitability in the restaurant industry

By using operational key figures, the organization aims at directing and developing the profitability of the operations by maintaining productivity and economy. As business becomes more complicated, it is even more important than previously that key figures are found that describe, as simply as possible, the economic success of the operations. With the help of key figures, the restaurant management can, in the midst of hectic work, receive a quick and accurate image of the economic success of the business without elaborate calculations and analyses.

Simple key figures facilitate the control of productivity and economy. The key figures that are in daily use in the restaurant industry are presented in Table 2.1.

Table 2.1
The key figures that are in daily use in the restaurant industry

Key figure	Formula
Key figures for the use of labour	
1. Sales/man-hour	Sales/worked man-hours
2. Sales/person (in time unit)	Sales output/number of staff in one single time unit (day, week, year)
3. Gross profit/person (in time unit)	Gross profit from sales/number of staff (in one time unit)
4. Labour costs/hour	Wages with related costs/worked man-hours
5. Labour costs/turnover percentage	Labour costs/turnover × 100
6. Food portions/man-hour in kitchen	Amount of sold portions/worked man-hours in kitchen
7. Food sales/man-hour in kitchen	Food sales/worked man-hours in kitchen
8. Beverage sales/man-hour in bar	Beverage sales/worked man-hours in bar
Key figures for the use of premises	
9. Sales/opening hour	Sales/opening hours
10. Sales/square metre	Sales/the area of the sales facilities in square metres
11. Number of customers in one time unit	Number of customers/time unit (hour, day)
12. Average cheque	Sales/number of customers
13. Sales/seat	Sales/number of seats (in one time unit)
14. Seat turnover	Number of customers/number of seats (in one time unit)
Key figures for the use of raw material and capital employed	
15. Turnover of inventory	Cost of sales/average value of inventory (in one time unit)
16. Cost of sales/portion	Total cost of sales/portions sold
17. Waste percentage	(Waste/use of raw material) × 100 (in one time unit)
18. Turnover of capital	Turnover/invested capital
19. The terms of payment of receivables	
20. The terms of payment for creditors	

The key figures in Table 2.1 could be termed hard figures, which are used in controlling, through numerical values, the relationship between input and output. Alongside the hard figures there are the soft figures that describe productivity, usually indirectly. With the help of the soft figures control can be exercised over (for example):

- customer satisfaction

- the working atmosphere in the organization

- turnover of staff and absenteeism

- the degree of innovation (the creation of new ideas).

The significance of these matters in the description of activities aimed at achieving efficiency goals is often of primary import-ance. It has been shown that in the hospitality industry a rise in the quality of products will lead also to a rise in productivity and improved customer satisfaction.

Cost of sales by product group

Cost-volume-profit analysis is one of the most commonly applied techniques in the field of accountancy when the aim is to achieve a more efficient use of raw materials in a restaurant. The goal of the cost-volume-profit analysis is to ascertain the turnover, cost of sales and gross profits and the possible waste of raw materials for each product group. In restaurants, the division into product groups may be done in the following fashion: food, coffee, alco-hol, wine, beer, soft drinks (water), cigarettes and other sales.

The product calculations are used especially in product develop-ment and selection, pricing and in the planning and control of prof-itability for each product. The sales information for each product needed as background information for the calculations is gathered daily with the help of the cash register system. If the company has in its use a comprehensive recipe and production control system, which is at its most efficient if functioning as a part of the cash regis-ter system, a numerical report of the cost of sales by product group is also generated. The calculation of the cost of sales is done through the following procedure: when for example a pepper steak is sold, the inventory control system deducts automatically the raw materials used for preparing the pepper steak (according to the recipe) from the value of inventory and adds these material costs into the control system of the cost of sales. With the help of this information, the product group-related and/or product-related gross profit can be monitored even daily. The gross profit thus cal-culated is also called the optimum gross profit.

The calculated results produced by the above mentioned system must be checked manually. Correspondence between reality and the calculation is compromised by many risk factors causing waste. Waste comes about, for example, in the reception of raw materials, storing, preparation and serving. It may also be caused, regrettably, by dishonesty among staff members.

In order to diminish the quantity of waste, the persons responsible for the production processes in the restaurant should mark down as precisely as possible all the events that have caused waste daily (e.g. had to discard 2 kg of spoiled salmon, 1 litre of stock was spilled on the floor). Only by registering this information is there sufficient knowledge and interest to reduce waste. Usually this is the only method of highlighting the importance of minimizing waste. Small mistakes cause, on a monthly and annual level, significant financial losses.

The frequency of taking physical inventories is dependent on the need for gathering this information, influenced by the fluctuations in the amount of sales and the total value of inventory, or the value of inventory of a certain product group. The ordinary inventory frequency is once a month. In the case of some product groups the inventory is done even daily (e.g. alcohol and cigarettes). The frequency is dependent also on the capacity of the organization. In a small restaurant, in which the gross profit is regularly at the desired level and the owner is at all times aware of the contents of the stock, inventories can take place even less frequently. The only legislation on the matter decrees that for making the final statement the stock value must be determined by inventory. Precision in the control of cost of sales is thus not required by law but for reasons of controlling the output. Good economy requires a precise control of raw materials and this in turn cannot be achieved without a frequent enough inventory.

Technically, the calculation of the values achieved by the operation as a whole and in the product group-related cost of sales is made using the method described in the following. In our example it is assumed that the restaurant controls the product group-related gross profit of three main product groups (alcohol, beer and food). The value of stock is calculated by inventory of each product group at the end of the control period.

For determining the use of raw materials the value of the inventory on the last day of the previous control period (which means the value of the opening inventory of the control period that is being examined) must be available, as well as the raw material purchases by product group during the control period. All the above mentioned information is processed without value added tax. Thus, the costs of sales are calculated as shown in Table 2.2.

Table 2.2
The actual use of raw materials by product group (€/November 200x)

	Alcohol	Beer	Food	Total
Opening value of inventory (1st November)	3 000	4 000	4 000	11 000
Add: purchases for November	15 000	18 000	17 000	50 000
Less: closing value of inventory (30th November)	2 000	4 000	3 000	9 000
Use of raw materials during November	16 000	18 000	18 000	52 000

To make a product calculation as well as a total gross profit calculation one must also know the turnover of the whole control period by product group. The product group gross profit calculation has the structure shown in Table 2.3.

Table 2.3
The actual product group gross profit calculation

	Alcohol	Beer	Food	Total
Turnover (€)	50 000	48 000	45 000	143 000
Less: cost of sales (€)	16 000	18 000	18 000	52 000
(cost of sales %)	(32)	(37.5)	(40)	(36.4)
= gross profit (€)	34 000	30 000	27 000	91 000
(gross profit %)	(68)	(62.5)	(60)	(63.6)

Differences between the actual gross profit and the optimum gross profit must be analysed after the calculations and the necessary sales and production decisions must be made on the basis of these differences. In practice, one must have one more profit concept, which is the targeted gross profit. It refers to the aimed level of gross profit, defined in the budget. The targeted gross profit is not the same as the optimum gross profit, but in it the presumed cost effect of waste has been observed. In the analysis stage, the actual gross profit will also be compared to the targeted gross profit before drawing any conclusions. The product-based calculated gross profits act as sign-bearers of disturbances in profitability. Therefore special attention must be given to controlling them.

In practice, the routine calculations in controlling profitability by product group are limited to calculating the gross profits only.

However, this does not mean that it would be unnecessary to find out the shares of single products or product groups in the joint costs (e.g. labour costs and other fixed costs). It is merely that the singling out of the product groups from the total costs is very demanding and time-consuming. Nevertheless, it would be wise to undertake this procedure. At least random check-ups of the quantity of input required by various product groups and products should be performed in order to find out the actual profitability. This can be done for example by defining the preparation time for each product by measuring the time needed for performing the various work tasks. The labour costs would also be measured by observing the time used. The estimation might cause, in the case of labour costs, the products being divided into groups according to the time needed for preparation. Then a gross profit percentage goal or a goal in euros could be defined in accordance with how much work it takes to produce the products of a given product group. The more time the preparation takes, the higher the gross profit should be, in order to ensure that the salary costs are covered.

Managing the use of staff

Of the operational costs of a restaurant, labour costs are the largest. It is of the utmost importance that these costs can be controlled in order to achieve productive and profitable operations.

The staff are the most important resource in the service industry. As an interest group, the staff come second in importance, directly after the customers. The importance of staff in running a profitable business shows also in the fact that the labour costs play an important part in the profitability structure of a restaurant. Together with the cost of sales, they make up 65–70 per cent of the turnover of the business. In some cases, depending on the business idea of the company, the staff may be even more important. For this reason the control of the use of work force should be very carefully analysed.

Controlling the use of work force is based on two elements: controlling profitability and the total labour costs. In order to achieve good profitability one must be able to plan the shift schedules such that the staff on shift and the number of man-hours corresponds as well as possible to the need for work force, in other words, the amount of sales. It is also necessary to control the hourly labour costs, i.e. the price of one man-hour, in order to control the total quantity of labour costs and the production economy.

Hourly labour costs depend on the structure of staff, in other words on which salary groups of the Collective Agreement the workers belong to. In practice, the salary grouping according to the Collective Agreement does not always give the correct picture of labour costs, because it is also the job market situation (whether it is a time of labour shortage or over supply) that determines the hourly wages of a skilled chef. The price of one man-hour (the hourly wage with additional labour costs) for one full-time worker is calculated by dividing the monthly labour costs by the so-called hourly wage denominator. For example in Finland, the hourly wage denominator is defined in the Collective Agreement for the restaurant industry to be 159 man-hours per month. The actual number of man-hours may vary somewhat on a monthly basis. In using the denominator of 159 hours it is assumed that the monthly costs of a worker do not include overtime costs.

For example, if the wages and additional labour costs of one worker add up to 2265 € per month, the price of one man-hour is:

2265 €/month: 159 h/month = 14.25 €/h.

It is sensible to use a higher price for one man-hour than the one indicated by the cost calculations as the real price of one man-hour (e.g. in making offers), to prevent possible errors. For example, instead of the previous example price, one could use the price of 20€/h. Thus it is possible to prepare for costs that exceed the estimates.

In day-to-day management, staff costs are not only affected by the hourly price but also by the number of hours done by the workers. The number of hours is dependent on, for example, the business idea of the restaurant (the service and product structure and opening hours), the organization of work, the functionality of the work facilities, professional skills, work efficiency, work motivation and success in teamwork.

Let us take a medium level food restaurant as an example of planning the use of labour. The cost structure including the profit after costs of sales and labour costs have been budgeted, using previous reports, as follows:

Turnover	*100%*
Less: cost of sales	*30%*
Gross profit	*70%*
Less: labour costs	*32%*
Profit after costs of sales and labour costs	*38%*

If the budgeted turnover for the coming week is 25 000 €, the labour costs can amount to 32% × 25 000 € = 8000 € and thus the shift schedule for one week can have 400 man-hours, according to the above mentioned 20 € hourly costs (8000 € : 20 €/h = 400 man-hours). The person drawing up the shift schedule must plan the use of hours for the week in question in accordance with the demand peaks. The work productivity figure for a restaurant, dividing turnover by man-hours, is therefore 62.50€/man-hour (25 000 €/400 man-hours = 62.50 €/man-hour).

Management itself plays a key role in the formation of this important part of the total costs. Under pressure to bring profit, the managers must be able to give the right emphasis to the importance of staff in achieving good results. The right motivation for the staff to reach the efficiency, and other goals, must be created. It must also be possible to estimate the relationship between price and quality of staff similar to the case of raw materials. The least expensive worker is not necessarily the best alternative from the point of view of achieving good results.

The regulations of the Collective Agreement and mastering the technique of making the shift schedules are vital to the successful planning of man-hours. There are special programmes for making the schedules that are often used to ease the technical side of the procedure. Technical aids do not, however, free the superior from the responsibility and duty to understand the special characteristics of the company's business idea, for without this understanding it is very difficult to achieve the profitability goals. The business must be controlled in order to be able to control the labour costs.

Extra workers and temporary workers are used as help in controlling the amount of man-hours. With the help of these employee groups the superior is better able to even out the differences between sales peaks and to ensure that the number of staff corresponds with the needs of different sales situations.

The balanced scorecard for efficient productivity control

The objects of control

To improve the control of profitability companies in the restaurant industry have also begun to make use of the balanced scorecard. The basic idea of the balanced scorecard is to use, alongside financial measures, non-financial measures to improve the control of operations. Instead of only economic control, businesses aim at a holistic control of their operations. The control model is used for bringing balance to quality and result measures, with the aim of optimizing long-term result developments.

In applying the balanced scorecard in practice, in addition to the economic figures, also, for example, customer and staff satisfaction, the functionality of the processes, the development of the quoted factors and figures describing environmental and social responsibility are followed.

It is challenging to attempt a control model that is a combination of so-called hard, numerical figures that reflect economic success and qualitative measures. It requires a continuity and systematic approach to product development. Without functional product development, the development of the whole business operation will remain (despite good measurement systems) deficient. As a prerequisite for being able to use the balanced scorecard, customer relations must be well taken care of. An advanced qualitative control system will benefit the management of a company only if customer relations are on the same level of good care. Naturally, this demands a great deal from the staff. Investment must be made in the professional skills and motivation of the staff. It is all in vain to invest in control systems if staff cannot be actively engaged in the development work. The commitment of staff is largely dependent on how well the management succeeds in communicating the strategy to the whole organization. Alongside staff commitment, it must be possible to ensure that the various departments or units of the organization function together. Synchronization of various activities must be mastered. The implementation of control procedures on multiple dimensions and levels requires a systematic approach. In practice it is not possible without a functional computer-based information system.

The measures of the balanced scorecard and their use

The traditional control system of operations is based on previous knowledge and the emphasis on financial measures is underlined. The danger in many situations is that economic figures are optimized short-sightedly, at the cost of long-term results. With the help of the balanced scorecard this will be prevented by taking the quality measures into account with the economic measures. In the balanced scorecard the significance of internal accounting and operating figures is emphasized instead of the production of mere figures by external accounting. The aim is also to deepen the analysis of the figures and thus improve precision in decision-making. In emphasizing the quality measures the aim is also to improve sensitivity to events in the market (customers, competitors). With the help of the balanced scorecard decision-making can be directed from assessment of the past to predicting the future and anticipating future events. In spite of the versatile nature of the balanced scorecard, the aim is always that the report material is clear and easy to use.

The use of the balanced scorecard begins with careful planning of the company's operations and definition of strategy. It must be possible to define the aims of the business, transform them into concrete goals and condense them into figures. These things must be communicated to the organization. Without the active engagement of the organization, the goals will not be reached and the balanced scorecard as a system will not function. During the whole process, feedback must be gathered so that mistakes can be corrected at as early a stage as possible. Often the new control system will first be used in a pilot unit. It is usually easier to solve planning mistakes in one unit than to correct them in all operational units at the same time.

What is required of good balanced scorecard measures? The basic definition for a measure is that it is a concise, verbal or numerical description of the observations. In order to function, the measures should also meet the following requirements:

- they are always based on the users' aims and needs
- there is a sufficient number of measures – but not too many
- the measures must take into account the various levels of the organization
- the measures must ensure the continuity, clarity and goal-orientation of the control procedures
- the measures of different aspects (profitability, customer and process-orientation, staff, innovation, information technology, environment) must be compatible.

Examples of measures of various aspects that might be used in a restaurant business are given in Table 2.4.

All control of the operations is made more difficult by large quantities of information and compatibility difficulties. The balanced scorecard has been designed to eliminate this problem as far as possible. When common values (on the basis of which the financial and non-financial goals have been formed) are carefully defined, it is easier to define and grasp the goals and the measures. Then also successes and failures will be understood in the same way. The benefit from the system will show in better and smoother cooperation and more productive operations.

The essential factor in all planning and control activities is to understand the relationships between cause and effect in practical everyday functions, business events and measures. Without understanding the nature and content of the operations – what the measures indicate – a business cannot be run successfully. No technical system can ever replace skilled management, but the balanced scorecard may, if used properly, be a fine aid for the management.

Table 2.4
Measures of various aspects that might be used in a restaurant business

Aspect	Measure
Profitability	Sales, wages, operating profit, € and %
	Profit before interest and taxes, € and %
Productivity	Sales/man-hour/person, €
Economy	Gross profit/product, € and %
Sufficient financing	Quick ratio
Financial stability	The gearing ratio
Customer	The marks received from customer satisfaction questionnaires
	Number of complaints
	Number of customers
Staff	Marks received from work atmosphere questionnaires
	The number of sick leaves
	Turnover
	The length of employment contracts
Process	Waiting times
	Seat turnover
	Turnover of inventory
Innovation	Variety of products
	The number of new products on e.g. the menu
	The further development of the business idea
IT	The number of PCs
	The extent of the e-mail system
	Usage periods of the technology
	The number and duration of function down-time
Environment	The amount of disposable products used
	The amount and level of sorting of waste

Hindrances to productivity in the restaurant industry

Success in the restaurant business is bound up with small details that should together constitute a functional enterprise, starting from the right colour of napkin to choice of premises and annual planning of the company. How can it be ensured that the effects of the above mentioned special characteristics are correctly observed in restaurant management? The best guarantee is professional, skilled management and staff, but that does not automatically bring economic success. Profitable and productive business comes about when both the technical and psychological factors are skilfully mastered.

In order to control productivity, profitability and quality the operational processes on the level of the company, the products and individuals must all be mastered. Process thinking should not stifle creativity in a restaurant, but it must bring steadiness, precision and accuracy into the operations in order to achieve high-quality, productive and profitable operations. In what follows, some typical hindrances to productive business and some solutions for removing them are presented.

Bad planning and indistinct business idea

The creation of an atmosphere favourable to success requires efficient, open communication. The organization must know and internalize its goals and the measures that must be taken in order to reach these goals. Regrettably often, particularly in small companies within the industry, this does not happen. The management does not, for example, bring the economic goals out into the open in the organization but keeps them hidden, thus creating a very difficult situation for the employees: results should be achieved, but how?

Open communications and management are important tools also in the creation of a good work atmosphere. Poor team spirit will lead to worse customer service and growth in the number of customer complaints. This will lead to two-fold losses: reduced sales and increased costs.

Too much diversity in operations

A too broad product selection or a too broad customer base may cause a control problem for the company. For example, good quality service cannot be guaranteed to all customers and the number of complaints grows, which results in less chances of success in the future. Too much diversity often leads to weakened control of profitability both on the level of the whole company as well as its products.

Lack of motivation

The restaurant staff and management must believe in what they are doing. They must have the firm conviction that the product being sold is the best on the market. Successful business is impossible without the staff believing in the product they are selling.

The management must be able to create an innovative and inspiring system of leadership and motivation. Through teamwork and commitment, a high-quality service organization is created, without forgetting the importance of strong, visionary management in the creation of a profitable, high-quality service product.

Deficient marketing and development work

Without life-span thinking, any development work carried out for the operational concept and units will remain deficient. Customers lose interest in a weakening product and sales diminish. Deficient market research leads to a lack of knowledge of the customers' needs and consequent erroneous management moves. The business will wither as profitability weakens.

Weak management

If the management of the company does not take its leadership role sufficiently seriously or cannot function as a democratic, stable figure, the leadership atmosphere in the company becomes lax and it becomes more difficult to reach the set goals. The superior must have the courage to expose her/himself to criticism and possible failure, for without courage it is not possible to run a successful business. The nature of strong leadership must be understood: it is not tyranny, but responsible and courageous engagement in the business activities in order to awaken the motivation in the employees of the organization.

Lack of delegation and focus

If the restaurant management attempts to do everything by itself, it will not be able to make use of the organization's skills widely enough. Then the management will not focus on the most essential tasks, but struggle to deal with matters that somebody else might do at lower cost, and possibly better. The restaurant's purchases should also be centralized with attention to quality and customer satisfaction as a factor guiding economy.

The management should concentrate on its own areas of expertise, i.e. the development of the restaurant product, and not, for example, on perfecting the technique of economic reporting. It is enough that superiors understand economic reporting so that they are able to assess and make use of it.

Too rapid growth

Economic growth as such should be a positive phenomenon, but this is not always the case. If the business grows too fast, there might be problems, for example in customer service and quality of products, profitability and sufficiency of funding. Controlled growth is used to help ensure that growth will continue also in the future. If growth is not controlled, it will lead before long to weakening sales opportunities.

Wrong investment decisions

Productivity weakens if the investments made do not serve the business idea. In renewing the restaurant units often all attention is given to renovating the customer facilities, whereas the processing facilities are left with too little attention. Expansion investments should be in the right relationship to the rationalization investments. Another possibility not sufficiently explored is the partial replacement of own production with subcontractors.

Large amount of fixed costs

Annual, weekly and daily variation in sales, so typical of the restaurant business, should be balanced by fixed costs that are as low as possible. The largest amounts come from employment costs and rents of premises. The more these can be made changeable, for example by using part-time workers and by negotiating leases in which the amount of rent is bound to the amount of sales, the economic risks of business are reduced and, at the same time, an opportunity is created for more productive operations.

Weak level of economic control

Productivity is based, first and foremost, on reporting that supports management. If reporting does not produce the right information to aid management or if reporting is not used enough in managing staff, productivity cannot be guided in the right direction.

Productivity comes from both customer and service provider satisfaction

Finally, the basis for the economic and qualitative goals of a restaurant business and, at the same time, for reaching the desired productivity can be summarized as follows: successful business activity is a triangle of the simultaneous satisfaction of the company, the staff and the customers. If one 'angle' of the triangle is weak, the others cannot, in the long run, remain satisfied. Keeping the business on a successful track demands that management maintains the satisfaction of all three groups.

Further reading

Aldrich, A. and Drysdale, J. (2002) *Profitable menu planning*, 3rd edn. Prentice Hall, Upper Saddle River.

Fitzsimmons, J. and Fitzsimmons, M. (1998) *Service management: operations, strategy and information technology*, 2nd edn. McGraw-Hill, Boston.

Giers, A., Koskinen, T. and Pöyhönen, M. (1991) *Tuottavuus majoitus – ja ravitsemiselinkeinossa.* Haaga Institute Polytechnic, Helsinki.

Heikkilä, P. and Viljanen, R. (2000) *Yritystoiminta hotelli-, ravintola-ja matkailualalla.* Vimark, Juva.

IAHMS Spring Conference (1995) *Productivity in the hospitality and tourism industry: trends, developments, proceedings.* Leeds.

Levesque, C., Mc Vety, P. and Ware, B. (2001) *Fundamentals of menu planning.* Wiley, New York.

Määttälä, S., Nuutila, J. and Saranpää, T. (2004) *Juhlapalvelu: suunnittele ja toteuta.* WSOY, Helsinki.

Ojasalo, K. (1999) *Conceptualizing productivity in services.* Swedish School of Economics and Business Administration, Helsinki.

Schutz, W. (1994) *The human element: productivity, self-esteem and the bottom line.* Jossey-Bass, San Francisco.

Uusi-Rauva, E. (1997) *Tuottavuus – mittaa ja menesty.* Kauppakaari, Helsinki.

Performance measurement in the international hospitality industry

Helen Atkinson

Introduction

Performance measurement is an important area of academic and practitioner activity. This chapter will review the weaknesses of traditional performance measures and evaluate a number of key frameworks. In the context of the hospitality industry characteristics and trends, it will review the hospitality literature in performance measurement and propose areas for future research.

A rationale for change

The measurement of corporate performance has been recognized as an important topic in management accounting for many years, but it was not until the late 1980s and early 1990s that the focus of both academic and practitioners' attention grew dramatically (Kaplan, 1994). Neely reported that between 1994 and 1996 publication volumes were equivalent 'to one new article on business performance measurement appearing every five hours of every working day' (1999:207). The move from the industrial age to the information age with the dramatic developments in the nature and intensity of business and commerce changed the way companies compete. It is no longer sufficient to be first to market with new technological innovations; to be successful companies now have to focus on customers not products, relationships rather than lead times and they need to 'exploit intangible or invisible assets' (Kaplan and Norton, 1996b:3).

Neely (1999) identified seven main reasons for this recent interest including: the 'changing nature of work increasing competition; specific improvement initiatives national and international awards and the power of information technology' (1999:210). Atkinson and Brander Brown (2001) argue that deregulation and privatization, globalization and product differentiation, increasingly sophisticated customers, increased emphasis on the supply chain and stakeholders has resulted in 'an emerging new competitive order' (2001:128), where companies are changing the way they monitor and measure performance.

Traditional performance measurement has been criticized for creating single focus, short-term orientation for companies that inhibits investment in new markets and new technologies and so reduces international competitiveness (Doyle, 1994; Cross and Lynch, 1992). Traditional performance measures that focus on financial performance and are dominated by the shareholders demands for return on investment have rapidly grown out of synchrony with the way companies are operating. A radical change was prescribed by Professor Robert Eccles for the way performance is measured; he advocated taking a *radical decision* where the status of financial measures must be subjugated to other measures which are more relevant in terms of the company's strategy and competitive arena. Thus 'giving them equal (or even greater) status in determining strategy promotions, bonuses and other rewards' (Eccles, 1991:131).

Atkinson and Brander Brown (2001:128) identified a number of fundamental weaknesses,

> including: limitations in their accuracy and neutrality; a dominance of lag/result over lead/determinant measures; an emphasis on the short term – often at the expense of strategic issues; little appreciation of the links and relationships between key areas and aspects of an organisation; and an overall lack of balance.

47

Furthermore, if what gets measured gets done (Eccles, 1991), it is important to focus management attention on the right things, thus companies must carefully select the right metrics to ensure their long-term business strategy is achieved. They must cease the 'folly of rewarding A whilst hoping for B' (Kerr, 1975:769). Measures such as customer satisfaction, market share and quality are arguably more important indicators of success than profitability. This is especially true when one considers the inherent weaknesses of the profit measure (Eccles, 1991; Kaplan and Norton, 1992) and the fact that measures such as customer satisfaction and market share are drivers of profitability, in other words are *lead* measures, whereas profit is a *lag* indicator (Fitzgerald et al., 1991). As these features become more important to the competitive advantage of companies, they must be incorporated into the performance measurement systems.

A range of models and frameworks has been developed to address the above weaknesses. Before entering into a critical review of these models and frameworks it is necessary to identify the key features of the hospitality industry and the future trends that provide a context for performance measurement systems review.

Hospitality industry characteristics and developments

The hospitality industry is a complex and multifaceted sector of the global economy. In the international arena, large corporate entities are developing strong brands and expanding through a range of mechanisms, such as franchising, whereas nationally in Europe and the UK there is still a large proportion of small and medium enterprise (SME) activity, in addition to the multi-unit chain operations which proliferate in the restaurant and public house sector. The characteristics and developments in the hospitality industry are having an impact on the performance measurement systems used and how effectively these are implemented.

The nature and characteristics of hospitality businesses

Hospitality businesses are multifaceted enterprises, for example, Harris (1995b) discusses the hotel industry where the product and service elements are complex and interrelated. Harris explains that a hotel product combines three different kinds of businesses in a single operation (Figure 3.1). Harris defines the accommodation or rooms division of a hotel as pure service. The Food and Beverage division or department encompasses restaurants and bars of various types and involves service, stock management and production functions. Each function presents different operational,

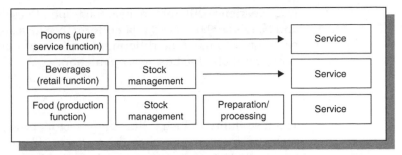

Figure 3.1
Hotel operation showing key activities and associated functions.
Source: Harris (1995:30).

managerial and financial issues and priorities and thus makes a hotel operation a complex business to manage.

In addition to the diversity of functions within the hotel operation, hospitality services generally cannot be stored, the perishability of the product/service adds another dimension to managing the business. The other features of services also apply. The involvement of the customer in the production process leads to two key characteristics. First, the unique nature of the service encounter (hcterogeneity) where every service encounter is different from the last. Secondly, services are produced and consumed at the same time (simultaneity) – this intensifies the impact of people in the process. The behaviour of both employee and customer and the way they interact will have a significant impact on performance. The intangible nature of services adds further to the complexity and difficulty of managing in a service environment. The high level of intangibles makes customer service and customer satisfaction key issues. Together these characteristics present particular demands on management, which are collectively unique to hospitality operations. These factors provide a challenging environment in which to develop effective performance measurement systems.

The hospitality industry is also populated by many high fixed cost businesses which, according to Kotas (1975), demonstrate a particular business orientation. Brander Brown and Harris (1999) argue that the combination of factors such as cost structure, demand fluctuation and capital intensiveness, result in a strong market orientation compared to manufacturing companies where the business focus is more cost orientated. However, they continue to point out that due to the complexity and multifunctional nature of hotels, in particular, the business orientation is not necessarily homogeneous within a hotel or across the sector. In congruence with Schmenner (1986), who classified service businesses into four different types and showed that different service businesses will experience different managerial imperatives, Brander Brown and Harris (1999) argued that performance measures will need to be tailored to meet the differing needs of not only the business context but also the business orientation.

Recent trends

The hospitality industry, like many sectors of the economy, has seen dramatic change over the last three decades; Harris and Mongiello (2001) identify a rise in market demand and customer expectations and the acceleration of globalization and product differentiation (Atkinson and Brander Brown, 2001). The hospitality industry, and in particular hotel sector performance, mirrors the business/economic cycle. Significant world events (such as the terrorist attacks in New York, the Iraq war and the Asian SARS epidemic) had dramatic effects in the early part of the 21st century, but Hans Lindh (2003:iv) reports that 'unlike in previous down turns there have not been a significant number of bankruptcies and closures, hospitality companies have emerged both learner and more focussed on maximising profitability by providing value to their guests, employees and owners'.

The hotel industry is characterized by large global brands and is experiencing developments in approaches to finance with increasing expansion through management contracts and an increasing trend to separate ownership from operation. This trend can lead to diverging interests and needs of hotel operators and hotel investment companies (Denton and White, 2000; Sangster, 2003) and thus put pressure on performance measurement systems. The demand for increasing return on investment (ROI) in conjunction with rising costs will lead to increased demand for the sector as a whole to improve productivity.

Competition is also intensifying in the restaurant and public house sector. There is increasing consumer spend associated with increased disposable incomes. Changing patterns of behaviour towards 'snacking and grazing' are leading to a decrease in fine dining and an increase in mid-scale and quick service restaurants (Ball and Roberts, 2003). Multi-unit operations (chains and franchises) are becoming increasingly significant, achieving economies of scale in production, system development and research and development, which enable these organizations to resist the effect of rising costs that is affecting the whole sector (Ball and Roberts, 2003). In the context of performance measurement, increasingly discerning consumers put the emphasis on brand standards and service quality.

Contract catering is dominated by two large players (in the UK and western Europe) and typifies the global local nexus where large international brands such as Compass provide a corporate umbrella for low scale relationship partnership businesses, operating in diverse business situations. Future trends include developments with 'blue chip organisations outsourcing their catering and support services on a multi-site basis throughout Europe' and the 'widespread bundling of catering with other support activities' (Quest, 2005:11), which provides opportunities for product and market development. This will lead to a greater need for brand standards to be maintained over wider service/product ranges and wider geographical and cultural landscapes.

The characteristics and trends described above result in key challenges, which will impact upon performance measurement systems. Brand equity needs maintenance through strict control of brand standards, which results in the need to develop and maintain global standards of performance. The importance of people, employees and customers in the production process combined with the perishable, real-time nature of operations results in a need for up-to-date information for decision-making. Changing patterns of ownership means that performance measurement at operational and corporate level may diverge.

Having identified key characteristics and developments in the hospitality industry there is now a clear context for the review of the performance measurement frameworks.

Performance measurement frameworks

The following frameworks have very different antecedents and reflect the discipline focus and context of the team developing them. They all possess, to a lesser or greater extent, the characteristics needed in contemporary performance measurement systems.

One of the earliest approaches to performance measurement was the Tableau de Bord, which was developed by process engineers at the turn of the century in France. They were concerned with understanding cause-effect relationships and developed a dashboard of measures to be used by managers to guide decision-making. Epstein and Manzoni (1997) report that this approach suffers from problems associated with an overemphasis on financial metrics, lack of brevity and internal focus. DuPont were famous for developing a structured financial analysis tool, which was the industry standard for performance management for many years. However, this was purely based on financial ratios and thus suffered from the weaknesses mentioned above.

Perhaps the most widely known measurement tool is Kaplan and Norton's Balanced Scorecard (Kaplan and Norton, 1992). This model, with its four distinct perspectives, has been implemented widely by consultants, such as Nolan and Norton who were linked to KPMG Peat Marwick. This framework will be explained in detail below.

Another well-respected formula is the Performance Pyramid developed by Lynch and Cross. This represents the whole business as a pyramid, starting at the top of the pyramid with Vision, which is built on the business unit level where key results and objectives are set on two key dimensions, Financial and Markets. The fourth level is set at departmental or work group level and encompasses four local operating performance criteria, which have internal and external perspectives. Quality and delivery focus on meeting external customer expectations and cycle time and waste represent tangible internal measures. One of the criticisms that can be laid at the performance pyramid is that, at the business unit level, two mutually exclusive features exist side by side. The financial and the market dimensions provide two divergent perspectives at this influential level. Giving these equal status could perpetuate conflict at the second level of the pyramid between finance and marketing. Thus, it could be argued that the performance pyramid does not do what Eccles (1991) was advocating, that is to subjugate financials within a set of broader measures at the critical small business unit (SBU) level. In addition, the performance pyramid is grounded in the manufacturing environment, although this model can apply to a mass service (Schmenner, 1986), such as a fast food restaurant, its application to a professional service firm, such as a solicitor, is more difficult. This model therefore would have limited applicability to the hospitality industry and will not be reviewed in detail.

The second model to feature in this chapter is focused on UK service businesses, called the Results and Determinants model. This model was developed by a multidisciplinary team and published by CIMA (Fitzgerald et al., 1991). It is based upon six dimensions for service businesses. The other key model, which will be described here, is the Performance Prism (Adams and Neely, 2002; Kennerley and Neely, 2002). This model takes a broader perspective of stakeholders while aiming to recognize the causal relationships that drive performance.

Other contemporary models and initiatives include Metapraxis' Performance Clusters, Foundation for Performance Measurement's Strategic Quadrants and The RSA's Tomorrow's Company, all of which attempt to address the weaknesses of traditional financial performance measures.

Balanced scorecard

The balanced scorecard approach provides a multifaceted view of the business. It provides a view of progress from a customer

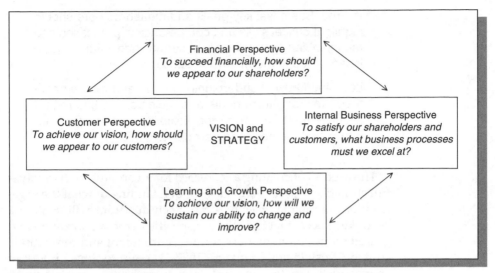

Figure 3.2
Balanced scorecard approach.
Source: Kaplan and Norton (1996:76).

perspective, a financial perspective, a business process/internal perspective and finally an innovation and learning perspective. The scorecard provides a link between strategy and operations by asking four key questions (Figure 3.2).

This notion of different perspectives is unique to the scorecard. Another important feature of the scorecard is the clear link between corporate strategy and measures throughout the organization. By focusing on the four perspectives, managers can articulate their core vision, strategy and goals before translating them into specific measures, targets and initiatives.

The structure of this framework enables companies to develop different measures within each quadrant. Atkinson and Brander Brown (2005) identified typical examples of the sorts of measures companies might include in their scorecard. These included:

> Financial: emphasising shareholder satisfaction, key goals and measures here generally involve [gross and/or net] profitability, return on capital employed, residual income/economic value added, sales growth, market position and share, cash flow etc.

> Customer: focusing on 'real' customer satisfaction, key goals and indicators here typically stress common customer concerns such as delivery time, quality, service and cost etc.

Internal Business: key goals and measures here should highlight critical skills and competencies, processes and technologies that will deliver current and future organisational [customer/financial] success.

Learning/Growth: underpinning the other three perspectives, key long-term goals and indicators in this regard typically relate to improving flexibility and investing for future development and new opportunities.

The process of creating a scorecard for an organization involves full strategic appraisal and clear understanding of what the organization's strategic objectives are. Each quadrant will contain a set of key success factors that are specific to the organization and geared to the company's corporate environment and competitive strategy. Epstein and Manzoni (1997:31) point to three important characteristics of the scorecard. First, it 'presents in a single document'; secondly, if implemented properly this document should be 'short and connected to the company's information system'; thirdly, it groups measures into 'boxes each, reflecting a distinct perspective' on the company's performance.

The other key feature of the scorecard is the focus (and limit) set on the number of measures being tracked at any one time. This ability to reduce strategy down to a handful of key measures and thus reduce managerial information overload is recognized by Brander Brown et al. (1996) and addresses issues raised by Geller (1985a–c) in his work on management information systems in the hospitality industry.

Importantly, it should also be noted here that a causal relationship is overtly recognized between the four perspectives, with innovation and learning being the driving force to deliver success in the internal processes, which then in turn will meet customer and shareholder needs (Kaplan and Norton, 1992).

The balanced scorecard is widely recognized and used (Marr and Schiuma, 2003). Several years ago it was already reported as being used by 60 per cent of Fortune 500 companies (Silk, 1998). It is argued that the balanced scorecard addresses a number of significant deficiencies associated with more 'traditional' performance measurement systems. For example, it provides a 'balanced' organizational assessment by recognizing a variety of key stakeholder views (Brander Brown and McDonnell, 1995; Ahn, 2001). In addition, by combining non-financial indicators like service quality, employee morale and customer satisfaction with financial performance measures it responds to Eccles' *radical* call to subjugate financial measures to be '… one among a broader set of measures …' (Eccles, 1991:131).

Furthermore, the balanced scorecard focuses management attention on the 'drivers' of performance by explicitly encouraging the inclusion of 'lead' as well as 'lag' indicators (Eccles, 1991; Fitzgerald et al., 1991; Atkinson and Brander Brown, 2001). In addition, by identifying the cause-and-effect relationships, important trade-offs between key goals and measures are highlighted. This is considered vital to identifying organizational priorities (Butler et al., 1997; Epstein and Manzoni, 1997; Mooraj et al., 1999). Significantly though, the balanced scorecard is also thought to be capable of acting as a powerful link between strategy and operations (Kaplan and Norton, 1996a; Brander Brown and Harris, 1998). Kaplan and Norton themselves acknowledge that the framework has evolved through use, with many companies employing it not only to measure performance but to develop, communicate and monitor strategy (Kaplan and Norton, 1996a).

Results and determinants model

The research underpinning Fitzgerald et al.'s Results and Determinants model (Figure 3.3) focused exclusively on UK service

	Performance dimensions	Types of measures
Re**s**u**l**t**s**	Competitiveness	Relative market share and position Sales growth Measures of the customer base
	Financial performance	Profitability Liquidity Capital structure Market ratios
De**t**e**r**m**i**n**a**n**t**s**	Quality of service	Reliability, responsiveness, aesthetics/appearance, cleanliness/tidiness, comfort, friendliness, communication, courtesy, competence, access, availability, security
	Flexibility	Volume flexibility Delivery speed flexibility Specification flexibility
	Resource utilization	Productivity Efficiency
	Innovation	Performance of the innovation process Performance of individual innovators

Figure 3.3
Results and determinants model.
Source: Fitzgerald et al. (1991:8).

industries and integrated new management accounting theories with operations management concepts and models. Fitzgerald et al. stated that, the competitive environment, competitive strategy and the service type would all determine the range of performance measures an organization should use.

Fitzgerald et al. acknowledge that the information set used to monitor performance must include both financial and non-financial metrics, address issues of feed forward and feedback and also be both internally and externally focused. Their ideas were synthesized into six generic performance dimensions: financial, competitiveness, quality, flexibility, resource utilization and innovation.

The six dimensions fall into two conceptually different categories – Results, which reflects the success of the chosen strategy and monitors the end results, and Determinants, which affects or potentially delivers competitive success, i.e. the means of achieving strategic goals. The choice of measures that are contained in each subset will be contingent upon the three key factors of the competitive environment, competitive strategy and service type and will of course vary from business unit to business unit. Although tailored to the UK service sector, there is no evidence that any hospitality companies have adopted it. One of the major criticisms of the R&D model is that it includes a large number of dimensions, which may not provide the focus that Kaplan and Norton (1996a), Geller (1985a–c) and others claimed to be important.

Performance prism

The performance prism has been developed by Neely in the light of experience and in response to the development of other models. In particular, it reflects changes in the corporate psyche that now recognizes the importance of a wider group of stakeholders in addition to shareholders. This model focuses on 'stakeholder satisfaction' (Kennerley and Neely, 2002:151) including 'other investors, customers, employees, and suppliers' and acknowledges the growing importance of regulators and pressure groups. Five key facets are identified and it is advocated that organizations consider the following questions when developing performance measures:

Stakeholder satisfaction – who are our key stakeholders and what do they want and need?

Strategies – what strategies do we have to put in place to satisfy the wants needs of key stakeholders?

Processes – what critical processes do we have to operate and enhance these processes?

Capabilities – what capabilities do we need to operate and enhance these processes?

Stakeholder contribution – what contribution do we require from our stakeholders if we are to maintain and develop these capabilities?

(Kennerley and Neely, 2002:152)

The model explicitly recognizes the causal link between stakeholder satisfaction and the other prism factors, showing that stakeholder value (a result) is created by the determinants, strategies, capabilities and processes. Recognition of the prism facets through all levels of the organization can ensure measures are 'integrated both across the organisation's functions and through its hierarchy' (Kennerley and Neely, 2002:153). The authors claim the framework is multidimensional and facilitates the use of financial and non-financial measures, balanced with 'external (stakeholder) and internal (strategy, process and capability) perspectives' (Kennerley and Neely, 2002:153).

Comparison and critique

The four models featured have similarities and differences. All these models have a variety of categories for measures and combine financial measures with non-financial measures, for example, innovation, quality and resource utilization. Kaplan and Norton's model is multirational in that it looks at performance from different perspectives, whereas Le Saint (1992) describes the model from Fitzgerald et al. as unirational. Lynch and Cross highlight the three sides of their pyramid, in an attempt to overlay the three key stakeholder perspectives, but it is not at all clear how the tensions between them can be resolved. Although Kaplan and Norton's model does reflect different perspectives, it does not recognize all stakeholders, ignoring employee and supplier's contribution and failing to identify the role of community (Atkinson et al., 1997; Mooraj et al., 1999; Nørreklit, 2000), whereas Kennerley and Neely's performance prism expressly focuses on a wider definition of stakeholders as well as recognizing the growing importance of regulators and pressure groups (Adams and Neely, 2002).

The scorecard intuitively recognizes that the way to compete and succeed is changing. It is predicated on the idea that the old ways of measuring, just like the old ways of competing (through the product and economies and scale) are no longer guaranteed to deliver success. In the future it will be quality, service and speed that matter. This future orientation is a key strength of Kaplan and Norton's scorecard model. The results and determinants (R&D)

model also recognizes the importance of competition. It goes further, explicitly and pragmatically, to recognize the service organization type as critical and to promote flexibility as central to longer-term success.

The results and determinants model focuses on causal relationships between the determinant dimensions and the results dimensions, making them explicit. Although Kaplan shows in his detailed work a link between quadrants, it is not evident on first inspection how causal relationships may arise. The performance pyramid does not appear to provide a structure overtly to recognize this, although the model is clearly linked to the value chain of operations, which in itself implies causality. The performance prism clearly recognizes the drivers of stakeholder satisfaction are the other prism facets (strategies, processes, capabilities and contribution), which are 'determinants' of performance.

All four models propose a range of measures, including financial and non-financial, internal and external and measures of efficiency and effectiveness. The scorecard and the results and determinants model explicitly recognize the trade-off between different measures and they all link strategy to operations. The scorecard is particularly succinct in this regard with strategy clearly at the centre of all scorecards.

To a lesser or greater extent these frameworks all have the potential to adhere to the key characteristics of performance measurement systems identified by Kennerley and Neely. For example they all provide:

1 a balanced view of the organization and

2 provide a comprehensive overview of performance in a multi-dimensional format with

3 either overt or covert recognition of the results and determinants of performance.

However, the key with all such systems is implementation. Recent feedback from the implementation process identifies some potential problems emerging.

Implementation experience and problems

The most widely used model is undoubtedly Kaplan and Norton's balanced scorecard. Smith (2005:27) states 'it remains the management accountants benchmarking tool of choice'. Inevitably then, most of the literature reviewing implementation of performance measurement systems relates to this model, but in principle could apply to any performance measurement framework.

Criticisms include the lack of balance, that despite attempting to follow the mantra, organizations fail to identify truly balanced measures, with financially orientated measures creeping into the other quadrants (Atkinson and Brander Brown, 2001). Lack of prioritization due to the desire to meet all stakeholders' needs (Gering and Mntambo, 2002), the tendency for top down approach and the lack of double loop learning (Nørreklit, 2000; Marginson, 2002), plus the interaction with other control systems (Otley, 1999; Ahn, 2001) have been identified as weaknesses in the implementation of scorecards. There is a call for more research into the cost benefit analysis of performance measurement systems (Mooraj et al., 1999) and, as yet, there has been little evaluation of the effectiveness of the balanced scorecard to deliver improved performance (Ahn, 2001). It has been suggested that perhaps it is the process of constructing the scorecard that is valuable in its own right, as it requires organizations to identify a 'more precise strategy' (Ahn, 2001:457).

The following section will describe and evaluate the state of the art of performance measurement research in the hospitality industry and will review the most recent research findings to identify successes, advances in thinking and avenues for further research in performance measurement systems.

Performance measurement in the hospitality industry

There has been much debate in recent years about the state of hospitality management research (Morrison, 2002; Olsen, 2002; Brotherton, 2003b; Jones, 2004; Littlejohn, 2004; Tribe, 2004). It is often felt by hospitality academics that this is a 'young' research area with a variety of epistemological assumptions. In particular, it can be argued that research and development in accounting in hospitality lags behind that in other industry sectors and generic research publications. However, there is a growing body of literature that, according to Morrison (2002:161), 'has made considerable advances and contributions to knowledge creation'. Olsen (2002:94) recognizes the dual demands of the academic community who have 'decades, even centuries of prior research experience' and the users of research who are 'very practical people who demand relevance and immediacy to the solution of their problems'.

In fact the hospitality industry has been in the forefront of accounting developments. Chin et al. (1995) recognize that the widespread use and acceptance of a standard chart of accounts in the form of the Uniform System of Hotel Accounts, has led to advances in competitive benchmarking. This 'significant development' (Harris and Brander Brown, 1998:162) has resulted in the development of common approaches to ratios and key statistics which, through the mediation of consultants, such as Pannell Kerr Forster, facilitates the production of industry statistics and competitive benchmarking. Despite recent evidence that such comparisons must be used with caution (Enz et al., 2001), there is widespread use of comparative data by managers, analysts and consultants, enabling the hospitality industry to integrate both externally and internally focused measures of performance for many years.

Some literature relating to performance measurement focuses on predicting failure (Adams, 1995) and managing through difficult trading conditions (Moncraz and Kron, 1993). The reported use of univariate analysis and multidiscriminant analysis to analyse profit statements and balance sheets, could indicate a more sophisticated approach to financial management (Adams, 1995; Moncraz and Kron, 1995). Harris and Brander Brown (1998) identify a myriad of examples demonstrating the increased use of more sophisticated financial statement analysis, but this is still predominantly financially orientated.

Clear identification of key performance indicators by Schmidgall (1988) showed differences in manager use in smaller versus large organizations with a bias towards cost orientation rather than market orientation. In 1995, Geller reviewed the use of critical success factors through research involving 27 hotel companies. This revealed that a range of critical success factors were being monitored including financial and non-financial factors. He identified the similarity among executives for a common set of goals which, when prioritized, showed profitability and return of investment (ROI) at the top, with guest satisfaction fourth and employee morale sixth. However, when focusing on critical success factors rather than goals, Geller found employee attitude as top of the priority list, with guest satisfaction second (1995a). The problem identified was that current management information systems were not providing good (timely and accurate) data to monitor these critical success factors and thus executives were not in a position effectively to monitor the things that mattered (1985b). Geller continued to prescribe a process for the review of executive information systems (1985c). The important issue here is that as early as 1985 it was clear what mattered and it was known that current management information systems were not delivering the right information.

Collier and Gregory (1995) identified a large amount of similarity within the hotel groups in terms of financial and non-financial measures adopted, although it is not clear what priority was placed on the different metrics. Importantly here, they noted that incentive schemes were invariably linked to budgetary control and thus financially orientated, which could imply that these organizations were still managing through financial measures.

Brander Brown and McDonnell (1995) show clearly that it is possible to develop a balanced and strategically focused performance measurement framework in the hotel context, although they too recognize the potential inhibition of hotel management information systems identified by Geller (1985b). Huckestein and Duboff (1999) report on the success at Hilton of implementing a balanced scorecard approach, which was at the centre of a review of their business model. This included a review of their value chain and establishment of a series of integrated initiatives to improve performance by focusing on key value drivers of brand management, revenue maximization, operational effectiveness, and value proposition. Interestingly, they identified the need to follow through and the need for this new approach to performance measurement and management to 'be ingrained in the business culture' (Huckestein and Duboff, 1999:38). They also recognized the need for such systems to evolve and acknowledged that as managers 'become more familiar' they adapt the measures to make the system more effective.

Despite this positive example, there is still evidence that progress is slow in the UK and Europe. Atkinson and Brander Brown's empirical study into UK hotels showed that there was still a 'predominance of financial and past orientated dimensions' and thus they are 'overwhelmingly dominated by result measures' (Atkinson and Brander Brown, 2001:134) with little or no adoption of new frameworks in a comprehensive or systematic way. The reasons cited include 'the influence of corporate ownership, as well as cultural and technological factors'.

In addition, work by Harris and Mongiello (2001) also identified an emphasis on financial metrics, although they identified differences at corporate and unit level. Haktanir and Harris (2005) observed the same variation between operational managers, focusing on customer satisfaction, and senior management, who focused on finance in the independent hotel sector.

Harris and Mongiello observed the juxtaposition between a market orientation and reliance on financial metrics, they identified the extent to which hotel company performance indicators were 'balanced' between finance, customer, human resources and operations. They found that some large hotel corporations were unbalanced with an emphasis on finance, whereas others were unbalanced towards the customer perspective. The most balanced companies showed equal status for finance and customers but these, arguably downstream, measures had lower weighting than operations and human resources. What is interesting about Harris and Mongiello's research is they found that even where financial indicators are used, they did not dominate the general manager's behaviour. A different profile of managerial actions was observed. 'These actions suggest that when general managers want to improve their business performance, they initially act on human resources … then marketing … and then on operations' (Harris and Mongiello, 2001:125). Harris and Mongiello claim that the hospitality industry has evolved and that managers are increasingly using managerial tools and 'their confidence in strategic issues seems greater' (Harris and Mongiello, 2001:127). What is also noteworthy is that both these studies show companies adopting functionally orientated scorecards which, it could be argued, have oversimplified Kaplan and Norton's original concept, losing the essence of innovation, growth and organizational learning in particular.

The above findings demonstrate how performance measurement is evolving in the hospitality industry and is backed up by recent research conducted by the author. Preliminary findings from this replicate research study reveal that the majority of respondent companies have adopted some formal model for performance measurement. Interestingly, those that have not adopted a formal model mainly operate in the restaurant sector. The research focused on those dimensions being measured and monitored and the relative priority given to them. Initial findings show revenue is top priority, followed by profitability and then liquidity and costs, with customer-orientated measures showing fifth in the priority order. As yet this research study is incomplete but initial findings show that financials still dominate corporate performance measurement agenda in the hospitality businesses.

As part of this ongoing research the in-depth interviews undertaken to date have revealed how the performance measurement system is being used and how it is integrated with other initiatives to deliver improved performance. One large hotel group identified a somewhat unbalanced scorecard with an emphasis on finance, customer and employees, but little real evidence of a focus on internal business and innovation and learning dimensions. However, detailed discussions revealed a series of 'off scorecard' activities that encourage innovation through a corporate university, learning zones in all major units, targets for staff development and continuous improvement initiatives teams, which does address this quadrant of the scorecard, although they did not have a formal mechanism for harvesting employee lead innovations.

The other very interesting pattern that is emerging in the hotel group detailed above is the increasing engagement with the scorecard as part of incentive programmes and the move towards the integration of more non-financial metrics. Traditionally, the incentive scheme has been based on budgetary system (as identified by Collier and Gregory, 1995) but, in recent years, the scorecard has been integrated into the incentive scheme rating system and each year its relative weighting has increased with 25 per cent of the bonus coming from the balanced scorecard scores. This still leaves 75 per cent of the incentive salary being driven by financial dimensions of performance, but the fact that in the last two years the weighting of the scorecard score has been increased.

Another interesting feature emerging is the move to a global scorecard for the whole company making a change from a global structure but with locally established measures and priorities. This is contrary to many research findings (Fitzgerald et al., 1991; Brander Brown and McDonnell, 1995; Olsen and Slater, 2002) and is a response to the identified trends of globalization and the increasing importance of brand standards. As one interviewee stated 'our customers are global, it doesn't matter to them what city or country they are in they want the same experience and the same feel from the hotel, they want our brand where ever they are'. This move to a standard scorecard for an entire company worldwide does seem to run counter to the accepted view of many researchers who claim contingent factors are important in performance measurement systems design (Fitzgerald et al., 1991; Brander Brown and McDonnell, 1995; Brignall and Ballantine, 1996; Harris and Brander Brown, 1998).

When it comes to monitoring the success of the scorecard, a review of literature shows a dearth of research (Atkinson and Brander Brown, 2005). Many researchers claim there is still little evidence of the efficacy of the balanced scorecard approach (Mooraj et al., 1999; Otley, 1999). But anecdotal evidence does exist and it is clear from Huckestein and Duboff (1999:36) that scorecard implementation is beneficial; 'without doubt, we conclude that the benefits far outweigh the time and resources required'. The benefits included managers taking long- and short-term views, increase in brand equity, improved teamwork and attuned employees to external competition, facilitated communication of how value is created throughout the company.

The latest research conducted by the author, implies that success stories with the scorecard continue. A representative from a large global hotel chain noted that the scorecard has 'refocused management on the things that drive performance'. Subsequent to the scorecard development and implementation, employee satisfaction became a key performance measure, regular satisfaction surveys revealed issues and concerns which were easily addressed and corrected by management; employees observed improvements and increased their engagement with the survey. Now there is a biannual staff questionnaire, which is completed by all staff and employee satisfaction is at an all time high. This achievement it is claimed is a direct result of the implementation of the scorecard.

Denton and White (2000) describe the balanced scorecard potential to mediate the tension between asset management and hotel operations. In an industry where increasingly hotel ownership is being separated from operation (Sangster, 2003), this case study shows the potential of the balanced scorecard framework to reverse 'the lodging industry's long standing trend that has seen alienation between' the interests of owners and management companies (Denton and White, 2000:107). Through the development of the scorecard, via the explicit identification of causal links and the correlation between dimensions of performance, such as guest satisfaction score and return on investments, it was possible to align the objectives of hotel managers with investment managers.

The above review illustrates the nature and diversity of performance measurement research in the hospitality industry. This research is typified by small-scale isolated research projects that generally paint a positive picture, but there is a need for more in-depth research.

Where next? The future for research

The above themes and issues coalesce with trends in the industry to set a future research agenda in the area of performance measurement and management. Five such areas are proposed below, although these are by no means exhaustive or exclusive but represent the author's view of the potential avenues for development.

It has been shown that the hospitality industry has, to varying degrees, embraced these new approaches to performance measurement, thereby addressing issues of balance, range, internal versus external, lead versus lag and financial versus non-financial measures. However, there is little systematic study of what is actually being measured. Evidence exists that some scorecards are still unbalanced (Harris and Mongiello, 2001) and there is also evidence that the two *lead* quadrants of the scorecard Learning Growth and, to a lesser extent, Internal Business perspectives are not being fully addressed. These are traditionally the hardest to identify and quantify (Denton and White, 2000). So there is still a need for research into what measures are being used in different business contexts and understand how these remain true to Kaplan and Norton's original concept and to establish common goals, CFS and performance measures relevant to each sector of the hospitality industry (Brander Brown and McDonnell, 1995).

There is clear coverage of the hotel sector but little published research about other sectors, such as the contract catering and restaurant and pub sectors. Although it is well known that the Compass Group, one of the leading contract catering organizations in the UK and Europe, use the scorecard throughout their organization, no studies have identified what are the particular issues and difficulties implementing a scorecard approach in this context. With the range of businesses within this group, which vary in terms of their business format and scale, concept and product/service, it would be interesting to find out how adaptive the scorecard is in this heterogeneous business context and how culture affects implementation. In addition, with global businesses, the effect of national cultural influences on the relationship to and interaction with performance measurement frameworks will become increasingly important (Harris and Brander Brown, 1998).

What is interesting in the latest research carried out by the author is the combined notion of organizational maturity and managerial trust in relation to the balanced scorecard. Organization maturity relates to how the scorecard is integrated into the management psyche and the extent to which management information systems have been developed to support scorecard use. Managerial trust relates to the extent to which the dysfunctional behaviour of managers associated with management control systems has diminished and the scorecard is accepted fully by managers. This will be evidenced by integration into incentive programmes and the use of non-financial measures as targets. Such a step change would necessitate true cultural acceptance rather than more pedestrian or worse 'lip service' managerial approach. Research into the human or 'soft' aspects of scorecard implementation reaches into human resource management and change management domains and would provide an ideal vehicle for addressing Neely's call for more interdisciplinary research (Neely, 1999).

It is claimed that the scorecard is 'instrumentation for a single strategy' (Kaplan and Norton, 1996b:75) and that the use of the scorecard has evolved from merely providing a balanced set of performance measures to become the 'cornerstone of a new strategic management system' (Kaplan and Norton, 1996b:75). Yet there has been little research into the relationship between the balanced scorecard, strategic controls and strategy implementation. Another key trend is the separation of hotel investment companies from hotel operating companies. This increasing phenomenon has implications for corporate objectives and goal congruence and endorses the need for more work, similar to that of Denton and White, to see how in practice scorecard and similar frameworks can mediate the potentially diverging objectives of different stakeholders.

Finally, there is a new requirement for statutory operating and financial reviews (OFR) taking effect from April 2005. Operating and financial reviews will put further emphasis on non-financial data collection and presentation (Barrett, 2005). This may further raise the profile of the scorecard and will certainly increase pressure for effective MIS to collect relevant data. There is still a need to look into the effect of technology and effective management information systems (Geller, 1985c; Atkinson and Brander Brown, 2001) and the role they play in improving performance reporting and, in particular, non-financial data reporting. Although there is a great deal of research activity in this important area of performance measurement, there is still only a small amount of research activity specific to the hospitality industry and so any additional investigations and discussions will be welcomed by the academic and practitioner community alike.

References

Adams, D. (1995) Methods of predicting financial failure in the hotel industry. In Harris, P. (ed.), *Accounting and Finance for the International Hospitality Industry*. Butterworth-Heinemann, Oxford.

Adams, D. and Neely, A. (2002) Prism reform. *Financial Management*, May, 28–31.

Ahn, H. (2001) Applying the balanced scorecard concept: an experience report. *Long Range Planning*, **34**, 441–461.

Atkinson, H. and Brander Brown, J. (2005) *Strategy implementation: a role for the Balanced Scorecard?* Conference paper presented at 12th Annual CHME Research Conference, 23–24 April 2003, Sheffield Hallam University: Trends and Developments in Hospitality Research.

Atkinson, H. and Brander Brown, J. (2001) Rethinking performance measures: assessing progress in UK hotels. *International Journal of Contemporary Hospitality Management*, **13** (3), 128–135.

Atkinson, A.A., Waterhouse, J.H. and Well, R.B. (1997) A stakeholder approach to strategic performance measurement. *Sloan Management Review*, Spring, 25–37.

Ball, S. and Roberts, L. (2003) Restaurants. In: Brotherton, B. (ed.), *The International Hospitality Industry: Structure, Characteristics and Issues*. Butterworth-Heinemann, Oxford.

Ballantine, J. and Brignall, S. (1995) An agenda for performance measurement research. In Tears, R. and Armistead, C. (eds), *Services Management, New directions, New perspectives*. Cassell, London.

Barrett, R. (2005) Technical matters: Corporate performance management. *Financial Management*, May, 34.

Brander Brown, J. and Harris, P. (1999) Hotel performance measurement in a competitive environment: a business orientation approach. *CHME Hospitality Research Conference Proceedings*, 2–12.

Brander Brown, J. and Harris, P. (1998) Relating business orientation and performance measurement design in a service industry context: theoretical and empirical perspectives from the hotel industry. *Proceedings of the Performance Measurement: Theory and Practice Conference*. Cambridge University.

Brander Brown, J. and McDonnell, B. (1995) The balanced scorecard: short-term guest or long-term resident? *International Journal of Contemporary Hospitality Management*, **7** (2/3), 7–11.

Brander Brown, J., McDonnell, B. and Lang, L. (1996) Performance measurement in UK hotel organisations: towards a balanced scorecard? Paper presented at the CHRIE annual conference, Washington, DC.

Brignall, S. and Ballantine, J. (1996) Performance measurement in service businesses revisited. *International Journal of Service Industry Management*, **7** (1), 6–31.

Brotherton, B. (ed.) (2003a) *The International Hospitality Industry: Structure, Characteristics and Issues*. Butterworth-Heinemann, Oxford.

Brotherton, B. (2003b) Finding the hospitality industry – A final response to Slattery? *Journal of Hospitality, Leisure, Sport and Tourism Education*, **2** (2), 67–70.

Butler, A., Letza, S.R. and Neale, B. (1997) Linking the balanced scorecard to strategy. *Long Range Planning*, **30** (2), 242–256.

Chin, J., Barney, W. and O'Sullivan, H. (1995) Best accounting practice in hotels: a guide for other industries? *Management Accounting*, **73**, 57.

Collier, P. and Gregory, A. (1995) *Management Accounting in Hotel Groups*. Chartered Institute of Management Accountants (CIMA), London.

Cross, K.F. and Lynch, R.L. (1992) For good measure. *CMA – The Management Accounting Magazine*, **66** (3), 20–24.

Denton, G.A. and White, B. (2000) Implementing the balanced scorecard approach to managing hotel operations. *Cornell HRA Quarterly*, February, 47–107.

Doyle, P. (1994) Setting business objectives and measuring performance. *Journal of General Management*, **20** (2), Winter, 1–19.

Eccles, R. (1991) The performance measurement manifesto. *Harvard Business Review*, January–February, 131–137.

Enz, C.A., Canina, L. and Walsh, K. (2001) Hotel-industry averages: an inaccurate tool for measuring performance. *Cornell Hotel and Restaurant Administration Quarterly*, December, 22–32.

Epstein, M. and Manzoni, J-F. (1997) The balanced scorecard and tableau de bord: translating strategy into action. *Management Accounting (USA)*, **79** (2), 28–37.

Fitzgerald, L., Johnston, R., Brignall, S., Silvestro, R. and Voss, C. (1991) *Performance Measurement in Service Businesses*. CIMA, London.

Geller, A.N. (1985a) Tracking the critical success factors for hotel companies. *Cornell HRA Quarterly*, **26** February, 77–81.

Geller, A.N. (1985b) The current state of hotel information systems. *Cornell HRA Quarterly*, May, 14–17.

Geller, A.N. (1985c) How to improve your information system. *Cornell HRA Quarterly*, August, 19–27.

Gering, M. and Mntambo, V. (2002) Parity Politics. *Financial Management*, February, 36–37.

Haktinar, M. and Harris, P. (2005) Performance measurement practice in an independent hotel context: A case study approach. *International Journal of Contemporary Hospitality Management*, **17** (1), 39–50.

Harris, P.J. (ed.) (1995a) *Accounting and Finance for the International Hospitality Industry*. Butterworth-Heinemann, Oxford.

Harris, P.J. (1995b) A development strategy for the hospitality operations management curriculum. *International Journal of Contemporary Hospitality Management*, **7** (5), 29–32.

Harris, P.J. and Brander Brown, J. (1998) Research and development in hospitality accounting and financial management. *International Journal of Hospitality Management*, **17**, 161–181.

Harris, P. and Mongiello, M. (2001) Key performance indicators in European hotel properties: general manager's choices and company profiles. *International Journal of Contemporary Hospitality Management*, **13** (3), 120–127.

Huckestein, D. and Duboff, R. (1999) Hilton hotels: a comprehensive approach to delivering value for all stakeholders. *Cornell Hotel and Restaurant Administration Quarterly*, August, 28–38.

Jones, P. (2004) Finding the hospitality industry? Or finding hospitality schools of thought? *Journal of Hospitality, Leisure, Sport and Tourism Education*, **3** (1), 33–45.

Kaplan, R.S. (1994) Management accounting 1984–1994: development of new practice and theory. *Management Accounting Review*, **5** (3/4).

Kaplan, R.S. and Norton, D.P. (1992) The balanced scorecard: measures that drive performance. *Harvard Business Review*, January–February, 71–80.

Kaplan, R.S. and Norton, D.P. (1996a) *The Balanced Scorecard: Translating Strategy into Action*. Harvard Business School Press, Boston.

Kaplan, R.S. and Norton, D.P. (1996b) Using the balanced scorecard as a strategic management system. *Harvard Business Review*, January–February, 75–85.

Kennerley, M. and Neely, A. (2002) Performance measurement frameworks: a review. In Neely, A. (ed.), *Business Performance*

Measurement: Theory and Practice, pp. 145–155. Cambridge University Press, Cambridge.

Kerr, S. (1975) On the folly of rewarding A, while hoping for B. *Academy of Management Journal*, 769–783, in Epstein and Manzoni (1997).

Kotas, R. (1975) *Market Orientation in the Hotel and Catering Industry*. Surrey University Press, Guildford.

LeSaint-Grant, F. (1992) Performance evaluation: all the answers? *Management Accounting*, **70**, 42–44.

Lindh, H. (2003) Challenges a plenty in the industry's most difficult years. Foreword. In Quest, M. and Needham, T. (eds), *The British Hospitality Association Trends and Statistics 2003*, p. iv. British Hospitality Association.

Littlejohn, D. (2004) The UK Research Assessment Exercise 2001: an analysis for hospitality research. *International Journal of Hospitality Management*, **23**, 25–28.

Lynch, R. and Cross, K. (1995) *Measure Up! Yardsticks for Continuous Improvement*. Blackwell, Oxford.

Marginson, D.E.W. (2002) Management control systems and their effects on strategy formation at middle management levels: evidence from a UK organisation. *Strategic Management Journal*, **23**, 1019–1031.

Marr, B. and Schiuma, G. (2003) Business performance – past present and future. *Management Decision*, **41** (8), 680–687.

Moncraz, E.S. and Kron, R.N. (1995) Operational analysis in hotels. In Harris, P. (ed.), *Accounting and Finance for the International Hospitality Industry*. Butterworth-Heinemann, Oxford.

Mooraj, S., Oton, D. and Hostettler, D. (1999) The balanced scorecard: a necessary good or an unnecessary evil? *European Management Journal*, **17** (5), 481–491.

Morrison, A. (2002) Hospitality research: a pause for reflection. *International Journal of Tourism Research*, **4**, 161–169.

Neely, A. (1999) The performance measurement revolution: why now and what next? *International Journal of Operations and Production Management*, **19** (2), 205–228.

Nørreklit, H. (2000) The balance on the balanced scorecard – a critical analysis of its assumptions. *Management Accounting Research*, **11** (1), 65–88.

Olsen, M. (2002) Hospitality research and theories: a review. In Lockwood, A. and Medlick, S. (eds), *Tourism and Hospitality in the 21st century*, pp. 94–105. Butterworth-Heinemann, Oxford.

Olson, E. M. and Slater, S.F. (2002) The balanced scorecard, competitive strategy and performance. *Business Horizons*, May–June, 1–16.

Otley, D. (1999) Performance management: a framework for management control systems research. *Management Accounting Research*, **10**, 363–382.

Quest, M. (ed.) (2005) *Food and Service Management Survey 2005*. British Hospitality Association, London.

Sangster, A. (2003) Splitting the bricks from the brains under fire. *BAHA Times*, November, 1–2.

Schmenner, R.W. (1986) How can service businesses survive and prosper? *Sloan Management Review*, **27** (3), 27–37.

Schmidgall, R.S. (1988) How useful are financial ratios? *The Bottom Line*, **3** (3), 24–27.

Silk, S. (1998) Automating the Balanced Scorecard. *Management Accounting*, **9** (11), 38–42.

Smith, M. (2005) The Balanced Scorecard. *Financial Management*, February, 27–28.

Tribe, J. (2004) The 4Ps of research: Practice, Policy, Principles and Positioning. Editorial. *Journal of Hospitality, Leisure, Sport and Tourism Education*, **3** (1). Accessed on line at http://www.hlst.heacademy.ac.uk/johlste/vol3no1/editorial.html on 29th June 2004.

Budgetary practice within hospitality

Tracy Jones

Introduction

Budgeting is generally believed to be the most widely used management accounting technique. Two surveys of management accounting within manufacturing show evidence of a 95 per cent usage of budgeting, in some form, by companies (Puxty and Lyall, 1989; Drury et al., 1993). It is a subject covered in detail by many management accounting textbooks and has been with us for many years. This chapter will consider 'textbook' theory concerning budgeting in addition to budgetary practice within the hospitality industry. It will also consider current developments within budgeting and whether it is still a useful management accounting tool in the 21st century.

Questions addressed in this chapter include:

- Why do companies use budgets?

- Can flexible budgeting ever be useful within hospitality, given the high fixed cost nature of the business?

- Is zero-based budgeting financially viable?
- How has budgeting changed over the past decade?
- How can the industry improve its budgeting practice?
- Is management participation essential for effective budgeting?

A content analysis of textbooks covering budgeting and two surveys of UK hotel organizations' budgetary practices (in 1996 and 2004) were undertaken. These, along with follow-up qualitative research with hospitality organizations' finance directors in 2004 and 2005, form the basis for the discussion and debate within this chapter.

The historical context of management accounting

Management accounting developed rapidly during the 19th and early 20th centuries to meet the changing needs for accounting information within the management hierarchy of organizations (Johnson and Kaplan, 1987). Johnson and Kaplan believed that, 'by 1925 virtually all management accounting practices used today had been developed' (Johnson and Kaplan, 1987:12). Management accounting theory originally developed to meet the needs of manufacturing industry during industrialization. Theory continued to be developed after 1925, but it moved away from being developed by industry to meet industry needs into generally being developed in an academic environment. While organizations grew increasingly complex due to multiple products, globalization and the emergence of service industries, management accounting theory developed within a model of a single product enterprise. The complexities of organizations made such theories difficult to implement and the theory itself became questioned (Johnson and Kaplan, 1987).

Significant management accounting literature during the 1980s and 1990s debated the gap between management accounting theory and practice (see for discussion Scapens, 1983; Drury and Dugdale, 1992; Dugdale, 1994; Ashton et al., 1995; Drysdale, 1996). As Drury and Dugdale (1992:327) emphasize, 'The perceived gap between management accounting theory, as portrayed in textbooks, and management accounting practice, however, appears to be based on anecdotal evidence ...' Although not *all* evidence is anecdotal (Drury et al., 1993), additional research to establish that such a gap exists, the nature of any gap, and its implications are essential in advancing theory in this area.

An issue in the theory/practice debate is whether the theory, or practice is 'right'. Scapens (1983:35) states, '[Such exercises] imply that management accounting practice is, in some sense, "wrong" and that the textbook provides the "right" answers'. Ashton et al. (1995:8) state, 'Current research is now more directed to understanding practice, whereas previous research was more concerned with prescribing managerial behaviour and developing normative models'. This view is supported by Drury and Dugdale (1992:334) who state '... there should be a change of emphasis from normative theory (what ought to be) to positive theory (what is)'. This view implies practice can become theory, as opposed to theory becoming practice. They go on to state, 'Theory should represent the desired state and practice should represent the current state' (Drury and Dugdale, 1992:334–345).

The interrelationship between management accounting theory and practice, as portrayed in the literature, is of a complex nature. The development of 'positive theory', through closer researcher and practitioner links within empirical research seems key in reducing the perceived gap between theory and practice within this field. Drury and Dugdale (1992:345) conclude, 'there is a need for researchers to investigate the nature of existing management accounting practice in order to lead to a better understanding of the situation and contexts in which particular theoretical techniques may be appropriate in practice'. For research in management accounting to be useful to both the academic researcher and the practitioner this interrelationship, the link between theory and practice, has to be acknowledged and researched.

Budgeting research in a hospitality context

In 1979, Kosturakis and Eyster considered operational budgeting within small hotel companies. By 1996, Schmidgall et al. identified that few hospitality educators had undertaken research into budgetary practices within the industry. Schmidgall's own work, with Ninemeier, published in 1987 and 1989 were the first major studies since that of Kosturakis and Eyster in 1979.

Schmidgall and Ninemeier's research (1987, 1989) considered aspects of the budgetary process in food service chains and hotel chains in America. This research was based on surveys conducted in 1986 and 1987, with responses from 30 hotel and 31 food service organizations across America. Schmidgall et al. followed up the research in 1996 when they compared practices in the USA with those in Scandinavia. These results were based on 179 questionnaires (a 24.4 per cent response rate in the USA and 9.5 per cent in Scandinavia).

Additional industry applied research in this area includes the work of Collier and Gregory (1995). Budgeting was part of a study into the practice of management accounting within hotel groups.

This was a case study investigation involving six organizations of different size and ownership.

DeFranco (1997) considered the importance and use of financial forecasting and budgeting at a departmental level in the hotel industry (USA), as perceived by hotel controllers. It was based on 140 returned questionnaires (35.6 per cent response rate) from unit level financial controllers.

The survey of UK hotel operators' budgetary practices by Jones (1997a,b, 1998) focused on many aspects of budgetary practice within the UK. The results were based on 44 completed questionnaires, representing a 45 per cent response rate.

More recent hospitality applied research into budgeting has been that of Brander Brown and Atkinson (2001). This focused on how budgeting could adapt better to meet the needs of managers to respond in an age of information, where response to market change demands a speedy response.

Budgeting within the UK hospitality industry

Since the initial work by Jones in the late 1990s, her research work has continued to focus on budgetary theory and budgetary practice within the hospitality industry (Jones, in progress). The results of this research are covered in detail within the chapter.

In order to identify any 'gap' between theory and industry practice, content analysis of textbooks was initially undertaken.

Content analysis of textbooks

To be able to make the statement, *'theory states budgets are produced to aid planning and control'* it must be substantiated, through evidence in such textbooks, that this is the *norm*, i.e. generally supported within management accounting textbooks as a whole and not merely the view expressed in an individual text (Jones, 2003). Several research methods were considered, but in order to provide substantive evidence concerning 'normative theory' of budgetary accounting theory 'content analysis' was viewed as the most suitable method.

Content analysis is a technique used within social science research and is particularly relevant when trying to establish meaning and patterns within text. The use of content analysis related to history and sociological studies, based on historic writings is well documented by Lewis-Beck (1994). The use of content analysis in management research is covered in 'Research Methods for Managers' (Gill and Johnson, 1991). Content analysis is also mentioned within 'The Handbook of Contemporary Hospitality Management Research' (Brotherton, 1999) in the context of hospitality research.

A framework was established to analyse the content of textbooks. The unit of *observation* was established as individual texts, while the unit of *analysis* was chapters and sections applied to budgeting. For each textbook the content was observed against 16 coded aspects of budgeting, which were further subdivided into 62 facets of budgeting. For each coded aspect a book was judge to either: cover it in detail; mention it briefly; not cover the topic; or to cover the subject negatively, i.e. not recommending its use.

The results from the content analysis informed the subsequent research conducted within the hospitality industry.

Researching industry practice

The survey conducted in 2004 covered varied hospitality organizations within the UK. Organizations ranged from those operating over 300 hotels, to those with one hotel. Sales revenue was from £3 m to over £600 m a year. Almost a third were PLCs, with the majority of the others being private companies. The vast majority (93.5 per cent) viewed hotels as major part of their business.

The survey was divided into three discrete sections. Section A concentrated on the process used in setting budgets in the organization. This was to identify what techniques were being used in the industry, including common practice. Section B focused on how budgets were utilized, once set. This section considered the monitoring process and the review of budgetary procedures used. Section C considered the more human and judgemental aspects of budgeting within the organizations.

This industry survey, along with those previously conducted related to the hospitality industry (Schmidgall and Ninemeier, 1987, 1989; Schmidgall et al., 1996; Jones, 1998) help to understand current industry practice. However, debate as to why this 'practice' exists and how it relates to theory is less well covered by such surveys.

This Jones (2004) survey was followed by qualitative research to establish why current industry practice existed and why in some cases this differed from 'textbook' theory.

Why are budgets produced?

Within the 2004 survey everyone cited, 'to aid control' as a reason why they produce budgets, closely followed by 'to evaluate performance' (96.8 per cent). The least frequently cited reasons were 'to coordinate the operation' and 'to communicate plans'. Table 4.1 compares, in rank order, the most commonly cited reasons for budgeting, as identified in textbooks and within industry in 1997 and 2004.

Table 4.1
Why do we produce budgets?

To:	UK industry survey 2004	UK industry survey 1997	Textbook content analysis
Aid control	1st	2nd	2nd
Evaluate performance	2nd	1st	4th
Aid long-term planning	3rd	4th	1st
Aid short-term planning	4th	5th	1st
Motivate managers	5th	3rd	5th
Communicate plans	6th	6th	6th
Coordinate the operation	7th	7th	3rd

Shown in rank order of most commonly cited reasons.

While there are differences between these three sets of data, are they significantly different? The data were analysed using a Spearman rank coefficient. In comparing the two sets of industry data (1997 and 2004) there is a strong correlation (0.86), with an R^2 of 73 per cent. However, if you compare either set of industry data with that from the content analysis the correlation is extremely low (1997 = 0.04/R^2 0%, 2004 = 0.43/R^2 19%). This identifies a statistically significant difference (a gap) between theory and industry practice in this regard.

Industry does not view budgets as an important aid in planning, but this is the most commonly cited reason for budgets in textbooks. Further industry research suggests planning happens well in advance of producing the annual budget and therefore this is the reason why they do not value it as a planning tool. Textbooks are 'process' driven and tend to group budgeting into a 'planning' and a 'control' phase. Such a breakdown relates to procedures in setting a budget and monitoring an existing budget.

What information is used in setting budgets?

The survey in 2004 showed all respondents used previous year's actual figures to assist in setting the budget. In-house market analysis, local economic indicators and industry statistics and indicators generally supported these. Least used were previous year's budgeted figures and national economic indicators. Previous year's budgeted figures were viewed as being too out-of-date to add value to the process, particularly in a fast changing environment.

The use of a top-down or bottom-up approach to budgeting

Textbooks discuss these alternative approaches. They emphasize the importance of full participation by managers in the budgetary process improves final acceptance of the budget. The bottom-up approach is viewed as the approach that best achieves full participation in the budgetary process. Previous research (Jones, 1998) noted less use of the bottom-up approach within the UK hospitality industry, compared to the industry in the USA. Over time this situation has not changed, indeed in 2004 significantly fewer organizations reported the use of this approach compared to previous research. These test results, as shown in Table 4.2, highlight there is not a single preferred approach commonly adopted across the industry. Using a chi-square, the results do not prove statistically significant, highlighting the range of approaches being used.

Table 4.2
A comparison of budgetary planning methods used (%)

	UK (Jones, 2004)	UK (Jones, 1997)	USA (Schmldgall et al., 1987)	USA (Schmidgall et al., 1996)	Scandinavia (Schmidgall et al., 1996)
Top-down	25.8	13.6	13.3	4.5	4.0
Bottom-up	35.5	54.6	56.7	79.5	64.0
Combination	38.7	31.8	26.7	16.0	28.0
Other	0	0	3.3	0	4.0
(Total not using bottom-up approach)	64.5	45.4	43.4	20.5	36

Of those using a combination approach, generally this involved benchmarks being set by head office, but detailed budgets being generated bottom-up. While industry strongly believed that participation is key in the budgeting process, they do not take the view that this is best delivered through a bottom-up approach to budgeting. There was a view that a bottom-up approach was not resource efficient. This approach was associated with either being time intensive or relying on managers further down the organization, who had insufficient training to generate an effective budget. Another view was that those participating in the budget must be the decision-makers. They argued if you have central buying responsibility, managers at unit level have less to add to the budget setting process. Many felt the combination approach allowed the organization to maintain control of the strategic direction by first setting overall targets and benchmarks. As a second phase, then allowing managers at unit level to provide an input into detailed budgeting at departmental level.

The use of zero-based budgeting

This is not a topic universally covered in textbooks, but those that do identify benefits associated with its use. These include more accurate budgeting, based on current needs, which avoids falling into the trap of 'rolling-forward' mistakes from previous years. Zero-based budgeting ensures each element is questioned and has to be justified while setting the budget.

The majority in the 2004 survey (58.1 per cent) did not use this method of budgeting. Of those that did use it, most only viewed it as a tool to be used for new hotels, projects or concepts, i.e. where no previous data exist. The main reason given was that the additional time involved was not worthwhile. Those using it considered it more valuable in relation to costs than to revenue budgeting. It was felt zero-based budgeting does allow a thorough review of costs and is a proactive approach. Interestingly, the previous year's data, combined with in-house assessments for the next year, were viewed as the best starting point for revenue based budgeting.

Preparation of short-term budgets

The vast majority (93.5 per cent) produced their budgets for the period of one financial year; others used either a six-month period or a rolling 12-month period. Most commonly, organizations started the process three months in advance of the budgetary period, with a third taking more than three months to complete the process. Anecdotal evidence suggests larger organizations, with more units and levels in the management, need to start the process earlier. This argument was dismissed by those questioned in industry. It was felt that modern technology now allows the data from ten or a hundred hotels to be uploaded in the same time, so size is not a factor. External factors, particularly requirements to lodge budgets with bankers or debt providers, were considered a greater influence on the timing of the process than size or the complexity of the business.

Figure 4.1 identifies, within the surveyed organizations, who is involved in setting the budgets. As might be expected, managers were more likely to be involved in budgeting at their own level within the organization than at others. Generally, there was more involvement downwards, rather than up the organizational

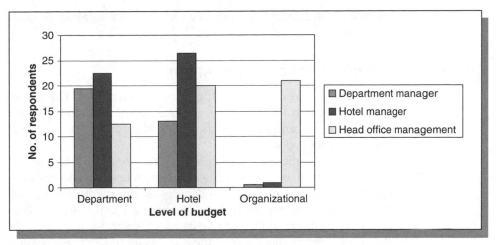

Figure 4.1
Participation in budget preparation.

structure. For example, a hotel manager is more likely to be involved in setting the overall hotel and hotel department budgets than involved at head office level.

Reforecast

Half of those surveyed reforecast their budgets on a monthly basis, with others undertaking this quarterly. Reforecasting was not undertaken by 29 per cent of the organizations surveyed in 2004. Generally, where reforecasting took place, the original budget was still used for performance measurement purposes. In this context the annual budget was viewed as a strategic tool, approved at a high level and often lodged with key players, such as banks, before the start of the financial year. In addition to the budget's role in evaluating organizational performance, management performance bonuses were linked to the budget in some circumstances. Exceptional, unexpected events (9/11 was quoted as an example) may lead to amendments of the original budget during a financial year, but this was certainly the exception to the rule.

Benchmarks for investigating variances

The majority (71 per cent) of organizations set specific benchmarks for triggering investigation into budgetary variances. Most popular was a combination of a per cent and £ benchmark, with the sole use of a per cent variance being next. When variances are identified action tends to be taken by managers with direct responsibility at that level and their own line manager. Accountants and controllers are often also involved in the investigation of such variances.

Budgets as a performance measurement

Textbooks pay attention to budgets as a control tool. The use of budgets to control and monitor organizational and management performance is emphasized, alongside the human behavioural aspects associated with this.

In the UK hospitality industry, all those surveyed in 2004 viewed budgets as the main performance indicator, or one of a few key indicators. Previous year's figures and budgeted figures are the key performance indicators used by those taking part in this survey. Few (16 per cent) reported the use of a balanced scorecard approach. As discussed later in this chapter, there has been research advocating fresh approaches to performance measurement and a move away from budgeting. Both within the survey and qualitative phases of this research, industry was clear that budgeting was an important part of performance measurement within their organizations. They believed budgets would continue to be consistently used across the industry, as a key performance measure, in the future.

Use of flexible budgets

Textbooks identify flexible budgeting as a way to use budgets as a performance measure, where the volume of activity (sales) varies from that set in the original budget. The technique uses the basic principle that, while fixed costs do not vary with volume of activity, variable costs should move in direct proportion to activity (sales) levels. The use of a flexible budget allows performance against budget to be undertaken by adjusting the total variable costs according to actual activity (sales) levels.

Of those surveyed, few organizations felt the need to use this technique, with 77.4 per cent stating it was not used. However, of those that did not use it regularly it was recognized as useful in exceptional conditions, such as after 9/11.

One argument is that there is less to be gained from flexible budgeting with a greater proportion of fixed costs. The nature of fixed cost in hotels, coupled with the cost of producing a flexed budget led organizations to believe it was not a cost effective tool for them to use.

Review of budgetary procedures

Only a third of organizations reviewed their procedure on a routine basis, generally annually. Of those that had reviewed their procedures this led to a variety of changes. Reasons given for not reviewing budgetary procedures included, 'if it is not broken why fix it?' Others felt incremental changes were made as they went along, so there was no need for a formal review.

Only a fifth of respondents used a budget committee or a budget manual to support the budgeting process. Likewise, only the minority of textbooks mention the use of budget committees or manuals to support the budgeting process. Organizations suggested a budget committee was just another level of bureaucracy that would not add to their budgeting process. Likewise some viewed manuals as, 'books that get dusty on top of shelves and are never used'. It was felt communicating procedures and processes directly, or in short briefing papers, was a far better approach than formal budgeting manuals.

The human face of budgeting

Organizations were asked to respond, using a scale, to a series of statements listed within the survey. Tested for statistical significance, using chi-square, these showed interesting results, as can be seen in Table 4.3.

As discussed previously, despite differing approaches to budgeting in use across the industry (top-down, bottom-up and a combination approach), those surveyed firmly believed budgets have a role to play in measuring management performance. The UK hospitality industry indicates that:

- Individual manager's authority and responsibility must be clear for budgetary control to work effectively

- Participation is key to managers accepting their budgets and considering them attainable

- Manager's performance bonuses should be linked to achieving their budgetary targets

- Having budgets that are achievable, but difficult to attain motivates managers

- Participation in the budgetary process is key when using budgets as a performance measure for managers.

Recognition by the industry of the importance of budgets to individual managers is significant. How this is achieved in practice is another issue, however.

Budgetary 'gamesmanship', where managers try to understate revenues and overstate costs is covered in some texts as another human aspect of budgeting (see Steele and Albright, 2004

Table 4.3
Human aspects of budgeting (results shown in number of respondents)

Question:	1 Strongly Agree	2 Agree	3 Neither Agree nor Disagree	4 Disagree	5 Strongly Disagree	Chi-square Is result statistically significant?
Individual manager's authority and responsibility must be clear for budgetary control to work effectively	15	14	2	0	0	Yes
Participation is key to managers accepting their budgets and considering them attainable	24	7	0	0	0	Yes
Budgetary 'gamesmanship', where managers try to understate revenues and overstate costs, is an issue for us	0	13	11	6	1	No
Manager's performance bonuses should be linked to achieving their budgetary targets	11	18	1	1	0	Yes
Having budgets that are achievable, but difficult to attain motivates managers	8	18	4	1	0	Yes
Participation in the budgetary process is key when using budgets as a performance measure for managers	17	13	0	1	0	Yes

Tracy A Jones, University of Gloucestershire.

for discussion). When asked if they believed this to be an issue within their own organization the results from industry were mixed, as shown in Figure 4.1. There is clearly a balance to be struck here. Using a strict top-down approach may avoid 'gamesmanship' opportunities within an organization, but in doing so reduces the opportunity for full participation by individual managers, thus leading to issues related to motivation, etc. as identified above.

Budgets clearly have implications associated with management behaviour, an issue organizations need to consider in the budgetary processes they use.

Beyond budgeting – can we live without the budget?

As stated earlier in this chapter, budgeting is the most commonly used management accounting tool. This research identified it is still firmly valued and used by organizations in the UK hospitality industry. Those questioned also believe it will retain this position, as a major performance indicator, in the future.

Are budgets merely produced because organizations feel it is expected of them, or are they adding value and fulfilling an important role? In 1993, Wilson and Chaua suggested budgets were political and symbolic processes in organizations. Over the last decade researchers have questioned the ritual of the annual budget.

Hope and Fraser (1997, 2003) are among those who have suggested alternatives to the budget and that, 'Budgeting, as most corporations practice it, should be abolished' (Hope and Fraser, 2003:108). They are not the only writers who feel we now need to look 'Beyond Budgeting'.

At the heart of this movement is the Beyond Budgeting Round Table (BBRT), who warn that, 'budgets are a relic from an earlier era' (CIMA-ICAEW, 2004:8). They, along with others, consider budgeting has many weaknesses, namely it is: too time consuming; too expensive; and out of touch with the needs of managers (CIMA-ICAEW, 2004). Partly, the argument lies in the conflicting dual roles budgets can play in an organization. Budgets can be a fixed target and provide financial incentives for managers, where bonuses are linked to performance against budgets. It is argued this can lead to management behaviour that 'may be at odds with the needs of the organisation' (CIMA-ICAEW, 2004:8).

Those who support 'beyond budgeting' suggest a model where companies move away from a model of a 'fixed performance contract' to a 'relative performance model' (Hope and Fraser, 2003). In such a model a manager's performance would not be related to achievements against a 'fixed budget' but against a relative model, where comparative performance against peers is considered more appropriate.

The joint Chartered Institute of Management Accountants (CIMA) and Institute of Chartered Accountants in England and Wales (ICAEW) event, along with their subsequent joint report, (CIMA-ICAEW, 2004) debated the traditional role of budgeting in organizations. They concluded that, 'budgets are in fact alive and well' and 'traditional budgeting remains widespread' (CIMA-ICAEW, 2004:2).

Research by Dugdale and Lyne (2004) also concluded general managers do not report dissatisfaction with budgeting and feel budgets have an important role to play. Therefore, while some believe we need to move away from budgeting in organizations, this is not a universally held view. Those that support the continuation of budgeting as a valuable management accounting tool believe we should be focusing on 'better budgeting' (Prendergast, 2000; CIMA-ICAEW, 2004; Dugdale and Lyne, 2004). The practice of budgeting can move forward and be enhanced but does not need to be replaced.

Conclusions

The views of managers questioned within the hospitality industry concur with the findings of others, that budgeting is a valuable management accounting tool. Budgeting is taking place widely across the industry and managers believe this will continue into the future. Organizations firmly believed the budget performed a valuable role as a Key Performance Indicator (KPI) within their business.

The demand for budgeting by external stakeholders should not be overlooked either. Several organizations reported bankers' requirement for an annual budget as the key driver in the timing of the annual budgetary process.

However, there is a need to be proactive in ensuring the budget continues to be a valuable management accounting tool for industry into the future. It is essential to question both the current theory and practice of budgeting in order to develop theory that will improve the budgeting practices within organizations in the future.

References

Ashton, D., Hopper, T. and Scapens, R.W. (1995) *Issues in Management Accounting*, 2nd edn. Prentice Hall International, London.

Brander Brown, J. and Atkinson, H. (2001) Budgeting in the Information Age. *International Journal of Contemporary Hospitality Management*, **13** (3), 136–143.

Brotherton, B. (1999) *The Handbook of Contemporary Hospitality Management Research*. Wiley, Chichester.

CIMA-ICAEW (2004) *Better Budgeting: A report on the Better Budgeting Forum from CIMA and ICAEW*. ICAEW/CIMA, London.

Collier, P. and Gregory, A. (1995) The practice of management accounting in hotel groups. In Harris, P. (ed.), *Accounting and Finance for the International Hospitality Industry*, pp. 137–159. Butterworth-Heinemann, Oxford.

DeFranco, A. (1997) The importance and use of financial forecasting and budgeting at the departmental level in the hotel industry as perceived by hotel controllers. *Hospitality Research Journal*, **20** (3), 99–110.

Drury, C. and Dugdale, D. (1992) Surveys of management accounting practice. In Drury, C. (ed.), *Management Accounting Handbook*, Chapter 15, pp. 327–347. Butterworth-Heinemann, Oxford.

Drury, C., Braund, S., Osborne, P. and Tayles, M. (1993) *A Survey of Management Accounting Practices in UK Manufacturing Companies*. Certified Research Report 22, ACCA.

Drysdale, L. (1996) Who sets the research agenda, academics or practitioners? *Management Accounting*, February, 20–21.

Dugdale, D. (1994) Theory and practice: the views of CIMA members and students. *Management Accounting* (British), September, 56–58.

Dugdale, D. and Lyne, S. (2004) *The Changing Roles of Company Budgets*, work-in-progress report presented to the Annual Congress of the European Accounting Association, Prague, 1–3 April.

Gill, J. and Johnson, P. (1991) *Research Methods for Managers*, Paul Chapman Publishing Ltd, London.

Hope, J. and Fraser, R. (1997) Beyond budgeting … breaking through the barrier to the 'third wave'. *Management Accounting*, December, 20–23.

Hope, J. and Fraser, R. (2003) Who needs budgets? *Harvard Business Review*, February, **81** (2), 108–115.

Johnson, H. and Kaplan, R. (1987) *Relevance lost – the rise and fall of management accounting*. Harvard Business School Press, Boston.

Jones, T. (1997a) UK hotel operators use of budgetary procedures. *EuroCHRIE & IAHMS Conference – Hospitality Business Development*, Sheffield.

Jones, T. (1997b) The practice of budgeting in UK hotels (workshop). *6th Annual CHME Hospitality Research Conference*, Oxford.

Jones, T. (1998) UK hotel operators use of budgetary procedures. *The International Journal of Contemporary Hospitality Management*, **10**, 96–100.

Jones, T. (2003) What the books say – the use of content analysis to establish textbook 'normative theory'. *12th Annual CHME Hospitality Research Conference*, April, Sheffield.

Jones, T. (in progress) *The development of positive budgetary theory within the UK hotel industry*. PhD thesis, University of Gloucestershire.

Kosturakis, J. and Eyster, J. (1979) Operational budgeting in small hotel companies. *The Cornell Hotel and Restaurant Administration Quarterly*, **19** (4), 80–84.

Lewis-Beck, M. (1994) *Research Practice – International Handbooks of Quantitative Applications in the Social Sciences Volume 6*. Sage Publications Ltd, London.

Prendergast, P. (2000) Budgets hit back. *Management Accounting*, January, 14–16.

Puxty, A. and Lyall, D. (1989) *Cost Control into the 1990s: A survey of standard costing and budgeting practices in the UK*. CIMA, London.

Scapens, R. (1983) Closing the gap between theory and practice. *Management Accounting*, January, 34–36.

Schmidgall, R. and Ninemeier, J. (1987) Budgeting in hotel chains: co-ordination and control. *The Cornell Hotel and Restaurant Administration Quarterly*, May, 79–84.

Schmidgall, R. and Ninemeier, J. (1989) Budgeting practices in lodging and food service chains: an analysis and comparison. *International Journal of Hospitality Management*, **8** (1), 35–41.

Schmidgall, R., Borchgrevink, C. and Zahl-Begnum, O. (1996) Operations budgeting practices of lodging firms in the United States and Scandinavia. *International Journal of Hospitality Management*, **15** (2), 189–203.

Steele, R. and Albright, C. (2004) Games managers play at budget time. *MIT Sloan Management Review*, Spring, **45** (3), 81–84.

Wilson, R. and Chaua, W. (1993) *Managerial Accounting: Method and Meaning*, 2nd edn. Chapman and Hall, London.

Benchmarking: measuring financial success in the hotel industry

Agnes Lee DeFranco

Introduction

Meaningful and useful financial measurements drawn from industry standards can help hotel executives gauge the performance of their properties and establish plans of action. Benchmarking is a method of comparing one's performance with itself, its competitors, or even with the entire industry, with the ultimate goal of identifying the strengths, weaknesses, opportunities, and threats of a hotel operation, establishing objective performance levels and formulating an appropriate course of action. Benchmarking is a beneficial process to any lodging operation. First, it measures the operation's performance and sets the bar or the standard. Then, by making the comparisons, on an internal, competitive, or industry-wide basis, the lodging operation will know where it is graded and what improvements are needed. Finally, with the improvement goals, action plans can be set to achieve them so that the total holistic return on investment of the operation can be improved (DeFranco et al., 2004).

The historical perspective: benchmarking

What is benchmarking?

According to Merriam-Webster Online (www.m-w.com), benchmarking is 'the study of a competitor's product or business practices in order to improve the performance of one's own company.' Therefore, benchmarking is to find the one appropriate reference in order for an entity to make improvement upon and such reference may not necessarily be the top or best performance point. It is also important to note that the definition says it is the study of product and business practices of one's competitor. In the hotel industry, a budget hotel and a resort hotel are both hotels but they are hardly competitors of each other. The same also holds true when considering the performance of a Chateau hotel in a wine region of France and a 4000-room mega casino hotel in Las Vegas. Therefore, finding the appropriate competitive set is critical in terms of comparing apples with apples.

Benchmarking in management literature

In management, benchmarking is a process that began in Japan and was adopted by Rank Xerox in 1979. When benchmarking was first introduced, financial metrics was not one of the top issues. Ten years later, Camp (1989) discussed the Xerox case in detail and defined three types of benchmarking as strategic, operational and management oriented. Camp defines strategic benchmarking as surveying competitors to find the best strategy for business; operational benchmarking as looking at costs and means of differentiating products; and management benchmarking as concentrating on support functions. Within operational benchmarking, relative cost was one of the areas to be measured.

Yasin and Zimmer (1995) also report on three basic types of benchmarking, but in a slightly different manner. They classify benchmarking into internal, competitive and functional. They define internal benchmarking as taking measurements and then comparing the results to the goals that are set for the organization. This is similar to the theory of management by objectives. In competitive benchmarking, Yasin and Zimmer compare one company to its direct competitors. It is identical to the internal benchmarking except that it is now more of an external effort. Finally, they define functional benchmarking as the process of comparison of measurements to set standards in a particular process or function rather than the entire company as a whole. In addition, since companies in different industries may share the same functions, functional benchmarking therefore can be internal, external and even comparing to companies not in the same industry. They also state in their research that benchmarking can be carried out in the operations subsystem and the service subsystem of a hospitality organization.

In determining the metrics to be measured, Yasin and Zimmer list nine factors, two of which include major cost drivers and the functions that represent the highest percentage of costs. In their suggested operations metrics, they include nine measurements, three of which (one third of the metrics) are financially related: percentage rework and costs, unit production costs and unit support costs.

The one benchmarking process that is most closely related to the financial segment of the hospitality industry is probably that of Schmidt's approach. Schmidt (1992) classifies benchmarking into strategic, cost and customer behaviour. In his strategic benchmarking, instead of looking into management strategies like Camp (1989), Schmidt includes financial accounting ratios such as return on capital, cost of capital, the market value to book value ratio and the highest average shareholder return in order to identify how well shareholder's value is being created strategically. However, similar in part to Camp's operational benchmarking, Schmidt's cost benchmarking also focuses on operational cost structure.

The process of benchmarking

So, how can hotels begin to benchmark? Should such process be internal, external, or even functional across other industries? What are the financial metrics that are useful and significant to hotel executives and is there accessible information available for hotels to begin their benchmarking process?

While studying the Xerox case, Camp (1989) identified the five steps of benchmarking as: planning, analysis, integration, action and maturity. To begin, planning is to decide what to measure. Once decided, the analysis phase will take place, where the necessary information needed will be collected. Each individual company will then use the published results and integrate the measurements into their own hotel properties and take appropriate action to maintain or better good performance or totally revamp poor results. After all positive steps have been taken and the best practices have been incorporated into the daily business, then the maturity stage sets in.

This is where the levels or measurements that the company was successful in achieving or meeting become the minimum standards for the ongoing operations of the organization.

Freytag and Hollensen (2001) put this process in more active terms and reduced Camp's (1989) five steps into simply benchmarking, benchlearning and benchaction. The term benchmarking is usually used when thinking about measurement. However, if nothing is learned and no action is being taken, the measuring process just produces a bunch of numbers. As noted, benchmarking is really the entire process, not simply collecting the data for the metrics or deciding what the best measurement is.

Commonly used benchmarking statistical reports for the hotel industry

Benchmarking statistics in the lodging industry are not new. They have been produced in some form since the 1930s (Corgel et al., 2001). As early as 1937, Harris, Kerr, Forster & Company, the predecessor of Pannell, Kerr and Foster (PKF) published the *Trends in the Hotel Business: Statistical Review 1929–1936*. At present, there are a number of sources where hotel companies can obtain information to gauge their progress and benchmark their performance.

Ernst & Young is one of the companies that provide hospitality industry statistics. Besides publishing its annual *National Lodging Forecast* in the United States, Ernst &Young offices worldwide also provide reports for various markets. For example, its Madrid office provides a study of economic indicators in hotels of the Spanish speaking Caribbean. In its Caribbean hotel report, properties are divided into categories such as 5-star, 5-star all-inclusive, 4-star, 4-star all-inclusive and so on. Besides the normally expected occupancy percentage and average daily rate, this report also discusses the net margin, the gross operating profit percentage, the distribution of income (rooms, food, beverage, shops or retail, others) and the distribution of expenses according to the categories of hotels. In addition, statistics regarding departmental operating profit percentage, staff productivity (income per employee, number of beds per employee, number of night stays per employees) and the distribution of workforce by department are all reported.

HVS International (Global Hospitality Consulting) is another source of information and various metrics. Since HVS specializes in hotel valuation, it produces a major US hotel transactions survey (sale of a single hotel at $10 million or greater, or a portfolio sale where the principals allocated an individual hotel at $10 million or greater). It also compiles reports on lodging property and lodging corporate positions compensation analyses and a separate property positions analysis of over 360 hotels throughout

Europe and the Middle East (www.hvsinternational.com). Like Ernst & Young, HVS also provides specific market analyses such as the *Sydney Market Analysis* and the *Canadian Lodging Outlook*.

Another major benchmark information provider is PKF Consulting. PKF Hospitality Research (PKF-HR), a division of PKF Consulting, produces monthly, quarterly, mid-year and annual trends. The annual trends are developed from a database of over 4500 income statements from lodging operations throughout the USA. The data are categorized by hotel type, geographic location, room rate, and size and analyses are performed on revenues, expenses and profits (www.pkfc.com). PKF-HR also offers customized reports such as the *Benchmarker, Price Ranger* report. The Benchmarker report, as its name suggests, can assist properties best in gauging their performance as this (customized) version allows any lodging company to set its own comparable (COMP) set and see exactly where they are performing when compared to their true competitors. The entire report can be about 12 pages in length as it gives the client a historical outlook of the hotel industry in the client hotel's geographical location, analyses the client hotel with its competitive set and even provides a competitive scoring system so that the client hotel can simply review the results and begin the 'action' part of the benchmarking process. Figures 5.1 and 5.2 are excerpts from a sample Benchmarker report. Figure 5.1 shows the comparison of the COMP set and the client hotel, while Figure 5.2 presents the variance calculations. As is apparent, there is no mathematical work required on the part of the hotels. Once the report is received, the client hotel can begin its benchaction phase.

The final company for the discussion of this chapter is Smith Travel Research (STR). Similar to PKF Consulting, STR produces a myriad of reports such as *Lodging Survey, HOST Survey, Lodging Review, Pipeline Report, HOST Study,* and *Local Market Reports for Convention & Visitor Bureaus, State Tourism Offices and Hotel Associations* (www.smithtravelresearch.com). Of all of the aforementioned publications, the *HOST Study*'s common-size income statement is the most useful for hotel comparisons as a property can compare its revenues and expenses, department by department, to industry averages. Since the numbers are expressed in percentages, the *HOST study*, like some other reports produced by the previously mentioned three companies, can pinpoint areas where a property can tighten up and improve or areas where it is outperforming industry. The other report that is most useful, especially with convention hotels, is the *Local Market Reports for Convention & Visitor Bureaus, State Tourism Offices and Hotel Associations*. In these reports, occupancy rate, room rate and

BENCHMARKER INCOME STATEMENT

REVENUES AND EXPENSES	AVERAGE OF 6 BENCHMARK PROPERTIES				HOTEL A			
Revenues	Year End 2002 ($)	Ratio To Revenue (%)	Per Available Room/Year ($)	Per Occupied Room/Day ($)	Year End 2002 ($)	Ratio To Revenue (%)	Per Available Room/Year ($)	Per Occupied Room/Day ($)
Rooms	5,928,239	68.3	26,154	98.85	5,725,000	60.8	25,905	117.34
Food	1,913,876	22.0	8,444	31.91	1,823,000	19.4	8,249	37.36
Beverage	419,662	4.8	1,851	7.00	1,315,000	14.0	5,950	26.95
Telecommunications	119,132	1.4	526	1.99	87,000	0.9	394	1.79
Other Operated Departments	141,203	1.6	623	2.35	469,000	5.0	2,122	9.61
Rentals and Other Income	162,128	1.9	715	2.70	0	0.0	0	0.00
Total Revenues	8,684,240	100.0	38,313	144.80	9,419,000	100.0	42,620	193.05
Departmental Costs and Expenses*								
Rooms	1,434,212	24.2	8,327	23.91	1,070,000	18.7	4,842	21.93
Food	1,440,000	75.4	6,000	24.07	1,643,000	80.1	7,434	30.87
Beverage	195,086	46.5	861	3.25	950,000	72.2	4,299	19.47
Telecommunications	57,047	47.9	252	0.95	87,000	100.0	384	1.78
Other Operated Departments	108,758	77.0	480	1.81	228,000	48.6	1,032	4.67
Total Costs and Expenses	3,238,406	37.3	14,287	54.00	3,978,000	42.2	18,000	81.53
Total Operated Departmental Income	5,445,834	62.7	24,026	90.61	5,441,000	57.8	24,620	111.52
Undistributed Operating Expenses								
Administrative and General	791,080	9.1	3,490	13.19	755,000	8.0	3,416	15.47
Marketing (Includes Franchise Fees)	772,708	8.9	3,409	12.88	760,000	8.1	3,439	15.58
Property Operation and Maintenance	412,591	4.8	1,820	6.88	666,000	7.1	3,009	13.63
Utility Costs	372,311	4.3	1,643	6.21	549,000	5.8	2,484	11.25
Other Unallocated Operated Departments	0	0.0	0	0.00	0	0.0	0	0.00
Total Undistributed Expenses	2,348,690	27.0	10,362	39.15	2,729,000	29.0	12,348	55.93
Income Before Fixed Charges	3,097,145	35.7	13,994	51.54	27,12,000	28.5	12,271	55.59
Mgmt. Fees, Property Taxes, & Insurance								
Management Fees	214,660	2.5	947	3.58	283,000	3.0	1,281	5.80
Property Taxes and Other Municipal Charges	400,279	4.7	1,001	0.01	280,000	3.1	1,326	0.01
Insurance	193,335	2.2	853	3.22	116,000	1.2	525	2.38
Total Management Fees, Taxes and Insurance	816,273	9.4	3,801	13.61	692,000	7.3	3,131	14.18
Income Before Other Fixed Charges	2,280,872	26.3	10,063	39.03	2,020,000	21.4	9,140	41.40
Average Daily Rooms Available	227				221			
Percentage of Occupancy	72.5%				60.5%			
Average Daily Rate Per Occupied Room (excluding complimentary rooms)	$99.39				$117.34			
Rooms RevPAR	$71.65				$70.97			

*Expressed as a per cent of Departmental Revenue

Figure 5.1

Benchmarker income statement.

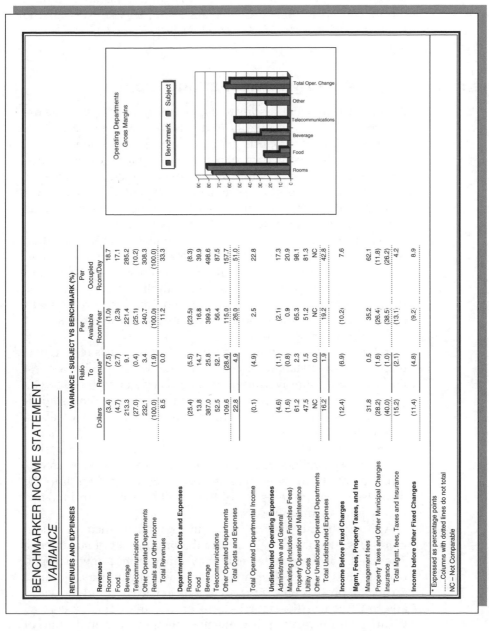

BENCHMARKER INCOME STATEMENT
VARIANCE

VARIANCE - SUBJECT VS BENCHMARK (%)

REVENUES AND EXPENSES	Dollars	Ratio To Revenue*	Per Available Room/Year	Per Occupied Room/Day
Revenues				
Rooms	(3.4)	(7.5)	(1.0)	18.7
Food	(4.7)	(2.7)	(2.3)	17.1
Beverage	213.3	9.1	221.4	285.2
Telecommunications	(27.0)	(0.4)	(25.1)	(10.2)
Other Operated Departments	232.1	3.4	240.7	308.3
Rentals and Other Income	(100.0)	(1.9)	(100.0)	(100.0)
Total Revenues	8.5	0.0	11.2	33.3
Departmental Costs and Expenses				
Rooms	(25.4)	(5.5)	(23.5)	(8.3)
Food	13.8	14.7	16.8	39.9
Beverage	387.0	25.8	399.5	498.6
Telecommunications	52.5	52.1	56.4	87.5
Other Operated Departments	109.6	(28.4)	115.0	157.7
Total Costs and Expenses	22.8	4.9	26.0	51.0
Total Operated Departmental Income	(0.1)	(4.9)	2.5	22.8
Undistributed Operating Expenses				
Administrative and General	(4.6)	(1.1)	(2.1)	17.3
Marketing (Includes Franchise Fees)	(1.6)	(0.8)	0.9	20.9
Property Operation and Maintenance	61.2	2.3	65.3	98.1
Utility Costs	47.5	1.5	51.2	81.3
Other Unallocated Operated Departments	NC	0.0	NC	NC
Total Undistributed Expenses	16.2	1.9	19.2	42.8
Income Before Fixed Charges	(12.4)	(6.9)	(10.2)	7.6
Mgmt, Fees, Property Taxes, and Ins				
Management fees	31.8	0.5	35.2	62.1
Property Taxes and Other Municipal Changes	(28.2)	(1.6)	(26.4)	(11.8)
Insurance	(40.0)	(1.0)	(38.5)	(26.2)
Total Mgmt. fees, Taxes and Insurance	(15.2)	(2.1)	(13.1)	4.2
Income before Other Fixed Changes	(11.4)	(4.8)	(9.2)	8.9

* Expressed as percentage points
.....Columns with dotted lines do not total
NC – Not Comparable

Figure 5.2
Benchmarker income statement – variance.

RevPAR for hotels in a particular market will be presented so a hotelier can get a full picture of the supply and demand changes in that one area. Since the *HOST study* is an annual report, really to benchmark and react positively in a timely fashion, tailored reports to a particular property are also available, such as the *Custom Trend Reports*, *Market Trend Reports*, *STAR Report*, *Daystar* and so on.

The making of hospitality benchmarking reports

Before deciding what reports to use or which firm to purchase the reports from, it is essential to understand how the data are collected and how the reports are compiled. As mentioned earlier, PKF began a limited version of benchmarking for the hotel industry in 1937 when they compiled, from over 100 sets of statements, a benchmarking report on revenues and expenses. Currently, for their *Annual Trends* report, they have a database of over 4500 statements from 200 plus different hotel companies.

PKF Hospitality Research uses a convenience sampling method where invitations are sent to all the major hotel companies and large or independent hotels that have a history with PKF-HR. In return, the participants will receive a complimentary copy of the study. Although it is a convenience sampling method, PKF-HR ensures that the various hotel segments are represented so that the data will not be skewed.

In the case of compiling data for the *Annual Trends* report, participants of the database can provide data by completing a questionnaire or by simply sending in a hard copy of each property's year-end financial statement. A team of accountants and statisticians at PKF-HR will then input the data into the database according to the classifications of the *Uniform System of Accounts for the Lodging Industry*. To ensure that all properties are classifying their costs similarly, the accountants at PKF may need to restructure the data from the statements before entering them into the database to ensure integrity of the results. As one can imagine, this is quite an arduous process.

Although some properties fax in or mail in their questionnaires, PKF would actually prefer the original set of statements. The length of these statements may range from a few pages to perhaps 300 pages. The accountants will then use a 'double scrubbed' process where they will look at each account individually and then in the aggregate to ensure the data are correct. Clearly, this process requires the most manpower from the part of PKF-HR and this proofing process is done both manually and by automation, however, this is an effective method of ensuring that the highest validity and reliability standards of data entry is attained (personal communication, Robert Mandelbaum and Claude Vargo, January 12, 2005).

Aside of these analyses, however, Ernst & Young focuses its data collection efforts to support its interpretation and analysis for private clients. Similar to PKF-HR, Ernst & Young used to do their own data collection and had their survey formulated according to the *Uniform System of Accounts for the Lodging Industry*, asking for key financial data and then calculating the ratios. However, in the mid-1990s, when STR had a database of an excess of 30 000 hotels, Ernst & Young began then to specialize only in the analysis of data and collaborated with STR in the data collection processes. Ernst & Young utilizes the data set from STR and concentrates its effort on benchmarking, interpretation and forecasting. Their *National Lodging Forecast* is based on raw input from STR; they input data into an econometric model to facilitate forecasts for 20 major gateway markets in the USA as well as report on market trends, new supply and relevant transactions.

Ernst & Young also performs customized benchmarking for consulting engagements. While in some ways they are similar to those of PKF-HR and STR, their benchmarking is rather specialized in nature as it forms the basis for comprehensive advisory procedures. An example could be that a themed upscale resort would like to benchmark its financial results. Instead of looking at resorts and hotels in the same area as a competitive set, Ernst & Young takes the approach of seeking out a representative set of the most comparable properties and customizes the metrics and format their client needs depending on the nature of the assignment. In other words, while STR and PKF-HR work with a specific database and may add additional data for their reports, Ernst & Young's reports normally all start from scratch in first hand data collection (personal communication, Mark Lunt, January 27, 2005).

Using the reports wisely: limitations of benchmarking

Knowing performance measurements is one thing, using them wisely is quite another. Numbers are only as good as they are being interpreted correctly and used appropriately. So, how should hotels interpret the data from the benchmarking reports? How should the reports be integrated into their operations? Before a hotel uses published or customized reports to perform benchmarking, there are several matters to consider.

Understand the methodology for data collection

First, a hotel needs to research to ensure it selects a company that has a good reputation in its market. As could be expected, most of the reputable companies will use a well-substantiated data collection process so that the numbers used to generate any form of general or customized report are likely to be valid and reliable. Validity in survey research means that the instrument used to collect data is actually measuring what the instrument intends to measure, while reliability refers to the degree to which the measurements are free from error and thus yield consistent results (Zikmund, 2003). In doing so, companies would have tested the instrument, making sure the questions do ask for the correct responses and are not confusing. In the case of all the reputable companies who have been in the research business for many years, the instruments have been validated many times so that there should not be an issue of data validity and reliability. Thus, a hotel company solicited by a new firm should ask how their instruments for measurements are developed and how they have been tested.

Choose the appropriate sampling technique and sample size

A sample should be representative so that data collected from that sample can be generalizable to the population and can be used effectively. Two pertinent issues regarding sampling are the technique used to determine the sample and the size of the sample. Recall that PKF uses convenience sampling for its *Annual Trends*, which is the one most used by other publishers. However, when it comes to their *Benchmarker*, specific properties that mirror the client hotel will be chosen as the sample for the report. Depending on the nature and objectives of the report, the sampling method may differ. In the hotel industry, given the various segments that define hotel properties, the stratified random sampling method would be ideal. However, from a practical standpoint, a thorough convenience sampling method, with follows through to ensure all categories are well represented is just as good. If a research firm simply has 100 hotels in the city of their home office to complete the questionnaire and then uses that same 100 hotel sample to put together a report, then that report will only be good for that city but the data are not representative of the entire hotel industry and cannot be generalized and used widely.

In terms of sample size, it is important to know how many properties make up the final 'one' average figure that is being reported. Again, depending on the intent of the report, the sample size can range from a few to a few thousands. A report that has a sample size of 3000, but they are all hotels from Europe, may be suitable for a European hotel, but hardly be relevant to a hotel in Orlando, Florida. Before using a report, it is important to read and understand previously published reports of that source and know what the sample is before accessing the current report. If the sample used does not fit the particular hotel property, even if the sample has 2000 responses, it will still be inappropriate for benchmarking purposes.

Compare apples to apples: the advantage of customized reports

While all reports are useful to a certain extent, the best report for benchmarking is really a customized report with the appropriate competitive set.

Comparisons are only valid if a hotel is comparing itself to the right sample. Using the room rates of limited service hotels and comparing that to the full service segment, for instance, is inappropriate. Some reports will have a very substantial sample for the entire USA. Then, they will go into different categories and classifications, such as by segmentation, geographical region, or size. In this case, it will still be beneficial as the report does provide the hotel an overview of the entire business. However, when it comes to the benchmarking process, it is imperative that individual hotels make comparisons to like ones. Figure 5.3 is a chart from a PKF Trends report on ratios to departmental revenues in 2003 for convention hotels in the USA classified by property size. If a property is a resort hotel, management should not use this page for benchmarking. However, if a hotel is a 750-room convention hotel, then the middle column in this chart will be the best information to use for benchmarking purpose.

Obviously, customized reports such as those offered by Smith Travel, PKF, Ernst & Young, HVS, or others would be the best. It is up to the individual hotels to look at the cost-benefit relationship as to how much they would like to invest in a customized report that would suit them perfectly.

Analyse all statistics: absolute and relative statistics

In using the reports effectively, hotels need to look at both the absolute and the relative statistics. Referring to Figure 5.1, the numbers in the first column, 'Year End 2002', are absolute statistics. In this case, the rooms revenue of $5 928 239 is the absolute average number that is reported by the hotels. Each sample hotel reports its rooms revenue and the total is then divided by the number of hotels reporting in order to derive the mean average. On the other hand, the numbers in the next column, 'Ratio to Revenue', are relative statistics. They are all relative to 'total revenues' which has been designated as the base at a value of 100 per cent. Any revenue will then be compared to the total in order to obtain a relative value. For instance, rooms has an

CONVENTION HOTELS – 2003

Ratios to Departmental Revenues

	Property Size Classifications		
	Under 500 Rooms	500 to 1000 Rooms	Over 1000 Rooms
Rooms Department:			
Rooms Net Revenue	100.0%	100.0%	100.0%
Departmental Expenses:			
Salaries and Wages Including Vacation	12.7%	11.8%	13.3%
Payroll Taxes and Employee Benefits	3.6	4.9	5.2
Subtotal	16.3%	16.7%	18.5%
Laundry, Linen, and Guest Supplies	3.0	3.4	3.7
Commissions and Reservation Expenses	3.0	4.7	4.7
Complimentary Food and/or Beverage Expenses	0.2	0.1	0.1
All Other Expenses	2.5	2.3	2.1
Total Rooms Expenses	24.9%	27.1%	29.1%
Rooms Departmental Income	75.1%	72.9%	70.9%
Food Department:			
Food Net Revenue	100.0%	100.0%	100.0%
Cost of Food Consumed	28.8%	25.2%	23.4%
Less: Cost of Employees' Meals	0.6	1.4	0.7
Net Cost of Food Sales	28.3%	23.8%	22.7%
Food Gross Profit	71.7%	76.2%	77.4%
Beverage Department:			
Beverage Net Revenue	100.0%	100.0%	100.0%
Cost of Beverage Sales	21.5	19.9	17.6
Beverage Gross Profit	78.5%	80.1%	82.4%
Food and Beverage Department:			
Total Food and Beverage Revenue	100.0%	100.0%	100.0%
Net Cost of Food and Beverage Sales	27.0	23.1	21.6
Gross Profit on Combined Sales	73.1%	76.9%	78.4%
Public Room Rentals	4.5	5.0	3.5
Other Income	26.4	19.2	13.6
Gross Profit and Other Income	103.9%	101.1%	95.5%
Departmental Expenses:			
Salaries and Wages Including Vacation	36.9%	38.0%	34.7%
Payroll Taxes and Employee Benefits	10.9	15.7	13.9
Subtotal	47.7%	53.7%	48.6%
Laundry and Dry Cleaning	0.9	1.0	0.7
China, Glassware, Silver, and Linen	0.7	0.9	1.1
Contract Cleaning	0.4	1.4	0.5
All Other Expenses	14.5	11.2	15.5
Total Food and Beverage Expenses	64.2%	68.3%	66.3%
Food and Beverage Departmental Income	39.7%	32.8%	29.2%

Figure 5.3
Ratios to departmental revenues.

absolute value of $5 928 239 and a relative value of 68.3 per cent. This means that the rooms division, in relation to the other departments, is bringing in 68.3 per cent of the total revenues.

Should attention be focused on the absolute mean or the relative value? Is it that important that we need both numbers? First and foremost, we need absolute numbers as they are concrete, and we know exactly how much we are off the target in the dollar amount whether we are at the average, below the average or above the average. Using Figure 5.1 as an example, if one simply compares the absolute value of the 'Income Before Other Fixed Charges' (last line item) of Hotel A to the average of the six benchmark properties, Hotel A is making less. When compared, the relative percentage of Hotel A's 21.4 per cent versus the average of 26.3 per cent, it is also less. In this scenario, Hotel A is not operating as effectively and efficiently as its competitive set. Clearly, Hotel A has some decisions to make in order to stay competitive. However, consider the following: Hotel B has an absolute value of $1 950 000 and relative value of 30.31 per cent in 'Income Before Other Fixed Charges'. In this particular case, although Hotel B may not be earning as much in terms of absolute dollar, it is actually bringing more of its revenues (4.0 per cent) all the way down to 'Income Before Other Fixed Charges', thus is more effective in managing its hotel. Of course, it would be best to have the absolute value higher than the average of the competitive set. However, the relative value does offer insight. On the other hand, if Hotel C has a higher absolute value but a lower relative value, it shows that Hotel C can probably improve in some areas to be more efficient and thus able to bring more 'absolute dollars' down to the bottom line – 'absolute' and 'relative', twins that are inseparable.

Useful hotel benchmarking metrics

Benchmarking tends to suggest numbers and metrics. While it is true that most benchmarks are quantitative measurements, it is pertinent to note that benchmarks can also be qualitative in nature. They are normally referred to as best practices. They are not numbers or measurements. Rather, they described a procedure or a method of doing a task or dealing with an issue. In the hotel business, qualitative benchmarks can be topics from how best to deal with express check-in on board an airport shuttle bus to a proactive property maintenance programme for the engineering department. These best practices are invaluable tools for management to use to improve their operations. In the accounting and finance areas, practices such as good electronic records management procedures, better budgeting and cost control procedures, or online integrated payroll accounting system can all be great qualitative benchmarking topics which will impact the financial success of a hotel. The process of data collection for qualitative benchmarks is quite similar. Hotels will be solicited to submit their success stories and, once published, other hotels that share similar characteristics can learn from each other.

As for quantitative benchmarks, they can be divided into two major areas: operations metrics and financial metrics. Operations metrics are ratios where management efficiency is measured. They can be further subdivided into activity ratios, profitability ratios and operating ratios. Activity ratios measure how well management uses the assets. They include metrics such as paid occupancy, average occupancy per room, employee turnover, daily seat turnover, multiple occupancy, inventory turnover, and fixed assets turnover. Profitability ratios measure the earning level management brings in terms of return on investments. Thus profit margin, operating efficiency, price-earnings ratio, earnings per share, return on equity, return on asset are all included. Finally, operation ratios include room rate, RevPAR (revenue per available room), labour cost percentage, room department profits, food profit percentage, beverage profit percentage, food cost percentage and beverage cost percentage.

In addition to the above, the two newer metrics are GOPPAR and RevPAC where GOPPAR stands for gross operating profit per available room and RevPAC is revenue per available customer. GOPPAR is preferred over RevPAR since it gives a better indication of a hotel's profitability. Unlike RevPAR that looks at revenues, GOPPAR reflects the operating profit potential of a hotel and therefore gives a better indication of the overall performance or cash flow potentials. It can also indicate management's use of expenses and whether such are controlled appropriately. In terms of RevPAR/RevPAC, due to double or multiple occupancies, it is sometimes considered better to measure revenue in terms of per available customer rather than per available room.

Singh and Schmidgall (2002) surveyed US lodging financial executives on their rating of ratios. On a scale of 0 to 5 where 0 means 'no opinion', 1 means 'unimportant' and 5 means 'crucial', only two activity ratios (paid occupancy and average occupancy per room) and one profitability ratio (profit margin) scored an average of above 4.00. However, all operating ratios as mentioned above scored an average of 4.15/5.00. This means that financial executives are very interested in daily operating statistics. On the pure financial side where liquidity and solvency ratios are included, Singh and Schmidgall did not record any of the ratios having a score of at least 4.00. The highest rated ratio was account receivables turnover at 3.55/5.00.

Since hotels are more interested in operational metrics, it is therefore no surprise that most reports lean toward the operational side and provide useful metrics such as occupancy percentage (Occ. Per cent), average daily rate, total revenues, revenue per available room. These reports are known as 'top line' reports as the metrics deal with revenues, the top line of any statement of operations.

Some reports provide more information and include the entire statement of operations detailing revenues and expenses from each major department, undistributed operating expenses, and management fees, property taxes and insurance, to end up with income before other fixed charges (IBFC). Some will even go into certain areas such as payroll and detail the payroll distribution of the sample hotels. Again, once a hotel finds its competitive comparison, then benchlearning, or conducting comparative or trend analyses, can occur.

Turning benchmarking to profits

As suggested by Freytag and Hollensen (2001), the entire process of benchmarking is not complete unless benchaction is achieved. Thus far in this chapter, the step of benchmarking the useful metrics, understanding how benchmarks are compiled and selecting the appropriate reports have been discussed. The crucial point now is how a hotel can utilize this process to enhance its performance, generate further actions, streamline its operations and to produce more profits.

Benchlearning: meaningful analyses

Benchlearning is analysing the data and identifying the gaps. Such gaps can be good or bad. Good gaps are where a hotel is outperforming its competitive set while the bad ones are the opposite. When analysing the data, there are two areas hotel management may want to look at: comparative and trends. It is true that integrating a hotel's data with those of the benchmarks is a comparative. However, a hotel may also want to compare two such sets of data, its performance and that of the competitors, with its budgeted figures. Hotels can also take the comparison one step further to include data of the same time period last year. Also, do not forget to compare both the absolute and relative figures. Customized reports, such as those from PKF, E&Y and STR, actually perform some of the benchlearning for the hotels in that they will, more often than not, include comparative analyses. As seen in Figure 5.2, the variances have been calculated for immediate management action. In cases where more generic reports or less customized information do not include comparative analysis, this is the time for management to do its own benchlearning to understand the data provided and then integrate its own hotel data with that of the reports and through trend and comparative analyses, see where the strength and weaknesses of the hotel lie. With the aid of a spreadsheet, the comparative analysis process should be quite easy to set up.

Trend analysis is the other integral half of data analysis. When a hotel compares its performance this year to that of last year's, it is the beginning of a trend analysis. Two years do not make a trend. A trend is a series of data over time. However, if a hotel is trying to trend its annual statistics on a monthly basis from January to December, then, two years with 24 data points can be a trend. Trend analysis is important as it aids hotel management to identify patterns so that they can act accordingly. For instance, if a trend exists that the occupancy rate of a hotel in a winter ski resort is very slow in the summer months, a hotel can plan accordingly for staffing, purchasing and even maintenance work.

Benchaction: let it rip

Once the comparisons are made and trends and patterns are identified, it is important to take action. Take an example where a comparative analysis indicates that a hotel is making money in the top line in revenues but is not taking as much to the bottom as its competitor. From here, management can begin to brainstorm the possibilities. If revenues are competitive, but the net profit is not, the issues then lie in the middle segment of the income statement: cost control. Management will then need to take a closer look at each of the line items and compare the relative statistics in food cost, labour costs, administrative and general, marketing, one by one until they can identify one with a large variance. What makes a large variance? Most would say around 1.5 per cent to 2 per cent. It may seem a very small amount. However, if each cost account is 1.5 per cent higher than the competitive set, ten accounts will yield a 15 per cent higher cost. This translates to 15 per cent lower in the net income. Once certain areas are identified, then further analysis need to be done by department to control the costs. Management will then need to devise action plans, communicate such plans to the staff, explain to the staff the reason for such plans, and execute the plans.

One important element in benchaction, as can be expected, is good communication. Management should have the commitment from all employees in order for any action plan to be successful. It may also be meaningful for management to track such successes in cost cutting or working on methods to increase more revenues and post them in the staff break area or cafeteria. Good news should be communicated to all. Some management feels that 'numbers' are secretive and are only the property of management and that line employees would not understand these trends or comparisons. If they would simply communicate in a simple manner via charts or graphs and share the success with the entire crew, it will actually enhance employee camaraderie and commitment.

In another example, a hotel is able to have a higher net profit percentage than the competitive set, but much lower as far as the dollar amount. In this case, the hotel is efficient in its operating, but the small revenues base will not allow the pass through of more absolute dollars to the bottom line. In this case, the issue may be in the pricing of the hotel rooms that affects the sales amount. Then, analyses will need to be performed to see what the competitors are charging for their room rates. This hotel may also want to analyse the demand elasticity to assess if a rate increase would be likely to result in a decline in business, how much would that be, and how would that decline affect the bottom line. These further analyses are part of the benchaction to see if any pricing changes will take place.

Conclusion

Benchmarking is here to stay. Mandelbaum and Vargo (personal communication, January 12, 2005) comment that this process has really been institutionalized to the effect that is now being written into contracts by major brands to be used to measure management performance for corporations and also management companies for owners.

It is also important to note that, as in any process, there is the involvement of human efforts. When it comes to formulating strategies and actions, making changes in the organization, and carrying out actionable activities, managers and owners cannot simply focus on the numbers. They also need to focus on their customers and employees. It is encouraging to produce better numbers, but it is also important that employees do not get burnout, thus causing errors. Proper human implementation is therefore of utmost importance (Elmuti and Kathawala, 1997).

An old Chinese proverb regarding victory says if one knows where one stands and also knows where the enemies stand, then this person can fight a hundred battles and will win all of them. Benchmarking is healthy for a hotel. Through evaluation and meaningful comparison, a hotel can continue to improve itself to enhance the products and services it provides to its guests.

References

Camp, R. (1989) *Benchmarking: The search for industry best practices that lead to superior performance*. ASQC, Quality Press, Milwaukee.

Corgel, J.B., Mandelbaum, R.M. and Vargo, C.R. (2001) *Benchmarking Hotel Profitability*. Hospitality Research Group, PKF Consulting, London.

DeFranco, A.L., Countryman, C. and Venegas, T. (2004) It's all about measurement: Benchmarking in the hotel industry. *Bottomline*, **19** (1), 26–28.

Elmuti, D. and Kathawala, Y. (1997) An overview of benchmarking process: A tool for continuous improvement and competitive advantage. *Benchmarking: An International Journal*, **4** (4), 229–243.

Freytag, P.V. and Hollensen, S. (2001) The process of benchmarking, benchlearning, and benchaction. *The TQM Magazine*, **13** (1), 25–33.

Schmidt, J. (1992) The link between benchmarking and shareholder value. *Journal of Business Strategy*, May/June, 7–13.

Singh, A.J. and Schmidgall, R.S. (2002) Analysis of financial ratios commonly used by US lodging financial executives. *Journal of Leisure Property*, **2** (3), 201–213.

www.hvsinternational.com. Website for HVS International.

www.m-w.com. Website for the Merriam-Webster Online Dictionary.

www.pkfonline.com. Website for PKF Consulting.

www.smithtravelresearch.com. Website for Smith Travel Research.

Yasin, M.M. and Zimmer, T.W. (1995) The role of benchmarking in achieving continuous service quality. *International Journal of Contemporary Hospitality Management*, **7** (4), 27–32.

Zikmund, W.G. (2003) *Business Research Methods*, 7th edn. Mason, Ohio, Thomson South-western.

Developing a benchmarking methodology for the hotel industry

Peter Harris and
Marco Mongiello

Introduction

In this chapter the concept of benchmarking and techniques of comparative analysis are addressed and
analysed with a twofold aim: (i) to evaluate benchmarking as a basis for assessment and management
of performance and (ii) to propose a technique of
comparative analysis specific to the hotel industry.

Benchmarking is defined in this context as a set of
activities that use performance indicators to assess
and to manage the performance of organizations.
Theoretical and practical points of view are addressed
for evaluating benchmarking, i.e. reference is made
to the viability of obtaining suitable information
for performance measurement and management.

The suitability of benchmarking is addressed by seeking the theoretical legitimacy of using benchmarks for assessing performance of individual organizations, while comparative analysis's viability is addressed with reference to the practical issues related to carrying out credible benchmarking processes. Hence, a judgement on benchmarking effectiveness is given as a result.

The assessment of the viability of comparative analysis is explained by presenting a major research project where: (i) a database of indicators for benchmarking is first designed and created, (ii) a technique for carrying out a comparative analysis is explained and (iii) considerations on the results are reported.

The matrix in Figure 6.1 indicates the structure of the research questions evaluated in this chapter.

	Suitability	Viability
Performance measurement	Is benchmarking theoretically legitimate and does comparative analysis provide suitable information for performance measurement?	Is there a credible technique that makes comparative analysis viable for measuring performance?
Performance interpretation	Do, in theoretical terms, benchmarking and comparative analysis provide a suitable base for performance interpretation?	Do the results provided by the application of the proposed technique of comparative analysis enable interpretation of performance?
Performance management	Is it theoretically legitimate to establish targets for improvement of performance based on the results of comparative analysis?	Do the results of the comparative analysis offer a basis for establishing viable targets aimed at improving performance?

Figure 6.1
The research questions.

The research approach in this chapter is a 'field research' method; the research was designed with the contribution of professionals and industrial associations, the aim of the project had been expressed by organizations' decision-makers over a number of years directly to us researchers on many and independent occasions, and the collection of data was carried out in the field via direct interviews supported by document analysis *in situ*.

With Young's (1999) words – and referring to Adler and Adler's (1987) framework – we too 'adopted an overt researcher role with the goal of objectively studying an organisation' (p. 79), probably because we too have been 'schooled in the logical empiricist tradition and thus, apply this world view to [our] field' (p. 80).

According to Young's (1999) taxonomy, the research we present in this chapter would be a 'Developing Theories' type of research, as in the example of Anderson's (1985) research on the adoption and adaptation of activity-based costing in specific industries. We propose a new system of comparative analysis, which is the development of techniques already existing in various industries but that have never obtained a theoretical analysis and legitimacy nor ever reached a satisfactory level of sophistication. We aim at giving theoretical legitimacy to the new system and at demonstrating its viability for managerial use. As we use a case study for demonstrating the viability of comparative analysis, we join the majority of the published research's approach as 'the majority of [benchmarking] research evidence presented tends to be case study based' (Longbottom, 2000:102).

About the suitability of comparative analysis for performance measurement and interpretation. A critical review of relevant literature

A wide literature, which spans some decades, is available on benchmarking – comprehensive literature analysis is offered in both Longbottom (2000) and Dattakumar and Jagadeesh (2003). On occasion of the birth of the *Benchmarking: An International Journal* (at that time the journal's name was *Benchmarking for Quality Management & Technology*) benchmarking was defined by Watson (1994:5) as 'a business practice which stimulates process improvement by determining best practices across organizations through performance measurement and understanding those factors which enabled the higher performance of the leading organizations'. Watson (1993) had previously identified a number of generations in the evolution of benchmarking along a scale of increasing sophistication. However, in the following years, starting from as early as Codling (1998:158), most of the attention has consistently been devoted to only one part of the definition, i.e. 'best practices', rather than the other aspect, i.e. 'performance measurement'. In an increasing number of industries, benchmarking of practices has been applied to higher and higher levels of sophistication, while the comparison of performance measures has been more and more considered as a too narrow and limiting approach to benchmarking. Meaningfully, Ahmed and Rafiq (1998) address benchmarking of performance indicators, but their explanation of the benchmarking process is only referred to practices not to performance indicators.

In fact, benchmarking of performance measurements has for long been said to be less than satisfactory for analysis purposes, as it overlooks the reasons of the variations between individual organizations and their benchmarks (Hinton et al., 2000:57). Anderson and McAdam (2004:467) mention conspicuous literature from the 1970s and 1980s in this sense and give ground to the advocates of balanced – financial and non-financial – approaches to perform-ance measurement, undermining the theoretical fundaments of comparative analysis of financial results.

On the other hand, Codling's (1998) concept of 'benchgrafting' – which refers to benchmarking being worthwhile only if it guar-antees that the 'transposition of best practice to the organization [must be possible] as a result of such systematic study' (p. 158) – paves the way for any new techniques of benchmarking to be a legitimate tool, as long as it supports improvement processes. In other terms, a technique of systematic comparison of indicators of performance is not valuable *per se* but for the process of improve-ment that it spurns; 'wherever possible benchmarking should not be restricted merely to comparisons of results but include an exam-ination of the underlying causal processes' (Hinton et al., 2000:59). This is the underpinning reasoning for financial comparative analysis to be considered a potentially revealing approach to per-formance assessment and management; the equation being that as benchmarking is in principle *acceptable* then also comparative analysis should be equally *acceptable*, under the condition that both benchmarking and comparative analysis must be support-ive to decision processes.

More recent contributions make even stronger the case for new techniques to be accepted and theoretically legitimated; in Kyrö (2003) the 'evolving and dynamic phenomenon' of benchmarking developed 'through action and for action' and the related 'scientific debate is for action and deduced from action', with the twofold aim, which we embrace in this chapter, 'to advance the theoretical discussion in this field and ... lead towards better practical appli-cations by means of advanced conceptualisation' (p. 212).

Our proposal of comparative analysis takes its moves from the acknowledgement that the actual and expressed needs of the decision-makers in organizations are the starting point of bench-marking, i.e. benchmarking is a phenomenon before being a theo-retical subject of analysis. We also acknowledge that the techniques of comparative analysis have developed in the last three decades under the pressure of the information needs of the decision-makers and their consultants, i.e. 'through action and from action'. We finally acknowledge that the technique of comparative analysis presented in this chapter finds its theoretical suitability in the extent of the details that it reaches as in this way it effectively sup-ports the investigation and implementation of continuous improve-ments in organizations.

Our step forward is that we move beyond the comparison of processes, which we consider the domain of the decision-makers in their own organizations, toward the comparison of financial performance indicators, which enable detailed investigation of the reasons of such performance. With Kyrö's (2004) words; we enter the 'interplay between science and practice in action research' (p. 54).

The human body metaphor, which is often used in organizational science, bears once again, an explanatory value; human bodies' health is assessed via comparison of bodies' 'performance indicators', such as temperature, pressure, pulse, against the norms that long medical experience has established. Departures from those norms are considered symptoms, which provide clues of potential diseases or indications of healthy metabolism. They are starting points for further investigations in the internal and individual processes. Similarly to physiological indicators, the financial ones give raise to valid interpretation when they are detailed enough to pinpoint specific symptoms, potential malfunctions or praiseworthy performances. The organization processes are and remain individual for each organization as well as their respective solutions and the solutions' implementation.

As opposed to the 'benchgrafting' metaphor of 'insertion of shoots or tissues from one body to another', by which Codling (1998:159) warns about the dangers of 'withering, infection setting in or rejection by the hosts' antibodies and immuno-defence system', our comparative analysis proposal recognizes the prime role of individuality in organizations avoiding the problem of intra-organization compatibility of processes, by pointing the attention to the financial norms only. The holistic approach to interpretation of organizations' behaviour, where multiple elements and processes are combined as one in each individual organization, the concept of 'equi-finality', whereby different organizations' routes are followed to reach similar results, and the similarity of performance results that the 'invisible hand' of competitive markets imposes, contribute to support the idea that financial results can be used as legitimate norms for individual comparison; they may prove valuable symptoms to uncover conditions, and also respect the individual differences in process.

About the suitability of comparative analysis for performance management. Some reflections

Once indicators have been gathered and compared with norms, the variations have been reasoned upon and a map for further investigation is designed, the main issue remains whether the results of comparative analysis are a suitable basis to produce new targets.

This is another difference between traditional process benchmarking and our proposal of comparative analysis. Best practices are suggested in the former, whereas there are no best norms in the latter. The aim of comparative analysis is to spurn a reasoned investigation into the processes that provoked the indicators, but does not provide immediate new targets. An indirect and more complex decision process leads to the definition of new targets which, compared with the norms, show if a sustainable picture of the organization is chosen.

So much of the norms *are not targets* in themselves, that the decision process started from the analysis of the variations (or departures of the actual results from the norms) may even aim at justifying the variations themselves, rather than creating new targets. In fact warnings have been expressed for the dangers of the so-called 'quick dip approach' to benchmarking, by which 'managers may misinterpret the data obtained and develop "stretch objectives" without really understanding true organizational capability (i.e. voice of the process)' (Zairi, 1994:13). Also the fourth of Maleyeff's (2003:20) benchmarking 'key principles' reinforces this point, by stating that 'if done improperly, [the setting of targets from] benchmarking can lead to poor morale among employees, and may cause workers to act in ways that degrade, rather than improve, customer satisfaction'.

The norms play the role of guidelines in the same way as, for example, the analysis of the break even point does, by indicating how far the organization is from making a loss; not only the volume of break even is not a target, but also a target below the break even point might occasionally be accepted as a component of a strategic design that requires the organization to work at a loss for a short period of time. Another example is the cost analysis applied to price decisions, where costs do not represent a target and yet they must be considered in order to check whether the market prices cover the relevant costs; prices are not decided on the basis of their related costs, but must be compared to costs that are *norms*, which can reveal whether the prices are sustainable or not. Both 'activity-based costing' and 'target costing' support this approach; the first as it indicates that more detailed costing serves for producing more valuable norms for checking the sustainability of the price policy, and the second, as it is an approach based on the prime role of pricing over costing, whereby the prices are the *norms* and the costs the consequence of the sustainability analysis.

Therefore, the concept of creating targets via elaborated decision processes – or 'sound programmes of quality policy deployment' (Zairi, 1994:14) – based on the analysis of norms, i.e. costs or prices as in the above examples, is not new to the management accounting literature (Walsh, 2000) and is the basis of our proposal of comparative analysis. In this chapter the suitability of comparative analysis for supporting new target decision processes is related to the level of detail that the comparative analysis information provides to the decision-makers.

About viability of comparative analysis for performance measurement and interpretation – a technique proposed and applied

Subsequent to the assessment of the theoretical suitability of comparative analysis, another equally important aspect must be solved; whether comparative analysis is viable for the purpose. It is a practical point that refers to the availability of: (i) management accounting data to form the basis for the norms; (ii) technical ability of researchers to elaborate the data and produce credible norms; and (iii) appropriate technology for making scientific elaboration and for presenting the results in a suitable fashion for decision-makers.

All these practical aspects are addressed through an experimental study; the aim being to demonstrate that an *ad hoc* designed study makes it possible: (i) to obtain data relevant for the production of comparative analysis norms; (ii) to design a series of norms with the level of detail useful for decision-makers; and (iii) to elaborate the data and present the norms in a suitable fashion for the decision-makers.

The case study was carried out in the hospitality industry where a tradition of benchmarking has been spreading over the last decades as a mechanism for performance assessment and continuous improvement. Performance measurement, also, has seen some recent important development in this industry, making it particularly suitable for this exercise (Harris and Mongiello, 2001).

The existing techniques involve the regular comparison of a firm's activities, such as services, processes and results, against best practice or some other predetermined standard. The benefits of comparative analysis, instead, would include:

- Highlighting areas of revenue, expenses and profit for improvement

- Identifying strengths and weaknesses against competitive set

- Stimulating continuous improvement.

For the case study the Italian hospitality industry was chosen, reasoned upon Italy not yet having any serious attempt of sophisticated comparative analysis but having shown a wide spread interest for it, mainly driven by its ties with world-wide hospitality organizations. Currently, benchmark reports are produced for the hotel industry in a number of countries in Europe and elsewhere. However, to date the content of the reports, including those featuring Italy, is too general to be of any real practical value as an operational benchmarking tool. For example, comparing the operating performance of a hotel in a city with the results generated from a sample of hotels taken from across the whole of a country or from the same city but with no analysis by price-based bands and with no analysis of cost items is of no practical use to the decision-makers.

In the case of the hospitality industry, benchmarks are often represented by other similar hotels inside the same organization. With this study other similar hotels drawn from a sample outside the hotel organization provide relevant data and contribute to the production of the benchmark for the competitive set – or 'benchmarking club or network' with Hinton et al.'s (2000) words.

The nature and sensitivity of management accounting data are the first obstacle to obtaining data, as in Hinton et al. (2000). Also, in terms of the quality and reliability of the information presented, it was essential for our study that the financial and operating benchmarks were produced as accurately as possible (precision being an illusion) and were comparable; 'like with like', 'apples with apples' (Hinton et al., 2000:57). It was, therefore, once again important that the research design incorporated a method of data collection and analysis that brought integrity and credibility to the process.

This was faced in the case study by presenting the managers with a process and a team that would make them perceive the highest possible level of confidentiality in the treatment of the data. The process – a pilot study – was made of two phases, i.e. data collection and data elaboration, which involved a globally recognized accounting firm for the collection and two foreign universities for the elaboration.[1] A trustworthy industrial organization was also involved and gave its endorsement to the project, encouraging its members to participate, but was not involved in collection nor elaboration of data, which were made anonymous during the elaboration process. The contribution of the industrial organization also helped to ensure that the 'organisational culture(s) [were] sympathetic to the ethos of benchmarking' (Hinton et al., 2000:59), by organizing workshops, to which the members were invited and where the project was explained in details.

Definitions in our proposal of comparative analysis

Comparative analysis of financial statements is concerned with comparing actual results against some predetermined 'standard' or 'yardstick' (Harris and Hazzard, 1992), such as past or budgeted performance, for the purpose of measuring the magnitude of the differences. The differences, or variations, can be calculated in two forms, i.e. 'absolute' or 'relative' variations. In a financial

---

[1]Data were collected in collaboration with Ernst & Young Italy in 2004 for a pilot study and the elaborations were made by Oxford Brookes University and the University of Westminister.

context, the absolute variation refers to the change in monetary value between actual results and (say) budgeted performance, whereas the relative variation refers to the percentage change between the figures; the relative change being determined by expressing the absolute variation as a percentage of the 'standard', i.e. budgeted performance.

The determination of absolute and relative variations of financial results provides each variation with a context in which to view the other variation, providing the basis for a more balanced and informed review of the change. For example, knowledge of (say) a €50 000 improvement in revenue against budget has limited meaning on its own. However, learning of a €50 000 increase in revenue against budget, representing a 2 per cent growth in business, provides a context for the change; seeing the bigger picture. Thus, although the additional €50 000 revenue increase is a considerable sum in monetary terms, seen in the context of the revenue budget, 2 per cent is a relatively small percentage change. It is, therefore, important to keep the comparison of results in perspective in order to avoid misinterpretation of the extent of changes.

Common-size financial statement analysis is concerned with facilitating the comparison of results between similar businesses of different sizes.

In order to undertake meaningful comparisons of financial results between businesses of different sizes or scale of operations (Jagels and Coltman, 2004), it is important the comparisons are assessed on a like-for-like basis, i.e. on a level playing field. For example, assume a company that owns two similar restaurants, with seating capacities for forty and seventy-five persons, wishes to compare the operating performance of each establishment, one against the other. If the larger of the two restaurants were to achieve higher levels of revenue, costs and profits, this, by itself, is unlikely to give a clear indication of the relative operating efficiency of the two establishments, because under normal conditions the larger establishment would be expected to generate higher revenues and, therefore, higher profits. Thus, notwithstanding the seating capacity of the restaurants, in terms of assessing efficiency, the problem of differing levels of business alone prevent an equitable comparison between the two establishments. However, the question of 'how do the two establishments compare in terms of operating efficiency?', e.g. costs and profits achieved as a percentage of revenue, or cost and profit per euro of revenue generated, addresses the level (scale) of business issue by focusing on the 'relative' (percentage relationship) level of business rather than the 'absolute' (numerical) value of the level of business.

In terms of implementation, the issue of operating efficiency can be addressed by the presentation of profit and loss statements in what is termed 'common-size' format. Total revenue is taken to represent 100 per cent and the various individual expense items are expressed in 'relative' terms as percentages of the total revenue. In the case of a multiple department hospitality business such as a hotel, the individual department revenues are regarded as 100 per cent and the associated direct department expenses are expressed as percentages of their particular department revenue, while the undistributed operating expenses (overhead) are expressed as percentages of total revenue. The individual department revenues are subsequently expressed as percentages of total revenue, commonly referred to as sales mix (or business mix). An alternative approach, as implied earlier, is to present the common-size profit and loss statement in terms of the cash value of costs and profit per euro of revenue generated. Clearly, the preferred method will depend on the context and purpose of the analysis.

With regard to hotels, however, the nature of the business offers another approach to the presentation of common-size profit and loss statements, based on the 'per available room' (PAR) concept. In this case, the various hotel revenues, expenses and profits contained in the profit and loss statement are presented line-by-line, in PAR terms, by dividing each line item by the number of available rooms in the particular hotel property under review. For example, if the annual profit statement of a 200-room mid-market hotel showed rooms department revenue €4 000 000; rooms department payroll €480 000; and other rooms department expenses (guest supplies, laundry, travel agent commission etc.) €360 000, the PAR common-size format for the statement would show RevPAR (revenue per available room) €20 000; CostPAR (cost per available room) – Payroll €2400; and CostPAR – other expenses €1800. The same principle is applied line-by-line to the food and beverage department, other operated departments (such as telephone department and leisure centre) and the undistributed operating expenses (overhead), down to gross operating profit (GOP).

The process of dividing the various revenues and expenses by the number of available rooms neutralizes the influence of capacity (size) and allows a hotel's financial results to be compared (benchmarked) against (say) other mid-market hotels (with differing numbers of rooms) PAR results in the same company. Alternatively, a hotel's results could be benchmarked against hospitality industry norms. Thus, once preparation of the PAR profit and loss statement is complete the results can be compared on an intra-company and industry basis using comparative analysis techniques.

The rationale for applying PAR as the basis for presenting the common-size format of hotel profit and loss statements is that room capacity, rather than (say) restaurant capacity, is normally the main 'driver' of a hotel business and, therefore, broadly considered to be the lowest common denominator. An alternative approach is to present the common-size profit and loss statements based on 'per occupied room' (POR). However, compared with the 'per occupied room' basis which only considers capacity utilization (room occupancy), the 'per available room' approach is regarded as more comprehensive as it incorporates both capacity utilization and total capacity (room occupancy and total room stock).

Comparative analysis technique

- *Revenue*: Apply the revenue per available room (RevPAR) under the appropriate room rate band of the benchmark sample and scale up (to the individual hotel room capacity) to determine the 'absolute' and 'relative' revenue variation (provides a meaningful basis to compare revenue (yield) management efficiency against competitive set – sometimes adjustments required in severe inflationary periods).

- *Expenses*: Apply expenses percentage of revenue figures and determine the 'absolute' percentage points variation (provides a meaningful basis to compare the level of key items of expenditure per €100 of revenue against competitive set – not generally affected by inflation).

- *Profits*: Apply both profit per available room (ProPAR) and profit percentage of revenue (because profit comprises both revenue and expenses so important to see 'absolute' magnitude of monetary value and the efficiency level of return on revenue – similar inflationary influences as above).

It is important to be aware of the benefits and limitations of comparative analysis. A major benefit of benchmark reports is the 'external', inter-firm comparison basis against which organizations can compare individual hotel property revenue, cost and profit performance line-by-line, year-on-year and, equally importantly in terms of trends against competitive set. Although in this chapter the examples refer to an analysis by rate band, also size, location, age and business mix can be included. When used thoughtfully, comparisons can offer insights into operating efficiency in terms of marketing and service delivery related to purchasing, productivity, sales promotion and pricing strategies.

Methodology of the case study

Thus, the method of data collection was fundamental to the quality and integrity of the benchmarking exercise. It was, therefore, decided that all financial and operating data would be collected by research analysts, in person, from each of the hotel properties participating in the study. This enabled face-to-face discussions that facilitated participants' understanding of the project and clarification and verification of anomalies and abnormalities found in records and results, thus providing greater confidence in the accuracy, consistency and comparability of data.

The presence of a research analyst was also found to be an effective vehicle to explain the purpose and benefits gained from contributing to the benchmarking scheme and to reassure participants as to the confidentiality and anonymity of their property and data. In addition, discussions between hotel participants and research analysts provided the opportunity to identify and reconcile incompatible results and encourage the introduction of standardized methods.

Although the hotels participating in the study were not explicitly operating the *Uniform System of Accounts for the Lodging Industry (USALI)*, the majority was either using hotel accounting software packages that appear to draw upon the *USALI* or, as a minimum, were operating a departmental accounting system which is the basis of the *USALI*.

Sample

The total sample in the pilot study, which was drawn from the North-East Veneto region comprised 29 properties.[2] In order to ensure direct comparability of results, hotel properties had provided two years operating data. Contributing hotel properties included both independent and group operated hotel properties.

Data analysis and presentation

The data used to compile the case study's report were structured so as to comply with the format of the ninth edition of the *Uniform System of Accounts for the Lodging Industry* (1996) and the statistical analysis in the report was presented in the form of averages (or 'norms') comprising 'medians' and 'quartiles'. For the examples of this chapter a sub-sample has been used.

Median

The median was determined by arranging data observations into ascending, or descending, order (known as an 'array') and locating the middle item.

---

[2] The results used for the purposes of this chapter – and reported in the appendix – refer to a sub-sample of the data collected for the pilot study.

Upper and lower quartiles

Quartiles were located half way between the end of an array and the median. For example, the lower quartile was found by locating the middle item between the lower end of the array and the median.

Statistical meaning

The median was selected for use in the report because it is a 'representative' average that is not normally influenced by extreme values in a sample. Whereas the quartiles were selected as they represent the dispersion (concentration) and skew of the values in the sample.

For example, looking at the hotels whose ADR (Average Daily Rate) was included between €70 and €140, the median ADR was €81, lower quartile is €77 and upper quartile is €128 as shown in Table 6.5 (see Appendix). As represented in the Figure 6.2, this means that the distribution of the values was skewed towards the lower extreme and more dispersed towards the higher extreme. The same explanation applies to the group of hotels whose ADR was below €70 and to those whose ADR was above €140.

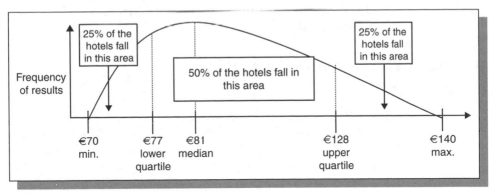

Figure 6.2
Distribution of statistical values.

The majority of the ADR values included between €70 and €140 were, therefore, concentrated around the median (€81) in a range of €77 and €128, i.e. a hotel with an ADR of €78 would say its ADR is lower than the median, but still among fairly frequent values, as opposed to a hotel with an ADR of €75, which would be 'out of the normal range of values'. Similarly a hotel with an ADR of €120 would say that its ADR is higher than the median, but still among fairly frequent values, while an ADR of €130 would be 'out of the normal range of values'.

The results of the analysis of the sample were presented as 'common-size' revenues and expenses in several detailed tables, which were grouped as: 'Percentage Tables', 'Per available room Tables' and 'Per occupied room Tables'. Each group including:

- Summary of Key Statistics Table (see Tables 6.3–6.5 in Appendix)
- Room Department Table (see Tables 6.6 and 6.8 in Appendix)
- Food and Beverage Table (see Tables 6.7 and 6.9 in Appendix)
- Telephone and Minor Operated Department Table
- Undistributed Operating Expenses Table.

In addition, each table presented the total sample in the first column and three bands of ADR values in the other columns and the results from the hotels in the sample were reported according to the value of the hotels' ADR, e.g. the results of a hotel with ADR equal to €78 would be included in the column headed '70 < ADR < 140', the results of a hotel with ADR equal to €155 would be included in the column headed 'ADR > €140'.

An extract of the tables is presented in the appendix of this chapter for the purpose of the example – the Virtual Hotel – whose explanation follows.

Benchmarking example: Virtual Hotel

Introduction

The following analysis is the result of the comparison of Virtual Hotel's data with their benchmarks (Tables 6.1 and 6.2). Virtual Hotel is a 100 room hotel located in the city centre and is open the whole year, its ADR is €76 and average occupancy 47 per cent. The restaurant serves guests and walk-ins.

Each benchmark is calculated as follows:

- If it is a revenue value, it is calculated as the figure PAR from the relevant column of the tables, i.e. the column where ADR is included between €70 and €140, multiplied by the number of rooms of the Virtual Hotel.

- If it is an expense, it is the figure PER from the relevant column of the tables, i.e. the column where ADR is included between €70 and €140.

- If it is a profit value, it is calculated both as the figure PAR multiplied by the number of Virtual Hotel's available rooms and as the figure PER.

Table 6.1

	Virtual Hotel 2003		Sub-sample report 2004		Variation	
					Absolute	Relative
	1 €	2 %	3 €	4 %	5 €/% points	6 %
Total revenue	**2 604 880**					
Room department						
Revenue	1 303 780		1 623 700		−319 920	−19.7
Payroll	450 000	34.5		19.8	14.7	
Other expenses	80 000	6.1		6.0	0.1	
Total expenses	**530 000**	**40.7**		**29.2**	**11.5**	
Departmental profit	**773 780**	**59.3**	**1 127 100**	**70.8**	**−353 320**	**−31.3**
Food & beverage department						
Food revenue	1 200 000	93.4	717 500	86.1	482 600	67.2
Beverage revenue	85 000	6.6	115 900	13.9	−30 800	−26.7
Total F & B revenue	**1 285 000**		**833 300**		**451 700**	**54.2**
Food cost of sales	400 000	33.3		29.2	4.1	
Beverage cost of sales	32 500	38.2		37.8	0.4	
Total cost of sales	**432 500**	**33.7**				
Food & beverage gross profit	**852 500**	**66.3**				
Public room sale	0					
Other income	0					
Gross profit & other income	**852 500**	**66.3**				
Food & beverage payroll	750 000	58.4		45.4	13.0	
Other F&B expenses	50 000	3.9		3.9	0.0	
Total F&B expenses	**800 000**	**62.3**		**60.7**	**1.6**	
F&B departmental profit	**52 500**	**4.1**	**67 500**	**16.4**	**−14 900**	**22.1**
Tel. + minor operated dept profits						
Telephone	12 000	30.0	11 400		600	5.3
Other operated departments	11 000					
Other incomes	0					
Gross income of tel. + minor oper. dept	**23 000**					
	849 280					
Undistributed operating expenses						
Administrative & general	200 000	7.7		3.7	4.0	
Marketing	30 000	1.2		3.0	−1.8	
Energy	150 000	5.8		5.2	0.6	
Property operation & maintenance	180 000	6.9		5.3	1.6	
Total U.O.E.	**560 000**	**21.5**				
Gross operating profit	**289 280**	**11.1**	**812 700**	**45.4**	**−523 420**	**−64.4**

Table 6.2

Per occupied room	Virtual Hotel 2003	Sub-sample report 2004	Variations
	€	€	€
Room department			
Payroll	26.23	15.17	11.06
Food and beverage department			
Payroll	43.72	13.78	29.94
Food revenue	69.95	33.65	36.30
Beverage revenue	4.95	5.43	−0.48

The variations of revenue are given in absolute (euros) and as relative (percentage), the variations of expenses are given as percentage points, the variations of profit are given in both absolute and relative.

Benchmarking technique (step by step)

Below is a guide to the main steps of benchmarking the results of an individual hotel property, such as the 'Virtual Hotel', using the sub-sample tables produced for the study (of which a sample is reported in the Appendix to this chapter):

1 Referring to Table 6.1, enter the actual annual operating results (revenues, expenses, profits and respective percentages) into columns 1 and 2, following the same format.

2 Benchmark room revenue and departmental profit (using 'per available room'): turn to Table 6.8 Rooms Department 'per available room' (RevPAR), refer to the column '70 < ADR < 140' (because Virtual Hotel's ADR is €76) and select the medians for 2003, 16 237 (RevPAR) against revenue and 11 271 against departmental profit, and multiply each figure by the number of rooms available in the hotel, thus 16 237 × 100 = 1 623 700 and 11 271 × 100 = 1 127 100 and enter the figures against room revenue and departmental profit respectively in column 3.

3 Benchmark room payroll and related, other expenses, total expenses and departmental profit (using 'percentage of revenue'): turn to Table 6.6 Rooms Department 'percentage of revenue', refer to the column '70 < ADR < 140' and select medians for 2003, 19.8% (payroll) and 6.0% (other expenses) 29.2% (total expenses) and 70.8% (departmental profit) and enter the percentages against room payroll and related, other expenses, total expenses and departmental profit respectively in column 4.

4 Benchmark food and beverage revenues and profits (using 'per available room'): turn to Table 6.9 Food and Beverage 'per available room', refer to the column '70 < ADR < 140' and select the medians for 2003, 8333 (food and beverage revenue), 7175 (food revenue), 1159 (beverage revenue) and 675 (departmental profit), and multiply each figure by the number of rooms available in the hotel, thus $8333 \times 100 = 833\,300$, $7175 \times 100 = 717\,500$, $1159 \times 100 = 115\,900$ and $675 \times 100 = 67\,500$ and enter the figures against food and beverage revenue, food revenue, beverage revenue and F + B Departmental Profit respectively in column 3.

5 Benchmark food and beverage revenues, expenses and profits (using 'percentage of revenue'): turn to Table 6.7 Food and Beverage 'percentage of revenue', refer to the column '70 < ADR < 140' and select the medians for 2003, 86.1% (food revenue), 13.9% (beverage revenue), 29.2% (food cost of sales), 37.8% (beverage cost of sales), 45.4% (F + B Payroll), 3.9% (other F + B expenses), 60.7% (total F + B expenses) and 16.4% (F + B departmental profit) and enter the percentages against the respective items in column 4.

6 Benchmark telephone profit (using 'per available room') and undistributed operating expenses (using 'percentage of revenue') using a similar technique as above.

7 Benchmark gross operating profit (using 'per available room' and 'percentage of revenue'): first, turn to Table 6.4 Summary of key statistics 'per available room', refer to the column '70 < ADR < 140' and select the median for 2003, 8127 against gross operating profit and multiply the figure by the number of available rooms to give $8127 \times 100 = 812\,700$ and enter against gross operating profit in column 3. Secondly, turn to Table 6.3 Summary of key statistics 'percentage of total revenue', refer to the column '70 < ADR < 140' and select the median percentage 45.4% (gross operating profit) and enter the percentage against the respective item in column 4.

Findings

The key findings that characterize Virtual Hotel are:

- Revenue is significantly below the benchmark
- Payroll per cents in all departments are higher than their respective benchmarks
- Other expenses are in line with the respective benchmarks.

Analysis and recommendations

The picture given by the item-by-item comparison of Virtual Hotel with its benchmark potentially shows that the capacity of Virtual Hotel is not exploited.

- Marketing activity to be enhanced and focused.

In order to generate new business some focused marketing effort is suggested. This could be coupled with a revision of the booking policy, e.g. allowing more advanced bookings in order to bring the occupancy up 10–15 points per cent, for a better exploitation of the capacity, without affecting (displacing) more profitable clients.

An increase in the volume of business in the rooms department should lead to less than proportional increase in the payroll costs, given the fixed costs components of the payroll. An increase in revenue, therefore, would reduce the gap with the revenue benchmark, reduce the payroll per cent and bring the departmental income closer and above the benchmark.

Virtual Hotel's restaurant's performance is, most likely, fuelled by walk-in customers, which give a positive effect on the Food revenue. Beverage revenue is suffering for both the 'scarce' amount of business in the hotel and a low beverage sale per occupied room. Although the performance of the Department is positive against the benchmark, the payroll once again proves to be out of line, leading to a negative figure for the overall performance of the Department.

- Intervention in the human resources policy

- 'Promotion' of beverages among the guests.

Explanation

Despite the total Food and Beverage revenue being higher than the benchmark, the payroll per cent is higher than the benchmark, as opposed to what should be expected. A revision of the human resource policies is, therefore, highly recommended. At the same time, the increase in business suggested above should contribute to reduce the lack of Beverage revenue. Also a 'promotion' of beverages among the guests is suggested, in order to increase the sales per occupied room.

Evidence is shown of a potential for increasing marketing expenses, which might increase at least in proportion with the envisaged increase in volume of business, if not more. General and administrative expenses are higher than the benchmark, most likely because of their significant fixed cost components, which make them increase disproportionately when the volume of business is lower.

- Monitoring general and administrative expenses.

A watchful eye should be kept on the general and administrative expenses, which should decrease in percentage with the increase of the volume of business.

Comparison (item by item)

Rooms Department

- Room revenue lower than the benchmark by approximately €320 000, which represents a value of 19.7 per cent less than the benchmark
- Room payroll is nearly 15 percentage points higher than the benchmark
- Room payroll per occupied room is €11.06 higher than the benchmark
- As a consequence the departmental income results are more than €350 000 lower than the benchmark, which represents 31.3 per cent less than the benchmark.

Food and Beverage Department

- The mix between food and beverage shows a disproportion towards food revenue and a significant variation is apparent in the size of the Food and Beverage department, which shows food revenue higher than the benchmark by more than 67 per cent and beverage revenue lower than the benchmark by 26.7 per cent
- Per occupied room: food is outperforming by approximately €36 but beverage is under-performing by approximately €0.5
- As a consequence the departmental revenue is outperforming the benchmark by €451 700, which represents more than 54 per cent above the benchmark
- Again payroll per cent shows 13 points above the benchmark
- Consequence of the above is the very thin profit of the Food and Beverage Department, which is nearly €15 000 less than the benchmark, i.e. more than 22 per cent lower than the benchmark.

Telephone and Minor Operated Departments

- No major variations are apparent.

Undistributed Operating Expenses

- Administrative expenses are higher than the benchmark by 4 percentage points
- Marketing expenses are just below the line of the benchmark by nearly 2 percentage points.

Gross Operating Profit

- The GOP of Virtual Hotel is significantly lower than its benchmark, i.e. a figure €523 420 lower than the benchmark, which creates a GOP of 11.1 per cent against the 45.4 per cent of the benchmark.

About viability of comparative analysis for performance management

The case study so far shows that a comparative analysis exercise is viable for measurement and interpretation of performance. The pilot study presented shows that it was possible to collect sensitive data and to elaborate and present them according to the design required by decision-makers for their activity. The response obtained when the pilot study report was presented corroborates the perception of viability of the comparative analysis of management accounting comparative analysis.

The last aspect to face at this point is whether the results of comparative analysis are also viable for managing performance. Definitive evidence of this is by now still to be obtained, as it is the subject of the phase that we are currently carrying out of the research project. However, some encouraging progress is already clear as the national industrial organizations have shown interest for the case study and support the nationwide expansion of the project on the basis that it would represent a tool for managerial control and decision-making.

Summary and final considerations

In this chapter we give new strength to 'result benchmarking', which we consider a *valid* tool for measuring and interpreting performance. We based this conclusion on the analysis of relevant literature, which demonstrated that benchmarking is in principle a valid method of measure and interpretation of performance and enabled us to draw the conclusion that, under certain conditions, comparative analysis has similar features and is, therefore, theoretically valid.

Also the suitability of comparative analysis for performance management was found sustainable, based on analogy with benchmarking literature and on logical reasoning.

We then addressed the aspect of viability of comparative analysis, by means of presenting the results of a case study – the pilot study of comparative analysis carried out in the North-East Veneto region of the Italian hotel industry – which showed that the comparative analysis is possible, or viable, for measuring and interpreting performance.

The viability of comparative analysis for performance management is only a speculation, by now, but is supported by promising actions of the industrialist.

Comparative analysis seems, therefore, to be an effective method and seems to result in an effective tool for measuring, interpreting and, although full evidence is to come, also managing performance.

Having established the principles, further research, which we are currently undertaking, will give further evidence of the effectiveness of comparative analysis and will also improve its methods. The immediate next phases are the expansion of the project nationwide in Italy and to follow-up those hotels that were involved in the pilot study to analyse how its results are influencing their performance management.

References

Adler, P.A. and Adler, P. (1987) *Membership Roles in Field Research.* Sage, Newbury Park, CA.

Ahmed, P.K. and Rafiq, M. (1998) Integrated benchmarking: a holistic examination of select techniques for benchmarking analysis. *Benchmarking for Quality Management & Technology,* **5** (3), 225–242.

Anderson, K. and McAdam, R. (2004) A critique of benchmarking and performance measurement – Lead or lag? *Benchmarking: An International Journal,* **11** (5), 465–483.

Anderson, S.W. (1995) A framework for assessing cost management system changes: The case of activity based costing at General Motors, 1986–1993. *Journal of Management Accounting Research,* **7** (1), 1–51.

Codling, B.S. (1998) Benchgrafting: a model for successful implementation of the conclusions of benchmarking studies. *Benchmarking for Quality Management & Technology,* **5** (3), 158–164.

Dattakumar, R. and Jagadeesh, R. (2003) A review of literature on benchmarking. *Benchmarking: An International Journal,* **10** (3), 176–209.

Harris, P.J. and Hazzard, P.A. (1992) *Managerial Accounting in the Hospitality Industry*, 5th edn. Stanley Thornes, Cheltenham.

Harris, P.J. and Mongiello, M. (2001) Key performance indicators in European hotel properties: general managers' choices and company profiles. *International Journal of Contemporary Hospitality Management*, **13** (3), 120–127.

Hinton, M., Francis, G. and Holloway, J. (2000) Best practice benchmarking in the UK. *Benchmarking: An International Journal*, **7** (1), 52–61.

Jagels, M.G. and Coltman, M.M. (2004) *Hospitality Management Accounting*, 8th edn. Wiley, New York.

Kyrö, P. (2003) Revising the concept and forms of benchmarking. *Benchmarking: An International Journal*, **10** (3), 210–225.

Kyrö, P. (2004) Benchmarking as an action research process. *Benchmarking: An International Journal*, **11** (1), 52–73.

Longbottom, D. (2000) Benchmarking in the UK: an empirical study of practitioners and academics. *Benchmarking: An International Journal*, **7** (2), 98–117.

Maleyeff, J. (2003) Benchmarking performance indices: pitfalls and solutions. *Benchmarking: An International Journal*, **10** (1), 9–28.

Walsh, P. (2000) Targets and how to assess performance against them. *Benchmarking: An International Journal*, **7** (3), 183–199.

Watson, G.H. (1993) *Strategic Benchmarking: How to Rate your Company's Performance against the World's Best*. John Wiley and Sons Inc., New York.

Watson, G.H. (1994) A perspective on benchmarking. *Benchmarking for Quality Management & Technology*, **1** (1), 5–10.

Young, S.M. (1999) Field research methods in management accounting. *Accounting Horizons*, **13** (1), 76–84.

Zairi, M. (1994) Benchmarking: The best tool for measuring competitiveness. *Benchmarking for Quality Management & Technology*, **1** (1), 11–24.

Appendix: Examples tables for comparative analysis*

Table 6.3
Sub-sample – Summary of key statistics – PER table

Summary of key statistics (percentage of total revenue)		Sub-sample		ADR < 70		70 < ADR < 140		ADR > 140	
		2003 (%)	2002 (%)	2003 (%)	2002 (%)	2003 (%)	2002 (%)	2003 (%)	2002 (%)
Total payroll	lower quartile	23.1	23.0	31.1	24.3	21.3	25.1	27.0	14.5
	median	32.2	29.8	32.2	30.4	23.1	35.0	32.9	26.4
	upper quartile	42.5	48.2	42.5	43.8	39.5	48.2	40.6	35.7
Total departmental operating profit	lower quartile	43.5	50.0	44.6	54.4	54.7	47.8	43.0	52.7
	median	59.3	60.8	45.6	60.2	59.3	59.3	59.7	62.6
	upper quartile	68.6	72.9	62.9	69.9	68.6	64.4	66.9	72.9
Total undistributed expenses	lower quartile	13.9	9.6	15.5	14.5	11.3	6.6	21.3	12.8
	median	21.3	13.0	20.2	21.4	13.9	9.7	24.5	19.2
	upper quartile	38.4	34.6	27.4	24.0	27.9	13.0	38.4	34.6
Gross operating profit (GOP %)	lower quartile	21.8	32.2	25.4	31.7	32.8	39.7	21.8	32.7
	median	32.6	38.8	32.6	38.8	45.4	47.5	28.4	36.3
	upper quartile	58.3	62.4	42.7	62.4	58.3	55.6	37.4	55.5

* *Note*: The 2004 Report contains 2003 and 2002 statistics.

Table 6.4
Sub-sample – Summary of key statistics – PAR table

Summary of key statistics (per available room – per annum)		Sub-sample		ADR < 70		70 < ADR < 140		ADR > 140	
		2003 €	2002 €	2003 €	2002 €	2003 €	2002 €	2003 €	2002 €
Total REVPAR	lower quartile	22 911	22 492	17 633	14 392	24 762	21 561	47 195	47 296
	median	28 857	25 714	20 637	15 378	27 088	22 972	81 087	70 414
	upper quartile	97 109	106 779	22 911	22 595	32 699	25 714	97 109	106 779
Total payroll	lower quartile	5 820	5 475	5 522	3 554	2 932	6 106	14 042	7 682
	median	9 558	9 047	6 641	4 672	6 143	7 595	21 861	17 821
	upper quartile	39 455	38 119	9 745	9 897	10 706	9 981	39 455	38 119
Total departmental operating profit	lower quartile	9 551	10 965	9 092	9 316	9 551	10 900	25 469	26 048
	median	18 697	16 340	9 205	9 371	13 556	13 711	41 747	41 279
	upper quartile	60 070	73 319	10 444	10 965	19 383	16 340	60 070	73 319
Total undistributed expenses	lower quartile	3 271	3 100	2 602	2 153	3 271	2 243	13 185	9 862
	median	6 284	4 575	2 957	3 298	4 540	2 508	19 879	11 506
	upper quartile	34 533	34 777	6 284	5 420	7 564	3 350	34 533	34 777
Gross operating profit (GOPPAR)	lower quartile	6 247	8 363	5 204	5 754	6 146	9 019	12 284	17 641
	median	9 077	12 511	6 247	5 963	8 127	11 468	21 163	27 823
	upper quartile	30 319	51 590	6 734	8 363	15 425	12 990	30 319	51 590

Table 6.5
Sub-sample – Summary of key statistics – POR table

Summary of key statistics (per occupied room – daily)		Sub-sample		ADR < 70		70 < ADR < 140		ADR > 140	
		2003 €	2002 €	2003 €	2002 €	2003 €	2002 €	2003 €	2002 €
Average daily rate	lower quartile	74.73	75.70	51.72	61.06	76.75	76.08	204.17	192.98
	median	84.60	85.64	60.50	68.07	80.73	78.70	289.66	259.20
	upper quartile	324.87	350.07	68.24	69.37	128.12	86.64	324.87	350.07
Total payroll	lower quartile	25.42	23.57	20.68	17.03	18.49	32.19	62.96	32.82
	median	38.57	43.11	25.42	20.43	35.06	39.09	94.16	70.83
	upper quartile	157.26	155.09	38.57	43.11	53.23	61.77	157.26	155.09
Total departmental operating profit	lower quartile	47.49	50.83	33.84	44.13	54.87	46.32	114.19	99.84
	median	78.27	92.88	34.37	47.76	57.85	56.71	166.40	167.02
	upper quartile	254.01	302.36	41.33	52.43	106.72	93.26	254.01	302.36
Total undistributed expenses	lower quartile	18.33	13.00	9.65	10.03	18.33	9.20	59.12	41.43
	median	24.87	21.36	10.70	14.42	18.67	9.86	82.04	47.40
	upper quartile	146.03	143.42	24.87	23.61	37.61	19.12	146.03	143.42
Gross operating profit (GOPPOR)	lower quartile	25.78	40.97	19.54	25.12	34.69	38.93	55.08	69.39
	median	46.63	54.05	22.61	26.08	46.63	47.51	84.35	109.98
	upper quartile	130.58	203.97	25.78	46.79	88.04	74.14	130.58	203.97

Table 6.6
Sub-sample – Rooms department statistics – PER table

Rooms department (percentage of revenue)		Sub-sample		ADR < 70		70 < ADR < 140		ADR > 140	
		2003 (%)	2002 (%)	2003 (%)	2002 (%)	2003 (%)	2002 (%)	2003 (%)	2002 (%)
Revenue (% of total revenue)	lower quartile	74.8	77.9	75.9	74.8	59.9	62.3	61.1	84.1
	median	81.1	82.1	76.6	80.4	70.7	70.9	85.5	91.0
	upper quartile	97.8	98.9	81.1	92.5	97.0	82.1	97.8	98.9
Payroll (% of rooms revenue)	lower quartile	11.7	10.4	23.7	17.0	10.6	23.2	11.7	9.1
	median	19.8	17.8	29.9	17.8	19.8	28.8	16.1	11.9
	upper quartile	35.7	40.7	35.7	29.4	24.9	40.7	26.8	25.7
Other expenses (% of rooms revenue)	lower quartile	6.0	2.6	12.0	5.7	2.7	2.0	7.1	5.6
	median	10.8	10.1	15.2	10.1	6.0	9.4	10.8	8.4
	upper quartile	22.9	17.3	21.8	12.2	22.9	17.3	13.3	13.2
Total expenses (% of rooms revenue)	lower quartile	26.1	23.5	35.7	25.0	25.1	26.7	26.9	24.0
	median	33.9	29.5	45.2	27.9	29.2	37.5	33.9	27.4
	upper quartile	57.5	56.9	57.5	41.7	47.5	56.9	40.1	38.9
Departmental profit (% of rooms revenue)	lower quartile	59.9	61.1	48.7	65.2	64.4	52.2	64.8	69.2
	median	66.1	70.5	54.8	72.1	70.8	62.5	66.1	72.6
	upper quartile	85.9	87.6	73.9	78.0	83.1	83.5	85.9	87.6

Table 6.7
Sub-sample – Food and beverage department statistics – PER table

Food and beverage (percentage of revenue)		Sub-sample		ADR < 70		70 < ADR < 140		ADR > 140	
		2003 (%)	2002 (%)	2003 (%)	2002 (%)	2003 (%)	2002 (%)	2003 (%)	2002 (%)
Food and beverage revenue (% of total revenue)	lower quartile	3.8	7.3	20.2	13.3	3.8	3.8	61.1	0.1
	median	18.7	16.9	21.7	19.2	27.0	28.9	13.4	7.6
	upper quartile	47.8	40.0	23.4	28.4	47.8	40.0	24.6	21.8
Food revenue (% of F + B revenue)	lower quartile	78.8	83.2	96.0	92.5	80.8	78.2	75.2	81.8
	median	89.1	91.5	100.0	98.8	86.0	89.6	76.4	85.3
	upper quartile	100.0	100.0	100.0	100.0	98.0	100.0	100.0	100.0
Beverage revenue (% of F + B revenue)	lower quartile	3.5	1.7	2.0	0.6	10.9	10.4	17.7	11.0
	median	13.9	14.2	4.0	1.2	13.9	17.5	24.8	18.2
	upper quartile	100.0	100.0	7.9	13.8	35.0	34.7	100.0	100.0
Food cost of sales (% of Food revenue)	lower quartile	25.8	22.0	32.4	32.3	24.0	22.5	17.0	12.3
	median	33.9	30.1	35.4	43.4	29.2	30.1	33.9	24.5
	upper quartile	91.2	91.5	37.7	91.5	91.2	39.4	35.4	32.5
Beverage cost of sales (% of Beverage revenue)	lower quartile	15.3	16.8	N/A	N/A	37.8	40.0	7.6	8.4
	median	30.6	33.6	N/A	N/A	37.8	40.0	15.3	16.8
	upper quartile	37.8	40.0	N/A	N/A	37.8	40.0	30.6	33.6
F + B Payroll (% of F + B revenue)	lower quartile	33.3	33.0	34.7	43.6	38.0	23.5	46.4	40.4
	median	47.1	48.0	47.1	46.6	45.4	41.0	68.5	64.1
	upper quartile	105.6	76.1	47.3	48.0	98.7	61.2	105.6	76.1
Other F + B expenses (% of F + B revenue)	lower quartile	0.0	0.0	0.0	0.0	0.2	0.0	0.0	0.0
	median	0.3	0.0	0.0	0.0	3.9	0.2	4.5	4.0
	upper quartile	23.1	15.8	7.6	10.1	23.1	15.8	19.3	15.2
Total F + B expenses (% of F + B revenue)	lower quartile	34.8	33.2	34.8	43.6	43.6	23.8	53.1	46.4
	median	54.7	56.6	47.3	46.6	60.7	41.2	82.6	68.1
	upper quartile	105.6	91.3	54.7	58.1	98.7	77.0	105.6	91.3
F + B Departmental profit (% of F + B revenues)	lower quartile	-15.4	-9.1	15.4	-10.5	-16.9	24.8	-35.5	-16.2
	median	15.0	12.9	15.9	10.0	16.4	39.0	-15.4	-0.4
	upper quartile	100.0	100.0	45.0	20.5	45.5	53.0	100.0	100.0

Table 6.8
Sub-sample – Rooms department statistics – PAR table

Rooms department (per available room per annum)		Sub-sample		ADR < 70		70 < ADR < 140		ADR > 140	
		2003 €	2002 €	2003 €	2002 €	2003 €	2002 €	2003 €	2002 €
Revenue	lower quartile	15 805	15 179	13 836	12 378	14 821	14 357	45 317	46 626
	median	17 510	19 262	15 805	12 398	16 237	16 410	68 011	62 415
	upper quartile	76 828	84 887	17 243	15 627	31 727	19 262	76 828	84 887
Payroll	lower quartile	2 616	2 607	3 615	2 101	2 000	4 022	8 996	5 217
	median	5 163	4 838	5 163	2 201	2 616	5 063	10 975	9 608
	upper quartile	15 490	15 363	5 641	4 598	4 356	5 313	15 490	15 363
Other expenses	lower quartile	1 861	1 588	1 831	709	400	1 165	3 196	2 269
	median	2 629	1 965	2 629	1 252	1 883	1 929	5 560	4 626
	upper quartile	9 169	9 194	3 446	1 913	3 710	3 338	9 169	9 194
Total expenses	lower quartile	6 238	5 313	5 446	3 090	2 535	4 612	15 941	11 502
	median	9 087	8 627	7 792	3 453	6 238	6 040	16 768	16 383
	upper quartile	24 659	24 557	9 087	6 511	9 250	8 627	24 659	24 557
Departmental profit	lower quartile	8 765	9 671	7 742	9 011	8 531	9 257	29 376	29 474
	median	12 314	12 671	8 765	9 117	11 271	11 481	48 013	45 314
	upper quartile	65 971	74 400	9 451	9 671	22 477	12 671	65 971	74 400

Table 6.9
Sub-sample – Food and Beverage department statistics – PAR table

Food and beverage (per available room per annum)		Sub-sample		ADR < 70		70 < ADR < 140		ADR > 140	
		2003 €	2002 €	2003 €	2002 €	2003 €	2002 €	2003 €	2002 €
Food and beverage revenue	lower quartile	3 605	3 460	3 605	1 970	5 123	4 557	8 968	10 369
	median	6 696	6 412	4 478	2 955	8 333	5 816	11 974	14 232
	upper quartile	23 890	23 234	5 371	6 412	13 786	10 286	23 890	23 234
Food revenue	lower quartile	4 435	4 065	3 427	1 964	4 421	4 525	10 574	13 225
	median	7 175	5 598	4 123	2 955	7 175	5 213	12 075	14 728
	upper quartile	17 671	18 166	5 371	5 525	8 964	6 714	17 671	18 166
Beverage revenue	lower quartile	331	231	355	231	702	666	1 528	1 140
	median	1 159	1 046	355	449	1 159	1 206	2 799	2 015
	upper quartile	6 219	5 068	355	887	4 821	3 571	6 219	5 068
Food cost of sales	lower quartile	1 368	1 197	1 246	1 029	1 275	1 429	4 662	3 290
	median	2 109	2 173	1 462	1 168	2 109	1 704	6 247	4 669
	upper quartile	9 228	10 028	1 580	1 284	3 036	2 643	9 228	10 028
Beverage cost of sales	lower quartile	492	370	N/A	206	237	508	1 589	598
	median	1 236	1 013	N/A	206	410	815	2 177	1 615
	upper quartile	6 163	5 764	N/A	206	1 821	1 429	6 163	5 764
F + B Payroll	lower quartile	1 601	1 684	1 146	888	2 055	2 132	10 046	9 178
	median	2 789	2 884	1 292	1 376	2 789	2 648	12 749	10 965
	upper quartile	17 938	17 674	2 529	3 078	4 637	4 209	17 938	17 674
Other F + B expenses	lower quartile	226	917	408	N/A	43	43	4 616	3 539
	median	408	1 791	408	N/A	43	43	4 616	3 539
	upper quartile	4 616	3 539	408	N/A	43	43	4 616	3 539
Total F + B expenses	lower quartile	1 631	1 694	1 146	888	2 088	2 164	10 580	9 729
	median	3 202	3 208	1 292	1 376	3 058	2 670	12 749	10 965
	upper quartile	22 554	21 213	2 937	3 726	6 940	5 294	22 554	21 213
F + B Departmental profit	lower quartile	-3 543	-2 001	631	-5	-357	1 469	-6 837	-5 157
	median	258	266	853	296	675	2 084	-6 814	-2 926
	upper quartile	6 279	3 564	2 017	1 312	6 279	3 564	258	1 768

Information Management

Managers who understand their business are more likely to be effective decision-makers. On this premise, information is addressed in this part of the book as a meaningful and valuable enabler of managers' decision-making. Introduced by an innovative approach to cost and revenue analysis that provides managers with a business insight for decision-making in the hotel industry, in chapter 7, a number of themes related to information management are subsequently addressed. First, techniques for cross-border reporting aiming at performance evaluation are presented and explained with examples in chapter 8. Secondly, the use of accounting information for cost allocation is presented in chapter 9, and a related critical review of the state of art of cost allocation techniques and cutting-edge applied research is presented in chapter 10. Thirdly, the use of accounting information is related to room pricing theories and practices in chapter 11, and to restaurant management in chapter 12. Then, the use of accounting information for supporting the increasing awareness of environmental and broader social responsibility in the international hotel industry is addressed in chapter 13. This part of the book closes with some reflections, in chapter 14, on the future of the figure of the hotel financial managers, the human assets who are responsible for producing financial information relevant for the decision-makers in a new and varied international arena.

11 Room rate pricing: a resource-advantage perspective

12 The relevance of restaurant accounting systems

13 Accounting for the environment: reflecting environmental information in accounting systems

14 Hotel unit financial management: does it have a future?

The profit planning framework: applying marginal accounting techniques to hospitality services

Peter Harris

Introduction

This chapter presents an approach to increase the effectiveness of managerial decision-making in order to enhance operational profitability in hospitality organizations. In particular, the purpose is to present the development and application of what can be termed a 'profit planning framework' of management accounting techniques which provide the basis for more informed routine planning and control decisions at the hospitality property level. The accounting techniques used to underpin the framework are evaluated in relation to their application in the decision-making process. However, for management accounting information to be perceived to add value to management decision-making it is essential that the information is related to the particular kind of product or business. Therefore, before engaging in the accounting techniques, it is important to reflect on the hospitality product as, from a management perspective, to 'understand the product' is to 'understand the accounting information', but if managers are not able to see the relevance of financial information, or relate to financial information in operational terms, the perception of its value is diminished.

Hospitality services

Key activities and products found in the hospitality industry relate to the provision of rooms, food and beverages. Although hotels, for instance, essentially represent a service industry product, closer examination reveals that in the provision of rooms, food and beverage services as a total integrated product a hotel encapsulates three significantly different kinds of industrial activity within a single arena (property), depicted in Figure 7.1.

For example, the provision of rooms constitutes a near 'pure service' product containing a high degree of service element similar to air travel or car rental. The provision of beverages also constitutes a service product but, in addition, incorporates a significant 'retail' function comprising the merchandising and stock management similar to that found in stores and supermarkets. The provision of food similarly constitutes a service industry product but, in addition to stock management, also comprises a 'production' function involving the purchase and conversion of raw materials into finished products, i.e. dishes and meals for distribution and service to guests. Although on a smaller scale, this activity has similarities with car manufacture and domestic appliance production. Thus, although from a consumer standpoint a hotel should represent a 'total seamless product', the distinct nature and underlying diversity of activities involved

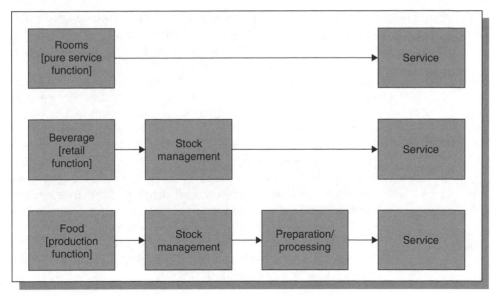

Figure 7.1
The hotel product: dimensions.

in product provision present a major challenge for operational management.

The diversity of activities dictates that, while the consumer perspective of a hotel product is gained from the receipt of a 'service', the actual rooms, food and beverage services – which are provided and consumed at the point of sale – are produced in-house by the range of production and service activities referred to earlier. By their nature these discrete industrial activities comprise different cost structures, which in turn reflect differing business orientations (discussed later). For instance, in general, room service provision contains a high fixed cost structure emanating mainly from the capital nature of the property infrastructure, with limited variable operating costs associated with the service provision.

Hotel accounting systems

Many hospitality organizations operate an accounting system based upon the *Uniform System of Accounts for the Lodging Industry* (1996), the industry standard used by most international hotel chains (Graham, 1995). Detailed budgets are submitted to the divisional or corporate office for approval and continually revised by unit management on a rolling basis during the budget period. Actual results are subsequently compared against budget in order to monitor operating performance. However, a number of limitations are apparent with this approach, due primarily to the fact that the budgets produced normally only classify costs into direct costs, i.e. by operating department and indirect costs, i.e. overhead – by service department groups. Due to the 'static' nature of the budgets produced (using direct and indirect costs), it is not easy to modify the initial budget estimates and, for example, assess the probable impact of alternative scenarios on profit levels, such as sales volume shortfalls or sales exceeding budget – an important implication for planning considerations. Also, managers are not able adequately to assess operating efficiency of hotel properties in terms of actual revenue, cost and profit performance against budgeted standards – an important implication for control decisions. Furthermore, it is difficult to determine a clear indication of the cost structure of particular property operations and brands in order to gain an insight into what Kotas (1973) identified as the 'business orientation' of an undertaking.

Development of the profit planning framework

Reviewing the upward reporting and control emphasis of the Uniform System and the importance of profit generation at the hotel property, it becomes apparent that there is a gap in the provision of accounting information for routine planning and business decisions. In view of the need to provide more relevant financial information for decision-making a 'profit planning framework' presented in Figure 7.2 was developed, based upon now well documented generic and applied marginal accounting techniques (see Eyster, 1974; Greenberg, 1986; Harris and Hazzard, 1992; Wijeyesinghe, 1993; Schmidgall, 1995; Harris, 1999; Kotas, 1999), but which are under-utilized in the practical decision-making situation in the hotel industry (Harris, 1999). The application of these techniques, with their emphasis on cost behaviour, facilitates a more informed understanding of the financial dimensions of the business and the implications of operational profit planning, control and improvement decisions taken by hotel property management teams; the kinds of decisions include negotiating new business, market share analysis, annual budget preparation and monitoring of interim results, sales volume and business mix decisions, pricing policies, *ad hoc* competitive price bids and cost management.

The purpose of the framework, the essence of which indicates the techniques that flow from the understanding of cost behaviour, is to provide a theoretical underpinning for decision-making activities – as Horngren (1977:777) pointed out: 'A knowledge of how costs behave under a variety of influences is essential to

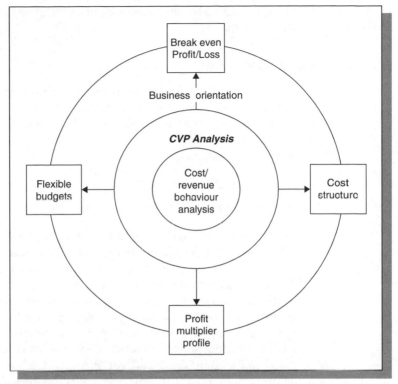

Figure 7.2
Profit planning framework (understanding the hotel business financial dimension).

intelligent predictions, decision making, and performance evaluation.' Once cost (and revenue) behaviour patterns are established it becomes possible to develop flexible budgets and apply a range of cost-volume-profit (CVP) techniques to determine cost structures, break even thresholds, profit and loss scenarios and profit multiplier profiles, all of which have a significant role to play in the decision-making process. Furthermore, as a result of applying a combination of these techniques, managers are able to gain a valuable insight into the financial and operating imperatives present in particular properties.

Applying profit planning techniques

Central to the implementation of the profit planning framework at the hotel property level is the understanding and application of marginal accounting techniques in terms of theoretical assumptions and limitations of marginal analysis, economic viability (cost/benefit) and data access from existing accounting information systems.

Method of cost behaviour analysis

The ability to analyse cost behaviour at the property level is fundamental to understanding the financial consequences of routine operating decisions. The three main methods available are as follows:

- technical estimate
- scattergraph
- statistical cost analysis.

The 'technical estimate' method is carried out in two stages using a historic or (preferably) budgeted profit and loss statement. First, by drawing upon knowledge of the operating conditions of the particular property, costs are classified into fixed, variable and semi-variable groups – in relation to sales volume – on a line-by-line basis (Harris, 1992). Secondly, each cost item in the semi-variable group is further analysed by estimating the fixed and variable proportions – again related to sales volume – and allocated to the main fixed and variable groups. For example, a key semi-variable cost in many hospitality businesses is payroll. In order to estimate the fixed element of restaurant payroll, determine the cost of the minimum number of staff required to 'open for business'. If this is compared with the current restaurant budget, the difference between the estimated fixed payroll and the estimated total payroll for the period will represent the variable payroll element. The analysis of revenues is similar in principle with the exception of items such as shop rents and display case rentals. Revenue is normally variable in that it varies with the volume of business. An example of semi-variable revenue is where, for instance, a hotel has an arrangement to charge an in-house shop a fixed annual rental, plus an agreed percentage of revenue.

While a major criticism levelled against the technical estimate method is the subjective nature of the analysis, it has the advantage of drawing upon the intimate operating knowledge and experience of property management teams and is straightforward to operate. As Eyster (1974:5) advised … 'keep in mind that we want to make our analysis as accurate as possible, but relatively simple to use'. Furthermore, since a relatively large number of significant hospitality operating and occupation costs can, for practical purposes, be judged to be wholly fixed or variable in nature, it is essentially the key remaining semi-variable costs, such as department payroll, department expenses and energy and utilities which normally require detailed analysis.

The 'scattergraph' method requires the cost data to be plotted against selected activity variables, e.g. monthly energy costs against number of room lets or occupancy. A trend line is fitted by judgement and the fixed and variable cost elements are determined from the total cost line. This method is less subjective than the technical estimate.

The 'statistical cost analysis' method is based upon linear regression and correlation techniques. A regression line is fitted to monthly data using 'method of least squares' in order to determine fixed and variable cost components ($y = a + bx$). The difference between the statistical analysis and the scattergraph method is that with the statistical analysis, the trend line (cost function) is calculated rather than judged and the method provides an objective fit to the data. The 'correlation coefficient' (r) and 'coefficient of determination' (r-squared) is used to measure the degree of association between variables (see Harris, 1995).

All the above methods have benefits and limitations, though with varying degrees of accuracy and objectivity. When introduced into the practical situation it may be prudent to introduce a simpler (more subjective) method and build up to the more sophisticated methods later; all methods are available with today's technology, e.g. statistical packages with spreadsheets. Once the practice of cost behaviour analysis is established, computer-aided graphical and statistical methods can be introduced to support the process and provide a 'second opinion' as to the degree of cost variability. However, such methods do not in themselves guarantee greater accuracy, but simply allow a more objective reading of cost-volume data available.

Flexible budgets

The analysis of cost behaviour from a profit and loss statement provides the basis on which to develop flexible (adjustable) budgets, a potentially powerful tool for both planning and control activities (Schmidgall, 1995; DeFranco, 1997; Harris, 1999). In planning terms, this allows the opportunity for initial budget projections to be revisited in order to assess the impact on profit of alternative scenarios, such as changes in prices and costs, sales volume and business mix, what Lee and Powell (1972) refer to as 'action' rather than 'reaction'. They suggest that reviewing the alternatives in advance should be an aid to maximizing potential profits as situations change. This is reinforced by Rust and Lefever (1988:73) who point out, 'As objectives change, the structure and level of costs will also change. A budget that includes fixed and variable components can be readily adjusted to accommodate changes in objectives'.

Thus, with the added assistance of computer spreadsheets flexible budgets facilitate financial responses to key 'what if' questions. For instance, 'what is the likely affect on profit of a 3 per cent shortfall in rooms revenue?' or 'how will profit change if a 5 per cent growth in total sales volume occurs?' This alerts managers to the critical areas of profitability and indicates which revenue and cost areas require greater attention for a given decision. It also enables management to gain an overall indication of 'profit stability' or 'profit instability' in relation to changes in revenue and cost items in particular properties, giving rise to a feeling of 'being more in control' when making decisions.

In terms of control, flexible budgets provide a useful basis on which to measure and evaluate operating efficiency. This is effected by flexing (adjusting) the original or revised budget to the actual level of activity achieved in a period (using budgeted standards for prices and costs) and by comparing actual revenue and cost results against the flexible budget revenues and costs (that should have been incurred) at the achieved level of activity. The calculation of flexible budget variances can provide useful indicators for management action. However, application of variance analysis is a subtle and complex area (Bastable and Bao, 1988; Ekas, 1996) and more research and development are required before the full benefits of analysis can be realized. Thus, in the initial implementation stage, property management teams were encouraged to attempt only a 'second level' of variance analysis (Horngren et al., 1994) in order to determine total sales volume and price variances and cost variances.

Applying cost-volume-profit techniques

Once managers engage in the understanding of cost-volume-profit relationships, a range of techniques are available to assist in the decision-making process.

Cost structure and business orientation

The classification of costs into their behavioural categories of fixed and variable provide the management teams with the basis to determine cost structure and gain an awareness of the 'business orientation' of their particular property – the cost structure of an undertaking refers to the distribution of fixed and variable costs to total cost. Kotas (1973) suggests that businesses with a high proportion of fixed costs to total cost are 'market/revenue oriented', whereas businesses with low proportions of fixed costs (or high proportions of variable costs) are 'product/cost oriented', depicted in Figure 7.3. The key point here is that market oriented businesses, such as hotels, are relatively revenue dependent in that they are normally required to maintain high revenue levels to break even (survive) and generate adequate profit returns. Added to this, they frequently experience profit instability (disproportionate profit variations) during periods of fluctuating demand.

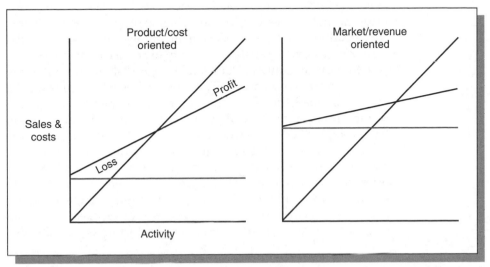

Figure 7.3
Hotel product: cost structure.

Thus, the presence of high fixed costs and the reliance on consumer demand normally make it essential for the management in these situations to be revenue driven – focusing on customer needs, competitor analysis and product differentiation. However, although the concept of market orientation focuses on revenue generation this does not imply that costs should be ignored – all costs are required to be controlled – but that the emphasis of managerial planning, decision-making and control should reflect the financial imperatives associated with the orientation of the particular business.

In the wider context of the hotel industry, the dimensions of business orientation tend to vary according to the kind of product, exemplified by the fact that the more up-market the hotel the higher the fixed cost structure tends to be. For example, comparison between budget and deluxe hotels normally indicates relatively 'low' and 'high' fixed cost structures respectively, reflecting the cost oriented nature of the former and market oriented character of the latter.

In effect, a transformation takes place in the cost structure of the hotels in that the more up-market the product (reflected in the rising average room rate) the greater the predominance of fixed costs and, therefore, the greater the degree of market orientation, whereas the further down-market the product the more the variable costs tend to dominate resulting in a greater degree of cost orientation. Ultimately, at the top end of the market – represented by five star and 'trophy' hotels – the predominance of fixed costs causes variable costs to pale into insignificance. This 'metamorphosis' in the cost structure is due to increasingly higher-cost locations, higher property and furnishing specifications, and more permanent highly-paid highly skilled labour necessary to satisfy the quality of service demanded.

Although generally, as depicted in Figure 7.4, budget hotels are determined to be cost oriented and deluxe hotels are deemed to be market oriented, the reverse can be the case. For example, limited-service budget hotels with restricted restaurant facilities will have a high fixed cost structure – due to the dominance of the rooms' activity – and a subsequent lack of variable costs associated with the food and beverage services, resulting in a market oriented business. Conversely, up-market hotels with a relatively small number of rooms offering extensive restaurant, banqueting and room service facilities may display a lower fixed cost structure and, therefore, tend to be more cost oriented. Again, this

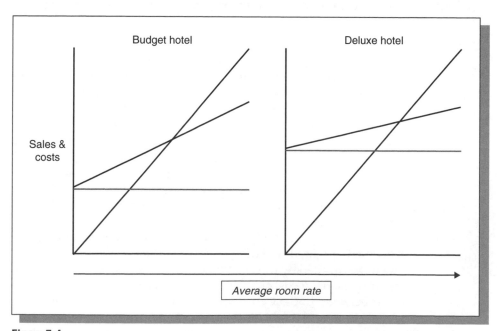

Figure 7.4
Hotel product: cost structure.

serves to reinforce the need for performance measurement to reflect business orientation in the context of the hotel product.

Break even, profits and losses

Knowledge of break even levels and profit and loss implications of different business scenarios are relevant if managers are to make informed decisions that ensure survival, optimize profit returns and limit risk.

After preparation of the annual flexible budget it is not only important to appreciate the impact on profit of possible sales and business mix changes, referred to earlier, but also to be aware of break even thresholds. However, some practitioners display a cynical disregard of the break even concept (Harris, 1999). They consider break even as an irrelevance and contend that a business exists to generate profits, not to recover costs. At first sight this argument is appealing, but on closer examination can be seen to be flawed, as until a business passes through the break even threshold profits will not be forthcoming. Hence, although break even is not an end objective in itself, it represents a critical intermediate point that must be reached before profits are realized.

The complexity of hotel operations in terms of the variety of products and services available is a challenge to the attempts to determine break even levels (referred to later). Nevertheless, the importance of the break even concept has for too long been underrated or ignored. The significance of the knowledge that above a given revenue level the contribution margins generated from additional revenue represents 'pure profit' which drops to the bottom line – gross operating profit (GOP) in the case of the organization's general managers – remains largely unknown, as little or no formal research has been carried out in the area. However, the conceptual context of the break even threshold, with its relevance to survival, suggests that it should not be casually disregarded in the profit planning process as it may prove to be a greater motivational driver of managerial decision-making than has previously been recognized.

There are a number of approaches that can be used to determine hotel break even levels. The method introduced to the property management teams is based on 'break even sales revenue' and 'break even occupancy' (derived from the flexible budget referred to earlier). Total revenue and variable costs are extracted from the flexible budget in order to determine the weighted contribution margin percentage (WCM%). Total fixed costs are then extracted and divided by the WCM% to give the total annual break even sales revenue. To determine break even occupancy, the total hotel contribution margin (CM) is divided by the number of rooms occupied for the period to give the CM per room occupied, and then the total hotel fixed costs are divided by the CM per room occupied and the result expressed as a percentage of rooms available. Hence, with reference to their flexible budgets, managers are able to review break even revenue and occupancies, and profit and loss scenarios as required. With this method the CM per room occupied combines the CM from rooms, food and beverage, and minor operated department sales to give the average total CM attracted by each room occupied.

Wijeyesinghe (1993) offers an alternative more simplified method of determining hotel break even levels. His approach modifies the traditional analysis of cost behaviour by making a global assumption that undistributed operating expenses are fixed costs and direct operated department expenses are variable costs, thus resulting in the gross operating income (GOI) substituting for the traditional contribution margin. This figure is divided by the number of rooms occupied to give, what he terms, the 'income per room let'. Finally, the fixed costs are divided by the income per room let and the result expressed as a percentage of annual room availability to give break even occupancy. Similar in principle to the above break even occupancy method, Wijeyesinghe's term 'income per room let' combines the GOI from room sales with the GOI from minor operated department sales to give the average total GOI generated by each room occupied.

As with most CVP applications, both break even methods contain assumptions and limitations in order to apply them in the practical situation. For instance, they assume cost (and revenue) linearity and, as Matz and Usry (1980:519) point out, … 'In most analyses, a straight line is adequate, because it is a reasonable approximation of cost behaviour within the relevant range'. However, the major difference between the two approaches considered here is that the method recommended for the company's properties attempts to analyse the fixed and variable components of both direct and indirect semi-variable costs where variation is perceived to be 'material', whereas the method advocated by Wijeyesinghe (1993) assumes all direct operating expenses are variable costs and all undistributed operating expenses (overhead) are fixed costs. Clearly, while both approaches offer valuable insights into the cost-volume-profit relationships of the properties, the choice of method will depend upon the operating characteristics and conditions of the particular situation, the decision under consideration and the degree of accuracy required.

Profit multiplier profile

The analysis of cost behaviour facilitates the use of another CVP technique to improve the decision-making activities, known as 'profit sensitivity analysis' (Kotas, 1978). By determining the profit multiplier profile of a business it becomes possible to measure the extent of the impact (sensitivity) of changes in key factors (such as price, room occupancy, restaurant covers, and fixed and variable costs associated with cost of sales, labour and overheads) on profit. With this technique the management teams are not only able to obtain a numerical expression of their property's business orientation (compared to the graphic approach referred to earlier under Cost structure implications) but, in addition, are able to assess a range of issues relating to product and service profitability, profit improvement and the effectiveness of alternative accounting procedures, control strategies and budget preparation methods (Harris, 1999; Kotas, 1999).

Conclusion

As indicated at the outset, the establishment of a profit planning framework is aimed at raising managers' awareness of the financial implications inherent in recurring planning and control decisions. Thus, with the selective use of marginal accounting techniques proposed in the profit planning framework, managers and financial controllers have the tools with which to gain greater insights into the orientation of their properties and to make more informed decisions in relation to routine profit planning, control and improvement activities such as break even thresholds on new business negotiations, make or buy, off-season closing, pricing policies decisions. However, the critical element common to all the component techniques contained in the framework is that of 'cost behaviour analysis'. The ability and preparedness to carry out a pragmatic analysis of operating cost behaviour forms the 'cornerstone' in the application of the techniques.

References

Bastable, C.W. and Bao, D.H. (1988) The fiction of sales-mix and sales quantity variances. *Accounting Horizons*, June, 10–17.

DeFranco, A.L. (1997) The importance and use of financial forecasting and budgeting at the department level in the hotel industry as perceived by hotel financial controllers. *Hospitality Research Journal*, **20** (3), 99–110.

Ekas, P. (1996) *Market Oriented Variance Analysis in Hotels*, Unpublished dissertation, Oxford Brookes University.

Eyster, J.J. (1974) Insuring your profit margins: restaurant cost-volume-profit analysis. *Cornell Hotel and Restaurant Administration Quarterly*, **14** (3), 3–11.

Graham, I.C. (1995) Financial management in an international environment: hotel 2000 NV, A case study. In Harris, P.J. (1995) *Accounting and Finance in the International Hospitality Industry*, pp. 239–260. Butterworth-Heinemann, Oxford.

Greenberg, C. (1986) Analysing restaurant performance: relating cost-volume-profit analysis. *Cornell Hotel and Restaurant Administration Quarterly*, **27** (1), 9–11.

Harris, P.J. (1992) Hospitality profit planning in the practical environment: integrating cost-volume-profit analysis with spreadsheet management. *International Journal of Contemporary Hospitality Management*, **4** (4), 24–32.

Harris, P.J. (1995) *Accounting and Finance for the International Hospitality Industry*. Butterworth-Heinemann, Oxford.

Harris, P.J. (1999) *Profit Planning*, 2nd edn. Butterworth-Heinemann: Oxford.

Harris, P.J. and Hazzard, P.A. (1992) *Managerial Accounting in the Hospitality Industry*, 5th edn. Stanley Thornes, Cheltenham.

Horngren, C.T. (1977) *Cost Accounting: A Managerial Emphasis*, 4th edn. Prentice-Hall International, London.

Horngren, C.T., Foster, G. and Datar, S.M. (1994) *Cost Accounting: A Managerial Emphasis*, 8th edn. Prentice-Hall International, London.

Kotas, R. (1973) Market orientation. *Hotel, Catering and Institutional Management Association Journal*, July, 5–7.

Kotas, R. (1978) The ABC of PSA. *Hotel, Catering and Institutional Management Association Journal*, February, 15–19.

Kotas, R. (1999) *Management Accounting for Hospitality and Tourism*, 3rd edn. Thompson Business Press, London.

Lee, R.W. and Powell, E.W. (1972) Profit planning: the continuing feasibility study. *Cornell Hotel and Restaurant Administration Quarterly*, **13** (3), 79–86.

Matz, A. and Usry, M.F. (1980) *Cost Accounting, Planning and Control*. South West Publishing, Ohio, USA.

Rust, D.B. and Lefever, M.M. (1988) International profit planning. *Cornell Hotel and Restaurant Administration Quarterly*, **29** (3), 68–73.

Schmidgall, R.S. (1995) *Hospitality Industry Managerial Accounting*, 3rd edn. The Educational Institute of the American Hotel and Motel Association, East Lansing, MI.

Uniform System of Accounts for the Lodging Industry, 9th edn. (1996) Educational Institute of the American Hotel and Motel Association, East Lansing, MI.

Wijeysinghe, B. (1993) Breaking even. *Hospitality*, 16–17.

Cross-border reporting for performance evaluation

Ian Graham

Introduction

In this chapter, we explore some of the knowledge management, financial management and control competencies required of an organization operating cross-border hospitality businesses.

Businesses operating in multiple sites differ from single outlet businesses in requiring data acquired at each site to be gathered, summarized and reviewed prior to being transmitted to the regional and corporate headquarters where the individual unit inputs are further summarized and reviewed. In this way the organization learns about its customers and competitors, manages its financial and other risks and organizes the cash required to keep the business alive. Both regional and corporate headquarters in their turn need to be able to organize data into information that is transmitted to the trading units and in some cases other headquarters offices. There may be further needs to accept data from third parties into knowledge, financial or control systems and there may be needs to transmit data to third parties, such as banks and suppliers, and customers. These processes apply to any multi-unit business operating in one single country and demand that a core competency of the organization and its executive team is the design, management and development of the underlying knowledge, finance and control processes and technologies in the context of the people organization.

But a further level of complication arises when such a multi-unit business is operating cross borders. In such a circumstance, the issues of currency, language, legal jurisdiction, tax systems and, to some extent, culture add a requirement for additional scope in the processes and systems deployed.

In the paragraphs that follow, through illustrations of best practice, we show how leading cross-border hotel operating and management businesses are implementing knowledge management, financial management and control processes and how the adoption of leading edge technologies is enabling the businesses to be closer to their customers, closer to the cash and closer to the control weaknesses. Some of the people issues that arise are also explored.

Four enabling technologies

There are four key technology elements that enable executives to assemble a solution that is flexible, yet meets the appropriate needs of their unique customer proposition (see Figure 8.1).

First, the ubiquity of the Internet as a communication channel, both between the hotel itself and all members of the extended enterprise (corporate sales, central reservations, headquarters), as well as between the hotel itself and all of its direct (business and leisure) and indirect (travel agents, tour operators, conference and convention planners, consolidators) customers.

Second, the emergence of open systems (ones that adopt the Open Travel Alliance standards and/or adopt Microsoft standards) allowing hotel companies to bundle the best applications to meet each business's needs rather than acceptance of a pre-bundled series of proprietary applications.

Third, the rise of the networked enterprise. This enables chains of hotels to reach the goal of a single image inventory and allows even the independent unbranded hotel to determine the distribution channels for its room inventory in the future. Seamless GDS distribution through Wizcom and Pegasus is now a utility on offer to all hotel operators. Owners and brand operators can decide to bundle all rooms in a city and/or in a segment and treat them as if

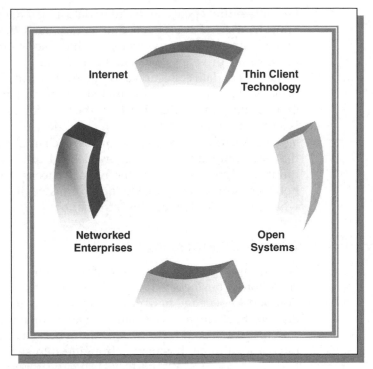

Figure 8.1
The four enabling technologies.

they are one single inventory – or can continue to ask unit management to drive inventory and pricing decisions.

Fourth, the adoption of 'thin client' web browsing technology that allows the application to be held on the organizations intranet server, or to be provided by an application server provider. This means that the business is no longer organized around the technology tools – with the tools becoming the servant rather than the master.

These technologies are increasingly put together to enable cross-border businesses to gather data from hotels around the world and assemble the data in one place – the executive's desktop. Whether you are a marketing executive, a finance executive or a human resource executive, if you have multi-property responsibility you can now turn on and tune into the information that you need – in real-time, with drill down to layers of data that underpin the top summaries, with an ability to communicate back to the trading hotel or the remote sales office – from the comfort of your own office, which of course may be your physical office or your virtual office.

And note the reference to time; technology has destroyed the barriers of time and space. Using the technology tools discussed here it is entirely possible to gather data generated by hotels operating in each of the global time zones, such that the CEO or, indeed, anyone else anywhere, can have access to any relevant data as they drive into work in the morning.

Barriers of data collection and integration, time and space have been destroyed – the international company has come of age. Outside the remit of this chapter is the question as to whether this is a good thing. An example from a sceptical author – some years ago, an executive from a well known French multinational boasted that the company systems allowed head office to learn of the number of lunch covers and the average checks at any one of their hotel restaurants by 3 p.m. He couldn't answer the question about what one would do with this information.

Key performance indicators

So if we now understand a little of the technology that enables a cross-border business to bring data home, convert it into information and knowledge and provide executives at all levels of the organization with access to data relevant to their roles and responsibilities, we need now to understand what data they are that the international hotel business is bringing into such an enterprise-wide database. The key performance indicators (KPIs) of success for a hotel or hotel company are, of course, likely to be no different whether the business is conducted in one location, in one domestic economy or around the world. The KPIs will be determined by the Board or chief operating officer and are likely to include data on customer satisfaction, competitive strength, employee satisfaction, product and service quality, profitability and cash flow. The headline statistics are usually assembled into a 'balanced scorecard' that allows a reader to gain a view of how the organization is performing across the whole range of key processes.

Role of functional currency

What though makes international operations unique? There are several factors and understanding currency is at the heart of understanding the implications. Some international hotel companies are headquartered in the USA, others in France and the UK, others in Hong Kong. The hotels that they operate, whether directly through management or indirectly through franchise agreements, are typically in many other countries. Let's use as an example a fictitious USA company with non-domestic operations in the UK, China, Australia and France. Its operations are conducted in at least four currencies – the US dollar, the pound sterling, the Chinese rimimbi, the Australian dollar and the euro. The company faces

Table 8.1
Currency movements

	Currency units per $		
	January 2005	January 2004	% Change
Australia	1.31	1.29	−1.6
China	8.28	8.28	0
France	0.77	0.79	+2.6
UK	0.53	0.55	+3.8

two challenges – the first to enable readers to compare and contrast and aggregate performance in five areas of the world and, secondly, to enable such comparisons over time and thus recognizing that currencies move against each other, all of the time. Table 8.1 illustrates the problem that needs to be solved.

We can see that the Australian dollar has devalued against the US dollar; the Chinese currency has remained pegged to the US dollar, while both the euro and sterling have appreciated against the dollar. Now let's imagine that our company's hotels have recorded the results shown in Table 8.2.

This is really difficult to interpret and react to. Some important things do stand out – the Australian hotel's RevPAR has fallen back in the year, while in the UK and China the business has grown well. But we cannot determine how well the overall business has done, and we cannot determine whether the Chinese performance is better than the UK performance; nor can we decide if the flat results in France are a matter of concern. Where should we be putting resources to leverage strengths and address weaknesses?

Table 8.2
Trading in local currency

	No. of rooms	RevPAR	
		Jan-04	Jan-05
US Hotel	250	US$105	US$105
Australian Hotel	200	AUS$100	AUS$90
Chinese Hotel	400	R800	R900
UK Hotel	300	£75	£85
French Hotel	350	€50	€50
Group Total	1500		

The first learning therefore is that we need to simplify the picture by using only one currency. The currency we use is called *the functional currency* and usually is the currency in use in the country of the parent company. So in our case, the functional currency would usually be the US dollar and that is what we will use as we continue this example. But if the currency of the country of the parent company had limited size as an international currency, then the functional currency might well be the currency used by most of the hotels.

So, if the US dollar is to be our functional currency, we need to convert all the results to this. And this gives rise to the next challenge – should we use the exchange rate applying in 2004 to convert the 2004 results or should we use the latest exchange rates, which are the 2005 rates. In Table 8.3 we use both exchange rates to illustrate the point in respect of the Australian hotel. In practice almost all companies will use the current exchange rate to convert historic results, as well as budgeted results and forecast results into the functional currency. Why? Well, because the current rate reflects the world as we are currently experiencing it and is, probably, the best guide to the future.

Table 8.3
Australian trading expressed in functional currency

	Exchange rate		No of rooms	RevPAR		RevPAR in functional currency		
						At historic rate	At current rate	At current rate
	Jan-04	Jan-05		Jan-04	Jan-05	Jan-04	Jan-04	Jan-05
Australian Hotel	1.29	1.31	200	A $100	A $90	$77.52	$76.34	$68.70

So if we now apply this approach to the results of all of our hotels (using the US dollar as the functional currency at current exchange rates) we can understand how the business as a whole has performed and how each country has performed. Table 8.4 provides this overview. We can see that the business has grown by 6.2 per cent, driven first of all by the UK and despite a downturn in Australia and flat results in both the USA and France.

By converting data into information using the current approach, we have generated knowledge that is actionable; and this is what business needs whether the decision-maker is in the corporate

Table 8.4
Group trading expressed in functional currency at current exchange rates

	At current rate Jan-04	At current rate Jan-05	Growth (%)
US Hotel	$105.00	$105.00	0.00%
Australian Hotel	$76.34	$68.70	−10.00%
Chinese Hotel	$96.62	$108.70	12.50%
UK Hotel	$141.51	$160.38	13.33%
French Hotel	$64.94	$64.94	0.00%
Group Total	$96.90	$102.87	6.17%

headquarters or in one of the hotels. We can allocate our scarce corporate resources properly.

Complexity

Before going further, it is worth emphasizing that the international hotel industry is, at least at one level, a simple business. All we are trying to do is:

- sell more rooms, and/or

- sell more services to each customer and/or

- make more profit from each service offered.

At a minimum, we need to meet customer expectations and to stay in business for any length of time, we need to anticipate and respond to future challenges.

All too often we make it a complex business. We cannot get our mind around the business model – are we in the real estate business, in the retail business, in the manufacturing business or in the brand business? Too often, executives in this industry are confused by the complexity of the business model and may fail to make the right decision because it is not clear which of these models we are focused on. As if this was not enough, we then compound the complexity by introducing different levels of economic interest – is the decision being made to maximize value to the owner, or to the operator or to the franchiser? In any event, it is unlikely to be shared evenly between all three. And then we compound the complexity yet further by operating internationally.

So the Board of Directors of the international hotel company has to find a way to identify separately the elements of value being created and attribute value to the correct party. In the next paragraphs we address how to simplify this complexity.

Let's consider the Australian hotel of our example international company – it is operated by one of the global operators and bears a name that includes one from their portfolio of brands. Let's further assume that the hotel is managed under a management contract, with the ultimate ownership of the hotel belonging to a Japanese shipping magnate. So we have a business in Australia, owned by Japanese interests, operated by an American company and using a brand owned by an American company.

Simplifying complexity

Earlier we have considered the role of a functional currency in reporting performance; now if we keep our eye on cash then we can report each party's interest correctly as the value is distributed. Figure 8.2 illustrates how value might be added in this hypothetical example.

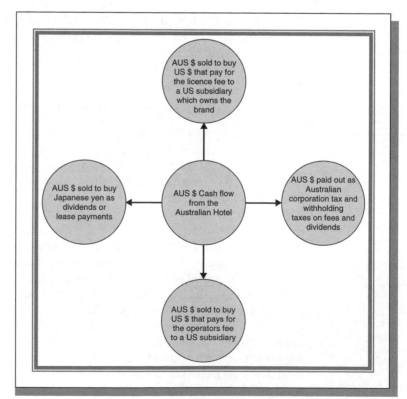

Figure 8.2
Currency cash flows to holders of interests.

The question you will rightly be asking is – so what? If we are concerned to monitor and report against the director of taxes' performance we have the source of the data and the currency of the data for this element of his or her performance. If we are concerned with the performance of the group treasurer, we have the source of the data and the currencies of the data for this element of his or her performance. If we are concerned with the performance of the brand manager we have the source of the data and the currencies of the data for this element of his or her performance. If we are concerned with the performance of the Australian director of operations, we have the source of the data and the currencies of the data for this element of his or her performance. Note that we would adopt the concept of a functional currency if the scope of someone's performance was being incurred in several currencies – but if the Australian director of operations has responsibility for the performance of pan-pacific hotels it may not be appropriate to use the US dollar as the functional currency since his business is not working in a US dollar environment, nor are his customers or suppliers.

Reducing the effective rate of tax

The example provided reflects the reality of the marketplace; cross-border organizations are structured internally in ways that are very different to that which appears at first sight. Usually, the internal organization of a business, the legal entity infrastructure, reflects an attempt to minimize the overall cost of corporation tax to the parent company. The company will be liable to pay corporate taxes, of course, but seeks to minimize the effective rate of tax by sometimes quite complex structuring. Thus we see in the example that the legal title to the brand has been separated to create a separate licence fee cash flow stream; the rights and obligations under the management contracts have been separated into yet another legal entity to which management fees are paid. These are structures within the global hotel operator to minimize tax; a further complication may be that the Japanese owner splits the return from the hotel, first into a lease to a company that owns the asset and secondly, as a dividend to the ultimate shareholder. Such structuring is part and parcel of international operations and can be very effective in driving down the effective rate of tax and therefore driving up the returns to equity holders.

So far we have seen how currency, legal entities and tax structuring impose particular challenges to managing the international hotel business and how these matters need to be taken account of in the design and implementation of reporting systems.

We have seen how such reporting systems can take advantage of 21st century technologies to deliver the right data to the right executive at the right level of detail at the right time and in the right currency; once the finance and information systems are established to accomplish this, the international executive is enabled to make the right decisions in the right context.

Act globally, think locally

But so far, our review has been insular to the business and its operating units as well as its own business partners. Perhaps unfortunately no such vacuum exists, and all businesses need to take account of the external environment if they are to succeed. In the external environment are such things as customers, suppliers and competitors – difficult at the best of times to understand and perhaps doubly so when the view is across borders.

If we return to our example, it is surely necessary to put the Chinese hotel's performance in context of the Chinese economy, of Chinese hotels, of the Chinese leisure industry, if a rounded assessment of its performance is to be made. And so too, but in a different way obviously, account of the performance of the Australian, American, British and French hotels has to reflect the local economic environments in which these hotels trade.

Hoteliers – operating only in a domestic environment or in an international environment – spend much time and energy in the continual drive for RevPAR penetration; building share of the market. Leading hotels contribute data to, and receive data about, competitor sets constructed by firms such as The Daily Bench, STR, Deloitte and MKG. At one level this is effective – the drive to build share of a market is a drive for relative value and is a far more valuable exercise than a simple drive for increasing occupancy, or drive for increasing average rate.

But the international business has also got to be able to judge performance across economies and allocate its scarce resources in those economies with the best long-term prospects and consider withdrawing or reducing its resources dedicated to economies and locations with poorer long-term prospects – consider the facts shown in Table 8.5.

So here we have it, the Chinese hotel with a 12.5% RevPAR growth (see Table 8.4 above) is only really keeping up with the economy, which is growing at 9.1% and there is price inflation of 2.8%; the UK hotel is shown to be clearly outperforming the general economy and may merit further resource such as sales and marketing being allocated to it, while the US, the Australian and the French hotels are all underperforming against their local economy. With a low growth rate and high unemployment, the

Table 8.5
Benchmarking economic performances

As at Jan 2005	GDP growth (%)	Interest rate (%)	Unemployment (%)	Inflation (%)
USA	3.5	2.6	5.4	2.4
Australia	3.0	5.4	5.1	2.3
China	9.1	2.4	N/A	2.8
UK	2.4	4.8	4.7	1.6
France	1.9	2.1	9.9	2.0

Board may think that it is going to be some time before the French hotel can do much better – time to withdraw resources?

A picture tells a thousand words

In our examples so far, we have used tables and charts to illustrate the point being made; this is in fact contrary to best practice, which recognizes that many international senior executives find it easier to absorb information that is presented graphically or in pictures. We have referred earlier to the idea of a dashboard – and within these tools many companies have adopted a traffic light approach to illustrating trends and data (Figure 8.3). Red requires attention, yellow is outside of expectations but not yet at danger levels and green is within expectations.

Figure 8.3
The traffic light.

Furthermore, it is generally better to show data as a trend rather than as an isolated piece of information; imagine if you are presented with Table 8.6.

Table 8.6
Cycles of RevPAR in London and Paris over a 15-year period

	1990	1991	1992	1993	1994	1995	1996
Paris RevPAR	130.4	116.1	111.7	100.8	92.8	89	87.4
London RevPAR	86.3	73.29	69.07	73.87	78.17	89.5	98

	1997	1998	1999	2000	2001	2002	2003
Paris RevPAR	95.7	121.3	124.7	136.8	129.9	125.5	100.2
London RevPAR	102.27	102.97	94.85	95.51	82.13	69.82	67.16

Get it? Now consider the power of the data that is revealed by Figure 8.4 which graphs 12 month RevPAR in both London and Paris against each other.

These thoughts are just as valid in a multi-unit company that is entirely domestic or even in a single unit business. But they are

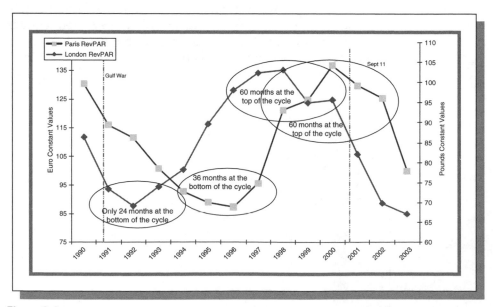

Figure 8.4
Cycles of RevPAR in London and Paris over a 15-year period showing heights and depths of the cycle, shapes of the valleys and troughs and Paris's tendency to follow London. Data from MKG Consulting, tri Hospitality Consulting.

certainly valid in international businesses where it is important to 'keep it simple'.

Cross-border investment appraisal

This prefaces changing the thought process to consider the most intellectually difficult issue. So far in this discussion we have concentrated on understanding how best to consider operating data across borders. As we come to the end of the chapter, let us spend some time considering how the knowledge we have now acquired should be applied to those cross-border investment decisions that face an international hotel company.

Let's assume that our example company has an opportunity to invest in a second hotel in the UK – to take advantage of the apparently good economic conditions. It would be normal for the Board to have determined that the appraisal should be conducted using a discounted cash flow methodology and it is outside the scope of this chapter to review this methodology as such. But it is very relevant to consider how the methodology should be applied.

Our example's parent company is located in an economy that is dollar denominated and has a short-term interest rate of 2.6 per cent; it is considering investing in an economy that is sterling denominated and where short-term interest rates are almost double those in the States at 4.8 per cent. It has almost certainly raised its equity in the USA, yet it would be normal in this case to raise loan finance in the UK (i.e. in sterling) thus enabling legal documentation to be put in place that requires appropriate charges and securities on the asset being bought.

The questions we have to answer are:

- What currency should be the basis of the cash flow analysis?

- What discount factor should be used to calculate the net present value of the proposal?

In this example, we have the choice of using the functional currency, the US dollar, or the local currency, the pound sterling. Adopting the adage think local, best practice will have the cash flows prepared in local currency, in this case pounds sterling. But it will also be important to identify the timing of cash flows to and from the parent company, e.g. dividends or management fees, since it is the timing of cash flows, rather than timing of the recognition of the liability that is important – and timing of cash flows to the US parent will be dependent on local UK legislation and banking practices rather than US corporate policies and procedures or even hotel trading performance.

Turning to the discount factor to use, we need to remember that a discount rate reflects the risk of the project; and in this case there is political and economic risk associated with investment in a foreign country as well as the more normal industry and economic risk of an investment in the hotel sector. This helps us to realize that we should use a discount that is specific to the UK because this will incorporate these risks.

The weighted average cost of capital (WACC), which underlies the discount rate, is composed of the cost of equity and the cost of debt. So in this case, we would determine the risk premium associated with a sterling denominated equity investment in the UK hotel market and the cost of sterling denominated long-term debt with a first charge on a UK asset. The WACC which we would use for the appraisal is thus a local WACC and will be different to the actual WACC of the parent company. It needs to be because the risks are different; and post acquisition the company's risk profile will be different forever.

Reference

Pizam, A. (ed.) (2005) *International Encyclopedia of Hospitality Management*. Elsevier/Butterworth-Heinemann, Oxford.

Cost analysis in the hotel industry: an ABC customer focused approach and the case of joint revenues

Paolo Collini

Profitability analysis and the classical division based approach

It is commonly believed that the development of management accounting in the last part of the 19th century, along with the emergence of large enterprises in industries like textile, railroads and steel (Taylor, 2000), was a consequence of the growing management's need for support of decision-making. The growing complexity of the business due to the enlarging scale of the activities and the consequential search for practical solutions is often seen as the driver of most of management development (Chandler, 1962), whereby the structure of profitability analysis was driven by needs like controlling internal efficiency in large decentralized organizations, and supporting adequate product decisions.

Johnson and Kaplan (1987) claim that management accounting was developed mainly for the manufacturing industry. The authors suggest that consequentially the accounting techniques were meant to focus on efficiency control of manufacturing processes (activities and production phases) and calculating total product costs.

Under these circumstances, it is not surprising that the structure of cost and profit analysis adopted by most firms has been mainly a cost centre based and product focused analysis. Therefore, efficiency (cost per unit of output) and effectiveness of organizational units (in terms of total volume and margin), along with product profitability, were the main areas managers had to monitor for maximizing short- and long-term company profitability.

It can be recognized that the traditional reporting approach (cost centre based product profitability analysis) is suitable for supporting the two main management's tasks: product decision along the product life cycle (pricing, promotion, R&D decision) and internal efficiency (products' unit cost). Products and organizational units (departments) were the most important cost objects for management accounting techniques, because they were the most important management's 'decision objects'.

Most of the development of management accounting in the last part of the 20th century has probably been driven by the growing complexity of management decision-making. Particularly, both the increase of the share of indirect costs in both manufacturing and non-manufacturing activities and the broader scope of management decision-making are some of the most important problems 'modern' management accounting systems had to face in the 1990s (Johnson and Kaplan, 1987).

The introduction of activity-based costing accounting techniques allows broadening of the scope of cost analysis, particularly in non-manufacturing activities. In this chapter some of the so-called 'modern' accounting techniques like activity-based costing will be used for improving the capability of accounting data in supporting management's decision in the hospitality industry. However, the aim of this chapter goes beyond the adoption in the service industry of already well known activity-based accounting techniques. The simple case presented in this chapter is not only the opportunity for seeing how an activity-based approach can change cost allocation in hospitality, but is also a way for proposing a different approach to profitability analysis, getting somehow away from the traditional department based profit analysis.

The classical product profitability reporting implies that managers are capable of taking specific product decisions (pricing, promotion) on individual products without affecting other products. Even though it is widely known that, very often, individual products have some degrees of interdependence, the traditional analysis tends to neglect the effect of decision-making on one product over other products. Only in the extreme case of 'joint production processes', in which all products must be produced together in a fixed proportion, are the interdependencies considered and individual products profit analysis is considered useless for decision-making.

In the hospitality industry, this 'accounting tradition' has led to the design of the *Uniform System of Accounts for the Lodging Industry*, an American based reporting scheme, mainly based on the two dimensions previously recalled: departments and services. In this reporting approach, in order to limit the effects of cost and revenues commonality, services are grouped on the basis of the departments in which they are mostly produced, i.e. rooms, food and beverages. Eventually, with the goal of focusing on management control and responsibility reporting, these two dimensions have led to a reporting structure in which divisions and service groups tend to overlap: departments and services are unified into a single report in which departments' efficiency and services' profitability are analysed.

Under this perspective, direct controllable costs are allocated over department/service groups with the purpose of identifying their contribution to the firm's overall profitability and organizational areas, and services that are not revenue generating are treated as pure overheads. This simple approach, where most costs are directly traceable to departments and very little allocation is required, allows managers to understand how different business areas and different responsibility centres contribute to the overall profitability of the firm.

In this chapter, following a simplified hotel case, different approaches to profitability analysis are presented and explained. Particularly, some peculiar characteristics of the customers' purchasing behaviour in the hospitality industry, i.e. the 'bundle' purchasing decisions, are considered. When bundle purchasing is considered, the interdependence across different services must be taken into account.

The case – introduction

The case presented in this chapter is a simplified example of cost and profit analysis in hotel operations. Most of the emphasis of the proposed analysis is on customers' purchasing behaviour; the case is an example of how some peculiar characteristics of customers' demand in the industry can be taken into account in both cost and profitability analysis.

The hotel is a small family owned hotel by the seaside of North East Italy. It has 40 bedrooms and provides accommodation, meals and beach service.

The accounting system provides the following cost information, which refers to the last financial period:

	Euros
Personnel	262 500
Food and beverage	115 000
Lining (leasing)	6 000
Electricity	24 000
Telephone	12 000
Services	4 500
Rent	75 000
Miscellaneous	10 000
Total	*509 000*

The structure of the management accounting systems identifies the following cost centres on the basis of the internal organizational structure, i.e. cost centres tend to identify with organizational units:

- Room division

- Restaurant

- Bar

- Beach

- Maintenance

- General overheads.

In Table 9.1, the costs directly traceable to the cost centres are presented.

The accounting report is structured around four management profit objects:

- Room division

- Restaurant

- Bar
- Beach.

Accordingly with this structure of the profitability analysis, revenues are accounted as follows:

Rooms	310 000
Restaurant	280 000
Bar	37 000
Beach	25 000

Table 9.1
Costs directly traceable to cost centres

	Room	Restaurant	Bar	Beach	Mainte-nance	Over-heads	Total
Personnel	85 000	75 000	25 000	25 000	2 500	50 000	262 500
Material usage	3 000	100 000	8 000	4 000			115 000
Towels and linen	4 500	1 000		500			6 000
Electricity						24 000	24 000
Various services					4 500		4 500
Telephone	6 000					6 000	12 000
Rent						75 000	75 000
Miscellaneous						10 000	10 000
Total	98 500	176 000	33 000	29 500	7 000	165 000	509 000

As a first step, a pure direct costing report is provided in Table 9.2, where each revenue generating department's direct costs are compared with their respective revenues and all other expenses are treated as general overheads.

Table 9.2
First step of pure direct costing

	Room	Restaurant	Bar	Beach	Total
Revenues	310 000	280 000	37 000	25 000	652 000
Expenses	98 500	176 000	33 000	29 500	337 000
Profit Margin	211 500	104 000	4 000	-4 500	315 000
Profit margin (%)	68.2	37.1	10.8	-18.0	48.3
Overheads					172 000
Net profit					143 000

As a second step, some indirect costs are allocated to profit centres on the basis of some cost drivers. More specifically, the selected drivers are the following:

- Rent expenses: square meters
- Electricity expenses: power of the equipment
- Maintenance expenses: number of hours of maintenance.

Table 9.3
Accounting process of cost allocation

	Room	Restaurant	Bar	Beach	Maintenance	Overheads	Total
Personnel	85 000	75 000	25 000	25 000	2 500	50 000	262 500
Material usage	3 000	100 000	8 000	4 000			115 000
Towels and linen	4 500	1 000		500			6 000
Electricity	16 438	3 288	1 644	0	0	2 630	24 000
Various services					4 500		4 500
Telephone	6 000					6 000	12 000
Rent	45 000	15 000	5 250	0	0	9 750	75 000
Miscellaneous						10 000	10 000
Total	159 938	194 288	39 894	29 500	7 000	78 380	509 000
Output					70		70
Unit cost (U per hour)					100		100
Total maintenance hours	40	15	5	3		7	70
Cost of maintenance	4 000	1 500	500	300		700	7 000
Total	163 938	195 788	40 394	29 800		79 080	509 000

Table 9.4
Final report of cost allocation

	Room	Restaurant	Bar	Beach	Total
Revenues	310 000	280 000	37 000	25 000	652 000
Expenses	163 938	195 788	40 394	29 800	429 919.9
Profit Margin	146 062	84 212	−3 394	−4 800	222 080.1
Profit margin (%)	47.1	30.1	−9.2	−19.2	34.1
Overheads					79 080
Net profit					143 000

The data for the allocation of indirect costs are the following:

Occupied space:

	Rooms	Restaurant	Bar	Beach	Maintenance	Common space	Total
Square meters	600	200	70	0	0	130	1000

Power of equipment:

	Rooms	Restaurant	Bar	Beach	Maintenance	Common space	Total
KW	5	1	0.5	0	0	0.8	7.3

Hours of maintenance:

	Rooms	Restaurant	Bar	Beach	Maintenance	Common space	Total
Hours	40	15	5	3	n/a	7	70

On the basis of this information, some of the costs previously included in 'overheads' are now allocated to profit centres/ departments.

Tables 9.3 and 9.4 show the accounting process and the final report.

The customers' profitability analysis in a case of 'bundling'

The profitability analysis based on a department's contribution to the total profit, shown in Table 9.2, is suitable for the need of supporting the managers' performance evaluation process. Individual department managers are responsible for achieving an adequate level of contribution to the firm's total profit. The actual margin produced by each profit centre (department) is compared with the goal set in the budget and individual performance is appraised accordingly. Therefore, the structure of the profit report is consistent with the structure of the responsibility within the organization and the final report highlights the performance of individual profit centres.

Usually, when tangible products are exchanged in a market, the characteristics of the products, and in particular the ability of decoupling production from consumption, allow consumers to express a specific demand for each single product, even though the consumption process implies a combination of different products at the same time. Customers have the capability of composing the desired bundle of products at a different time and place from the ones in which they buy them. Under this perspective, customers are able to formulate specific independent demand for individual products, evaluating price and values of each product separately.

Under these circumstances, producers can evaluate the profitability of each individual product and production and marketing decisions can be taken independently for each single product.

It is easy to recognize that this approach to profitability analysis does not appear very consistent with the structure of decision-making in the market related decisions for many service industries, and particularly in hospitality, where not only consumption and production cannot be decoupled, as in all services, but the whole value for the customers is produced by a combination of services that must be obtained together, and for which customers are not capable of expressing independent demands. In fact, the immateriality of services implies that the production process and the consumption process take place jointly and therefore, when different services are part of a set of items meant to satisfy a single set of a customer's needs, as it is in hospitality, no separate purchasing decision can be taken by the customers: all services have to be acquired at the same time in the same place and from a single source, i.e. services have a complementary relationship, they are acquired in a bundle.

This introduces the concept of complementarity relationship among different products. Complementarity can take place at the technical level, when products interact with each other physically or at the customers' utility function level, when customers are perceiving a higher level of satisfaction by purchasing together different services than acquiring them individually (Guiltinan, 1987). As a matter of fact, we should recognize that most services provided by hotels have a high degree of complementarity: it is often quite difficult to imagine the different services offered by a hotel (accommodation, restaurant, bar and other amenities) being offered independently from each other. Moreover, it is quite difficult to imagine customers expressing an independent demand for each specific service. The case for a high degree of complementarity is strongly supported by the fact that several services are provided by hotels at no charge, i.e. as part of the whole service, even though they are not unavoidable in a customer's view. The distinction between independent services and services that are part of a whole product is hard to find. However, when specific services are perceived as unavoidable, they can be seen as part of the 'main product' and therefore customers do not express an independent demand for them. In this case, these services are offered as additional attraction factors and they contribute to building the customers' opinion of the other services. These complementary services contribute to justify the price of the main service to which they are linked. These services are seen as part of a complex product and clearly their profitability cannot be evaluated individually. When no independent demand can be expressed by the consumers, customers' perceived value does not reflect into prices and therefore no independent profitability analysis can be carried out. This consideration can be extended to the case of services that are provided at a price, but are perceived by customers as strongly complementary with other services and therefore customers do not assess individually the value of each specific service. The fact that some services are revenue generating, when a high level of complementarity is recognized, makes this service's profitability as difficult to evaluate as the one of services that are free of charge because prices do not represent customers' perceived service value.

Taking a company's perspective, the main consequence of this consumer behaviour lies in the fact that no independent market effort can be taken by the producer: decisions on one service are involving, to some extent, other services included by customers in the same bundle. As a consequence, the profitability analysis of each individual service might not be useful in supporting market related decision-making, because of joint demand that customers express for a bundle of services. In order to comply with this bundle effect of demand, several strategies can be chosen by a company (Bojamic and Calantone, 1990):

1 pure bundling strategy, in which services can be sold as a package at a given price

2 pure components strategy, where products are sold and priced independently

3 mixed bundling strategy, in which services are offered both individually and in a bundle at a discount price.

In the case of the hospitality industry, it has to be recognized that normally, the firm's strategy can be seen as a mixed strategy: some services are offered as a bundle at a specific price and others are supplied on demand and charged accordingly. In a pure bundle strategy, the packages can be seen as a complex product and profitability can be analysed by individual package as if they were 'simple' products. When packages are made of a variable combination of elements and single elements participate in more than one package (as it happens in most cases), they can be seen as modular products in which the cost of each package is the sum of the cost of individual modules.

Much attention has been devoted in the literature to the profitability analysis of bundle strategies; bundle strategies are seen as particularly useful when both the ratio of fixed to variable costs and the degree of cost sharing are very high (Guiltinan, 1987). Given the level of fixed and common costs, in the short run, profitability is mainly a matter of sale volume and therefore the company has little interest in reducing individuals' demands on some services by pricing. Bundle pricing is often a way of maximizing sale volume by providing additional services that have no marginal costs in the short run and that can attract more customer demand.

The case of the hotel that we are considering in this chapter, can be seen as a case of mixed strategy in which several services are provided, sometimes at a price and sometimes at no charge, in a situation in which customers do not express an independent demand for each service, but the mix, i.e. the amount of each service required by an individual customer is set by each individual customer according to his or her needs. Regardless of the fact that a price might or might not be charged for individual services, a profitability analysis in which cost and revenues are analysed in terms of 'service' or 'service group' does not help the company in understanding 'where' it is producing more value. Of course, taking into consideration some of the consequences of a customers' bundle purchasing approach does not imply that a product or service focused cost and revenues analysis is an important source of information for managing efficiency and for performance appraisal within the organization: the point here refers only to profitability analysis as a source of information in product and service decision-making.

From product and service profitability to customers profitability analysis

Several authors have noted how customers vary, in general, in terms of profitability (Cooper and Kaplan, 1991; Slywotzky and Shapiro, 1993) because they do not generate the same level of revenues and costs. In general, profitability varies across different customers because they express a demand for different products with different individual profitability. In other terms, profitability varies among customers (if products have different contribution margins) because of the different product mix they purchase. Consequently, companies have been considering the search for profitable customers as an important marketing goal along with the 'usual' search for profitable products.

The customers' purchasing bundle approach, regardless of whether the firm chooses to adopt or not to adopt a bundle pricing strategy, highlights the need for refocusing profitability analysis, moving from product and service focus to customer focus. The whole customers' bundling demand becomes the focus of management attention in supporting decision-making, because products and services are not independent objects of customers' buying decisions. The main purpose of any product and service policy is no longer to sell profitable products and services, but to attract customers who buy products and services in a profitable mix. The customers are potential buyers of a range of services from the company and, therefore, profitability should not be seen only as the relation between costs and revenues of each product, but as the relation between costs and revenues of the whole with reference to a specific individual customer with a specific purchasing mix. Concepts like 'relationship management' and 'system selling' are becoming popular among marketing managers in the service industry (Guiltinan, 1987) along with the idea of customer relation management, clearly supported by a customer profitability analysis. The marketing effort should not be driven towards selling products and services, but towards both attracting customers with a high 'potential' in terms of purchasing attitude and broadening the firm's relationship with its profitable customers. A marketing policy should be evaluated in terms of capability of attracting 'good' customers. The concept of 'good' customers refers to attributes like loyalty (or repurchasing attitude) and customer profitability.

This approach was first developed in the banking industry in the early 1990s, when all costs and revenues of each individual customer were re-unified in one single record. Having understood that about 50 per cent of customers were unprofitable (Storbacka et al., 1994), banks have been trying to encourage a relationship with profitable customers. Thanks to the information provided by such a customer profitability analysis, banks have been able to develop marketing strategies for specific groups of customers that appeared to be more profitable than others. Under this perspective, the profitability of each product is just a contribution to the total profitability of a single customer. As mentioned before, a customer's profitability depends on two main factors: individual service profitability and a customer's purchasing mix. Products that might not appear very profitable *per se*, might be part of the purchasing bundle of customers who show a high profitability in the whole set of products and services they buy and, therefore, might be seen as an important factor of attraction of profitable customers. Clearly, this approach might significantly change the management's perception about what produces value.

The issues of joint revenues

When the bundle purchasing approach is taken into consideration, it becomes clear that an individual product's profitability has only a limited capability in explaining a firm's profitability. In fact, customers do not mind much the individual prices of single products or service they acquire, but focus their attention in terms of the value-to-cost relation of the whole bundle of products they purchase.

Therefore, the profit of individual products or services does not guarantee that the value customers received from that specific item is bigger than the price they pay: customers could buy a service (and pay the price) because of the value they received from the other related services. Under these circumstances, there is a strong interdependence among the revenues generated by the different products and services acquired by a single customer. This interdependence is so strong that revenues have to be considered jointly, as any attempt to separate them would not be consistent with the customer's bundling approach: this case can be defined as a case of conjunction of revenue due to the purchasing process. Similarly with the case of joint costs in production processes, it is possible to refer to the case presented here, as a case of joint revenues. The case of joint costs refers to production processes in which several independent (in terms of market demand) products are produced in a single process with common resources without any reasonable way of distinguishing the contribution of common resources to each product. The most cited case of joint production costs is the case of an oil refinery in which, from a given amount of crude oil, several products (like gasoline for cars, burning oil, coal tar, lubricants) with different market demands and prices, are produced (Collini, 2001). It is well accepted in the accounting literature that the profitability of joint products must be assessed jointly, given that there is no meaning in individual products' profit (NACA, 1957). Technically, joint products are linked to each other by the technical characteristics of the production process: in the case presented here, the conjunction is due to the way the demand is expressed by the customers. Alfred Marshall (1923:192) defines technically joint products as products for which 'it is not practicable . . . to produce any one (member of the group) without, at the same time, producing the others'; joint products 'because of demand' can be defined as those for which it is non-practicable to sell any one without selling all or some of the others. Given that all the consequences of conjunction are due to the fact that when one product is produced and sold, some of the others must be produced and sold, it is clear that whether their conjunction is originated either by production or by demand does not change the consequences in terms of profitability analysis of the products; therefore, it has to be recognized that cost and revenue relations of individual products cannot be analysed when products are joint products, regardless where the conjunction is originated.

The fact that the mix among different products and services might change from one customer to another does not necessarily imply that the assumption about joint revenues has to be dismissed: even in the case of joint costs, a flexible mix (within a range) does not change the need for a joint evaluation of the economic consequence of production, as long as the linkages are strong enough to make Marshall's statement applicable.

When a customer focus profitability analysis is considered, the way individual service's profit is seen has to change: the existence of a positive profit margin on individual products and services does not imply that they are part of a positive customers' value production process. Profitable products and services could be part of a non-profitable customer's purchasing bundle and, therefore, their contribution to value production is unclear because the contribution of each individual product or service to the production of value is not automatically measured by the revenues it appears to generate. Their contribution is related to both the influence they have on the customer's purchasing decision of the bundle of products and the value the customer attributes to the whole bundle.

The profit analysis scheme

Having dismissed the idea of evaluating services contribution to the overall profit only in terms of individual services profitability, the profit generation analysis has to be performed according to the need of supporting 'customer relation management'. In 'customer relation management', customer selection based on profitability is seen as a key point (Kaplan and Norton, 2001): most of the marketing effort has to be devoted to attract profitable customers. A customer profitability analysis can help in evaluating different 'customer segments' and detecting the customers' characteristics that appear to have a positive relation with profit.

In order to analyse the profitability of different groups of customers, the management accounting system must compute costs and revenues by individual customer, making each individual customer a profit object. Having available a data set on individual customer's profit, any group analysis can be performed by grouping together customers with the same characteristics (like geographic origins, distribution channels, age, family size, time of the year, time of booking, etc.).

Short-term and long-term analysis

Profitability analysis is based on detecting the contribution to profit of changes in volume of products and services sold in a period of time. It is widely known that this analysis requires *ex ante* the definition of the time horizon of such an effect. In the so-called 'short-term', fixed costs are not affected by any decision and action regarding sale volume and, therefore, their effects on profit are measured in terms of contribution margin (difference between changes in revenues and changes in variable costs). As mentioned above, in service organizations, and particularly in the hospitality industry, pure variable costs are a small share of total costs and therefore, contribution margin analysis has a limited capability of explaining profitability, given that margins tend to equal revenues. Customer management (selection, acquisition, retention) tends to maximize the value of the customers, and therefore the value creation in general (Kaplan and Norton, 2003) in the long run. These actions require mainly a long-run mind set because they tend to show their effects over time. Even though some action (like selection) might produce some effects in the short run, the firm should focus on long-term value production by selecting customer groups capable of producing value in the long term. All these reasons are suggesting that a 'data warehouse' with detailed information regarding long-term profitability of each individual customer should be put in place for supporting decision-making in the marketing area. In order to develop such analysis, a full cost approach is required. Full cost, when carefully done, allows the understanding of the implications of customers' behaviour on resource usage in the long run. Of course, when a long-run approach is taken, the short-term relation between costs (fixed and variable) and volume is neglected and all costs are seen as variable.

It is widely recognized that an activity-based cost system is the most suitable accounting approach for cost allocation in this case (Kaplan and Narayanan, 2001). An activity-based cost system is particularly suitable for cases in which the degree of cost commonality among different products and services is high, as is the case in the hotel industry.

As it is well known, an activity-based cost system requires the allocation of indirect costs over a set of activities by 'resource drivers' and, afterwards, the allocation of the cost of activities to processes on the basis of the individual activity's contribution to each process, measured by the activity drivers (Turney, 1992). In the hotel industry, each customer can be seen as a process where the different services are considered as activities performed by the company and consumed by the customer. When an activity-based approach is applied, the individual customer's value chain can be analysed in terms of cost of the activities and total revenues regardless of any allocation of value on individual activities/services.

The case – continued

In the simple case presented in this chapter, a set of activities has been identified. Activities have been selected because they both consume resources and are supposed to produce value for the customers. The following activities were selected for the design of an activity-based cost system:

Room division

- Reception and check-in and out
- Room cleaning
- Room service
- Mini bar refurnishing
- Luggage service to the room.

Restaurant

- Meal service
- Breakfast service.

Bar

- Service.

Beach service

- Check-in (preparing the contract at the beginning of the stay)
- Parasol setting (daily)
- Chair setting (daily).

After having selected the relevant activities, working time is chosen as resource driver for allocating departments' costs over activities. According to activity-based costing terminology and techniques, resource drivers are used in order to allocate resources over activities. Resource drivers should measure the effort, in terms of resources, carried out by individual organizational units, in performing individual activities. The amount of activities used by each process (customer) is measured in terms of activity drivers. The amount of activity drivers causes a proportional use of the activity. The 'effort' of each department in performing the different activities was measured in terms of total working time devoted to each one. On the basis of a 'one time analysis', the amount of time was measured and the percentages of total working time devoted to each activity was calculated, as shown in Table 9.5.

The consumption of each activity is measured by a specific activity driver. Drivers are based on units of activity performed during the period of time of the analysis. In Table 9.6, the drivers selected for the chosen activities are shown.

Table 9.5
Allocation of time to activities

Division	Activity			
	Room division	Restaurant	Bar	Beach
Reception and check-in and out	15%			
Room cleaning	70%			
Room service	10%			
Mini bar refurnishing	3%			
Luggage service to the room	2%			
Meal service		90%		
Breakfast service		10%		
Bar			100%	
Contract (at the beginning of the stay)				10%
Parasol setting (daily)				35%
Chair setting (daily)				55%
Total	100%	100%	100%	100%

Table 9.6

Activity	Driver	Number of driver
Check-in and out	Number of customers	570
Room cleaning	Number of days per room	2880
Room service	Number of calls	470
Mini bar refurnishing	Number of items sold	820
Meal service	Number of meals	8812
Breakfast service	Number of breakfasts	4896
Bar	Number of items sold	2450
Contract (at the beginning of the stay)	Number of contracts	403
Parasol setting (daily)	Number of days per chair	1728
Chair setting (daily)	Number of days per chair	2419
Luggage service to the room	Number of deliveries	270

Some costs (like the cost of food at the restaurant) can be seen as direct costs and charged directly to each individual customer (on the basis of actual or standard consumption) and therefore are not included in activities' costs. All non-direct costs are considered activities' costs and therefore allocated according to the percentage of effort (resource driver) over the activities. On the basis of the available data, the costs of activity and the cost of each unit of activity (also called cost driver) can be calculated as in Table 9.7.

Table 9.7

The cost of each unit of activity, i.e. cost drivers

	Room	Restaurant	Bar	Beach	Total
Total division costs	163.938	195.788	40.394	29.800	429.920
Customer's direct costs	–	100.000	8.000		108.000
Customer's cost of activities	163.938	95.788	32.394	29.800	321.920
Check-in and out	4.591	–	–	–	24.591
Room cleaning	114.757	–	–	–	114.757
Room service	16.394	–	–	–	16.394
Mini bar refurnishing	4.918	–	–	–	4.918
Luggage service to the room	3.279	–	–	–	3.279
Meal service	–	86.209	–	–	86.209
Breakfast service	–	9.579	–	–	9.579
Bar	–	–	32.394	–	32.394
Contract (at the beginning of the stay)	–	–	–	2.980	2.980
Parasol setting (daily)	–	–	–	10.430	10.430
Chair setting (daily)	–	–	–	16.390	16.390
Total costs of activities	163.938	95.788	32.394	29.800	321.920

As an example, three customers have been selected in order to develop the profitability analysis (Table 9.8). For the purpose of calculating the full cost of servicing these clients, the specific service consumption profile (in term of number of activity drivers)

Table 9.8

Example of profitability analysis based on three customers

	Customer 1	Customer 2	Customer 3
Number of days per room	12	6	2
Number of meals	12	6	4
Number of breakfasts	12	6	4
Number of contracts	1	0	1
Number of days per parasol	6	0	2
Number of days per chair	12	0	4
Room service: number of calls	0	0	1
Luggage: number of deliveries	1	0	1
Bar: number of items sold	4	2	2
Mini bar: number of items sold	2	1	2
Total revenues	1290	600	230
Direct costs	310	97	70

of each customer is presented. Obviously, this calculation should be carried out for each individual customer in order to create the required data set of customers' profitability.

On the basis of these data, the profitability of these three customers can be calculated as in shown in Table 9.9.

Clearly the three customers present different levels of profitability due to a different level of service usage and different revenues. Each customer has his or her own profile of activities consumption and revenues due to the mix of services he or she required. When this analysis is developed for all customers, the management can, by analysing profitability by specific groups of customers, identify some characteristics like age, nationality, distribution channel (tour operator, travel agency, walk in clients) and any other characteristic that might be perceived as a factor to which a peculiar consumers' behaviour can be associated.

The issue of activities' value

Having accepted the idea that individual service profitability cannot completely satisfy the need for analysing value production in the *case of bundling*, the problem of understanding how the value added is produced remains unsolved. The example of customer profitability analysis has shown how different customers might affect a firm's profitability according to their different activity consumption profile, but the contribution of individual activities to the production of value remains unclear. In other words, the analysis has suggested the existence of a positive (or negative) value added for each customer/process, but it has not shown how activities contribute to the production (or destruction) of that value. As clarified earlier in this chapter, it does not make sense to pursue the goal of calculating the value added of each individual activity – i.e. not sold and priced individually – because prices, when they exist, do not represent a measure of the recognized customer's value produced by each activity. In a joint process, the contribution of individual elements of the process cannot be identified.

Even though any attempt to solve this problem might appear to neglect the original assumption about bundling on customer behaviour, some ideas regarding the contribution to value production of the individual activities can be found in the value of the processes to which the activities contribute. The data set of individual customer's profitability can be used for understanding how much value is produced in those customers/processes to which each individual activity contributes.

Following this approach, the consumption of a specific activity by a customer is identified as a grouping factor: in other words, all customers that have used a specific service item (unit of activity)

Table 9.9
Profitability calculated in the example of three customers

		Customer 1			Customer 2			Customer 3		
		Driver	Number	Cost	Driver	Number	Cost	Driver	Number	Cost
Check-in and out	Check-in	43.14	1	43.14	43.14	1	43.14	43.14	1	43.14
Room cleaning	Number of days per room	39.85	12	478.15	39.85	6	239.08	39.85	2	79.69
Room service	Number of calls	9.78	12	117.40	9.78	6	58.70	9.78	4	39.13
Mini bar refurnishing	Number of items sold	1.96	12	23.48	1.96	6	11.74	1.96	4	7.83
Meal service	Number of meals	7.39	1	7.39	7.39	0	0.00	7.39	1	7.39
Breakfast service	Number of breakfasts	6.04	6	36.22	6.04	0	0.00	6.04	2	12.07
Bar	Number of items sold	6.78	12	81.31	6.78	0	0.00	6.78	4	27.10
Contract (at the beginning of the stay)	Number of contracts	34.88	0	0.00	34.88	0	0.00	34.88	1	34.88
Parasol setting (daily)	Number of days per parasol	12.14	1	12.14	12.14	0	0.00	12.14	1	12.14
Chair setting (daily)	Number of days per chair	13.22	4	52.89	13.22	2	26.44	13.22	2	26.44
Luggage service to the room	Number of deliveries	6.00	2	12.00	6.00	1	6.00	6.00	2	12.00
Direct costs				310.00			97.00			70.00
Total cost				1174.11			482.10			371.82
Total revenues				1290.00			600.00			230.00
Profit margin				115.89			117.90			−141.82
Profitability (% of revenues)				9			20			−62

are included in a group and the profit of the group is the sum of the profit of all customers included in the group. In this way, the profitability of the customers taking advantage of a specific activity can be seen as a hint of the contribution to the value producing process of that specific activity. Even though it would be quite hazardous to jump to the conclusion that an activity participating to some processes with high profitability is a value added activity, it might be a useful piece of information to know that an activity participates in processes in which production of value (for the firm) is high, low or negative. In the example presented in this chapter, several groups of customers could be identified on the basis of the services they consumed during their stay at the hotel. As an example, three possible groups have been analysed:

- Customers requiring room service
- Customers using the parking facility
- Customers requiring luggage room service.

The data regarding the three possible groups are presented in Table 9.10.

Table 9.10
Three possible groups of customers

	Room service	Parking	Luggage service
Number of days per room	120	240	80
Number of customers	24	36	30
Number of meals	180	400	70
Number of breakfasts	120	230	80
Number of contracts	18	31	30
Number of days per parasol	90	220	70
Number of days per chair	175	260	120
Room service: number of calls	50	3	7
Luggage: number of deliveries	25	12	30
Bar: number of items sold	55	98	72
Mini bar: number of items sold	45	53	28
Total revenues	15 200	31 500	12 250
Direct costs	2 345	5 192	1 342

The different levels of profitability of the three groups are shown in Table 9.11 and Figure 9.1.

From the data it emerges that customers showing interest in different activities performed by the hotel have a different level of long-run profitability. On the basis of this knowledge the company

Table 9.11
Profitability of the three groups of customers

Activity	Driver		Customers' groups (by activities)					
			Room service		Parking		Luggage service	
			Driver	Cost	Driver	Cost	Driver	Cost
Check-in and out	Check-in	43.14	24	1 035.36	36	1 553.04	30	1 294.20
Room cleaning	Number of days per room	39.85	120	4 782.00	240	9 564.00	80	3 188.00
Room service	Number of calls	9.78	50	489.00	3	29.34	7	68.46
Mini bar refurnishing	Number of items sold	1.96	45	88.20	53	103.88	28	54.88
Meal service	Number of meals	7.39	180	1 330.20	400	2 956.00	70	517.30
Breakfast service	Number of breakfasts	6.04	120	724.80	230	1 389.20	80	483.20
Bar	Number of items sold	6.78	55	372.90	98	664.44	72	488.16
Contract (at the beginning of the stay)	Number of contracts	34.88	18	627.84	31	1 081.28	30	1 046.40
Parasol setting (daily)	Number of days per parasol	12.14	90	1 092.60	220	2 670.80	70	849.80
Chair setting (daily)	Number of days per chair	13.22	175	2 313.50	260	3 437.20	120	1 586.40
Luggage service to the room	Number of deliveries	6.00	25	150.00	12	72.00	30	180.00
Total cost of activities				13 006.18		23 521.18		9 756.80
Direct costs				2 345.00		5 192.00		1 342.00
Total cost				15 351.40		28 713.18		11 098.80
Total revenues				15 400.00		35 000.00		13 750.00
Profit margin				48.60		6 286.82		2 651.20
Profitability (% of revenues)				0.32		17.96		19.28

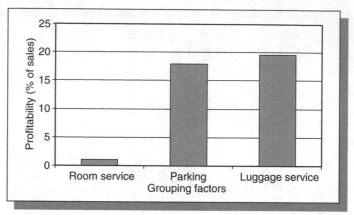

Figure 9.1
Profitability of different customers' groups.

could evaluate the opportunity of committing resources in activities that appear not to be part of value added processes. In the example, customers using parking facilities and luggage room service appear to be much more profitable than those that require room service. This could lead to the conclusion that, even though it is impossible to assess the value of parking in a customer's 'utility function', those customers that appreciate these services appear to be more profitable than others and therefore, it would be possible to conclude that parking and luggage service participate to high value added processes.

Obviously, customers included in one group can be included in another group (there are no reasons why customers parking the car are not asking for room service) and therefore it would be important to check not only the average profitability of the group, but also the variability around the mean in the group: a quite high variability could suggest that the grouping factor might not explain the level of profitability of the group of customers.

References

Bojamic, D.C. and Calantone, R. J. (1990) A contribution approach to price bundling in tourism. *Annals of Tourism Research*, **17** (1), 528–540.

Chandler, A.D. (1962) *Strategy and structure: The History of the American Enterprise*. The MIT Press, Cambridge, MA.

Collini, P. (2001) *Controllo di Gestione e Processi Aziendali*. CEDAM, Padova.

Cooper, R. and Kaplan, R.S. (1991) *The Design of Cost Management System*. Prentice Hall, Englewood Cliffs.

Guiltinan, J.P. (1987) The price bundling of services: a normative framework. *Journal of Marketing*, **51** (4), 74–85.

Johnson, T.H. and Kaplan, R.S. (1987) *Relevance lost. The rise and the fall of management accounting*. Harvard Business School Press, Boston.

Kaplan, R.S. and Narayanan, V.G. (2001) Measuring and managing customer profitability. *Journal of Cost Management*, September/October, 5–15.

Kaplan, R.S. and Norton, D.P. (2001) *The Strategy Focused Organization*. Harvard Business School Press, Cambridge.

Kaplan, R.S. and Norton, D.P. (2003) *Balanced Scorecard Report*. May–June. HBS Publishing Co., Cambridge.

Marshall, A. (1923) *Industry and Trade*. McMillian Ltd, London.

NACA (1957) *Joint Cost*. National Association of Cost Accountant, Chicago, USA.

Slywotzky, A.J. and Shapiro, B.P. (1993) Leveraging to beat the odds: the new marketing mind-set. *Harvard Business Review*, September, 97–106.

Storbacka, K., Strandvik, T. and Gronroos, C. (1994) Managing customer relationships for profit. *International Journal of Service Industry Management*, **5** (5), 21–28.

Taylor, T.C. (2000) Current development in cost accounting and the dynamics of economics calculation. *Quarterly Journal of Australian Economics*, **3**, 3–19.

Turney, P.P.B. (1992) Activity based management. *Management Accounting*, January, 20–25.

Customer profitability accounting in the context of hotels

Vira Krakhmal

Introduction

To improve financial performance, hotel companies often target multiple customer segments by expanding their product features and services. The logic underlying this strategy is that revenue maximization requires attracting more guests, which is accomplished by targeting new customer segments and offering a wider variety of products and services. This chapter will emphasize that, although revenue enhancing techniques are important in the present day hospitality market, even more important are the analytical methods that help managers determine the segments that generate the greatest profit contribution to the bottom line. As a result, the information requirement on the relative profitability of a segment or customer group has to take into account the costs that would be incurred as a result of decisions made by management.

Marketing planning in hotels usually focuses on customer market segments, with specific marketing activities and packages being directed towards individual market segments (e.g. business, leisure or conference segments). The marketing plan also generally shows the marketing activities planned according to the identified market segments (Ward, 1989). Although the *Uniform System of Accounts for the Lodging Industry* provides the basis for one dimension of analysis, namely recording, controlling and benchmarking the product mix, i.e. rooms, food and beverage, leisure and minor operated departments, it is not designed to facilitate the introduction of the second dimension analysis, namely planning and optimizing the customer mix, i.e. market segment and customer profitability. As a result, accountants are producing information for departments while managers are making decisions based on market segments, thus creating a mismatch between the 'provision' and 'use' of routine information at the hotel property level (Downie, 1997).

Recent developments in customer profitability accounting allow for more focus on the customer segments, a system of analysis in which the individual customers comprise the unit of analysis. The main benefit of customer profitability analysis for hotel companies is that it provides management and other decision-makers with customer-related information, which in turn enables the management of yield from a profit perspective; allowing management to focus and consider revenues, costs and profits from a customer perspective. This information relating to profitability of customers can be applied in the decision-making process to support a range of long- and short-term customer related decisions. Following the shift in business towards customer orientation, the concept of understanding customer and market segmentation is becoming key to the improvement of hotel operating performance.

Accounting information systems in hotels

Three major types of accounting information systems are in current use. The most common is the traditional custodial system, which provides financial reports relating to the condition of an organization at a given point of time (Kirpalani and Shapiro, 1973). This system is designed primarily to generate the balance sheets and income (profit and loss) statements required by external interests such as stockholders, securities exchanges and government agencies.

Performance accounting is a less common, but still widely employed accounting information system. Its purpose is to match the performance of cost and profit centres (such as service and operating departments) against the plans, standards and budgets previously formulated for such centres. Thus, centres serve as the basic collection units for both cost and revenue data with reports subsequently being made available on the performance of each centre (Mossman et al., 1974).

The third type of accounting information system, one that is still in relatively limited use, can be characterized as decision-oriented and contribution-based. In such a system accounting, operating and statistical information is used primarily to evaluate alternate courses of action. The system relies heavily on contribution accounting, whereby all unavoidable costs functionally related to the product or service are allocated to it. Decisions based on contribution accounting have particular relevance in the areas of product introduction and abandonment, in pricing and generally, in the determination of the appropriate level of marketing effort (Mossman et al., 1974).

The hotel industry uses the *Uniform System of Accounts for the Lodging Industry* (1996), which originated in the USA and was first published in 1926. Although several editions have been published since then, the basic principles have remained the same. The *Uniform System of Accounts for the Lodging Industry* sets out in some detail recommendations on how particular transactions should be dealt with in accounting terms. Results of hotels are reported using standard formats that are therefore instantly comparable with results of other hotels.

One of the main features of the Uniform System is the hotel property results are reported by department, in line with the traditional organizational structure found in most hotel operations. All expenses attributable to (and controllable by) a particular department are allocated against the revenues of that department to arrive at a departmental operating profit.

In the hotel industry, like in any other industry, the financial results are simply a reflection of the underlying operations. By including operational statistics in the same reporting packages as the financial information, it is much easier to focus on why, for instance, financial performance is poor and to use the information as a basis to find an appropriate means of improving performance.

The Uniform System provides an accounting and reporting format which enables all interested parties, from managers and operators to owners, financiers and auditors, to assess performance of the hotel against past performance, or that of direct competitors (similar quality, size and location) and across the industry as a whole (where such directly comparable information is available). Allocation of revenues and costs enables the management to attribute responsibility for results to individual department heads who can directly influence, and be accountable for, the results of their department. Reports of operational performance then give managers the relevant information on how each of the constituent departments of the hotel is performing in order that problems, and indeed their resolution, can be identified promptly by the manager responsible.

However, operating profit by department does not go far enough in deriving a full contribution analysis. For example, each department uses a proportion of energy cost and derives certain benefits from marketing spend (assuming this is accounted for as a support cost). The administrative function exists to support the operating departments, but allocating these costs to departments is subjective and the costs are not necessarily within the control of the departmental manager.

There is a danger that too dogmatic an approach to a department analysis obscures an assessment of the hotel's performance as a whole. For example, a marketing promotion that leads to reduced room rates may increase restaurant covers and overall profitability as well as encouraging repeat business. Furthermore, a hotel should be seen to provide a seamless overall service to the customer and, in order to achieve this, all departments should be pulling in the same direction; a departmental structure does not encourage the sharing of resources between departments to optimize the benefit to the whole entity.

Yield management approach

Yield management has received considerable recognition from industry professionals as a sophisticated marketing tool. It is an effective method of evaluating sales and pricing alternatives. Demand forecasting and revenue projections are used to evaluate sales alternatives in terms of revenue maximization. Hotels attempt to achieve the optimal mix of group and transient business that maximizes room revenue and average rate. Revenue maximization is an attractive goal, since it increases the amount of money flowing from existing demand (Regan, 1989).

The market demand pricing strategy that is the basis of yield management is ineffective for long-term pricing decisions. In the competitive markets that virtually all hotels face, market demand pricing eventually results in deep discounting that erodes profit margins (Jones and Hamilton, 1992). Market demand pricing is an appropriate short-term strategy, but to remain profitable in the long run, hotels must achieve an average rate that covers both fixed and variable costs. Although hotel financial systems accumulate the revenue and expense information that is essential for cost analysis, such information is reported by operating department rather than by market segment and overhead expenses are not distributed to the various segments.

Costs need to be identified to support the yield management decisions that are being made, not just for rooms (by segment), but for all ancillary revenue areas. These should include all support and fixed costs as well as the specific variable costs associated with delivering the product. This focus on cost, as well as revenue management, should improve the contribution to hotel profits and increase the overall efficiency of the hotel property. This approach is supported by Donaghy et al. (1995) who suggest a 'yield focused approach' to the profitability of market segments which identifies all product costs; a process that should 'add value' to the yield management decision. A segmentation approach is essential, however, as different segments may incur different types of costs – with marketing being a good example. The yield management approach does not, however, identify how the costs should be determined.

Customer profitability approach

Why is it important to understand the concept of customer profitability and to determine the profitability of customers? Although the customer profitability concept is not equally important in all industries, it is important in a number of service industries such as banking, healthcare and education and is growing in importance with regard to other service businesses such as hospitality.

The importance of the approach depends, in part, on the strategy a company has adopted toward its customers. In circumstances where companies claim to be customer-driven and service-oriented and are devoting significant labour, capital and time to their customer base, or planning to provide special treatment to certain customers, then customer profitability can prove to be particularly useful. In such cases, customer profitability analysis should also be included as one of the ongoing management reports, presented routinely.

The reason customer profitability analysis is needed and should be used is that it aids companies in avoiding losses and allows them to improve profitability (Riley, 1999). Foster et al. (1996) stated that 'customer account profitability' represents an important future direction in management accounting. Paradoxically, most management accounting systems focus not on the customer, but on the products, departments, or geographic regions. Only rarely can a management accounting system produce customer profitability figures.

As the companies become more customer and service-oriented, they frequently invest capital and labour into the management of their customer base. The key to being successful in customer management by means of a customer profitability approach is a successful shift from being product-centric to a customer-centric focus. In many industries customer service has become a key element in the battle for both volume and margin (Bellis-Jones, 1989). As companies shift from traditional product focus to customer focus, the understanding of customer relationship management in terms of customer behaviour and profitability represents a fundamental change which affects virtually every aspect of an organization (Gurau and Ranchhod, 2002). In an effort to delight customers, companies often overlook whether they are actually making money from 'the business of providing additional delight' (Kaplan and Narayanan, 2001). If a company does not in any way estimate or record how much labour or capital has been invested per customer, then it will be unable to assess how much its investments in clients have yielded. Usually, little or no knowledge is gleaned about whether the investments were made in the right customers. The investments might have been made in the customers or customer segments that are unprofitable to the company.

The 'why?' of the customer profitability analysis can be reduced to the simple statement that revenue does not contribute equally to profit. Profitability depends not only on the unit cost of a product or service, but also on the extra services required. The customer profitability approach allows the identification and measurement of the profitability of each customer group and, although it is especially useful for service companies (Kaplan and Narayanan, 2001), it is also relevant to a growing number of other companies in all industries. For hotel companies, customer profitability is far more important than product profitability, because the costs of providing the service are usually determined by customer behaviour.

Sales and marketing have long craved a decent yardstick to measure effectiveness of their inputs to the company sales. Customer profitability is the key to aligning incentives between companies and their customers. When companies understand the drivers of individual customer profitability, they can take a variety of actions to transform unprofitable relationships into profitable ones (Kaplan and Narayanan, 2001).

Why do customer-related costs matter?

On the surface, it is not readily apparent. The best customers are not necessarily the ones who spend the most money. They are the ones who return the most bottom-line value to the organization. Their value stems from multiple-cost and revenue factors that have traditionally been elusive and difficult to capture and rarely assembled into a customer view.

How much does it cost to market to customers?

Was that brochure just mailed a waste or did it hit gold? How much spend is appropriate? Where is the highest payback? Are high-value customers being attracted? These questions are fundamental to effective marketing, but many marketing organizations still answer them with intuition, imperfect metrics, anecdotal information and a history of unpredictable and non-repeatable events.

How can one add value to each customer relationship?

Naturally, an increase in customer profitability results from cross-selling and up-selling of services and from preventing good customers from leaving. However, being successful at these efforts might not increase profitability if the cost-to-market or cost-to-serve is too high.

How much does it cost to serve customers?

The cost of serving varies widely from one customer to another. Some customers tie up call centres by raising objections to every bill or by seeking a high level of technical support. Other customers procrastinate before paying every bill. Some may use so many resources that cost-to-serve exceeds revenue related to such customers. If there is a potential to track costs to the customers who consume them, then it is at least theoretically possible to make informed decisions, such as where to control or even reduce the growth of the customer base and the diversity of the customer mix and where to enable and increase it.

Increasing the profitability of each of its customers, not simply its products, is a way to sustain long-term economic-value growth for the enterprise and its investors. Customer profitability analysis can help companies achieve such growth by providing answers to numerous questions: How much profit is being earned from each customer (or at least each customer segment) today and how much can be earned in the future? What kind of new customers are being added and what is the growth rate of additions? How and why are customers migrating through segments over time?

As a result of varying customer demands for different levels of service, the cost-to-serve component of each customer's profit contribution requires measurement and visibility. As increasing variation in customization and tailoring for individuals becomes widespread (e.g. the American company Wyndham Hotels and Resort provide guest recognition programmes 'By Request' designed to customize each stay to customers individual tastes and preferences), how will companies distinguish their profitable customers from their unprofitable ones? Companies now need financial measures for how resource expenses are uniquely consumed, below the gross margin line, by each diverse customer.

The problem, however, is that the managerial accounting systems of most companies concentrate on product or service line costs (which, as was noted earlier, are flawed and misleading by arbitrary cost allocations) because regulatory financial accounting rules require such compliance. Accountants must begin applying the same costing principles for product costing, typically activity-based costing principles, to types of customers so there is visibility to all traceable and assignable costs. Activity-based costing data are essential to the process of validating and prioritizing the services to be added for particular customers, because some customers may purchase a mix of mainly low-margin products and service lines. After considering the 'cost-to-serve', such as extra services for customers, transactions exclusively in high-cost channels or in special requirements channels, some customers actually may be unprofitable. Likewise customers who purchase a mix of relatively high-margin products may demand so much in extra services that they also could be unprofitable.

To be competitive, a company must know its sources of profit and understand its cost structure. A competitive company must also ultimately translate its strategies into actions. For blatantly unprofitable customers, a company might explore passive options of substantially raising prices or surcharging customers for the extra work. In the long run, the company may also be more assertive and terminate the relationship with a customer. For profitable customers, a company may want to reduce customer-related causes of extra work for its employees, streamline its delivery process so it costs less to serve customers, or even attempt to alter the customers' behaviour so that they place fewer workload demands on the company.

Activity-based costing

Criticism of the conventional management accounting was widely brought out by Johnson and Kaplan in their almost legendary book 'Relevance Lost – Rise and Fall of Management

Accounting' (1987). Their research started the process that led to the birth and further development of activity-based costing by the middle of 1990s. The key concepts underlying the activity-based costing method were mainly introduced by Johnson and Kaplan and still remain the same – give up on classification of costs into fixed and variable, accept anything as a cost object and recognize that the majority of traditional fixed costs such as sales, general and administrative costs are not driven by the volume of the products sold or services provided (Howell and Soucy, 1990).

Activity accounting is built on the three-stage principle:

1 products, customers, or other cost objects consume

2 activities, whereas activities consume

3 resources (Brimson and Antos, 1994).

Costs are allocated to the cost objects using three-level, resource activity cost object allocation (Figure 10.1).

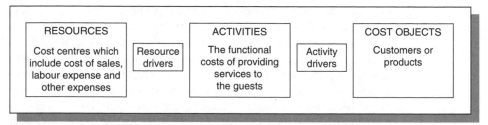

Figure 10.1
Basic elements in activity-based cost allocation.

The term 'resources' in activity-based costing method generally corresponds to the general ledger entries, i.e. financial resources in cost centres and bookkeeping accounts. 'Activities' are performed by the organization and can be any task or operation in a company that is seen important enough to be recorded separately. Activities use resources, and costs from the resources are allocated to activities based on resource usage indicated by 'resource drivers'. An example of a resource driver could be the number of check-ins and check-outs of customers performed in a hotel. This resource driver would be applied to an account called 'labour cost of front office department' to allocate the costs to the activities that use those functional costs.

Likewise, 'cost objects' can be any final costing objects that the company wants to measure. Often cost objects are products and customers. Cost objects are assumed to use up the activities. The costs associated with the activities are allocated to the cost objects according to their use of activities. Activity usage is indicated by 'activity drivers' (Atkinson et al., 1997). An example of an activity driver could be a number of rooms sold to customers.

Through the three-step allocation, all costs are allocated to the cost objects according to their activity usage and activities are charged with costs according to their incurred costs. With such detailed allocation, most fixed costs become 'variable' and thus potentially allocable through the activity-based costing using drivers.

According to the conventions of the activity-based costing, the small number of costs for which a reasonable cause and effect relationship with cost objects cannot be found should not be allocated. These expenses should be covered by a company's overall operations margin.

The implementation of activity-based costing within a hotel environment necessitates a change in current accounting approaches to revenue and cost allocation. It requires an adjustment from the way in which revenues and expenses are traditionally recorded by operating and service departments, to the identification and recording of expenses by customer group. Figure 10.2 illustrates the essence of activity-based costing, which is designed to move from the way revenue and cost are traditionally recorded in accounting systems, by operating department and overhead categories (as represented by the traditional accounting approach of Figure 10.2), to reporting each by customer group (Noone and Griffin, 1998).

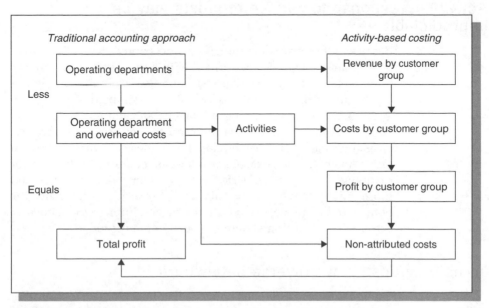

Figure 10.2
Activity-based cost assignment in hotels.

Although revenue data by customer group can be sourced directly from many property management or yield management systems, the key to activity-based costing lies in the selection of an appropriate method of matching costs with customer groups. The hotel industry has several distinctive characteristics when compared to other industries. These characteristics should be identified in order to design a more effective activity-based costing system for the property. Three characteristic challenges should be considered when implementing an activity-based costing system.

Output is often hard to define

Output in the service industry is sometimes described as the 'package of service benefits', with many benefits being intangible. Intangible benefits include: speed of service, friendliness of staff, and overall satisfaction received by a customer. In addition, each guest may have a different interpretation of the output received. Such lack of definitiveness may present difficulties when management attempt to trace the activities involved and resources consumed with the potentially associated outcome. Hospitality services are therefore quite different from the tangible product received and produced in the more manufacturing-oriented industries.

Activity in response to service requests may be unpredictable

Because hotels provide a mix of products and services to a broad based market, activities performed within the organization are not only likely to change continuously, but also likely to vary significantly depending on the individual requests made by a guest. Although product-sustaining and facility-sustaining activities usually do not change much over time and are performed on a regular basis, unit-based and batch-related activities will vary widely. In fact, some hotels can execute activities as requested, without prior planning. The activities performed on a more frequent level, and those activities that are especially costly to execute, will provide the hotel with the greatest area for tracking and improvement once an activity-based costing system has been implemented.

Transient guests have diverse behaviours

One qualitative difference between the hotel industry and other industries' cost systems is the need to model customer behaviour when analysing sources of demand. Which customers are more profitable to have? Which services or customers are the most profitable? Will guests use other products and services within the hotel? Such variable behaviour by guests can make it exceedingly difficult to target and minimize the costs associated with transient customers. The business segment customer groups, however, provide the largest opportunity for hotels to benefit from an activity-based costing system, because almost all functions associated with the business segment are commonly scheduled far in advance, which allows for better forecasting of activities and more efficient and cost effective resource allocation and consumption.

In addition to having distinct characteristics that present challenges to activity-based costing implementation, the hotel industry presents some strong opportunities for activity-based costing to assist in cost reduction and well-informed managerial decision-making. Three conditions in the hotel industry that could be readily addressed by the implementation of an activity-based costing system have been identified.

Fixed overhead is a large proportion of total costs in a hotel

Indirect labour and fixed overhead represent a large proportion of the total costs in hotels. Management should focus on elimination or reducing overhead, which in turn requires the identification and addressing of the real cause of overhead. Most hotel companies have set up their accounting systems to meet the requirements for the *Uniform System of Accounts for the Lodging Industry*. However, under the Uniform System the indirect overhead costs are not allocated to the departmental level. Costs that escape departmental tracking usually include: administrative and general, data processing, human resources, transportation, marketing, guest entertainment, energy costs and property operation and maintenance. Typically, these costs average 25 per cent of the total costs associated with the property. The distribution of overhead costs to the departments and activities that drive them would be a major advantage for the hospitality industry. By implementing the activity-based costing system, hotel companies could begin to realize true profitability of departments, outlets and market segments and to make profit-maximizing decisions accordingly.

Activity focus can potentially improve the service delivery to customers

Customer service is the key element in the battle for volume and margin in the hospitality industry. Within each property type and each market segment, a level of service is expected by the customers. To maintain a property's market share, the managers need to embark upon operational improvements that streamline the hotel's cost structure without decreasing the level of service received by the guest. Activity-based costing increases management's focus on all of the activities performed within the organization. Through this focus, management can begin to eliminate non-value adding activities, cut out operational excesses and reduce unnecessary service delays or repetitions. These changes will assist management in meeting its goal of maximizing profits while maintaining or improving service quality for the customer and thus maintaining or increasing market share.

Hotel managers can increase operational efficiency and decrease costs by shortening the service delivery cycle. Processes should be kept down to as few activities as possible. By timing processes from start to finish, management can better track operational improvements.

Large improvements in measures of profitability for market segments are available

Currently, management reports for hotels do not match costs with related revenues for each market segment; hotel managers are not aware of the profitability of different market segments. Managerial decisions, therefore, about long-term pricing of hotel rooms and, to what extent which markets should be targeted with advertising dollars, are based on inaccurate cost information. Measurement of profitability of market segments is yet another one of numerous benefits which hotels could gain from an activity-based costing system.

Long-range planning for group business, along with the utilization of an activity-based costing system, would allow the hotel to forecast the resources that will be consumed and the resulting costs. As a result, the hotel would be better able to estimate profit margins for particular market segments and group business. Sales managers involved in contract negotiations should utilize activity-based costing in order to target the most profitable groups.

The process of booking clients and signing contracts represents a relatively fixed cost. The variable costs come into play during contract negotiation. If a sales manager had to select between two customer groups, normally, the highest revenue-producing group would get the contract. If the members of that higher revenue-producing group had made different requests for services throughout the duration of their stay, however, the customer group bringing in the highest revenue may not be the most profitable.

The importance of understanding the activities customers request and utilize, and the resulting costs of each activity, cannot be underestimated. By correctly applying a customer profitability model, the sales manager can estimate the amount of hotel resources that will be consumed and the profit margin earned. For instance, if an activity-based costing system were utilized, the sales manager could gauge the costs of requested activities such as nightly turndown, or the profitability impact and implications of a buffet versus sit-down dinner. In order for a hotel to turn the focus on activities and profitability, the compensation system for the sales force should incorporate profit-related factors as well. Sales managers should not be given revenue-based incentives. Once the activity-based costing system is implemented, managers can assess the profitability of all activities requested by a particular group and book accordingly.

The framework for activity-based costing traces segments and reassigns costs based on the cause-and-effect demands triggered by customers and their orders. As previously described, activity-based costing refers to these triggers as 'activity drivers'. When the cost of processing a customer's request is subtracted from the sales amount for those requests, a company can really know whether it actually made or lost money on a transaction. A company might even estimate prospectively whether an accepted price quote for a future customer order will be profitable or not.

In addition, the customer profitability models, by taking into account some of the overhead expenses and by assigning them to specific activities, could prevent unproductive inter-departmental competition that does not reflect the fully distributed costs of the activities in which each department is engaged. The benefit of the profitability model is not only determining the profit contribution of customers, including accurate costs for the services they buy, but also understanding the elements of customer-specific work that make up the entire costs to serve each customer. It is no longer acceptable not to have a rational system of assigning so-called non-traceable costs to their sources of origin, whether those sources are products or customers.

Customer profitability information

Customer profitability information is obtained almost as a by-product of an activity-based costing model. After an activity-based costing model has been built the last few steps to form customer profitability are fairly straightforward. The key requirement to obtaining customer profitability is the presence of a customer account. The objective of customer profitability analysis is to assign the revenues, expenses, assets and liabilities of an organization to the customers who cause them (Howell and Soucy, 1990). The customer profitability for any time period can be expressed as Storbacka (1994) puts it:

$$Customer\ profitability = Relationship\ Revenue - Relationship\ Cost$$

Both relationship revenues and relationship costs consist of several underlying items that are specific to the activities in a particular organization. First, to record customer profitability, the company needs a marker or an indicator to distinguish positively its customers from each other, which in the context of computer systems implies the presence of the company-wide customer coding. With coding, systems are able to transfer data reliably. Second, besides positive identification, a customer account is also needed. Usually the account's number is the customer's code in the system. The account is created at the same time as the customer is created in the account system and becomes the company's client. The purpose of an account is to accumulate customers' periodic profitability data. Every month (or other period) customers' periodic profit is accounted for and accumulated to the account.

In the activity-based costing model, all customers, or customers as segments, are usually included. In the model they are cost objects, in the same way as the company's products are. The costing model that is built to interface with the activity-based costing software, allocates costs to the customers according to their activity usage. Activities customers use are, for instance, work performed for them by the company, financial investments made by the company, or special treatment received. Special treatment can be made for the price discounts and free services provided by the sellers. Because all activities have some costs associated with them, all costs incurred are transferred to the customer's account.

While activity-based costing calculates costs, revenues are usually handled by the sales systems. A sales system typically produces highly detailed data by types, units, sales prices and order quantities. When this revenue information is consolidated with the costing information, the two systems together form the customer profitability model. Figure 10.3 illustrates an example of a customer profitability account.

A periodic customer profitability account figure is created by subtracting periodic customer costs from revenues produced by the customer during the same period (Howell and Soucy, 1990). The individual items in a calculation can vary greatly from company to company. Also, annual figures are basically formed as a sum of monthly (or other periodic) results. When estimating customer profitability at some periodic level, there is the need to verify that the costs for activities that are carried out less frequently, are

Customer profitability:

        sales revenue from customer

    + other income from customer

    − discounts

    − direct marketing support

    − customer distribution costs

    − cost of sales

    − equipment costs

    − inventory holding costs

    − service costs

    − credit costs

    − other costs

    − etc.

    = customer profitability

Figure 10.3
Formation of periodic customer profitability information.

accounted for. These activities are carried out maybe only once a year. A carefully designed activity-based costing model should be able to account for these costs also.

Customer base analysis

What does ready access to customer information usually reveal? First, the information quantifies what most may already have suspected: all customers are not the same. Some customers may be more or less profitable based strictly on how demanding their behaviour is. Although customer satisfaction is important, a longer-term goal is to increase customer and corporate profitably. There must always be a balance between managing the level of customer service to earn customer satisfaction and the impact from doing so that will have on stakeholder wealth. The somewhat elusive goal is to increase customer satisfaction profitably. Because increasingly more customers will expect and demand customization rather than standard products and services, therefore, understanding this balance is important. Activity-based costing data facilitate discussions and potential actions needed to arrive at that balance.

Most importantly, if a customer group is revealed to be unprofitable, then the company should not necessarily abandon the customers and refuse doing business with that group. The lack of profitability might be a result of the company's own pricing policies. Customers are unprofitable only because company strategies and forms of operation make unprofitable customer behaviour possible (Storbacka et al., 1999). Flawed pricing policies are also usually responsible for the top profit customers being vulnerable to defection to competitors because the customers are being underserved (Zeithaml et al., 2001).

Maintaining a positive attitude towards unprofitable customers is essential. After profitability figures are utilized by the company, one pitfall to be avoided is letting the company personnel regard or treat the unprofitable customers as 'bad' customers. Poor treatment and reduced service may only further aggravate the profitability problems. It is therefore important for a company to view even an unprofitable customer in a positive light. Unprofitable customers are company acquired customers, and often represent the greatest profit potential a company has (Storbacka et al., 1999).

Ideally, the aim of a hotel company should be to maximize retention of existing profitable customers and to increase the rate at which new profitable customers are added. Existing unprofitable customers are, however, important because much less labour and capital resources are required to develop an existing unprofitable customer into a profitable one, compared to finding a new profitable customer. In addition, a customer may be unprofitable in the short run (especially a newly acquired customer), but may turn out to be profitable in the long run. Some customers may also act as important referrals and attract other customers, who could be profitable (Campbell, 2001).

Often customers do not want to be considered unprofitable, because they are aware that being considered unprofitable has adverse effects on the service they are able to receive from the provider (Storbacka et al., 1999). Customers are thus often truly interested in making their relationship profitable if the profitability issue is addressed with them. The measures have to be focused on mutually trying to find an agreement that both parties can accept. Even though some of the academic literature suggests such an open approach, it may not always be appropriate.

Several approaches to analysing customer profitability are suggested. One of these is to determine the course of action needed by comparing the customers in a matrix that combines customer profitability and the level of customer focus (Figure 10.4) (Kaplan and Narayanan, 2001).

Figure 10.4 provides a two-axis view of customers with regard to the two layers of the 'composite margin' of what each purchases (reflecting net prices to the customer) and its 'cost-to-serve'. Each quadrant of the matrix represents a zone in which four different

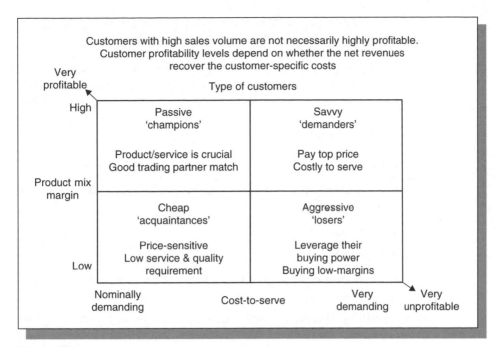

Customers with high sales volume are not necessarily highly profitable. Customer profitability levels depend on whether the net revenues recover the customer-specific costs

Figure 10.4
Activity-based costing customer profitability matrix.

types of customers can exist. Figure 10.4, of course, contradicts the general assumption that customers with the highest sales usually generate the highest profits.

For each customer group in Figure 10.4, the company should follow several recommended actions:

- *Champions* – the best type of customers. They are loyal, purchase a lot and can be nearly effortless to service.

- *Demanders* – *savvy* customers that may generate positive profits, but who make heavy uncompensated demands on resources. It is necessary to grow their revenues, but manage how they cause costs.

- *Acquaintances* – the eponymous *cheap* customers. It might be dangerous to build business based on them, but might be necessary to have them because they contribute marginal profits with relatively low maintenance. Growing revenues associated with such customers is a positive factor – but the growth must be done economically. Such customers are price-sensitive and may not put much importance on levels of service or quality.

- *Losers* – *aggressive* customers who drain resources and time yet provide little – and probably negative – financial return. Their

205

size and volume may have exacted a negotiated pricing discount beyond what was perceived as profitable.

Figure 10.4 shows various customers as points of an intersection on the matrix. The objective is to make all customers more profitable, represented by driving them to the upper-left corner. Although this is a partial list, making customers more profitable can be accomplished by:

- Managing each customer's 'costs-to-serve' to a lower level
- Establishing a surcharge for or re-pricing expensive 'costs-to-serve' activities
- Reducing services
- Raising prices
- Increasing costs on activities that a customer shows a preference for
- Shifting the customer's purchase mix toward richer, higher-margin products and service lines
- Discounting to gain more volume with low 'costs-to-serve' customers.

Another technique to analyse the customer base is to plot the company's customers in a matrix of customer strategic significance and customer profitability (Figure 10.5) (Cokins, 2004). The arrows in the matrix signify the customer development directions.

Note that migrating customers to the upper-left corner is equivalent to moving individual data points in the profit profile in Figure 10.5 from right to left and bottom to top. Knowing where customers are located on the matrix requires activity-based costing data.

Individual customers have the potential to produce even greater profits in the future beyond simply providing additional profits from incrementally higher revenues from their additional purchases. Other tangential profits come from the following:

- Reduced operating costs from economies of scale
- Word-of-mouth referrals by the customers to others who become new customers
- Premium pricing that can be achieved with loyal customers.

The combined effect of these sources of profit generated from a single customer highlight the importance of high customer retention

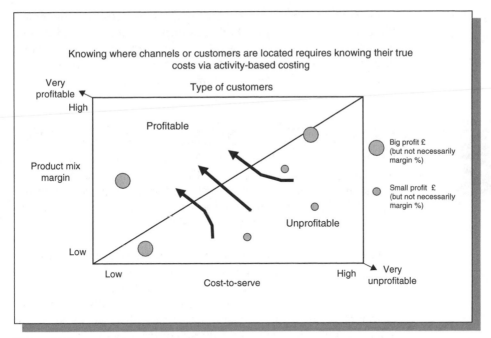

Figure 10.5
Migrating customers to higher profitability.

rates, the value derived from customer loyalty and the opportunity cost of losing profitable customers.

Some customers may be located so deep in the lower-right corner of the customer profitability matrix that the company will conclude that it is impractical to achieve profitability with them and they should be terminated. After all, the goal of a business is not to improve customer satisfaction at any cost, but rather to attempt to manage customer relationships to improve long-term corporate profitability.

Another critical reason for knowing where each of the customer groups is located on the profitability matrix is to protect the most profitable customers from competitors. If, in a business, very few customers account for a significant portion of the profits, the risk exposure could be enormous. The farther to the left side of the customer profitability matrix (Figures 10.4 and 10.5) the customer is located, the more sensitive the bottom line profit is to competitor attacks on key customers.

In addition, customer profitability analysis is already itself a very useful and revealing tool for the account manager to improve customer profitability. Using customer information, the account manager can attempt to convert an unprofitable account to a profitable account in several ways. It is possible, for instance, to increase revenues or cut costs by reducing activities that cause the account to be unprofitable. Examples of activity reductions are changing delivery schedule or delivery methods to more affordable ones, reducing sales personnel services for the customer, managing product price and managing service price.

Conclusion

For customer profitability analysis the process of maturation has only started. The discipline is still developing and commonly agreed models are yet to be established. In defining the customer equity and profitability, and the coexistence of the two, many theories are still searching for their place and new ones are being developed.

Most hotel companies still do not calculate customer profitability, and neither have they installed the systems required. This is possibly because there are still many companies that do not use activity-based costing, which is often seen practically as a precondition to accumulating customer profitability information, at least in a somewhat meaningful and continuous manner.

Customer profitability analysis is not without problem areas which are in its more involved and somewhat convoluted accounting. In addition, the method is somewhat complicated and requires the constant updating of the accounting model (usually within the activity-based costing software application) according to the changes in the real operations. If the updating is not performed, the model will produce erroneous results. The danger of not having a fully implemented customer profitability system is the possibility of mistaken management decisions. Therefore, to assure the correct accounting of the 'driver' information, customer profitability relationship requires a much closer relationship between the accounting department and all other departments of the hotel than before. Such a closer relationship is not the responsibility of the accounting department alone, but rather rests in the decision-making and operations of all departments that interface with the customer. A big challenge for hotel organizations is to make customer-oriented departments work routinely, smoothly and efficiently together.

References

Atkinson, A., Banker, R., Kaplan, R. and Young, M. (1997) *Management Accounting*. Prentice-Hall, Englewood Cliffs.

Bellis-Jones, R. (1989) Customer profitability analysis. *Management Accounting*, **67** (2), 26–28.

Brimson, J. and Antos, J. (1994) *Activity-Based Management for Service Industries, Government Entities, and Nonprofit Organisations*. John Wiley & Sons, New York.

Campbell, A. (2001) Generational revenue analysis. *CPA Journal*, **71** (2), 58–61.

Cokins, G. (2004) Are all your customers profitable to you? *SAS White Paper*.

Donaghy, K., McMahon, U. and McDowell, D. (1995) Yield management: an overview. *International Journal of Hospitality Management*, **14** (2), 139–150.

Downie, N. (1997) The use of accounting information in hotel marketing decisions. *International Journal of Hospitality Management*, **16** (3), 305–312.

Foster, G., Gupta, M. and Sjoblom, L. (1996) Customer profitability analysis: challenges and new directions. *Cost Management*, **10** (1), 5–17.

Gurau, C. and Ranchhod, A. (2002) How to calculate the value of a customer – measuring customer satisfaction: a platform for calculation, predicting and increasing customer profitability. *Journal of Targeting, Measurement and Analysis for Marketing*, **10** (3), 233–249.

Howell, R. and Soucy, S. (1990) Customer profitability as critical as product profitability. *Management Accounting*, **72** (4), 43–47.

Johnson, H. and Kaplan, R. (1987) *Relevance lost: the rise and fall of management accounting*. Harvard Business School Press, Boston.

Jones, P. and Hamilton, D. (1992) Yield management: putting people in the big picture. *The Cornell Hotel and Restaurant Administration Quarterly*, **33** (1), 89–96.

Kaplan, R. and Narayanan, V. (2001) Measuring and managing customer profitability. *Journal of Cost Management*, **15** (5), 5–15.

Kirpalani, V. and Shapiro, S. (1973) Financial dimensions of marketing management. *Journal of Marketing*, **37** (2), 40–47.

Mossman, F., Fischer, P. and Crissy, W. (1974) New approaches to analyzing market profitability. *Journal of Marketing*, **38** (2), 43–48.

Noone, B. and Griffin, P. (1998) Development of an activity-based customer profitability system for yield management. *Progress in Tourism and Hospitality Research*, **4** (3), 279–292.

Regan, R. (1989) *Hotel Revenue Management*. Revenue Dynamics, Seattle.

Riley, M. (1999) Know your customer. *Financial Executive*, **15** (1), 38–42.

Storbacka, K. (1994) *The Nature of Customer Relationship Profitability*. Swedish School of Economics and Business Administration, Research Report 55, Helsingfors.

Storbacka, K., Sivula, P. and Kaario, K. (1999) *Create value with strategic accounts*. Kauppakaari Oyj, Helsinki.

Uniform System of Accounts for the Lodging Industry, 9th edn. (1996) Educational Institute of the American Hotel and Motel Association, East Lansing.

Ward, K. (1989) *Financial Aspects of Marketing*. Butterworth-Heinemann, London.

Zeithaml, V., Rust, R. and Lemon, K. (2001) The customer pyramid: creating and serving profitable customers. *California Management Review*, **43** (4), 118–146.

CHAPTER 11

Room rate pricing: a resource-advantage perspective

Jean-Pierre I. van der Rest

Introduction

'Economic theory, or more specifically the theory of price, is not an exact science. It is a conglomeration of principles and assumptions concerning the behaviour of individuals and firms put together in a specified paradigm to 'explain' the behaviour of prices in markets (Narasimhan, 1984:S27). Therefore, economic models and theories do not claim to describe the processes by which people in firms actually make decisions. They claim rather to explain why certain decisions persist.

Economic models are not designed to describe realistically the way firms make pricing decisions or the way consumers respond. Economic models are abstractions: they exclude or hold constant many real variables that are not germane to the theoretical objectives. Consequently, they rarely provide practical algorithms for implementing pricing decisions.

(Nagle, 1984:S3–S4)

In practice, the pricing decision tends to be the responsibility of the marketing manager who sets a price within the context of his overall marketing strategy. He seeks a practical solution to the problem of finding a 'right' price level at which to sell the good or service.

(Dorward, 1987:66)

[M]arketing academics and practitioners, whose goal is to help firms make better pricing decisions, can little afford to ignore the interrelationships between price and other marketing variables that economists hold constant.

(Nagle, 1984:S4)

This does not suggest that economic models and theories are irrelevant to practical pricing problems. 'Economic models may be weak in specific prescriptions for individual action, but they are strong in useful heuristics for understanding the consequences of action' (Nagle, 1984:S4). Economics contributes a set of elementary concepts and insights, analytical methods, paradigms and guides useful in various pricing decisions. Ultimately, company pricing policy is the task of marketing. Economics provides a sound foundation of theory that proves the marketer's task less strenuous. 'In the extreme, price theory in economics deals with how markets behave, while price theory in marketing science deals with how managers should act' (Hauser, 1984:S65). Economists aim to analyse broad economic changes and to evaluate existing and prospective social controls. When they study market forces they typically simplify the model of the manager's task. However, when marketing managers study the way their actions impact upon profits, they typically simplify the model of the market mechanism (Hauser, 1984). '[T]hey advocate principles of pricing which they believe are applied by *the better firms*' (Smyth, 1967:117, emphasis added). In contrast, economic theory 'is more impressed by what the *majority* of firms *appear* to do' (Smyth, 1967:117, emphasis added). As a result, price theory cannot function as a practical instrument to describe or prescribe the pricing decision in practice (Gutenberg, 1928; Harper, 1966; Langholm, 1969; Cyert and Hedrick, 1972; Said, 1981).

This chapter, therefore, proposes a new perspective to the study of room rate pricing by drawing on a different and more general theory of competition (Hunt and Morgan, 1995) – as an alternative to price theory in neoclassical economics – to enable the exploration of room rate pricing practices in 'the better firms' (i.e. hotels with superior performance). This theory is referred to as the 'comparative advantage theory of competition', or 'resource-advantage theory'. Its major advantage is its ability to build upon existing knowledge while addressing limitations previously ascribed to the economic paradigm. The chapter synthesizes a meta-analysis of pricing theory with a large-scale interview study in an international hotel group.

The multifaceted character of price

Economists define price as 'what must be given in exchange for something' (Bannock et al., 1992:336). That is, they consider price 'as a ratio indicating the quantities of money needed to exchange a given quantity of goods or services' (Monroe, 2003:5).

Figure 11.1 illustrates the economist's definition of price as a ratio of two 'get components'. A price-setter can change price, or the value-in-exchange, by altering the numerator or the denominator. In behavioural marketing theory, however, it is common to consider price only as a 'give component' (Ahtola, 1984). Thus, from a *guest's* perspective, a *room* price is what is given up or sacrificed to make use of a room for one night. (Cox (1946) and

$$Price = \frac{Quantity\ of\ money\ received\ by\ the\ seller}{Quantity\ of\ goods\ and\ services\ received\ by\ the\ buyer}$$

Figure 11.1
Price as a ratio of two 'Get Components'.
Source: adapted from Monroe, K.B. (2003) *Pricing: making profitable decisions*. McGraw-Hill.

Harper (1966) argue that the denominator of ratio 11.1 includes all elements of the service offering.)

Typically, but not exclusively, sacrifice refers to the perceived *monetary* sacrifice. Time cost, search costs, convenience cost, and psychic costs may enter either explicitly or implicitly into the guest's perception of sacrifice (Down, 1961; Mincer, 1963; Linder, 1970; Mabry, 1970; Nichols et al., 1971; Gronau, 1973; Leibowitz, 1974; Leuthold, 1981). Monetary price is therefore not the only sacrifice perceived by the guest (Zeithaml, 1988:11).

The model in Figure 11.2 illustrates the role of room rate on the guest's perceptions of quality, sacrifice, value and willingness to book. The model suggests that a guest's willingness to pay a particular rate is determined by his perceived value judgement. Nagle

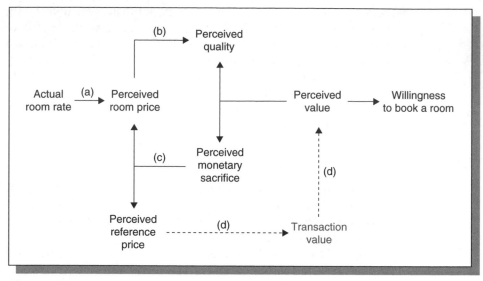

Figure 11.2
Relating price, quality and value.
Source: adapted from Monroe, K.B. (2003) *Pricing: making profitable decisions*. McGraw-Hill, pp. 101–199 and Zeithaml, V.A. (1988) Consumer perceptions of price, quality and value: a means-end model and synthesis of evidence. *Journal of Marketing*, **52**, pp. 2–22.

and Holden (1995:77–94) summarize considerations that mitigate the importance of value relative to the importance of other factors (e.g. effects of perceived substitutes, unique value, switching cost, difficult comparisons, price quality, expenditures, end-benefits, shared costs, fairness, and inventories). This judgement involves a mental trade-off between the perceived quality or benefits a guest receives in the room night relative to the (monetary) sacrifice he perceives by paying the rate. What constitutes customer value appears to be very personal and idiosyncratic. Guests may define it as 'low room price', 'whatever I want in a room night', 'what I get for what I give', or 'the quality I get for the room price I pay' (and, even within these definitions, guests may differ in opinion). However, value and quality are not the same. Perceived value is more individualistic, personal and difficult to measure. Value (unlike quality) involves a trade-off (Zeithaml, 1988:13–14).

The model posits that willingness to book a room is positively related to perceived value. In addition, it suggests that perceived room price, rather than actual (objective) room rate, is the guest's relevant decision-making variable (Jacoby and Olson, 1977). The model presumes a positive relationship between perceived room price and perceived quality, and perceived room price and perceived monetary sacrifice. Thus, guests may use perceived price as an indicator of quality, i.e. an attracting attribute, as well as a measure of perceived sacrifice, i.e. a repelling attribute (Leavitt, 1954; Dodds and Monroe, 1985; Erickson and Johansson, 1985). Monroe (2003) argues that it is this dual, conflicting nature of price that complicates understanding of how (room) rates affect booking decisions. Linkage:

1 signifies that perceived room price has a meaning that is distinct from its objective meaning in terms of perceived monetary sacrifice, e.g. the psychophysics of prices (Monroe, 1971, 1973), price consciousness (Gabor and Granger, 1961; Monroe et al., 1986), encoding (Jacoby and Olson, 1977)

2 symbolizes the notion that perceived quality is a function of price (e.g. Scitovsky, 1944; Gabor and Granger, 1966; Lambert, 1980)

3 represents the supposition that guests may evaluate prices by comparing actual room rates to some price frame of reference (e.g. Ginzberg, 1936; Scitovsky, 1944; Adam, 1958). When this reference price is larger than the perceived room price, it is argued that perceived value may be supplemented by a so-called transaction-value (Thaler, 1985; Monroe and Chapman, 1987; Mano and Elliott, 1997). The concept of a reference price would only be valid, however, under the assumption that guests are capable of remembering room rate price information

4 has, therefore, been marked by a dotted line.

It thus appears that there is more to the setting of a room price than simply establishing a monetary rate to be exchanged (Monroe, 2003). In practice, pricing is about setting value and not price (Leszinsky and Marn, 1997). This is because price has a dual, relative and conflicting role in the consumer buying decision-process.

A conceptual framework for room rate pricing

Although economic theory may not be very helpful to prescribe the room rate pricing decision in practice, however, it can be extremely useful to identify the general forces or factors that are relevant to a *conceptual framework* for pricing decision-making (Hawkins, 1940).

Figure 11.3 suggests that there is a hotelier's maximum (theoretical) initial price discretion. This discretion is defined by customer-value produced (utility/preferences ceiling) and value sacrificed (cost floor). Utility determines the absolute highest room price a guest is willing to pay. Costs (direct variable) determine the absolute lowest rate a hotel can offer without making a loss (in the short term).

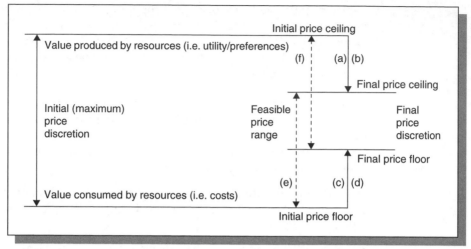

Figure 11.3
Conceptual framework for room rate pricing.
Source: adapted from Monroe, K.B. (2003) *Pricing: making profitable decisions*. McGraw-Hill,
pp. 11–21, Ingenbleek, P.T.M. (2002) Money for value. CentER: Tilburg University, p. 37 and
Dutta, S. et al. (2002) Pricing as a strategic capability. *Sloan Management Review*, **43**, pp. 61–66.

In practice this initial price discretion will be influenced by a
number of factors and forces that affect the hotelier's ability to build
and maintain successful relationships with guests. The existence
and dynamic nature of these influences – which are internal and
external to the hotel's operating environment – lower the maximum and raise the minimum level of the price discretion, thereby
narrowing down the range of feasible room rate prices. Internal
factors, indicated by (a) and (c), involve the company's tangible
and intangible (i.e. relational and competences) resources. External
factors, shown by (b) and (d), comprise demographic, regulatory,
economic, technological and social forces, factors that impact upon
the nature of competition, as well as various actors such as customers, competitors, suppliers and intermediaries. It is, therefore,
the hotelier's arduous job to discover his real and feasible (non-
theoretical) price range (i.e. the final price discretion). This ultimate discretion, or 'range of mutual benefit' (Boulding, 1966:34), is
made of those room rates where the rates at which a guest will
book the room (e) equal the rates at which the hotelier will sell (f).
Finding this range, then, is the root of all theoretical and practical
pricing problems. Once a range of feasible prices is established,
the consequences of most actions can be understood by the application of (neoclassical) concepts and insights, analytical methods,
paradigms and guides available in the empirical literature.

The notion of a price discretion has been a very important innovation in pricing theory (Ingenbleek, 2002). A hotel with relatively

high costs and relatively low customer value produced will have a relatively smaller range of feasible room prices. For such a hotel, room rate pricing will be more difficult as the statistical chance of finding the range of mutual benefit will be relatively lower. The opposite also holds. A hotel that consumes relatively low costs and produces relatively high customer value will have a bigger range of feasible room prices. This hotel will have relatively fewer difficulties due to a relatively higher statistical chance of finding the range of mutual benefit.

A price discretion refers to the ability or power to make informed pricing decisions. The literature on pricing suggests that there is no single, universal approach to make well-informed room rate pricing decisions (Oxenfeldt, 1973). Every approach is, however, in essence the same: a process of collecting, exchanging and inter-preting information. Room rate pricing is an organization process involving the discussions and negotiations between different business functions such as marketing, sales, accounting and finance (Pearce, 1956; Hague, 1971). Hoteliers can base their judgement (i.e. the end-state decision) on three types of information: customer value (i.e. benefits to the guest), competition, and costs. Recent findings indicate that these types are not mutually exclusive (Noble and Gruca, 1999). The hotelier's discretion depends on a certain degree of information of each type. This concept of information type is essential as it represents the hotelier's internal and external operating environments which constitute the room rate discretion. Therefore, it is better to refer to cost-informed, competition-informed and value-informed room rate pricing, instead of the neoclassical economic nomenclature cost-based, competition-based and value-based pricing (Ingenbleek et al., 2001).

Room rate pricing as the fundamental basis of organizational efforts

'A hotel or motel may be viewed as offering a product line con-sisting of different types of rooms and different types of occu-pancy, usually single or double' (Monroe, 1990:312). Such product line poses two particular pricing problems: perishability and bind-ing capacity constraints. These problems encourage a business orientation in which hotels attempt to fill room capacity. To fill room capacity profitably, hotels use complex pricing systems administered by a computer. These so-called yield management systems employ techniques such as early discounting, overbooking and limiting early sales (Desiraju and Shugan, 1999). The practice of using the techniques is referred to as yield management (Lieberman, 1993). A yield management system can be viewed as a tool for implementing an optimal, multi-period pricing strategy in which each room price is a function of forecasted excess capacity (Desiraju and Shugan, 1999:45). 'Yield management is a revenue maximization technique which aims to increase net yield through the predictive allocation of available bedroom capacity to predetermined market segments at optimum price' (Donaghy et al., 1995:140).

Over reliance on revenue maximization techniques holds the danger of a too strong inside-out emphasis. A true market-oriented business sets value, not revenue. Setting value requires a comprehensive outside-focus, a real understanding of the customer. Just like pricing, '[t]he process of managing yield is basically a human activity' (Yeoman and Watson, 1997:80). Therefore, 'a successful yield-management system depends on people as much as on sophisticated technology' (Jones and Hamilton, 1992:95). As Relihan (1989:40) argued, 'yield management can dramatically increase revenues for a hotel operator. But it's not a substitute for poor marketing or poor sales'. For example, it may motivate a suboptimal desire to serve additional customer segments (Enz et al., 1999). It may also give rise to a loss of competitive focus, customer alienation and severe employee morale problems. Inside-out reasoning may even induce unacceptable practices such as 'offering insufficient benefits in exchange for restrictions, imposing too severe a restriction on discounts and not informing the customer of changes in the reference transaction' (Kimes, 1994:29). Those practices hold a real danger of overlooking price fairness issues which play an important role in the customer value process (Kimes, 1994, 2002; Oh, 2000). Therefore, Orkin (1988:56, italics added) must be disagreed with, 'Yield management is not merely an adjunct to traditional managerial approaches. Instead, it represents a *fundamental* basis for concentrating organizational efforts'. Choi (2004) argues that variable pricing practices do not result in lower perceptions of fairness.

This belief has coloured the way practitioners and academics have viewed room rate pricing. For example, pricing is considered 'a purely financial decision' (Rogers, 1976:226) or 'conceptually a straightforward process' (Weatherford et al., 2001:53). But, as Professor Bill Quain most aptly stated (2003:173):

> I believe that it is getting harder and harder to find employees who have the drive to sell, the drive to create profits, and the drive to satisfy customers by filling more of their needs with ever improving products and services. This is a basic problem for revenue managers. It is not enough to create revenue-raising programs by manipulating prices. To be truly successful, hospitality operators must break the cycle of price consciousness that is so deeply

ingrained in both our customers and our employees. True success, the ability to maximize profits versus the expenditure of energy and resources, will take time. It will take training. Most of all, it will take a constant battle to link outcome with effort.

While discovering the range of mutual benefit, hoteliers must study the way room rates impact upon profits, revenue and yield. But, they need also to consider factors that no yield management system can appreciate. Revenue management is inherently quantitative. '[I]ts implementation involves serious issues arising from marketing, organizational behaviour, human resources, and information technology' (Kimes, 2003:137).

'Pricing is not merely a financial decision but must be fully integrated with other aspects in the marketing mix' (Rogers, 1977:16). As Rogers (1976:229) argued 'each pricing decision is specific and should be made with reference to the qualitative features of the individual unit and its sales mix'. In practice 'pricing is a marketing tool' (Lewis, 1986:21) calling for 'a strong understanding of what the various hotel guest segments value' (Varini et al., 2003:47). This tool can be supported by heuristics (Bitran and Mondschein, 1995; Weatherford, 1995; Baker and Collier, 1999), multiple-stage process models (Rogers, 1975; Kim et al., 2004), and guides for analysis (Lesure, 1983; Dunn and Brooks, 1990; Russo, 1991; Quain, 1992; Shaw, 1992; Wijeyesinghe, 1993; Cross, 1997; Lewis and Shoemaker, 1997; Orkin, 1998). Contemporary room rate pricing requires the thorough understanding of consumer behaviour and network organization principles (Enz, 2003). It involves the integration and alignment of internal operations, human resources and technologies (Enz et al., 1999). Moreover, it demands appropriate precautions to protect the various valuable revenue management system trade secrets (Kimes and Wagner, 2001). But, most and above all, it needs a strategic perspective which is quite different from 'discounting' room rates (Abbey, 1983; Nelson, 1992; Hanks et al., 1992, 2002; Enz et al., 2004).

A strategic marketing perspective to the study of room rate pricing

In the contest to capture the customer, hotels increasingly use room rate prices as a tactical weapon. Price effects are 'more immediate and direct, and appeals based on price are the easiest to communicate' (Rao, 1984:S39). Frequently, however, the skirmishing degenerates into a 'price war' (Rao et al., 2000:107). This has made economists and practitioners recognize 'that price is a dangerously explosive and complex variable' (Oxenfeldt, 1973:49).

Price is, however, only *one* aspect of competitive behaviour and studied independently will give a partial picture at best. It will be necessary, therefore, to study room rate pricing in the context of a more general theory of competition.

Hunt and Morgan (1995:1) argue that the marketing strategy literature 'is evolving toward a new theory of competition – one that has significant advantages over neoclassical theory'. They label this theory the 'comparative advantage theory of competition', or 'resource-advantage theory' (R-A theory). This theory is aimed to 'satisfactorily explain the micro phenomenon of firm diversity' (Hunt and Morgan, 1995:2). This diversity may exist across but also within industries. It may manifest itself through differences in size, scope, methods of operations, or financial performance. In other words, R-A theory seeks to explain, for example, why some firms, relative to others, achieve superior financial performance.

As Figure 11.4 illustrates, competition 'is a constant struggle among firms for com*para*tive advantages in resources that will yield marketplace positions of com*peti*tive advantage for some market segment(s) and, thereby, superior financial performance' (Hunt, 2000:135, emphasis added). Thus, some firms achieve superior financial performance because they have a relative competitive advantage arising from a relative comparative advantage in resources. As organizational learning is endogenous to the process of R-A competition, a certain level of performance may generate knowledge about the competitive position and the specific resources

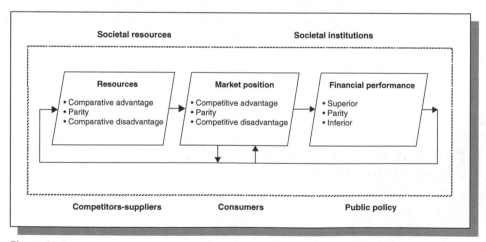

Figure 11.4

Resource-advantage competition.

Source: Hunt, S.D. and Morgan, R.M. (1997) Resource-advantage theory: a snake swallowing its tail or a general theory of competition? *Journal of Marketing*, **61**, 78.

on which this position is based. A firm may also learn in which resources it should invest in order to improve its market position. These resources include all means for the performance of value-adding, and extracting (i.e. pricing) activities.

As Figure 11.5 illustrates, nine possible competitive positions can result from the firm's resources. The figure should be read as follows: '[t]he marketplace position of competitive advantage

| | | Relative resource-produced value | | |
		Lower	Parity	Superior
Relative resource cost	Lower	1 Indeterminate position	2 Competitive advantage	3 Competitive advantage
	Parity	4 Competitive disadvantage	5 Parity position	6 Competitive advantage
	Higher	7 Competitive disadvantage	8 Competitive disadvantage	9 Indeterminate position

Figure 11.5
Competitive position matrix.
Source: Hunt, S.D. and Morgan, R.M. (1997) Resource-advantage theory: a snake swallowing its tail or a general theory of competition? *Journal of Marketing*, **61**, 78.

identified as Cell 3 results from the firm, relative to its competitors, having a resource assortment that enables it to produce an offering for some market segments that (1) is perceived to be of superior value and (2) is produced at lower costs' (Hunt and Morgan, 1996:109).

Ideally, a firm would prefer a competitive advantage as indicated by cell 3, but positions identified as cells 6 and 2 may also bring competitive advantage and superior returns. Conversely, a firm would try to avoid a competitive disadvantage as indicated by cell 7, although positions identified as cells 8 and 4 may also lead to a competitive disadvantage and inferior returns. Cell 5 represents the unlikely parity position which produces average returns. Firms occupying positions 1 and 9 may or may not achieve superior performance. For example, in cell 1, lower relative resource costs correlates with a sacrifice in relative value for consumers. Offering relatively lower prices to attract customers, the extent to which the price reduction is smaller, equal, or bigger than the relative advantage in resource costs, positions of competitive advantage, parity, or competitive disadvantage are achieved.

The role of room rate pricing in R-A theory

Price only receives implicit attention in R-A theory. This reflects the businessmen's preference for non-price rather than price competition (Oxenfeldt, 1975). The international hotel operating environment makes room rate pricing, however, relatively important. It assumes that firms that achieve superior financial performance also ask appropriate prices. If prices are too high, customers may shop at competitive firms which may affect financial performance. If prices are too low, the competitive advantage may not result in superior financial performance. Furthermore, it assumes that pricing practices are influenced by the various factors stipulated in Figure 11.4. Inflation, anti-trust legislation, customers' price sensitivity, competitive (re)actions, to name a few, may create unique and complex pricing problems for each decision process.

R-A competition suggests that the hoteliers' price discretions (i.e. ranges of mutual benefit) of rooms in parity market positions (cell 5) are identical because competing hoteliers have similar value and cost considerations. It also suggests that the price discretions of rooms in indeterminate market positions are either downward skewed (cell 1) or upward skewed (cell 9). Room rate discretions in competitive advantage market positions (cells 3,2/6) and competitive disadvantage market positions (cells 7,4/8) are respectively wider and narrower. Assuming a categorical scale, these suggestions are illustrated by Figures 11.6 and 11.7.

The arrow-headed lines in Figure 11.6 illustrate the width and position of each range of feasible room rates as derived from each hotel's market position cell. Cells 1, 5 and 9 have room rate discretions equal in width but at different positions within the maximum price discretion (see Figure 11.3). The widest room rate discretion exists in a competitive advantage market position (cell 3), and the narrowest in a competitive disadvantage market position (cell 7).

Assuming that a relative narrow price discretion (e.g. cell 7) reduces the success of setting appropriate room rates, it can be inferred that room rate pricing may be a more important resource

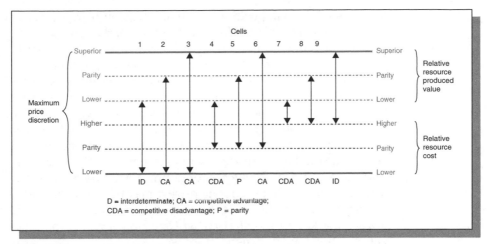

Figure 11.6
The room rate price discretion per market position.
Source: Rest, J.I. van der (2005) Room rate pricing in an international hotel group. (Oxford Brookes)

	Relative resource-produced value		
	Lower	Parity	Superior
Lower	**1** Downward skewed price discretion	**2** Wide price discretion	**3** Wide price discretion
Parity	**4** Narrow price discretion	**5** Similar price discretion	**6** Wide price discretion
Higher	**7** Narrow price discretion	**8** Narrow price discretion	**9** Upward skewed price discretion

Relative resource cost

Figure 11.7
The price discretion in the competitive position matrix.
Source: Hunt, S.D. and Morgan, R.M. (1997) Resource-advantage theory: a snake swallowing its tail or a general theory of competition? *Journal of Marketing*, **61**, 78.

to hotels with weak positions, than to hotels with strong market positions (*ceteris paribus*). Hotels with weak market positions may benefit from superior room rate pricing resources as it may enable the transformation of a weak into a strong market position. A superior pricing resource, however, will not compensate a position of competitive disadvantage. Competitive (dis)advantage is a function of relative cost and value, not of room rate prices. A superior resource may optimize financial performance, but it will not generate long-term superior returns for hoteliers in competitive disadvantage market positions. Assuming that a relative wide price discretion increases the success of setting appropriate room rates, it can be inferred that room rate pricing may be a less demanding activity to hotels with strong market positions, than to hotels with a weak market position (*ceteris paribus*). Hotels with strong market positions may benefit from superior room rate pricing resources as it may increase the financial returns that flow from this market position.

R-A theory suggests that a hotelier should reconsider room rate prices when his competitive position matrix is altered. As reconsideration implies both initial and subsequent processes, we may distinguish between room rate price *setting* processes and room rate price *changing* processes. Setting refers to a planning process, whereas changing signifies a tactical process. Reconsideration may or may not lead to alterations in room rate prices.

R-A competition also suggests that room rate prices result from organizational processes which are rooted in tangible and intangible pricing resources. Although an enumeration of room rate pricing resources is unavailable from the literature, a first step may be the recognition of Day's (1994) work on *capabilities*. Day made a classification based on the assumption that three types of capabilities can be identified in all businesses. His classification, as illustrated by Figure 11.8, has been adapted to a hospitality service context. Depending on the orientation and focus of the processes, inside-out, outside-in and spanning capabilities can be distinguished. For example, a yield management capability is deployed from *inside-out* and activated by market requirements, competitive challenges and external opportunities. The focal point of, let's say, a sales directors' market sensing capability is, however, almost exclusively outside the hotel. The purpose of this *outside-in* capability is to connect the processes that define the other organizational capabilities to the external operating environment and to enable the hotel to compete by proactively anticipating market(ing) requirements and creating long-lasting relationships with key clients and third-party distributors. A *spanning* capability is needed to integrate the inside-out and the outside-in capabilities. Room rate pricing, for instance, must be informed by both external and internal capabilities.

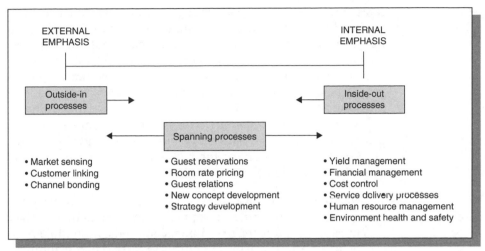

Figure 11.8
Room rate pricing as a spanning capability.
Source: adapted from Day, G.S. (1994) The capabilities of market-driven organisations. *Journal of Marketing*, **58** (10), 37–52.

Room rate pricing as a spanning capability is a specific pricing resource which enables the hotelier to organize the pricing processes in ways that enable understanding of the room rate price discretion *and* extraction of value created. This process evolves through the process of learning right and wrong things (Hunt and Morgan, 1996). Hotels with a clear market-orientation may have superior outside-in capabilities that inform and guide both spanning and inside-out processes. 'The effect is to shift the span of all processes further downward the external end of the orientation dimension' (Day, 1994:41). The spanning and inside-out capabilities of internally focused hotels, however, may be poorly guided by external considerations which confines them to the internal end of the orientation spectrum. Room rate pricing is, however, different from other spanning processes. For example, guest reservations, guest relations and strategy development may recognize, create, or deliver customer value. Room rate pricing only extracts customer value. The concept of transaction-value (see Figure 11.2) suggests that pricing may involve more than value appropriation.

Exploring the room rate pricing capability

To understand what a hotel can do to discover its range of mutual benefit, it is necessary to first describe the processes by which room rate prices are set or changed in practice. Describing how the hotel properties in an international hotel group go about room rate pricing is, however, not a straightforward task. Managers who are involved in the pricing of room rates often find it difficult to formalize their thinking. Intuitive judgements bulk the decisions which are dependent on a great many variables. Moreover, the extraordinary complexity of pricing precludes presenting the entire process behind the spanning capability. Nonetheless, for exploratory purposes, it may be possible to identify the major dimensions of a room rate pricing capability. This capability comprises pricing processes at both the head-office and the individual property level of the hotel group. At the head-office level several pricing activities are carried out including:

1 developing a general pricing policy, approving property pricing strategies and offering support to individual hotels. These activities constitute the first dimension. At the individual property level various pricing activities are carried out including:

2 determining and adjusting a pricing strategy

3 learning and fine-tuning prices

4 negotiating and explaining prices to the market.

These activities constitute the other three dimensions.

With the determination of these four dimensions it may be possible to identify resources that help or prevent the process of discovering the range of mutual benefit and, ultimately, the setting and changing of appropriate room rate prices. Following the resource-advantage view outlined in the previous sections, it is suggested that these resources may explain the diversity in room rate pricing processes by which individual properties in an international hotel group seek to discover the range of feasible prices. More specifically, it is argued that some hotels may have better knowledge of the range of mutual benefit because they enjoy a *comparative advantage* in these resources.

In the field of strategic management there is no generally accepted classification for resources. However, distinctions between tangible versus intangible resources and relational resources versus competences are commonly made (De Wit and Meyer, 2004). Tangible resources include materials and computer systems. Intangible resources include relational resources and competences. Relational resources comprise internal relationships (i.e. intra-organizational, team, or direct), external relationships (i.e. inter-organizational or direct). (There was limited evidence available on reputation sources.) Competences include knowledge (i.e. know-how, know-what, know-where, know-when, know-why), skills (i.e. the ability to carry out a narrow task or activity), and attitude (i.e. mind set, disposition, or will). Table 11.1 illustrates the various

Table 11.1
The resource base for room rate pricing practice in an international hotel group

Spanning activities	Tangible resources	Relational resources	Competences
Developing pricing policy, approving pricing strategy and offering support	Materials: • strategic pricing handbook • revenue management library	Internal relationships: • intra-organizational (property management, regional management)	Knowledge: • insight in participants' preferences Attitude: • mind set to learn from critical comments
Determining and adjusting pricing strategy	Materials: • business plan • budget and forecast Computer systems: • rate positioning diagram • rate effectiveness tool • accounts performance tool • stay and spend tool	Internal relationships: • team (revenue management team) External relationships: • direct (clients, business community, government agency, rivals) • inter-organizational (travel industry)	Knowledge: • competitor pricing (history), product (hard- and software), clients feeder markets, channel inter-mediaries and demand generators • own property's relative hard- and software Skills: • selecting competitors, making relevant comparisons, determining general price levels • establishing (tacit) information sources • performing financial analyses communicating price changes • establishing routines to resolve goal conflicts Attitude: • will to commit to action plan

(Continued)

Table 11.1
(*Continued*)

Spanning activities	Tangible resources	Relational resources	Competences
Learning and fine-tuning prices	Materials: • revenue diary • market outlook report • third-party statistics • Internet links Computer systems: • revenue management system • displacement analysis tool • forecasting tool	Internal relationships: • direct (inbound-outbound sales • team (revenue management team) External relationships: • direct (travel industry, government agency, rivals)	Knowledge: • focal points and tacit coordination Skills: • yielding, forecasting and managing revenue • tracking and assessing competitive price information Attitude: • disposition to span sales and revenue concerns
Negotiating and explaining prices	Materials: • accounts record • sales gift	Internal relationships: • direct (sales revenue) External relationships: • direct (clients, travel industry) Reputation: • sales • hotel and brand	Knowledge: • client (organizational) characteristics • customer budget and wants • alternative competitive offer(ing) Skills: • collecting and assessing customer information • establishing lowest rate and negotiation strategy • maintaining goal congruence (sales revenue) • educating and convincing the market Attitude: • will to creatively and proactively close a deal

pricing resources encountered in the international hotel group. The remainder of this section provides a commentary on each capability dimension.

Developing pricing policy, approving pricing strategy and offering support

Pricing is a human interactivity process which is subject to constant change. As the status quo of pricing knowledge across the group varies significantly, head office may decide to develop a general corporate pricing policy. The process of improving room rate pricing practice throughout the hotel group, however, will not be an easy task. It will take time and expertise to develop corporate guidelines which are broad enough to include the multiplicity of pricing environments, while at the same time being meaningful to hoteliers who face special pricing problems. The group may have to develop a strategic pricing handbook and an online revenue management library which will likely be the result of a continuous learning process specific to the hotel group. For example, the routines to get approval, to accept and implement a new directive, can be the result of intra-organizational relationships that often take years to develop. Understanding that some properties prefer certain strategies – and that these hotels may be reluctant to accept other directives from head office – the head office will have to recognize that it too needs a mind set to learn from critical comments. This mind set may be key to building relationships in which mutual trust and respect contribute to the development of goal congruence and an advance in room rate pricing practice.

A corporate pricing policy may also receive criticisms because it may lead to an individual business unit's range of mutual benefit which may be considered to be too small for practice by property management. That is, most hotels occasionally need additional business which is generally taken from the lower segments that fall outside of the planned range. Although this phenomenon has been encountered less often at hotels with wide price discretions, the interview results also indicate that, for all hotels, demand uncertainty hinders the discovery of the range of mutual benefit and the selection of the ideal business mix.

Determining and adjusting pricing strategy

When one asks a hotelier about the process of collecting data the answer will be that it is no *sinecure*. It requires mutual beneficial relationships with clients, government agencies and the business community (including rivals) to exchange the vital information that is often only accessible to internal parties. But, even with the right information available, it is still hard to interpret the information and make better pricing decisions. Evaluation of segments, the selection of the competitive set and the comparing of competitive products and prices are generally subjects of considerable debate and twist. Disputes follow naturally from the goal conflict between sales and revenue. Room rate pricing, therefore, requires the building of internal relationships. General managers need to understand the specific dimensions of internal conflicts in order to establish routines that resolve such goal conflicts. Moreover, it may take time to develop computer systems that support the improvement of market knowledge. During the field study it became clear that revenue managers with the best reputation in the hotel group were also the ones who stayed at one property for long periods, sometimes more than 10 years. Furthermore, the determination of a pricing strategy is considered very much a group process of information collecting, interpreting and negotiating (i.e. agreeing). Competitor information seems to be very important in this process. It is considered more objective and reliable. 'We can rely on what our rivals will do. What we cannot rely on is what our customers will do.' The process of obtaining competitors' price information seems to require special skills and relationships. Strictly speaking it is not always possible to get this type of information. Nonetheless, hoteliers seem to be very resourceful in this matter. Interpretation of competitor information and prices can be problematic. The information does not always match the features and attributes of the own market's products and services. Furthermore, there is every appearance that the notion of a fair market share is influential in the determination of the room rate pricing strategy. A too aggressive strategy may upset rivals and lead to a price war. In addition, it was found that in distressed markets hotels are forced to 're-invent' themselves. Further, revenue managers seem particularly to benefit from annual accurate and well thought-out on-site inspections at rival sites. On the other hand, sales managers appear to benefit from a greater understanding and involvement in the cost and revenue implications of the offers that are made to the clients. These findings suggest the importance of the spanning capability. The study also suggests that there is a continuing tension between market sensing information, which is of an anticipatory and estimative nature, and yield and revenue management information, which is more of a historical nature. In many cases, the social relationships and managerial attitudes influence towards which end on the oriental dimension the various processes shift. When, for example, the general manager has a strong background in sales, pricing is likely to become more market-oriented. Conversely, when general management is weak in sales and financial management,

pricing tends to become more 'spread-sheet' driven (i.e. sophisticated analysis of numbers without considering value implications: inside-out). Finally, the determination of a rate structure is
considered very difficult. Sales typically examine the practical
and saleability of the structure. Revenue management focuses on
the financial implications of the structure proposal.

Learning and fine-tuning prices

Learning and fine-tuning is aimed at the superior appropriation
of value. The findings indicate that the revenue manager is key to
this process. Fine-tuning takes place via displacement analysis and
yielding. The process involves the active scanning of the environment. In some cases the study finds that revenue managers develop
specific systems to enhance the accuracy of the information and
the decisions. The rest of the management team and other hotel
staff is typically part of those systems. The observation that such
systems are valuable is obtained only after investing long periods
of time. Sales and revenue managers who do not believe in such
systems tend to work more individually. Findings suggest that in
these circumstances it becomes harder to span the inside-out and
outside-in processes. Fine-tuning processes often start using
some form of referent or goal. Indices on RevPAR, ADR, occupancy and market penetration are collected and interpreted on a
regular basis. Tracking competitors' prices is next. Learning
occurs through the constant investigation of deviations and the
weekly evaluation of forecast and performance data. The study
finds that some general managers deliberately force all members of
the revenue management team to articulate, examine and eventually modify the thinking of how markets work, i.e. how competitors and channel intermediaries will react. Under these
circumstances there appears to be much more of a balance between
market sensing and revenue management perspectives. In all situations where these balanced perspectives evolved, both internal
relationships and performance had improved. In addition, both
learning and fine-tuning seem to benefit from a well-determined
pricing strategy. Such strategy creates a mind set to stick to the
plan. This attitude stimulates the search for proactive and creative
tactical pricing solutions. During the interview study, it was often
remarked that in pricing changing 'you need ice in the stomach'.
Given some focal points established through past experience and
given that all hotels are reluctant to initiate downward price spir-
als, all that is needed for coordinating tacitly is sometimes to wait
and see whether a competitor is really wrong or right in his
(downward) price action. Then again, the choice to wait and see
may be based on the wrong information, especially considering

the difficulty of tracking and assessing price information. The process of adjusting prices is, therefore, often a team process. Participants in this process frequently disagree on how customers and competitors will react. It is thus important to establish field contacts to triangulate the various internal viewpoints. An expertise in managing revenue is not sufficient. Empirical results clearly indicate that revenue managers must also employ a will to integrate both sales and revenue concerns. The use of tools and materials may aid this process. Sales may improve their knowledge of costs and revenues. Revenue managers may increase their scope from solely monitoring and analysing figures and indices to a fuller understanding of the peculiarities of market reality.

Negotiating and explaining prices

Determining and adjusting prices only initiates the room rate pricing process. Hoteliers also know that they need to 'sell' the prices to customers. The hotel, therefore, needs to build an ability to convince the customers of the logic behind the pricing strategy and fine-tuning actions. To convince customers, it needs an ability to agree internally on the room rate pricing policy. The field results unmistakably show that there is a lot of disagreement, especially among sales people, with how the corporate pricing policy affects their ability to negotiate and explain prices. In addition, convincing customers involves the ability to cope with the consequences of selling room rate prices to buyers which themselves may not be the (end)users and/or the payers of the room offering. This matter requires a skill to understand *whose* value arguments are involved. To develop such skill, reliable (tacit) resources are necessary to get an accurate picture of customers' budgets, wants and alternative competitive offers. Furthermore, the study indicates that it is not easy to develop knowledge of middlemen and decision-makers. It takes time to be able to assess each player's reaction to a pricing action. Personal reputation is vital to the process of convincing and negotiation. For example, after an industry decline, relationships often form the basis for convincing clients that the brand's reputation to be expensive is not correct (anymore).

Some tentative conclusions

Room rate pricing in an international hotel group seems to occur via processes and resources that are idiosyncratic to the individual hotel properties. These processes and resources can be identified via four dimensions. The dimensions are, however, only dimensions. Viewed separately, they only provide partial understanding. On the whole, pricing seems to require an explicit combination of knowledge, skills and other resources in order to extract value from customers. It appears to be very much an organizational process of information gathering, exchange and interpretation that involves discussion and negotiations both inside and outside the hotel. This process is complicated by the dual, relative and conflicting role of the room rate price in the consumer buying decision-process. To discover 'better' the range of mutual benefit it is important to develop the processes and resources that make up the room rate pricing capability. To develop a pricing capability, it seems to be necessary to invest in tangible resources, relational resources, knowledge, skills and attitude.

The interview results combined with the resource-advantage view suggest that hotel (group)s cannot easily imitate pricing resources without investing significant resources over time. As Dierickx and Cool (1989:1507) illustrate by the following dialogue between a British Lord and his American visitor:

> 'How do you got such a gorgeous lawn?' 'Well, the quality of the soil is, I dare say, of the utmost importance.' 'No problem.' 'Furthermore, one does need the finest quality seed and fertilizers.' 'Big deal.' 'Of course, daily watering and weekly mowing are jolly important.' 'No sweat, just leave it to me!' 'That's it.' 'No kidding?!' 'Oh, absolutely. There is nothing to it, old boy; just keep it up for five centuries.'

In following other work on pricing capabilities (e.g. Dutta et al., 2003), it is therefore argued that room rate pricing resources are subject to so-called time decompression diseconomies. The study supports the notion that, in addition to investing in value-creating processes and resources, to develop a superior value proposition, it is also important to invest in value-extracting processes and resources. However, the study also suggests that without investments in value-creating processes and resources (e.g. the room product, the service level, the appearance of the building), room rate pricing becomes much more difficult as:

1 the market position will gradually erode in the competitive process

2 narrowing the final room rate pricing discretion

3 making it harder to span market sensing and revenue management processes

4 decreasing the funds available to invest in the pricing resources required to extract value.

References

Abbey, J. (1983) Is discounting the answer to declining occupancies? *International Journal of Hospitality Management*, **2** (2), 77–82.

Adam, D. (1958) *Les Réactions du Consummateur devant le Prix*. SEDES, Paris.

Ahtola, O.T. (1984) Price as 'give' component in an exchange theoretic multicomponent model. In Kinnear, T. (ed.), *Advances in Consumer Research*, vol. 11. Association for Consumer Research, Ann Arbor.

Baker, T.K. and Collier, D.A. (1999) A comparative revenue analysis of hotel management heuristics. *Decision Sciences*, **30** (1), 239–263.

Bannock, G., Baxter, R.E. and Davis, E. (1992) *The Penguin Dictionary of Economics*, 5th edn. Penguin, London.

Bitran, G.R. and Mondschein, S.V. (1995) An application of yield management to the hotel industry considering multiple day stays. *Operations Research*, **43** (3), 427–443.

Boulding, K.E. (1996) *Economic Analysis: Vol 1 – microeconomics*. Harper & Row, New York.

Choi, S. and Mattila, A.S. (2004) Hotel revenue management and its impact on customers' perceptions of fairness. *Journal of Revenue and Pricing Management*, **2** (4), 303.

Cox, R. (1946) Non-price competition and the measurement of prices. *Journal of Marketing*, **10**, 370–383.

Cross, R.G. (1997) Launching the revenue rocket: how revenue management can work for your business. *Cornell Hotel and Restaurant Administration Quarterly*, **38** (2), 32–43.

Cyert, R.M. and Hedrick, C.L. (1972) Theory of the firm: past, present, and future. *Journal of Economic Literature*, **10** (2), 398–412.

Day, G.S. (1994) The capabilities of market-driven organizations. *Journal of Marketing*, **58** (10), 37–52.

Desiraju, R. and Shugan, S.M. (1999) Strategic service pricing and yield management. *Journal of Marketing*, **63** (1), 44.

De Wit, B. and Meyer, R. (2004) *Strategy: process, content, context*. Thompson, London.

Dierickx, I. and Cool, K. (1989) Asset stock accumulation and the sustainability of competitive advantage. *Management Science*, **35**, 1504–1511.

Dodds, W.B. and Monroe, K.B. (1985) The effect of brand and price information on subjective product evaluations. *Advances in Consumer Research*, **12**, 85–90.

Donaghy, K., McMahon, U. and McDowell, D. (1995) Yield management: an overview. *International Journal of Hospitality Management*, **14** (2), 139–150.

Dorward, N. (1987) *The pricing decision; economic theory and business practice*. Harper & Row, London.

Down, S.A. (1961) A theory of consumer efficiency. *Journal of Retailing*, **37**, 6–12.

Dunn, K.D. and Brooks, D.E. (1990) Profit analysis: beyond yield management. *Cornell Hotel and Restaurant Administration Quarterly*, **30** (2), 23–34.

Dutta, S., Bergen, M., Levy, D., Ritson, M. and Zbaracki, M. (2002) Pricing as a strategic capability. *Sloan Management Review*, **43** (3), 61–66.

Dutta, S., Zbaracki, M.J. and Bergen, M. (2003) Pricing process as a capability: a resource-based perspective. *Strategic Management Journal*, **24** (7), 615.

Enz, C.A. (2003) Hotel pricing in a networked world. *Cornell Hotel and Restaurant Administration Quarterly*, **44** (1), 4.

Enz, C.A., Potter, G. and Siguaw, J.A. (1999) Serving more segments and offering more products. *Cornell Hotel and Restaurant Administration Quarterly*, **40** (6), 54–63.

Enz, C.A., Canina, L. and Lomanno, M.V. (2004) Why discounting doesn't work. *The Center for Hospitality Research Reports*, **4** (7), 1–28.

Erickson, G.M. and Johansson, J.K.A. (1985) The role of price in multi-attribute product evaluations. *Journal of Consumer Research*, **12** (20), 195.

Gabor, A.N. and Granger, C.W.J. (1961) On the price consciousness of consumers. *Applied Statistics*, **10** (3), 170–188.

Gabor, A.N. and Granger, C.W.J. (1966) Price as an indicator of quality. *Economica*, **33** (1), 43–70.

Ginzberg, E. (1936) Customary prices. *American Economic Review*, **26** (2), 296.

Gronau, R. (1973) The intrafamily allocation of time: the value of the housewife's time. *American Economic Review*, **63** (4), 634–651.

Gutenberg, E. (1928) *Die Unternehmung als Gegenstand Betriebswirtschaftlicher Theorie*. Habilitationsschrift, Universität Münster.

Hague, D.C. (1971) *Pricing in Business*. Allen and Unwin, London.

Hanks, R.D., Robert, G.C. and Moland, R.P. (1992) Discounting in the hotel industry: a new approach. *Cornell Hotel and Restaurant Administration Quarterly*, **33**, 15–23.

Hanks, R.D., Cross, R.G. and Noland, R.P. (2002) Discounting in the hotel industry: a new approach. *Cornell Hotel and Restaurant Administration Quarterly*, **43** (4), 94.

Harper, D. (1966) *Price Policy and Procedure*. Harcourt Brace & World, New York.

Hauser, J.R. (1984) Pricing theory and the role of marketing science. *Journal of Business*, **57** (1), 65–71.

Hawkins, E.R. (1940) Marketing and the theory of monopolistic competition. *Journal of Marketing*, **4** (4), 382–389.

Hunt, S.D. (2000) *A General Theory of Competition: resources, competences, productivity, economic growth*. Sage Publications, Thousand Oaks.

Hunt, S.D. and Morgan, R.M. (1995) The comparative advantage theory of competition. *Journal of Marketing*, **59**, 1–15.

Hunt, S.D. and Morgan, R.M. (1996) The resource-advantage theory of competition: dynamics, path dependencies, and evolutionary dimensions. *Journal of Marketing*, **60**, 107–114.

Hunt, S.D. and Morgan, R.M. (1997) Resource-advantage theory of competition: a snake following its tail of a general theory of competition? *Journal of Marketing*, **61**, 74–82.

Ingenbleek, P.T.M. (2002) *Money for Value: pricing from a resource-advantage perspective*, PhD. Tilburg University (CentER), Tilburg.

Ingenbleek, P.T.M., Debruyne, M., Frambach, R.T. and Verhallen, T.M.M. (2001) *On Cost-Informed Pricing and Customer Value: a resource-advantage perspective on industrial innovation pricing practices*. The Pennsylvania State University, University Park.

Jacoby, J. and Olson, J.C. (1977) Consumer response to price: an attitudinal, information processing perspective. In Wind, Y. and Greenberg, M. (eds), *Moving Ahead with Attitude Research*, pp. 73–86. American Marketing Association, Chicago.

Jones, P. and Hamilton, D. (1992) Yield management: putting people in the big picture. *Cornell Hotel and Restaurant Administration Quarterly*, **31** (1), 89–95.

Kim, W.G., Han, J.H. and Kyun, K. (2004) Multi-stage synthetic hotel pricing. *Journal of Hospitality and Tourism Research*, **28** (2), 166–185.

Kimes, S.E. (1994) Perceiving fairness of yield management. *Cornell Hotel and Restaurant Administration Quarterly*, **35**, 22–29.

Kimes, S.E. (2002) Perceived fairness of yield management. *Cornell Hotel and Restaurant Administration Quarterly*, **43** (1), 21.

Kimes, S. E. (2003) Revenue management. A retrospective. *Cornell Hotel and Restaurant Administration Quarterly*, **44** (5/6), 131.

Kimes, S.E. and Wagner, P.E. (2001) Preserving your revenue-management system as a trade secret. *Cornell Hotel and Restaurant Administration Quarterly*, **42** (5), 8–15.

Lambert, D.R. (1980) Price as a quality signal: the tip of the iceberg. *Economic Enquiry*, **18** (1), 144–150.

Langholm, O. (1969) *Full Cost and Optimal Price*. Scandinavian University Press, Oslo.

Leavitt, H. (1954) A note on some experimental findings about the meaning of price. *Journal of Business*, **27**, 205–210.

Leibowitz, A. (1974) Education and home production. *American Economic Review*, **64**, 243–250.

Lesure, J.D. (1983) Break-even analysis: a useful tool in the lodging industry. *International Journal of Hospitality Management*, **2** (3), 115–120.

Leszinski, R. and Marn, M.V. (1997) Setting value, not price. *The McKinsey Quarterly*, **1**, 98–115.

Leuthold, J. (1981) Taxation and the consumption of household time. *Journal of Consumer Research*, **7**, 388–394.

Lewis, R.C. (1986) Customer-based hotel pricing. *Cornell Hotel and Restaurant Administration Quarterly*, **27** (2), 18–21.

Lewis, R.C. and Shoemaker, S. (1997) Price-sensitivity measurement. *Cornell Hotel and Restaurant Administration Quarterly*, **38** (2), 44–54.

Lieberman, W.H. (1993) Debunking the myths of yield management. *Cornell Hotel and Restaurant Administration Quarterly*, **34** (1), 34–41.

Linder, S.B. (1970) *The Harried Leisure Class*. Columbia University Press, New York.

Mabry, B.D. (1970) An analysis of work and other constraints on choices of activities. *Western Economic Journal*, **8** (3), 213–225.

Mano, H. and Elliott, M.T. (1997) Smart shopping: the origins and consequences of price savings. *Advances in Consumer Research*, **24**, 504–510.

Mincer, J. (1963) Market prices, opportunity costs, and income effects. In Christ, C.F. (ed.), *Measurement in Economics: studies in mathematical economics and econometrics in memory of Yehuda Grunfeld*, pp. 67–82. Stanford University Press, Stanford.

Monroe, K.B. (1971) Psychophysics of prices: a reappraisal. *Journal of Marketing Research*, **8** (2), 248–250.

Monroe, K.B. (1971) Measuring price thresholds by psychophysics and latitudes of acceptance. *Journal of Marketing Research*, **8** (4), 460.

Monroe, K.B. (1973) Buyers' subjective perceptions of price. *Journal of Marketing Research*, **10** (1), 70–80.

Monroe, K.B. (1990) *Pricing: making profitable decisions*, 2nd edn. McGraw-Hill Book Company, New York.

Monroe, K.B. (2003) *Pricing: making profitable decisions*, 3rd edn. McGraw-Hill Book Company, New York.

Monroe, K.B., Powell, C. and Choudhury, P.K. (1986) Recall vs. recognition as a measure of price awareness. *Advances in Consumer Research*, **13**, 594–599.

Monroe, K.B. and Chapman, J. (1987) Framing effects on buyer's subjective product evaluations. *Advances in Consumer Research*, **14**, 193–197.

Nagle, T.T. (1984) Economic foundations for pricing. *Journal of Business*, **57** (1), 3–26.

Nagle, T.T. and Holden, R.K. (1995) *The Strategy and Tactics of Pricing: a guide to profitable decision making*, 2nd edn. Prentice Hall, Englewood Cliffs.

Narasimhan, C. (1984) Comments on 'economic foundations for pricing'. *Journal of Business*, **57** (1), 27–34.

Nelson, R.P. (1992) Current issues in hotel room discounting. *Journal of Hospitality and Leisure Marketing*, **1** (1), 71–75.

Nichols, D., Smolensky, E. and Tideman, T.N. (1971) Discrimination by waiting time in merit goods. *American Economic Review*, **61**, 312–323.

Noble, P.M. and Gruca, T.S. (1999) Industrial pricing: theory and managerial practice. *Marketing Science*, **18** (3), 435–454.

Oh, H. (2000) The effect of brand class, brand awareness, and price on customer value and behavioral intentions. *Journal of Hospitality and Tourism Research*, **24** (2), 136.

Orkin, E.B. (1988) Boosting your bottom line with yield management. *Cornell Hotel and Restaurant Administration Quarterly*, **28** (4), 52–56.

Orkin, E.B. (1998) Wishful thinking and rocket science. *Cornell Hotel and Restaurant Administration Quarterly*, **39** (4), 15.

Oxenfeldt, A.R. (1973) A decision-making structure for price decisions. *Journal of Marketing*, **37** (1), 48–53.

Oxenfeldt, A.R. (1975) *Pricing Strategies* AMACOM, New York.

Pearce, I.F. (1956) A study in price policy. *Economica*, **23**, 114–127.

Quain, B. (1992) Analysing sales-mix profitability. *Cornell Hotel and Restaurant Administration Quarterly*, **33** (2), 57–62.

Quain, B. (2003) No one ever made money by discouraging their customers from spending it! *Cornell Hotel and Restaurant Administration Quarterly*, **44** (5/6), 166.

Rao, A.R., Bergen, M.E. and Davis, S. (2000) How to fight a price war. *Harvard Business Review*, **78** (2), 107.

Rao, V.R. (1984) Pricing research in marketing: the state of the art. *Journal of Business*, **57** (1 pt.2), 9–60.

Relihan, W.J. (1989) The yield-management approach to hotel-room pricing. *Cornell Hotel and Restaurant Administration Quarterly*, **30** (1), 40–45.

Rogers, A.N. (1975) *Pricing in the Hotel Industry: a theoretical and empirical investigation*, Mphil. University of Surrey, Guildford.

Rogers, A.N. (1976) Price formation in hotels. *Hotel, Catering and Institutional Management Review*, **1**, 227–237.

Rogers, A.N. (1977) Psychological aspects of pricing. *Hotel, Catering and Institutional Management Journal*, **5**, 15–16.

Russo, J.A. (1991) Variance analysis: evaluating hotel room sales. *Cornell Hotel and Restaurant Administration Quarterly*, **32** (1), 60–65.

Said, H.A. (1981) *The Relevance of Price Theory to Pricing Practice: an investigation of pricing policies and practices in UK industry*, PhD. University of Strathclyde, Glasgow.

Scitovszky, T. (1944) Some consequences of the habit of judging quality by price. *Review of Economic Studies*, **12** (2), 100–105.

Shaw, M. (1992) Positioning and price: merging theory, strategy and tactics. *Hospitality Research Journal*, **15** (2), 31–39.

Smyth, R. (1967) A price-minus theory of cost. *Scottisch Journal of Political Economy*, **5**, 110–117.

Thaler, R. (1985) Mental accounting and consumer choice. *Marketing Science*, **4**, 199–214.

Varini, K., Engelmann, R., Claessen, B. and Schleusener, M. (2003) Evaluation of the price-value perception of customers in Swiss hotels. *Journal of Revenue and Pricing Management*, **2** (1), 47.

Weatherford, L.R. (1995) Length-of-stay heuristics: do they really make a difference? *Cornell Hotel and Restaurant Administration Quarterly*, **36** (6), 70–79.

Weatherford, L.R., Kimes, S.E. and Scott, D.A. (2001) Forecasting for hotel management: testing aggregation against disaggregation. *Cornell Hotel and Restaurant Administration Quarterly*, **42** (4), 53.

Wijeyesinghe, B. (1993) Break-even. *Hospitality*, February, 16–17.

Yeoman, I. and Watson, S. (1997) Yield management: a human activity system. *International Journal of Contemporary Hospitality Management*, **9** (2), 80–83.

Zeithaml, V.A. (1988) Customer perceptions of price, quality and value: a means-end model and synthesis of evidence. *Journal of Marketing*, **52** (3), 2–22.

CHAPTER 12

The relevance of restaurant accounting systems

Tommy D. Andersson

Introduction

People are different as are restaurants. By producing meal experiences with unique characteristics, restaurants cater for the needs of specific customer categories. A look at the restaurant market of a city gives a fascinating illustration of the culture and diversity of that city.

From an economic point of view, this diverse supply of meal experiences is perfectly rational when the demand is equally diverse and customers are prepared to pay a premium price for the extra; be it an extra service experience, an extra culinary experience or an extra aesthetic experience of an elegant dining room.

A problem in an economic context, as often in economics, is information. Restaurant managers must not only know the preferences and the needs of their customers, but also allocate resources in a way that makes it possible to produce the particular meal experiences that their customers expect.

Accounting systems provide an instrument for budgeting and for an efficient allocation of resources. A restaurant manager must be aware of the fact that customers normally do not come only to eat, but come for a multidimensional experience and restaurant managers should, therefore, plan and budget multidimensionally.

Accounting systems provide information about goal achievement and signals for management control. A multidimensional budget will force managers to follow up activities in detail and assess whether resources efficiently perform or support the specific activities they are allocated to. Traditional management control is concerned with cost of resources, e.g. food cost and cost of labour, whether management control related to customer experiences should be concerned both with the cost of resources and the value of the meal experience created for the customer.

Accounting systems also provide necessary information for cost-based pricing. The price charges the customer for the cost of producing a meal experience. Traditionally, restaurant managers determine a cost-based mark-up price by adding 150–300 per cent overhead charges on the food cost. Apart from the fact that this practice ignores the value of the customer experience, it can, from a theoretical point of view, be criticized for a number of reasons.

The focus of the following discussion will be:

1 an analysis of the value that customers attach to a meal experience and to the various aspects, or dimensions, of the meal experience

2 a discussion of the recent development of restaurant accounting systems in relation to recent accounting research

3 an assessment of the implications on budgeting, management control and pricing if the traditional uniform system of accounts is adjusted to new ideas and alternative approaches to accounting.

The value of meal experiences

To understand customer needs should be an essential part in understanding customer value of services and goods. We must understand *why* we consume. Economists may tell you *how much* and to *what price* you will consume, but do not seem to have much of an answer to the question *why*.

A psychological model of well-being

Our sense of well-being may be described in terms of arousal and stimulation. There is, according to psychological theories, an optimal level of arousal (OLA) which implies that we could experience too much as well as too little arousal. We do continuously regulate our level of arousal by various means and amounts of stimulation. The objective is for each individual to seek or avoid stimulation in such ways that his level of arousal is, as much as possible, close to this optimum.

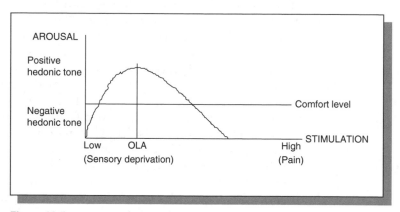

Figure 12.1
Arousal as a function of stimulation (Eysenck, 1976:113). OLA, optimal level of arousal.

Theories of arousal have been discussed and developed during the last 50 years (Moruzzi and Magoun, 1949; Lindsley, 1951; Berlyne, 1960; Zuckerman, 1979; Farley, 1981; Strelau, 1985; Björck-Åkesson, 1990) and much attention has been paid to biological and biochemical processes in the brain that reflect the level of arousal.

The optimal level of arousal is individual and so is the need for seeking and avoiding stimulation. There is a large body of psychological research dealing with a discussion of personality vis-à-vis optimal level of arousal (Guilford, 1967; Cattell and Kline, 1977) and OLA seems to depend on introversion/extraversion (Eysenck, 1976) and/or other factors.

As demonstrated in Figure 12.1, Eysenck (1976) values the level of arousal in terms of a 'positive hedonic tone' and a 'negative hedonic tone'. Part of our consumption can thus be explained by a need for seeking stimulation to overcome a negative hedonic tone, i.e. to relieve hunger, thirst etc., whereas other parts of our consumption only serve the purpose of an increased well-being, i.e. to increase the positive hedonic tone. The dividing line between negative and positive hedonic tone we call *comfort*, thus indicating a level where we are comfortable but not excited.

These models from physiological psychology thus give a clue to *why* we consume. Stimulation from goods and services seems to be necessary in order to overcome a negative 'painful' hedonic tone and attain (at least) the comfort level of our needs. These underlying needs thus hypothetically direct our consumption of goods and services.

This discussion of how stimulation influences arousal and how it affects our sense of well-being has so far been one-dimensional, but human needs may be of various kinds. Well known is the classification into five basic needs by Maslow (1954): physiological, safety, belongingness and love, esteem and self-actualization needs. Scitovsky (1985) suggests personal comfort, social comfort and stimulation as three categories of human satisfaction. These categories will henceforth be used, although somewhat renamed:

Physiological needs are based on the satisfaction of biological needs and desires. Food, drink, clothing and health in required amounts form the basis of physical comfort as do machines and services that reduce unpleasant levels of physical effort.

Social needs are based partly on our sense of belonging to groups that we wish to belong to, and partly to our self-esteem based on our ranking in the hierarchy of those groups. These needs may be satisfied by memberships, titles, status symbols and conspicuous consumption, but also by a multitude of 'non-economic' activities performed within a group in order to gain appreciation from other group members.

Intellectual needs are based on all sources of interest, entertainment and excitement. Danger and novelty of an appropriate degree (i.e. not too much) can be essential ingredients in entertainment and excitement. Enjoyable work, music, literature, watching sports, gambling, arts and so on may satisfy intellectual needs.

These three categories are not intended to classify goods and services, although such examples were used above, but primarily to classify human needs, which are often satisfied by goods and services. Many goods and services provide some degree of satisfaction for all three needs. Dining out, for example, will satisfy *physiological needs* by relieving hunger, it might satisfy *social needs* if we go to a restaurant highly approved by our group and/or if we go there with friends (group members). *Intellectual needs* may also be stimulated through novel and delicious dishes, an exciting milieu or an entertaining evening with our companions.

Previous studies of customer value of meal experiences

Based on the notion that demand is related to needs and need satisfaction, Andersson (1991) analysed the consumer value of a meal experience. Willingness to pay was used as a measuring instrument thus making the value comparable to the cost. By asking customers to assess the value for five hypothetical meal experiences it was possible to break down the total value (willingness-to-pay) of the experience into the value of five parts. A comparison of lunch customers and dinner customers revealed significant differences regarding the value that the customers attach to the various parts of the total meal experience. Table 12.1 illustrates the average values as well as the customer evaluation of the various parts of a lunch and an evening meal experience.

Table 12.1

A *relative* comparison of various aspects of the dining experience. Values are calculated as percentages of total willingness to pay for the total experience

	Average rest. % of total	Lunch rest. % of total	Evening rest. % of total
Food and beverage	35	46	15
Service	6	6	11
Culinary finesse	18	18	16
Aesthetics	19	14	32
Good company	22	16	26
Total	100	100	100

Most striking is the increase in willingness to pay for stimulation of social and intellectual needs (i.e. milieu, ambiance and good company) during an evening meal compared to a lunch. This difference comes out even more clearly when the two types of restaurants are compared in monetary terms illustrated in Table 12.2.

Table 12.2

A comparison of values customers put on various aspects of a lunch and an evening meal experience in *absolute* monetary terms (GBP)

	Average rest.	Lunch rest.	Evening rest.
Food and beverage	2.40	2.30	3.20
Service	0.50	0.30	2.40
Culinary finesse	1.25	0.90	3.50
Aesthetics	1.15	0.70	6.80
Good company	1.50	0.80	5.60
Total	6.80	5.00	21.50

Whereas the willingness to pay for physiological comfort (i.e. to relieve hunger) only changes moderately by a factor 0.4, the willingness to pay for intellectual and social stimulation increases dramatically; there is a fourfold increase in willingness to pay for a good chef, a sevenfold increase for good company and a 10-fold increase in value placed on an aesthetic milieu (all differences are significant at 1 per cent level of significance).

Mennell et al. (1992) focused on social needs in a study of eating habits and believed that 'sharing food is held to signify *togetherness*, equivalence among a group that defines and reaffirms insiders as socially similar' (1992:115). Eating patterns define the boundaries of class, ethnic, religious, age and sexual groups.

A survey by Payne and Payne (1993, cited in Beardsworth and Keil, 1997) ranked important reasons for selecting a restaurant and found the main reasons to be (in descending order of importance): quality of food, value for money, range of menu, attentiveness of service, overall atmosphere, the welcoming of families, availability of parking and convenience of location. The atmosphere matters for choosing a lunch place. It should be relaxed and harmonic so that people can enjoy the food and the lunch hour. The staff and the service of the place need to be of high quality.

Mischitelli (2000) argued that quality of service, food quality, a good cook and the menu are essential and pointed out that a restaurant's atmosphere, warmth and comfort is important for people's choice of restaurant. Furthermore, he argued that cleanliness in the dining area, the entry ways and the restrooms is a big word-of-month consideration.

Westman and Skans (2001) pointed out the same factors as Mischitelli, regarding the choice of a lunch place. They found that the *social atmosphere* was critical when people made their choice regarding where to eat. It was also important for many to eat with colleagues they enjoy eating with. Marshall and Bell (2002) studied the location factor and concluded that location appeared to be more influential in driving the choice of restaurant for lunch, compared with other eating occasions.

In a study of 342 lunch customers in Sweden, Börjesson et al. (2004) found price and location to be top priorities followed by culinary finesse, cleanliness and good ingredients out of twelve issues for the selection of a lunch restaurant. The authors also found significant gender differences with women being more concerned about the restaurant interior and cleanliness, whereas men care more for food on the plate, both in terms of food quality and portion size.

A study of 310 restaurant customers in Gothenburg, Sweden (Andersson and Mossberg, 2004) assessed six dimensions of the dining experience by using willingness-to-pay and methods similar to Andersson (1991). The average results in terms of percentages as well as monetary values of total willingness to pay in Table 12.3 refer to an ideal experience and the value of a full-fledged dining experience.

There are interesting differences between a lunch and a dinner regarding the value that customers place on stimulation. The

Table 12.3

A *relative* and an *absolute* comparison of the customer value of various aspects of a perfect dining experience

	Lunch		Dinner	
	% of total	in GBP	% of total	in GBP
Food	43	3.48	13	3.76
Service	8	0.68	19	5.78
Fine cuisine	25	2.00	13	3.90
Aesthetics	7	0.57	11	3.28
Good company	12	1.00	28	8.30
Other guests	5	0.38	17	5.05
Total	100	8.12	100	30.10

difference is largest in the willingness to pay for stimulation of social and intellectual needs (i.e. restaurant aesthetics, service, other guests, and good company) during a dinner compared to a luncheon. The importance of 'other guests in the restaurants' (an aspect that was not included in the Andersson, 1991 study) is strong for an evening meal. When the two meal experiences are compared in monetary terms, the willingness to pay for physiological comfort (i.e. to relieve hunger) remains virtually the same, whereas the willingness to pay for intellectual and social stimulation increases dramatically. These results strongly support the results of the previous study by Andersson (1991).

A conclusion from the results was that it is possible to study the restaurant as an arena for a multidimensional experience. Customers expect evening restaurants to satisfy mainly social and intellectual needs, whereas lunch restaurants mainly must cater for physiological needs (see Tables 12.1, 12.2 and 12.3).

It may be tempting to disregard dimensions such as *Dining company* and *Other guests in the restaurant* on the grounds that these factors are beyond the control of restaurant managers. However, at a second thought, restaurant managers certainly can influence these dimensions a great deal and successful managers (and restaurant concepts) also do so. The results of the study suggest that these dimensions are important for the total experience and have not yet got the research attention they merit.

Research on restaurant accounting systems

The Uniform System of Accounts for Restaurants (USAR), presented in Table 12.4, provides a well-established framework for restaurant accounting systems. Other national standards have been produced, e.g. in the UK through the Economic Development Committee for Hotels and Catering, but USAR, originating from the National Restaurant Association of the USA, has been the most widely used standard internationally.

Table 12.4
An income statement according to the uniform system of accounts for restaurants – USAR

Sales
Food sales
Beverage sales
Misc.

Cost of sales
Food cost
Beverage cost
Misc. variable

GROSS PROFIT ON SALES

Controllable expenses
Payroll
Direct operating
Music & entertainment
Repair & maintenance
Administration & general
Advertising

PROFIT BEFORE OCCUPATION COST

Occupation cost
Property taxes
Rent
Insurance
Lease
Interest
Depreciation
Other income or expenditure

PROFIT BEFORE INCOME TAX

The uniform system of accounts for restaurants provides little opportunity to analyse cost behaviour and no prescription for how fixed and operating costs should be controlled according to Potter and Schmidgall (1999). In spite of the fact that fixed costs are very dominating in the hospitality industry, detailed analyses of fixed cost and fixed cost behaviour are lacking. A poor understanding of cost behaviour limits the managers' ability to identify areas for cost reduction and improved efficiency.

The hospitality industry seems, in this respect, to be a number of years behind the manufacturing industry where new methods for a critical examination of cost behaviour were discussed 20 years ago. These new methods were developed to respond to changes in the cost structure of the manufacturing industry where fixed cost had grown in importance and had become much more dominant at the same time that variable costs had become much less important. Traditional methods for product costing had therefore 'lost relevance' (Johnson and Kaplan, 1987). The new methods were based on a more thorough analysis of cost behaviour in order to understand the drivers of fixed cost. These cost drivers were used for a more relevant distribution of fixed cost in product costing. This method is called activity-based costing (ABC).

Activity-based costing has developed into ABM – activity-based management (Cooper and Kaplan, 1991) with a broader scope, not only limited to costing but including also budgeting and management control (Gupta and Galloway, 2003). ABM is, just like ABC, based on an examination and an analysis of the production process with the objective to identify activities that add value and use resources.

The ability of ABC/ABM to solve cost management problems was probably overestimated in the 1990s and much consultancy work in this area has been futile. Armstrong (2002) points at a danger of underestimating the value of an activity if it is difficult to identify its cost driver. Staff activities that are not clearly performed for specific products may be considered less valid and, with a parallel development in favour of 'lean production', the destruction of many valid staff functions has been a harmful consequence of ABC/ABM.

Activity-based costing has been implemented in the health care sector (e.g. Chan, 1993) and in the airline industry (Tsai and Kuo, 2004). In an explorative study of management accounting systems in the hospitality industry (Mia and Patiar, 2001), information on customer satisfaction was rated as the most important by the general managers, followed by 'profitability of operating departments'. A study of the use of accounting information in the hospitality sector underlines the need to develop appropriate accounting information for managers (Downie, 1997). Another field study of management control systems in a restaurant chain (Ahrens and Chapman, 2004) looked at coercive and enabling uses of accounting systems. It was found that managers achieved flexibility and efficiency by using accounting systems in an enabling way.

A consequence of the lack of analysis regarding fixed cost, dominating the hospitality industry, is that cost based pricing remains underdeveloped since there are no appropriate accounting data available. Food and beverage cost, which is central to traditional accounting systems (USAR) as the dominating variable cost will carry all the overhead cost as the only direct cost providing a basis for overhead charges (e.g. Schmidgall, 1990). This will imply overhead charges of 150–300 per cent which will cause the same type of cost distortion that Johnson and Kaplan brought to the attention of the manufacturing industry in 1987.

In an extensive review of research and development in hospitality accounting, Harris and Brander Brown (1998:175) concluded that one future challenge in this area is:

> … to understand the relationship between quality/guest satisfaction/employee morale and profit … Other areas include the application of 'new' techniques in service situations such as activity-based costing (ABC) and more comparative work with other industries in both domestic and international settings.

The results of a more recent explorative study (Raab and Mayer, 2003) of 24 restaurants in the USA are disappointing since the use of ABC is almost non-existent, although, as Raab and Mayer point out, restaurants may be an ideal setting for the application of ABC tools due to the inherent characteristics of the industry.

Implications of accounting for customer experiences

For a manager who wishes to create a restaurant experience that meets the needs of the customers, a traditional accounting system provides little guidance. The focus on cost of resources, such as food, beverage and labour without any relation to the functions these resources are expected to perform or support will miss the point that a manager should not only minimize the cost of resources but also maximize the customer value (and as a consequence of this also an opportunity to maximize restaurant revenue).

A shift of focus from cost of resources to cost of functions will be suggested here. Compared to ABC, the 'accounting unit' is not the activity performed but the value of the customer experience that is supported by performing a function and using a resource. The shift is illustrated in Figure 12.2.

There is no one-to-one correspondence between resource cost items and functional cost items. Labour cost (payroll) is, for example, absorbed by several functions depending on what function labour is used for; skilled and talented kitchen staff produce culinary experiences; unskilled kitchen staff help in providing basic services in the kitchen. Skilled and talented waiters provide quality services. Production of aesthetic experiences may incur, on the other hand, depreciation, interest rates as well as lease costs.

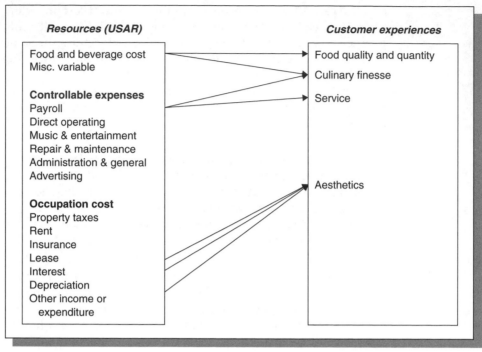

Figure 12.2
Shifting the accounting focus from resources to the support of customer experiences. The illustration
is incomplete in details.

Traditional budgeting versus budgeting for experiences

Budgeting is primarily an instrument for incremental changes.
Budgets are based on previous year's performance and on the direction the company wishes to go next year. A restaurant manager with
focus on customer satisfaction and with an ambition to provide the
necessary support in order to give the customer a memorable meal
experience may be helped by a budget for experiences. To illustrate
the ideas, it is assumed that a lunch restaurant with an annual
expense budget of £5 806 000 wishes to make a budget for experiences. It is also assumed that the four aspects of a dining experience
discussed in previous sections are selected as relevant functions.

Please note that Table 12.5 is only meant to illustrate the reasoning. The traditional resource cost (columns 1 and 6) is a much
simplified version of Uniform System of Accounts for Restaurants
and the number of relevant functional areas is limited to four.
Resource costs such as cost of repairs, advertising, taxes and rent
are missing as are experiences related to for example location,
administration, and entertainment.

Table 12.5

An illustration of how a transformation from a traditional restaurant budget (columns 1 and 6) to a restaurant budget for experiences (columns 2–5) can be made

Column	Food quality and quantity	Culinary finesse	Service	Aesthetics	Total resource budget
1	2	3	4	5	6
Cost of sales					
Food and beverage cost	£1 824 000 (80%)	£456 000 (20%)	£0	£0	£2 280 000
Controllable expenses					
Payroll	£630 000 (30%)	£630 000 (30%)	£840 000 (40%)	£–	£2 100 000
Direct operating	£18 000 (30%)	£12 000 (20%)	£12 000 (20%)	£18 000 (30%)	£60 000
Occupation cost					
Lease	£1 800 (30%)	£1 200 (20%)	£–	£3 000 (50%)	£6 000
Interest	£36 000 (30%)	£24 000 (20%)	£–	£60 000 (50%)	£120 000
Depreciation	£372 000 (30%)	£248 000 (20%)	£–	£620 000 (50%)	£1 240 000
Total functional budget	**£2 891 800**	**£1 371 200**	**£852 000**	**£701 000**	**£5 806 000**
… as a percentage of total (%)	50	24	15	11	100

The assumptions made in Table 12.5 regarding the distribution of costs are:

- *Food quality and quantity* absorbs most of the cost of raw material (80 per cent) as well as the cost of unqualified kitchen staff. A certain share of direct operating cost as well as depreciation, lease and interest for kitchen equipment are also allocated to 'Food quality and quantity'.

- *Culinary finesse* requires some specific extra cost for raw material (20 per cent) as well as qualified kitchen staff, i.e. the chef(s). Part of the kitchen equipment is also assumed to be needed for culinary finesse.

- *Service* mainly absorbs costs for service staff (40 per cent of total payroll).

- *Aesthetics* will require capital cost (depreciation + interest) for investments in furniture and interior decoration. Direct operating cost will also be affected by the standard of chinaware, table-cloths and cutlery.

A manager thinking in terms of creating dining experiences for the customers may use the budget in Table 12.5 and spend 50 per cent of the expense budget on 'the basic kitchen' (i.e. raw material, equipment and unqualified kitchen staff). Another 24 per cent should be spent on 'extras in the kitchen', i.e. a skilful chef, culinary ingredients and special equipment. Aesthetics is allocated 50 per cent of the capital cost budget and there is room for considerable investments to upgrade the standards of the dining room, clothing attire for the staff, table decorations etc. The implications of this type of budget are mainly that a manager with a focus on customer experiences gets an instrument using the same frame of mind and analysing the restaurant work from a customer perspective.

Budgeting is a typical marginal process and, in a longer-term perspective, the interesting aspects will be how the budgeted expenses in the four areas will vary from year to year depending how it is perceived that customers' meal experiences can be enhanced most effectively. Where, in what aspect of the total meal experience, will a marginal increase in expenses generate most marginal customer value?

Traditional management control versus management control of the meal experience

Management control of the meal experience must focus on the allocation of resources and whether customer value produced by the resources is larger than or equal to the cost of the resources. It will be a central task for the controller to gauge customer satisfaction and understand the aspects of a dining experience that are important for the particular clientele of the restaurant. The basic creed of a management controller should be that the marginal value must always be larger than or equal to the marginal cost.

This means that it is not necessarily efficient to achieve the optimum level of arousal (see Figure 12.1) at all times and from all resources. When the marginal arousal value of, for example, a culinary experience is compared to the marginal cost of ingredients, different levels of arousal are economically justified (Figure 12.3).

Since the price of salt is almost nil, the saltiness of the dish should be just right at the OLA (optimal level of arousal). Note that the marginal value of salt above the OLA is negative since the OLA of the culinary experience will be reduced by too much salt. The price of truffle is, however, considerably higher than the price of salt and it may be necessary from a management control perspective to limit the amount and achieve less than OLA in order not to misallocate resources to activities that produce a marginal arousal value less than the cost of the resource. This argument is relevant for all resources used to create experiences. There may, however, be a difference between a lunch and an evening restaurant in this respect. Lunch customers are price sensitive and the amount of truffle must be limited, whereas the willingness to pay at the evening restaurant may permit the chef to make a perfect truffle pâté. Alas!

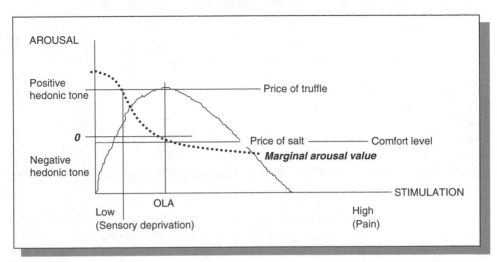

Figure 12.3
The marginal arousal value of a culinary experience compared to the marginal cost of ingredients.

In the study of customers' willingness to pay for various aspects of a restaurant experience (Andersson, 1991), cost accounting data were also collected from the same restaurants that customers visited. Using the cost accounting scheme described above, the restaurants were analysed in terms of four functional areas: food quality and quantity, culinary finesse, service and aesthetics.

Customer values are assessed using monetary measures for willingness-to-pay and are thus commensurable with the expense budget and actual expenses. There are clear advantages in conducting customer surveys in terms of monetary measures since it gives the management controller clear indications about the customer value that is created by restaurant resources. It is not possible to use industry averages since restaurants must work on their own unique profile and attend to their own customers with specific expectations on the meal experiences.

Table 12.6 illustrates the opportunities for management control that a well conducted survey gives. 'Customer actual value' and 'customer ideal value' have been estimated asking questions about customers' monetary evaluation both of the actual lunch experience at the particular restaurant and about an imagined ideal lunch experience. These evaluations can easily be carried out regularly at low cost and provide excellent information to assess and control the success of restaurant management focused on providing support for customer experiences.

Table 12.6
A comparison of the budget for the lunch restaurant (Table 12.5), actual restaurant cost (% of total cost) and customers evaluation (% of total willingness to pay excluding 'good company') for the actual as well as an ideal meal experience

	Budget (Table 12.5)	Actual expenses	Customer actual value	Customer ideal value
Food quality and quantity	50	42	55	52
Culinary finesse	24	19	20	30
Service	15	13	8	10
Aesthetics	11	16	17	8
Total	100%	100%	100%	100%

An analysis of the budget year described in Table 12.6 reveals a successful basic work in the kitchen (food quality and quantity). The actual customer value is higher than the ideal in spite of the fact that the actual expenses are lower than budgeted. Thus, a well managed basic economy in the kitchen, but the culinary finesse aspect needs more attention. The actual evaluation is 10 per cent below the ideal and the actual cost is 5 per cent below budget. It is advisable to increase these expenses during the next budget period since the marginal value of an increase is likely to be higher than the cost.

Investments in aesthetics have been considerable, but to a certain extent misdirected since it is much more than customers prefer. It may be good economy to upgrade the facilities completely at one time and this is probably what has happened during the past year since both the budgeted and actual values are more than needed. Probably, these expenses will be much reduced in next budgets and resources should be reallocated to culinary experiences. Service expenses are also higher than necessary, which probably is a reflection of lunch customers' preferences for self-service to speed up the process.

Traditional cost-based pricing versus experience pricing

Traditional cost-based pricing is based on the idea that indirect cost (a cost that cannot be directly associated with a particular product) should be allocated to products based on direct cost. In the restaurant industry, food and beverage costs are considered as the only direct cost that can be associated with a dish or a drink in mark-up pricing (e.g. Schmidgall, 1990). Since indirect cost for a restaurant is much larger than direct cost, this will lead to very high overhead charges of at least 150–300 per cent. The precision of the cost allocation is lost with overhead charges of that size (Johnson and Kaplan, 1987).

When all overhead is charged on the basis of food cost, dishes with low food cost will be priced much lower than dishes with high food cost. This will influence demand and unduly favour cooking with cheap ingredients. Quality food will subsidize junk food. This may also imply that the demand, compared to the budget, will be skewed towards cheap dishes (with a comparatively low overhead in monetary terms) and as a result of this, indirect cost may not be recovered.

A functional approach starts from the needs of the customer and an analysis of what is needed to give the customer a top dining experience. With a budget based on functions performed to support customer experiences instead of resources, costs can be allocated to dishes in a different way.

The cost of each function performed needs to be analysed in relation to the customer value it creates. Such an analysis will also indicate how costs can be distributed. The experience of top service may, for example, depend on number of service encounters. An entertainment experience and an aesthetic experience may be time dependent and should be distributed according to the time customers spend in the restaurant. In a recent work, Kaplan and Anderson (2004) advocate a new approach to ABC with a much stronger emphasis on time-driven activity-based costing.

Returning to our example of a lunch restaurant with an annual expense budget (see Table 12.5) of £5 806 000 and food cost of £2 280 000, the traditional overhead charge would be:

$$(5\,806\,000 - 2\,280\,000)/2\,280\,000 = 155\%.$$

- A price based on the meal experience would include the direct food cost, plus basic cooking cost which is called 'food quality and quantity' in Table 12.5. This requires an analysis of how kitchen capacity is used. In this example, it is assumed that basic cooking requires the same resources for all dishes and, therefore, a fixed charge similar for all dishes is used.

- Culinary finesse is assumed to be related to the value of raw material and the cost is distributed as an overhead percentage charge based on direct food cost.

- Service is probably not related to the value of the dish, but rather depending on the number of encounters, which should depend on number of dishes served. Thus, a fixed charge per dish seems more reasonable than a percentage on food cost.

- Aesthetics, finally, is assumed to depend on time spent in the restaurant. Thus, it is reasonable to have either a charge per dish consumed or a fixed charge for lunch and another (maybe three times higher) for an evening meal.

To illustrate the difference between a traditional full-cost price and a price based on functional cost, two different dishes will be used as examples:

- *Bratwurst mit Kartoffelsallat* will represent a dish with low cost of food ingredients (£0.85 per dish)

- *Turbot meunière with a sauce based on horse-radish* represents a dish with more expensive ingredients (£1.90 per dish) and prepared with more culinary finesse.

In Table 12.7, the two different ways of cost pricing are illustrated with numbers. For the traditional pricing method, an overhead charge of 155 per cent is used and for the experience pricing method, the following charges are used:

- Food quality and quantity costs £0.75 per dish for basic kitchen work

- Culinary finesse costs 47 per cent of the food cost based on required skills

- Service costs £0.40 per dish served based on number of service encounters

- Aesthetics cost £0.34 for a lunch customer based on time used for dining.

Table 12.7
A comparison of cost-based pricing of two dishes using different approaches

	Traditional cost pricing		Experience pricing	
	BW m. K	Turbot meu	BW m. K	Turbot meu
Food cost	£0.85	£1.90	£0.85	£1.90
Traditional overhead (155%)	£1.32	£2.95	n/a	n/a
Food quality and quantity (£0.75/dish)	n/a	n/a	£0.75	£0.75
Culinary overhead (47% of F&B)	n/a	n/a	£0.40	£0.89
Service charge (£0.40/dish)	n/a	n/a	£0.40	£0.40
Aesthetics charge (£0.34)	n/a	n/a	£0.34	£0.34
Full cost	**£2.17**	**£4.85**	**£2.74**	**£4.28**
Profit margin (10% of full cost)	**£0.22**	**£0.48**	**£0.27**	**£0.43**
Cost based price	**£2.40**	**£5.30**	**£3.00**	**£4.70**

One typical implication of the experience pricing method is that the price differences between the two dishes will be reduced. This should be a clear advantage and better reflect the cost of producing the two meal experiences. The price difference between the two dishes is reduced from £2.90 to £1.70, which presumably will also increase the demand of the quality dish (the *Turbot meunière*) and thus the total revenue. The sum of the two prices is equal for the two different methods. A crucial question is still, of course, whether the prices reflect the cost. If not, a change in demand may cause higher costs than budgeted and cause inefficiency. A conscientious cost analysis must, therefore, be carried out regularly in connection with management control in order to arrive at prices that both cover the costs fairly, for different dishes, and also stimulates demand for various menu items that creates a capacity utilization that is optimal for the restaurant.

Conclusions

It is now more than 40 years since Feigenbaum discussed customer satisfaction and quality in terms of: 'the degree to which the product in use will meet the expectations of the customer' (Feigenbaum, 1961:13). No doubt, customer expectations are a central issue for many restaurant managers today, but these managers get little information and support from the accounting system in their efforts to create memorable meal experiences for their customers.

A major point of this chapter has been to examine critically how the development of accounting systems has responded to the challenges from a more customer oriented and experience oriented style of restaurant management. A literature survey of previous research on how new accounting ideas are introduced into the hospitality industry is depressing. Ideas that have been discussed in the manufacturing industry for almost 20 years are unheard of in the hospitality industry (Raab and Mayer, 2003). At the same time as research indicates that managers are highly concerned about customer satisfaction (Downie, 1997; Mia and Patiar, 2001), it is evident that the development of accounting systems has not responded at all to this situation.

Against this background, the objective of this chapter has been to discuss how an accounting system can be constructed based on the value of customer experiences. The starting point was thus an analysis of the value of a meal experience followed by a discussion of how the accounting system can reflect the activities a restaurant must perform in order to generate memorable customer experiences.

The meal experience was analysed and categorized into four parts: the food quality and quantity experience, the culinary experience, the service experience and the aesthetic experience. These four dimensions were then used to construct an accounting system based on four major functional areas in a restaurant. The implications of this approach were discussed in relation to expense budgeting, management control as well as cost-based pricing. This analysis is inspired by activity-based costing (Johnson and Kaplan, 1987), but slightly different in the sense that the 'final accounting unit is the value of customer experiences in the restaurant and not the cost of a manufactured product. Thus, the value (which is the central issue here) may be more or less depending on the cost. A pinch of salt costs nothing, but may make a large contribution to the experienced value of a bowl of lobster soup.

The example used for discussing the implications refers to a highly simplified case of a lunch restaurant. This case is to some extent based on average values from an empirical study, but also, to a large extent, based on theoretical assumptions. This is of course a weak point. To understand better how different functions are performed in a restaurant, more data as well as more refined methods for statistical cost analysis (Harris, 1995) are needed.

Another important input for an accounting system based on the value of customer experiences is close monitoring of the customer expectations and the customer assessments of the meal experiences that a particular restaurant is able to provide. These evaluations must be unique for each restaurant since the diversity of the restaurant market drives each restaurant to create and refine its own unique profile. This profile must fit its clientele and just as every restaurant is unique, so is every meal experience. The meal experience offered by a restaurant should be just as special as the expectations of the restaurant's customers and, furthermore, they should, as much as possible, coincide.

References

Ahrens, T. and Chapman, C.S. (2004) Accounting for flexibility and efficiency: a field study of management control systems in a restaurant chain. *Contemporary Accounting Research*, **21** (2), 271–301.

Andersson, T.D. (1991) Dining quality: Do customers get value for money? *Journal of Hospitality Financial Management*, **1** (1), 3–14.

Andersson, T.D. and Mossberg, L. (2004) The dining experience: do restaurants satisfy customer needs? *Food Service Technology*, **4**, 171–177.

Armstrong, P. (2002) The costs of activity-based management. *Accounting Organizations and Society*, **27** (1–2), 99–120.

Beardsworth, A. and Keil, T. (1997) *Sociology on the Menu: An Invitation to the study of food and society*. Routledge, London and New York.

Berlyne, D.E. (1960) *Conflict, Arousal and Curiosity*. McGraw-Hill, New York.

Björck-Åkesson, E. (1990) *Measuring Sensation Seeking*. Acta Universitatis Gothoburgensis, Göteborg.

Börjesson, F., Csanaky, T. and Vinni, M. (2004) Crunch your lunch. *Master Thesis 2004:54*. School of Economics at Gothenburg University, Gothenburg.

Cattell, R.B. and Kline, P. (1977) *The Scientific Analysis of Personality and Motivation*. Academic Press, Washington.

Cooper, R. and Kaplan, R.S. (1991) Profit priorities from activity-based costing. *Harvard Business Review*, **69** (3), 130–135.

Downie, N. (1997) The use of accounting information in hotel marketing decisions. *International Journal of Hospitality Management*, **16** (3), 305–312.

Eysenck, H.J. (1976) *The Measurement of Personality*. MTP Press, Lancaster.

Farley, F.H. (1981) Basic process individual differences: a biologically based theory of individualization for cognitive affective and creative outcomes. In Strelau, J., Farley, F.H. and Gale, A. (eds), *Psychology and Education: The State of the Union*. McCutchan Pub. Corp, Berkley.

Feigenbaum, A.V. (1961) *Total Quality Control*. McGraw-Hill, New York.

Guilford, J.P. (1967) *The Nature of Human Intelligence*. McGraw-Hill, New York.

Gupta, M. and Galloway, K. (2003) Activity-based costing/management and its implications for operations management. *Technovation*, **23** (2), 131–138.

Harris, P.J. (1995) Statistical cost estimation and prediction in hotels. In Harris, P.J. (ed.) *Accounting and Finance for the International Hospitality Industry*. Butterworth-Heinemann, Oxford.

Harris, P.J. and Brander Brown, J. (1998) Research and development in hospitality accounting and financial management. *International Journal of Hospitality Management*, **17** (2), 161–181.

Johnson, H.T. and Kaplan, R.S. (1987) *Relevance Lost: The Rise and Fall of Management Accounting*. Cambridge, Harvard Business School Press.

Kaplan, R.S. and Anderson, S.R. (2004) Time-driven activity-based costing. *Harvard Business Review*, **82** (11), 131.

Lindsley, D.B. (1951) Emotion. In Stevens, S.S. (ed.), *Handbook of Experimental Psychology*. John Wiley & Sons, New York.

Marshall, D. and Bell, R. (2002) Meal construction: exploring the relationship between eating occasion and location. *Food Quality and Preference*, **14**, 53–64.

Maslow, A.H. (1954) *Motivation and Personality*. Harper and Rowe, New York.

Mennell, S., Murcott, A. and van Otterloo, A.H. (1992) *The Sociology of Food: Eating, Diet and Culture*. Sage, London.

Mia, L. and Patiar, A. (2001) The use of management accounting systems in hotels: an exploratory study. *International Journal of Hospitality Management*, **20** (2), 111–128.

Mischitelli, V. (2000) *Your New Restaurant*, 2nd edn. Adams Media Corporation. Massachusetts, Avon.

Moruzzi, G. and Magoun, H.W. (1949) Brain stem and reticular formation and activation of the EEG. *Electroencephalography and Clinical Neurophysiology*, **1**, 455–473.

Potter, G. and Schmidgall, R.S. (1999) Hospitality management accounting: current problems and future opportunities. *International Journal of Hospitality Management*, **18** (4), 387–400.

Raab, C. and Mayer, K.J. (2003) Exploring the use of activity based costing in the restaurant industry. *International Journal of Hospitality & Tourism Administration*, **4** (2), 79–96.

Schmidgall, R.S. (1990) *Hospitality Industry Managerial Accounting*. Educational Institute of AHMA, East Lansing.

Scitovsky, T. (1985) *Human Desire and Economic Satisfaction*. Wheatsheat, London.

Strelau, J.E. (1985) *Temperamental Bases of Behavior: Warsaw Studies on Individual Differences*. Swets & Zeitlinger, Lisse.

Tsai, W.H. and Kuo, L. (2004) Operating cost and capacity in the airline industry. *Journal of Air Transport Management*, **10**, 271–277.

Westman, C. and Skans, M. (2001) Val av lunchratt., *Sifo Research and Consulting*, Projekt Nummer 3615210, version 2. http://www.slv.se

Zuckerman, M. (1979) *Sensation Seeking: Beyond the Optimal Level of Arousal*. Erlbaum, Hillsdale.

Accounting for the environment: reflecting environmental information in accounting systems

Rebecca Hawkins

Introduction

There has been a growing realization among a number of hospitality businesses that utility costs have not been managed in the same targeted manner as other cost centres. Events in recent years (and especially in the last two years when oil prices in Europe at least have rocketed) have seen a sharp increase in the price of basic utilities such as electricity and gas. These in turn have had an impact on profitability and some global businesses are quoting the change in global oil prices and subsequent increase in energy costs as one reason for their relatively poor performance. These events have spawned an increasing realization that good management of utility costs can both help to enhance the reputation of a company (and we have recently seen the term reputation management coined as one way of describing environmental programmes) and reduce financial risk.

To date, however, there have been no standardized approaches that have been embraced by the industry to account for the costs of utilities and other environmental assets. Some mistakenly assume that these issues are embraced within 'environmental accounting'. This term, however, refers to a very specific type of activity (identifying in financial terms the environmental costs of the operation). Some approaches towards minimizing the rising costs of 'environmental' assets (such as gas, electricity, fresh water) are under development (see, for example, www.hospitableclimates.co.uk, the International Tourism Partnership's work on benchmarking due for release in the next few months), but until these are fully developed and embrace the wide range of environmental issues, companies will continue to devise their own ways of identifying the costs and benefits that accrue from programmes to protect the environment.

This chapter aims to identify the type of savings hotel businesses can gain by implementing environmental programmes. It then identifies the steps that are necessary for hotel businesses (and especially international hotel businesses) to implement if they wish to reduce utility costs and improve environmental performance.

Have you heard the story about the hotel business that implemented an energy efficiency programme and reduced its energy bills by 10 per cent? If you haven't, it's time to take on the jargon of sustainable development and reap the rewards of being an environmentally aware citizen!

Fifteen years ago, the words 'environmental management' would scarcely have been mentioned in the Board Room of any of the major international hotel companies and, if it had, for most it would probably have been considered to be a cost for shareholders. In 2005, the tables have turned and the chief executives of most of the major global hotel companies in the world are fully conversant with the terms environmental management, corporate social responsibility and ethical business; many have developed comprehensive policies and programmes to deal with these issues and many will explain that, contrary to popular belief over a decade ago, environmental programmes at least can contribute significantly to the bottom line and to shareholder value.

Coupled with this growth in environmental awareness has been an understanding that utility costs are not fixed (at around 4 per cent of turnover in the case of energy), but are a realistic target for cost reduction. Those companies that have excelled at utility management could report energy costs as a little over 2.6 per cent of turnover in 2003. The most enlightened companies of all have gone further than to look at energy costs alone. They have reviewed their policies towards water, waste, purchasing and the way they interact with their employees and communities. Many (including Hilton, Radisson, Accor Hotels, Inter-Continental, Taj Hotels, Resorts and Palaces) have emerged with comprehensive programmes that demonstrate ethical, environmentally friendly or socially responsible credentials. Published information that is now available from a wide range of companies includes:

- Accor Hotels's Social and Environmental Report

- Hilton's Environmental Policy

- Radisson's Responsible Business Programme

- Whitbread's Corporate Responsibility Programme.

Some businesses have been able to target very specific niche markets through their initiatives, for example the carbon neutral conferencing option that is now available in Canada for businesses seeking to reduce their own carbon footprint or eco-rooms featuring water and air filters, alongside ethical products and environmentally benign cleaners etc. in hotels. Others have been able to register their commitment by being quoted in social responsibility indexes (e.g. FTSE4Good) with many aspiring to join these indexes.

Three corporate routes to reducing environmental impacts

Throughout this chapter, you will find reference to three types of corporate approaches to the environment. These are (in no particular order of importance):

Environmental programmes

Companies have made claims to be implementing environmental programmes for over a decade. Internationally, hotel companies really started to champion the environmental cause in 1992 with the formation of the International Hotels Environment Initiative (now the International Tourism Partnership). Embraced within environmental programmes are the core issues of energy, waste and water management alongside strategies to reduce the impacts of purchases on the environment and to manage landscapes responsibly. The former three actions at least are claimed to provide clear cost reduction benefits. Some environmental programmes also embrace the issues of being a good neighbour and making a contribution to the community in which the business is based.

Corporate social responsibility programmes

These programmes are a more recent phenomenon. While corporate social responsibility programmes can and usually do address environmental issues, they also embrace the wider issues of how the business integrates with communities, how labour standards are applied, the company's approach to philanthropy and so on. The costs and savings of operating corporate social responsibility programmes are less clear cut and are rarely presented in the public domain.

Ethical programmes

These overlap in many ways with corporate social responsibility programmes and are the most recent development. Environmental issues may be embraced within an ethical programme, but the main focus is on how the company behaves as an employer, how it deals with its supply chain, how the communities in which the business is based are treated. The costs and savings of ethical programmes are rarely presented in the public domain, but it is likely that, unless environmental savings are included within the data, ethical programmes will operate at a net cost to the company. For many companies, these costs will be worth bearing as they will be off-set by less tangible benefits such as reputation management, improved recruitment and reduction of risk.

Seven reasons to don your green coloured spectacles

There will be few readers who are surprised at the reasons that many hotel businesses have converted to the principles of environmental management. Some businesses are undoubtedly motivated by strong ethical or environmental beliefs that underpin their whole business model, most are seeking the cost savings that can be accrued by careful management of costly resources such as energy and water (and in the view of the author there is nothing to be ashamed of in this fact); and the savings claims that are made are significant. It is claimed that a hotel that adopts a comprehensive energy management programme (including investment in new energy efficient equipment and building refurbishment) can reduce its energy consumption by up to 40 per cent. For a mid-range hotel with about 100 rooms, a health suite, swimming pool and restaurant service this saving can equate into a cost saving – at 2004 costs – of up to £16 000 per annum on electricity alone (without taking investment in the refurbishment into account). For a hotel that is one of a chain of 20 hotels, and if the actions are replicated across the business, this can equate to £320 000 per annum; a significant sum. Even if the more common saving level of 10 per cent is achieved, the savings to that hotel could be just under £4000 per annum; and the really good news is that, quite aside from the moral high ground that can be claimed by those companies that consume less energy and, therefore, pollute less, these energy savings can be accrued year-on-year for minimal additional investment. Furthermore, energy is not the only issue on which substantial savings can be made. If the claims are to be believed, savings of 40 per cent on water costs and 25per cent on waste disposal costs can also be made for only a little effort and minimal investment.

With figures of this magnitude, there can be little doubt why so many large corporate hotel companies have taken up the mantle of environmental responsibility. Indeed, the factors encouraging businesses to adopt environmental programmes have only increased in recent years. Companies (in all sectors, but including hotels) are pushed on by:

- An increase in energy costs. Few can doubt that the days of cheap energy have gone, for the short term at least. Over the last two years, energy costs have soared and some hotel companies in the UK are finding themselves paying 30 to 40 per cent more for their electricity and gas now, than a year ago. For a large London hotel with an energy bill in the region of £300 000 these costs instantly add up to £120 000 to the hotel bill – the equivalent of selling 600 rooms at £200 per night.

- Water and waste water treatment costs have also increased apace and now represent a growing proportion of the turnover of an average hotel.

- An increase in taxation. Companies in the EU at least will be familiar with the commitment at state level to reducing emissions of carbon dioxide – one of the main gases implicated in climate change. In many countries, this commitment is underpinned by a tax or levy on consumption of energy from non-renewable resources. In the UK, this is known as the Climate Change Levy and is set at £0.0015 per kilowatt hour (kWh) of gas and £0.0043 per kWh of electricity consumed. For hotels, the levy represents in the region of a 15 per cent increase in energy costs. Add this to the 30 per cent or so increase in electricity costs and you begin to get a picture of unprecedented rises in energy costs which, if left unmanaged, have the potential to undermine business profitability and shareholder value.

- Energy is not the only resource that is taxed. Waste disposal is also subject to a tax (albeit in the UK one that is often invisible to the hotel disposing of the waste). The Landfill Tax was one of the first environmental taxes to be introduced in the UK. Currently set at £18 per tonne of waste sent to landfill, it is on an escalator and will increase by at least £3 per tonne in the following years until it reaches a medium-to-long-term rate of £35. The tax is paid by the waste disposal contractor, but is passed onto businesses (including hotels) in the form of increased waste disposal bills.

- An increase in regulation and the costs of regulatory compliance. More than 100 pieces of environmental regulation have passed through the EU. These deal with a wide range of activities from how a company manages potentially hazardous chemicals, how its vehicle fleet is maintained, to how much it pays for its energy or waste disposal. This level of regulation – and the flurry of activity around Kyoto and other environmental issues – would illustrate that the trend towards regulation for environmental issues is here to stay and will increase the costs of compliance for all businesses. The costs of non-compliance can be significant with punitive fines and negative publicity befalling those businesses that break the law, whether by accident (e.g. failing to provide evidence of compliance with Packaging Waste Regulations) or deliberately (e.g. discharging chlorinated swimming pool water to the mains without the appropriate consents, allowing asbestos to be removed without appropriate consents/procedures).

- A push from other businesses who have their own ethical, corporate social or environmental policies and who ask their suppliers (including hoteliers) about their environmental commitment.

- The growing importance of reputation management. A truly 21st century concern which is inspired by the misfortunes of companies like Shell and Nike, both of whom fell foul of pressure groups and both of whom lost some market share (albeit for a short time period) and had to invest in rebuilding their image. No international hotel company has yet really incurred the wrath of the environmental or ethical movement, but there are few who would want to risk their reputation and their image in the growing face of environmental concerns.

Six steps to successful environmental programmes (for utility costs at least)

Given what has been presented above, there would be (and indeed are) few hotel groups that, when pressed, would not claim to implement some type of programme to minimize resource consumption (whether motivated by cost or other reasons). The ways in which these programmes are implemented, however, varies significantly between businesses and it is becoming evident that it is only those businesses that have the most rigorous procedures for managing utility costs that are successful at achieving savings as well as reducing environmental impacts. It is this rigour that is as essential to any element of environmental programmes as it is to any other part of a hotel's operation.

Over the years, a small number of hotel groups and external programmes have emerged as the front-runners in terms of delivering environmental improvements and cost savings. Some of these are described briefly below.

Accor Hotels

A member of the United Nations Tour Operator Initiative and the Prince of Wales' International Tourism Partnership, Accor Hotels has made a firm commitment to sustainable development and its strategy became fully operational in 2003. Managed by a dedicated sustainable development organization and using the Global Compact as a guiding principle, the commitment to sustainable development is wide reaching and embraces:

- The way in which the organization purchases goods and services (focusing on the environmental and employment practices of its suppliers and fostering the use of Fair Trade products)

- The way in which it recruits, trains and treats its staff

- The approach to quality and safety

- The approach to corporate social responsibility

- Promotion of initiatives to reduce exploitation of communities (and especially to implement the ECPAT compact on the sexual exploitation of children)

- The way in which it impacts on the environment (energy, water consumption, waste production).

The programme is underpinned by a number of tools at corporate level, including:

- A corporate commitment to sustainable development (including a policy statement known as the Hotel Environmental Charter)
- Training materials for hotel managers
- Training materials for employees
- Monitoring reports benchmarking consumption in different parts of the business
- An annual sustainable development report providing quantitative data on progress towards achieving targets. This includes information on energy and water consumption and it is the approach to these issues that has provided major opportunities for both protecting the environment and producing cost savings.

National divisions are responsible for implementing different elements of the overall sustainable development programme. In the UK and Ireland, the Technical Services Director is responsible for energy and water management specifically. His approach to these issues has delivered significant cost savings for the business. Accor Hotels UK and Ireland start their energy and water management programmes from the premise that the costs of these activities are major, but are often not managed as well as other cost centres. In the case of Accor Hotels in 2002, the combined costs of energy and water were £4.2 million or 2.7 per cent of turnover.

The costs are mainly incurred by electricity (57 per cent of the total) with gas and water accounting for 21 per cent and 22 per cent, respectively. Within the UK and Ireland division, the strategy for managing energy and water has six core elements.

Policy

Any energy efficiency policy requires the buy in of senior executives of the company and this is achieved through the sustainable development policy statement (which in the case of Accor Hotels is supported by a head office based sustainable development implementation team, which not only monitors the policy and reports results, but also provides support to those responsible for implementing the policy within individual hotels). Accor Hotels calls its policy statement the Hotel Environment Charter – this has nine commitments, which relate directly to energy and water management. Annual targets are set for achievements across the business as a whole to ensure ongoing implementation of the policy.

Monitoring

Implementation of the policy and achievement of targets can only be assessed if rigorous procedures are in place to monitor consumption and ensure achievement against targets. In Accor Hotels UK and Ireland energy and water consumption is measured on a monthly basis. Simple spreadsheets containing pre-programmed tariff costs enable these to measure not only consumption units, but also costs (Figure 13.1). Data are collated for the current month and compared to consumption for the same month in the previous year and for the year to date. Excessive consumption is immediately investigated to find the cause.

Benchmarking

At a national level, energy consumption data are correlated and league tables of good and poor performers are compiled (Figure 13.2). Benchmark figures take into account geographical location (by making adjustments for degree days) and building type. Accor Hotels benchmark their energy consumption per sleeper, most hotel companies choose to benchmark per square metre of serviced space. The important fact is not the unit of measurement, but the consistency and accuracy with which the data are collected.

Partnerships

Within operating countries, Accor Hotels have forged partnerships with agencies that have similar objectives. In the UK and Ireland, it has formed a partnership with Hospitable Climates. A programme delivered by the Hotel & Catering International Management Association (HCIMA) on behalf of the Carbon Trust, Hospitable Climates aims to negate the impact of the Climate Change Levy on operating costs by helping hospitality businesses reduce their energy costs through improved energy efficiency. This partnership has provided general managers in all Accor Hotels with regular energy efficiency training materials/seminars (and in so doing kept energy management high on the corporate agenda), provided free energy audits to hotels to target specific energy management issues and provided access to tools to help hotel managers benchmark their own energy performance against other non-Accor hotels. Overall, membership of Hospitable Climates

KEY: Let = room let

MAY — HOTEL

	Current Month				Year To Date		
	ACTUAL	BUDGET	LAST YEAR		ACTUAL	BUDGET	LAST YEAR
RMS SOLD	3,242	3,650	3,011		14,880	15,766	14,420
SLEEPERS	5,876	6,224	5,189		26,560	29,349	25,605
ELECTRICITY							
TOTAL KWH	87,989	3,650	78,895		426,278	0	389,199
TOTAL £	£ 3,684	£ 3,974	£ 3,325		£ 17,845	£ 16,351	£ 16,398
KWH/RM Built	710	-	636		688	-	628
KWH/Let	27.14	0.00	26.20		28.65	0.00	26.99
£/Let	£ 1.14	£ 1.09	£ 1.10		£ 1.20	£ 1.04	£ 1.14
GAS							
TOTAL KWH	85,678	0	85,266		547,404	0	587,993
TOTAL £	£ 989	£ 1,010	£ 984		£ 6,320	£ 4,157	£ 6,788
KWH/RM BUILT	691	-	688		883	-	948
KWH/LET	26.43	0.00	28.32		36.79	0.00	40.78
£/LET	£ 0.31	£ 0.28	£ 0.33		£ 0.42	£ 0.26	£ 0.47
WATER							
Total M3	1,292	0	1,040		6,082	0	5,071
Total £	£ 1,595	£ 2,192	£ 1,510		£ 7,468	£ 8,758	£ 6,459
M3/LET	0.40	0.00	0.35		0.41	0.00	0.35
M3/SLEEPER	0.22	0.00	0.20		0.23	0.00	0.20
£/LET	£ 0.49	£ 0.60	£ 0.50		£ 0.50	£ 0.56	£ 0.45
TOTAL £/LET	£ 1.93	£ 1.97	£ 1.93		£ 2.13	£ 1.86	£ 2.06

Figure 13.1

Accor spreadsheet containing pre-programmed tariffs that enable the company to measure consumption units and cost.

Hotel No.	UK Hotels	Elec kWh	Elec £	Gas kWh	Gas £	Water m³	Water £	Rooms	Sleepers	Utility cost	Elec kWh/Let	Gas kWh/Let	Total kWh/Let	Water m³/Sleeper	Water m³/Let	Utility Cost/Let
1	Hotel A	519 833	£20 309	668 231	£8717	4959	£7966	13 222	17 571	£36 992	39.32	50.54	89.86	0.453	0.602	£2.80
2	Hotel B	499 598	£29 791	571 169	£7968	3584	£5791	17 473	23 505	£43 550	28.59	32.69	61.28	0.246	0.331	£2.49
3	Hotel C	240 961	£10 515	676 022	£8819	2461	£3304	7104	10 077	£22 638	33.92	95.16	129.08	0.328	0.465	£3.19
4	Hotel D	257 921	£10 867	533 404	£6958	2438	£2779	6455	8132	£20 604	39.96	82.63	122.59	0.342	0.431	£3.19
5	Hotel E	326 753	£13 715	508 281	£6630	2713	£3355	9627	12 228	£23 700	33.94	52.80	86.74	0.274	0.348	£2.46
6	Hotel F	152 465	£9476	272 310	£4066	1087	£1865	5022		£15 408	30.36	54.22	84.58	DIV/0!	0.371	£3.07
7	Hotel G	512 344	£21 267	722 481	£9425	4417	£3721	15 210	20 830	£34 413	33.68	47.50	81.19	0.179	0.245	£2.26
8	Hotel H	670 453	£28 397	438 945	£5897	2900	£6350	18 926	25 812	£40 644	35.42	23.19	58.62	0.246	0.336	£2.15
9	Hotel I	537 178	£20 872	580 662	£7680	5438	£7155	18 520	27 995	£35 708	29.01	31.35	60.36	0.256	0.386	£1.93
10	Hotel J	2 402 087	£97 147	4 384 232	£57 192	20 605	£22 778	54 288	84 464	£177 117	44.25	80.76	125.01	0.270	0.420	£3.26
11	Hotel K	415 510	£15 515	584 346	£6098	6160	£6347	13 163	5306	£27 960	31.57	44.39	75.96	1.196	0.482	£2.12
12	Hotel L	291 209	£11 784	480 355	£6266	2041	£3987	8329	11 225	£22 038	34.96	57.67	92.64	0.355	0.479	£2.65
13	Hotel M	468 453	£15 468	666 605	£8956	2564	£3391	7467		£27 816	62.74	89.27	152.01	DIV/0!	0.454	£3.73
14	Hotel N	370 225	£14 557	694 993	£9057	3037	£2532	9941	11 773	£26 155	37.24	69.91	107.15	0.215	0.255	£2.63
15	Hotel O	298 884	£12 169	628 195	£8258	2997	£2966	8400	11 627	£23 394	35.58	74.79	110.37	0.255	0.353	£2.78
16	Hotel P	261 465	£12 692	578 149	£6959	2988	£5200	5800	8055	£24 851	45.08	99.68	144.76	0.646	0.896	£4.28
17	Hotel Q	242 686	£9787	542 342	£7075	1425	£3373	6097	8036	£20 235	39.80	88.95	128.76	0.420	0.553	£3.32
18	Hotel R	465 315	£16 958	598 292	£7805	4398	£5969	14 315	18 039	£30 733	32.51	41.79	74.30	0.331	0.417	£2.15
19	Hotel S	386 129	£15 031	535 022	£22 483	3974	£4717	11 595	15 774	£42 232	33.30	46.14	79.44	0.299	0.407	£3.64
20	Hotel T	310 636	£13 866	479 489	£5877	2454	£2804	8152	5769	£22 547	38.11	58.82	96.92	0.486	0.344	£2.77
21	Hotel U	344 032	£14 511	618 105	£8112	3557	£3817	10 424	123 913	£26 440	33.00	59.30	92.30	0.296	0.366	£2.54
22	Hotel V	337 205	£13 189	444 370	£5796	4790	£4609	11 638	20 684	£23 594	28.97	38.18	67.16	0.223	0.396	£2.03
23	Hotel W	394 560	£8054	352 337	£5232	3718	£4753	12 694	3991	£18 039	31.08	27.76	58.84	1.191	0.374	£1.42
		10 705 902	435 940	16 558 337	231 338	94 705	119 529	293 862	363 806	786 807	36.43	56.35	92.78	0.329	0.407	£2.68

Figure 13.2
ACCOR UK energy and water – 2003 summary for April.

contributed towards a 4.8 per cent energy saving across UK and Ireland hotels in 2002. Partnerships ensure that all forms of tax relief on energy efficient investments are claimed (e.g. in the UK, through the Enhanced Capital Allowance programme).

Targeted investments

Many extravagant claims are made about the benefits of specific energy saving technologies and these are sometimes not supported by the evidence. Technologies often require appropriate technical support, commissioning and maintenance and these costs can outweigh the potential saving, unless appropriately costed in. Accor Hotels have a targeted approach to investments. They test technologies in a small number of hotels to monitor results and to identify their potential contribution to different brands. Such tests in 2003 for energy efficient lamps in five hotels resulted in the decision to install such lamps in 50 per cent or more hotels across the brand with a targeted saving of 15 per cent on electricity costs. Tried and tested technologies are then included within the new build and refurbishment criteria to ensure continual upgrade of the hotel stock.

Staff awareness and training

It is a surprise to many that guests are not always the most significant consumers of energy and water. Employees are very significant consumers and without continuous awareness raising activity can contribute to spiralling utility costs. Commitment needs to be kept alive at all levels of the hotel, and the tools to do this vary. General managers and accountants are inspired by cost savings and need to be able to scrutinize energy and water bills to verify data; staff are often motivated because they make a contribution to environmental protection or to the quality of their community. All employees are usually receptive to benchmark league tables (as long as they are presented positively) and respond well to target setting. Even without any investment, awareness and training programmes among staff can deliver energy and water savings of up to 10 per cent and so the importance of this activity can never be forgotten.

Through their programme and rigorous implementation of these six steps, Accor Hotels have achieved significant savings. In UK and Ireland alone in 2002, they estimated that their staff awareness raising programme accounted for 8 per cent of their total saving on energy costs; and their experience is not an isolated example.

The Inter-Continental Hotels and Resorts experience

Inter-Continental Hotels and Resorts was the first hotel group to publicize its entry into the environmental arena and it was its environmental reference manual that instigated the formation of the International Hotels Environment Initiative (now known as the International Tourism Partnership). Embracing a wide range of core environmental issues (Table 13.1), Inter-Continental Hotels and Resorts also developed a comprehensive programme in 1992 to track utility costs as a part of their sustainable development initiative. Although implemented by global executives – a director with board level responsibility for sustainable development was identified with support from relevant technical individuals – the programme had the following core components in common with the Accor Hotels' approach.

Table 13.1
Issues covered in the Inter-Continental Hotels & Resorts Environmental Reference Manual (1992)

Introduction and policy statement

1 Waste management
2 Product purchase
3 Indoor air quality
4 Air emissions
5 Energy conservation
6 Noise
7 Storage tanks
8 Asbestos
9 PCBs
10 Pesticides and herbicides
11 Hazardous materials
12 Water
13 Community action
14 Laundry and dry cleaning
15 Checklist of actions

Policy

A commitment throughout the company to reducing environmental impacts and minimizing resource consumption costs. Annual targets were set for achievements across the business as a whole to ensure on-going implementation of the policy.

Monitoring

Inter-Continental Hotels measured energy and water consumption on a monthly basis. Simple spreadsheets containing pre-programmed tariff costs enabled these to measure not only consumption units, but also costs.

Benchmarking

At an international level, energy consumption data were correlated and league tables of good and poor performers were compiled. Benchmark figures took into account geographical location (by making adjustments for climate zone) and building type.

Partnerships

The partnership with International Hotels Environmental Initiative enabled ICH to share its experiences with other hotel companies globally.

Targeted investments

ICH also had a programme to test carefully technologies (for quality and performance) prior to investment across the company.

Staff awareness and training

Training was a core tenet of the ICH's programme and was reinforced by the development of Green Teams with representation of all hotel departments within each hotel. Subscription to Green Hotelier magazine, posting of benchmark results, the selection of environmental champions, the launch of an environmental report (the first for the sector) and a well respected award programme were all essential in delivering the cost savings and in driving the environmental programme forward to meet the challenges of specific hotels. The environmental reference manual was the core tool through which achievements were tracked and measured within each hotel (supplemented by the benchmark data for energy and water consumption).

51 Buckingham Gate, London

Other hotel groups have encouraged their national hotels to take individual approaches to environmental issues and have driven their initiative through a Green Team based within the hotel. Taj Hotels, Resorts and Palaces is one such group and while there is a policy – Eco Taj – within the group to reducing negative environmental impacts, individual hotels respond in the way that best suits their business model. Some hotels in the group have gained registration to the ISO 14001 environmental management standard, but others have taken more pragmatic (but no less strategic approaches) to environmental issues. The diversity of properties within the group means that corporate benchmarking of the performance of all would not be constructive and so individual hotels have been encouraged to take their own initiatives and to log into the mechanisms that have been established by national governments to bring about reduction in environmental impacts.

The flagship London property 51 Buckingham Gate has been a leader in environmentally responsible practices over the last five years. In recognition of its achievements, it won the Considerate Hoteliers Award for both Environmentally Friendly Hotel of the Year and Considerate Hotelier of the Year in 2004 (see the website – www.51-buckinghamgate.com – for more details). The approach for this hotel is driven by a Green Team with the full support of Bernard de Villèle, Vice President Business Development and Operations for Europe and Americas and General Manager of 51 Buckingham Gate. Mr de Villèle is committed to the hotel's environmental programme and has been often quoted in his views on the responsibility of the industry:

> Unless every individual pays their fullest attention to green issues, our future generations are due to witness a disaster on a global scale. As an industry we are not doing enough and we have a corporate responsibility to set targets and constantly review and update our green practices. Commitment to environmental issues can often be achieved without a financial investment through simple action plans – and the great thing is that the benefits are not only environmental, but financial in terms of real savings.

The hotel has implemented the same processes as the Accor Hotels and Inter-Continental case study, but targets have been agreed and driven at the property level rather than corporately. It is the Green Team that is responsible for both managing and implementing the environmental policy and it does this by encouraging each department in the hotel, including human resources and engineering, to be represented. The Green Team does not necessarily comprise senior representatives from management, but it does have a high level of enthusiasm and a commitment to tackling a wide range of issues from maintaining the environment in the area in which they are located, to ensuring the courtyard garden is managed using organic means and managing the all important utility costs. The Green Team has developed an environmental policy for this hotel specifically and has implemented a process for monitoring and reporting results (known as the Green-o-meter, which provides a monthly statement of all of the hotel's green initiatives, measuring the financial and environmental impacts – this information is included in the monthly profit and loss statements). It also sets annual targets for Green-o-meter budgets by department in order to achieve the targets. Targets for 2004 included to:

- increase recycling of paper
- introduce recycling programmes for other wastes including plastic bottles and discarded hotel equipment
- establish green targets for each department
- recruit more members to the Green Team
- introduce energy-saving targets in line with an audit by Action Energy.

Each quarter the Green Team then focuses on a specific resource issue (energy, water, gas, paper recycling) and tries to generate improvements across the hotel on this issue.

Partnerships are forged to tackle specific issues. For example, 51 Buckingham Gate has joined the Hospitable Climates Programme (see below) with a view to reducing its energy consumption. With an energy bill in the region of £333 000, energy costs are a natural target for reduction. The partnership with Hospitable Climates delivered an audit of how energy is used in the hotel. Benchmark data were derived using UK specific standards for luxury hotels. These made it evident that, while the hotel was relatively efficient in its use of gas, its ranking for electricity consumption was poor. A range of recommendations were highlighted (Figure 13.3a and b), including many which would have an immediate payback for limited investment (e.g. it was estimated that improved staff training to ensure that equipment is switched off when no longer in use could bring about cost savings of £10 000). Some unexpected failings in internal processes have been illustrated through the energy audit. For example, it was evident that a computerized system for logging faults reported to the housekeeping department was not being properly updated and used and so a manual system, involving a complaints book and relevant telephone conversations with the engineering department, is now being used to good effect and equipment that is faulty is rapidly repaired, thus reducing energy wastage.

The hotel is now testing specific recommendations to ensure that they do not adversely impact upon the guest experience before implementing them throughout the whole business. New targets are agreed annually and investment decisions are made by head office to facilitate the achievement of these targets.

Description of recommendation	Estimated annual savings			Estimated cost	Payback period (years)
	£	kWh	CO$_2$ (tonne)		
Measures with no capital expenditure					
Promotion of energy awareness and switch off programme to all staff	10 000	277 777	144		
Continually review and adjust as necessary the operation of the HVAC systems in line with building occupancy and good practice guidance	8000	395 616	124		
Measures with rapid payback (<1 year)					
Implement a continuous commissioning strategy to ensure that the building services are delivering occupant comfort using minimum energy consumption	30 000	1 490 134	465	25 000	0.8
Measure such as draft stripping and improving insulation levels where necessary will reduce heat loss and improve building performance	6000	298 026	92	3000	0.5
Improved metering of services will provide detailed data for analysis and may be used to provide energy reduction incentives	6000	298 026	92	6000	1.0
Further staff awareness and green housekeeping motivational training to include 'carbonsense' TM awareness training of senior hotel management	10 000	496 661	155	4000	0.25
Measures with longer payback (<5 years)					
Audit and examine all existing light fittings and retrofit or upgrade with dimmable ballasts and control where necessary	33 000	916 666	476	100 000	3.0
Install systems that control lights in accordance with occupancy and daylight presence detection and photocell sensing in appropriate areas	8000	222 222	115	40 000	5.0
Audit and examine condition of main energy using plant – hot water, air conditioning and heating and bring forward replacement date of same, to include additional investment in upgrade to energy efficient plant, e.g. condensing boilers and novel cooling solutions	15 000 to 115 000	745 066 (based on £15 000)	232	30 000 to 250 000	2 years

Figure 13.3a

Recommendations made in an energy audit for reducing energy consumption in the Crowne Plaza London St James and 51 Buckingham Gate.

Benchmarks for luxury hotels				
KWh/m^2	Good	Fair	Poor	St James Court
Gas	<300	300–460	>460	130 (GOOD)
Electricity	<90	90–150	>150	191 (POOR)
Cost £/bed				
Gas	<£260	£260–£400	>£400	£112 (GOOD)
Electricity	<£360	£360–£600	>£600	£554 (FAIR)

Figure 13.3b

Comparison of energy consumption with benchmark data – 51 Buckingham Gate. (Figures prepared by Nicolas Heidrich, Cormac O'Doherty, Mohamed Berrazouane and Alex Jones).

Government initiatives

Many national governments have become aware of the significant impacts that hotels collectively can have on the environment. National initiatives have now taken on board some key elements of the environmental management programmes that hotels have implemented to make them available to all hotel companies regardless of size. Hospitable Climates is one such initiative promoted by the UK government and now proven to be a successful and practical energy management programme provided to the sector. Implemented by the Hotel & Catering International Management Association on behalf of the Carbon Trust, Hospitable Climates helps all businesses:

- develop and implement appropriate policies

- establish monitoring processes and produce benchmark reports of possible savings (Figure 13.4)

- develop partnerships with the Government or other energy advice services

- target investments – and ask appropriate questions of technology providers (see www.hospitableclimates.co.uk)

- implement staff awareness and training through easily accessible materials (see www.hospitableclimates.co.uk).

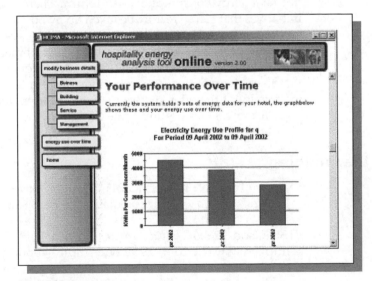

Figure 13.4
HEAT On-Line. Hospitable Climates tool to help hotel businesses benchmark their energy consumption against other similar businesses.

These programmes offer help to all hotel businesses regardless of size and can help them achieve cost savings alongside environmental improvements in the core area of energy management. They can even provide benchmarking data. What is required to complete the equation is the refinement of these benchmarking data and their extension to other areas aside from energy management to help hotels target realistic savings and ensure that they contribute towards environmental improvements. Some progress is being made on this front through ongoing development by Hospitable Climates, the Environment Agency (http://www. environment-agency.gov.uk/netregs/) and the International Tourism Partnership (www.internationaltourismpartnership.org), however, standardization of processes would help international hotel businesses to have confidence in the results and would also help us to factor changing utility costs into business accounting models.

The future's bright – but it is not Orange!

… It's green and environmentally responsible! Managing and accounting for the savings from environmental programmes is not rocket science, just good management practice. Having travelled so far over the last two decades or so, it is unlikely that the mindset brought about by low utility costs, a belief that consumers (especially in other businesses) pay little attention to the ethical stance of a business and a view that Governments would not tax energy consumption will return. There are few win-win initiatives that can so readily be taken up by hotels as environmental programmes. The clear need now is to find ways to encourage a large number of businesses to protect the environment and enhance their bottom line. Most businesses that take action on this front find that they lower not only their utility costs, but they also improve the quality of the offer, reduce risk and improve their credentials with insurers, investors and some clients.

Further reading

Fairmont Hotels & Resorts (2001) *The Green Partnership Guide – A practical guide to greening your hotel*, 2nd edn. Fairmont Hotels & Resorts, Toronto.

FTSE4Good (2005) *Impact of new criteria and future direction*. http://www.ftse.com/ftse4good/future_report.pdf

Global Reporting Initiative (2002) *Sustainability reporting guidelines – hotels*. GRI, www.globalreporting.org

Green Hotelier http://www.greenhotelier.com/

Hospitable Climates www.hospitableclimates.co.uk

International Hotels Environment Initiative (1996) *Environmental Management for Hotels – the industry guide to best practice.* Butterworth-Heinemann, Oxford.

International Tourism Partnership www.internationaltourism-partnership.org.

Kirk, D. (1996) *Environmental Management for Hotels – a student handbook.* Butterworth-Heinemann, Oxford.

UK Environment Agency www.environment-agency.gov.uk/netregs/

United Nations Tour Operator Initiative www.international-tourismpartnership.org

Webster, K. (2000) *Environmental Management in the Hospitality Industry – a guide for students and managers.* Cassell, London.

CHAPTER 14

Hotel unit financial management: does it have a future?

Cathy Burgess

Introduction

Earlier chapters have discussed a range of issues that may well have a significant impact on the financial aspects of the hotel industry in the future. But what do these, and other, changes in financial approaches mean for the finance function within the hotel unit?

Traditionally many hotels were self-accounting (Burgess, 2000a) with only a minor proportion of the functions being performed at a head office (if part of a group), the vast majority being performed on-site. Trends in the generic accounting area have resulted in management concentrating on 'core' functions with the impact of organizations now considering whether certain functions can be outsourced – either within the company or totally externally. Latterly, hotel groups have also considered whether this approach might also be appropriate for their accounting functions and have explored the potential for outsourcing or centralizing some or perhaps most of their accounting processes. The result has been that far fewer functions are now performed internally, and so there is less perceived need for unit-based management of the control and finance processes, with more regionally or centrally-based financial management.

But what about the future? Will there be one, as far as financial management within the unit is concerned? Will the trends of recent years continue, with a move away from control within the units to external offices, both in generic accounting and in hotels. With the reliance on systems – whether technological or procedural – to direct the financial aspects of daily hotel operations, will financial management in the unit become redundant? Are there differences between hotels that are part of a large chain and those that operate independently? In turn, what does this mean for financial controllers and their role, and will they then have a greater or lesser need for professional qualifications in this new environment?

This chapter looks at the impact of current and potential changes on the management of the finance function within the hotel unit and on the future role of the hotel financial controller. First, a brief review will be made of recent changes to accounting, followed by some general trends in outsourcing accounting functions. Consideration will be given as to the relevance for this in generic management and then to hotels, given the rather limited research in the area. The impact on the financial management will be reviewed, first from previous sources and then via a series of small research projects performed within the hotel industry, assisted by the membership of the professional association for hotel controllers, BAHA (British Association of Hospitality Accountants). The term 'financial controller' is used to denote the financial manager within the unit, whether or not formally qualified as an accountant.

Changes in accounting

Technology has speeded up accounting functions. Many basic tasks have become automated and routine and, providing that systems are effective and rigorous, may not need to be performed within the operating unit. This has resulted in a division between the two aspects of accounting into those that are concerned with *accounting* (i.e. processing data to produce reports) and those that are concerned with analysis and planning – *financial management* (Scapens and Jayazeri, 2003).

Where there is less need to perform the basic ('accounting') tasks in-house then consideration is given as to whether these may be performed externally to the unit and what benefits are gained from such an approach. Businesses are increasingly looking to save costs, both short term and longer term, through changes in approach and management. One approach to achieving cost reduction is to establish what functions are 'core' ('does it add direct value to an enterprise's goods and services?' CIMA, 2001) and hence need to be managed in-house, and what may be managed externally from the unit so that businesses can then focus on their core functions or products.

The move of functions off-site is generally known as 'outsourcing' which means 'procuring a good or service from third party rather than generating this internally' (CIMA, 2001). This may mean moving functions to a full external provider or to an office that is owned or managed by the parent company ('in-sourcing' or 'centralization', the benefits of which are discussed further below). Although initially companies have turned to outsourcing for economic reasons, later emphasis has been on longer-term benefits, so that the decision to outsource is seen to be more of a strategic decision (Kakabadse and Kakabadse, 2000, 2002) than a purely operational one in order to ensure success.

Accounting has been cited as one of the key areas of business that can be outsourced, whether as a whole or only partially. Processes such as payroll and data processing have been outsourced for many years, but other accounting tasks that do not require on-site activity are now feasible, such as payables and receivables, preparation of financial statements and tax. Other functions such as budgeting and cash management are also potential outsourcing candidates. It is not only cost benefits that are seen (Clott, 2004) but also improved management information (PricewaterhouseCoopers, 2002) and access to external expertise and up-to-date systems. Although in the past it was thought (Beasley et al., 2004) that only major groups could benefit from outsourcing, more recently the improvements in technology have resulted in reduced cost and hence made outsourcing affordable to most organizations.

However, outsourcing accounting may also have some perceived drawbacks. One of the main issues is a reduction in control and, as the business still has the responsibility for maintaining customer service, there may be conflicts (Robertson, 2003). As an example, loss of data, cash flow, revealing of confidential information and lack of on-site control are all cited (Beasley et al., 2004) – all of which have the potential to affect delivery of core services.

Given the concerns about loss of control due to outsourcing to an independent third party, an alternative approach is to consider internal outsourcing or centralization, whereby activities for the group are consolidated at a single, company-owned site. This aids in cost reduction (of staff, premises, technology) and also facilitates standardization of processes and reports, with a consequent improvement in speed and efficiency, while minimizing risk by retaining internal control (Davis and Albright, 2000). To achieve maximum benefit, processes must be integrated and carefully planned and managed for effective results. There is a potential danger that companies may 'over-centralize' with senior management imposing processes that 'inhibit junior managers' (CIMA/ICAEW, 2004). Hence a mix of centralized systems but with local management can optimize decision-making (Matejka and De Waegenaere, 2000) so that managers do not 'lose touch' with their customers.

Accounting and management

Inevitably the impact of outsourcing or centralizing various accounting functions has affected the management of the accounting area which is 'changing fast' (Herbert et al., 2003). In theory, outsourcing finance processes 'frees up finance staff' (CIMA, 2001) but the reality has been a reduction of staffing levels to realize the cost benefits. This has principally been at the lower, clerical, levels but some higher-paid jobs (Allott et al., 2001) may also be lost within organizations and there may well be fewer accountants in the future.

Within the unit, these changes have meant that the controller has moved from being a 'number cruncher' to being much more of a business advisor (Chaston and Mangles, 2001) with 'management accounting becoming management' (Allott et al., 2001). Financial managers have a wider role in their organization and consequently gain in importance in assisting in the management of the business.

In terms of skills, this changing role will mean that financial managers will need to develop further their business skills in analysis and problem solving rather than being just providers of information. They will need to become more 'interdisciplinary and analytical' as well as managing and coordinating systems and procedures (McIvor and McHugh, 2002). There is still a need for the financial manager to have effective internal controls (Pierce and O'Dea, 2003) while contributing to the strategic and business management decisions (CIMA, 2001) that are important to the long-term success of the organization. As a result, financial managers need 'sound commercial judgement' (Jackson, 2004) as well as developing improved technological skills and strategic planning and other non-accounting skills.

This, in turn, raises questions as to the ongoing need for qualifications and development. Inevitably, the professional associations see the gaining and maintenance of qualifications as crucial to the continuance of the profession (CIMA, 2004; ICAEW, 2004) and little evidence is found to the contrary from any other sources.

Accounting in hotels

Over previous years the trend had been for the hotel accounting function to be moved from a centralized or regional office to being operated within the unit – becoming more 'self-accounting' (Burgess, 2004) – aided by improved standardization of systems and reporting processes. However, further increases in the availability of effective technology have enabled different approaches to be considered. Additionally, recent global events have resulted in new economic pressures (Tri, 2005), with hotels increasingly needing to find more effective ways of managing costs in a very volatile market, as has occurred in the generic accounting area. Again, these are seen as strategic issues that require high-level decisions (Espino-Rodriguez and Gil-Padilla, 2005).

Hotels have traditionally managed almost all of their guest service operations on-site, with the exception of cleaners for rooms and public areas, and security. However, they are now also considering the 'core/non-core' arguments and considering whether some functions may be better performed externally, with a consequent save in operating costs (Gallagher and Kelly, 2003). Researchers such as Mirchandani and Liggett (2002) suggest that 'being a truly full-service organization is an admirable goal but rarely possible' and that outsourcing or centralization may well give them additional resources that they cannot afford in-house, despite the potential difficulties of loss of control. This is a particular benefit for small hotel groups (Paraskevas and Buhalis, 2002), which allows flexibility while minimizing resources.

There are few objective articles that consider outsourcing or centralization for hotel accounting functions (although rather more has been written by interested parties such as suppliers or consultants). Given that accounting is not a core hotel function, the evidence from generic sources suggests that this is highly suitable for outsourcing or centralization, particularly given the rapid improvements in technology that will provide information to aid in managing the business. Cline and Warner (1999, 2001) have shown that hotels should consider focusing on core services (such as guest service) and outsource support services such as accounting, with cost reduction seen as a key benefit, although the savings are debatable and again there are concerns about loss of management control (Peacock and Kubler, 2001) of systems and technology.

In 2001, Graham suggested the potential splitting of the basic accounting functions, some aspects (such as guest billing) remaining in-house with the production of final management reports being performed externally. Although there may be a reduction of control from some respects (Ahrens and Chapman, 2004), there is increased control in others – by focusing on day-to-day operations the business can improve its service to its customers. There is also ongoing access to business expertise as well as processes – execution as well as support and advice. Carl Weldon (1999) considered that, for his organization, the technological aspects were only part of the decision. The culture of the organization and attitudes towards both control and the management of it also contribute to this strategic decision. Again, the accounting functions were seen as a support service, providing useful and timely information to help managers run the business, rather than 'top-down' management of the accounting process.

These limited findings from hospitality literature support those from the generic sources in showing that hotel accounting may be subject to outsourcing or centralization (Andersen, 2001) with a consequent shift in the controller's role. There has been only minimal research reviewing the changing role of the controller (other than that by the author) with technology and outsourcing being key issues affecting the role. The trend in recent years has been for the controller to become much more of a business advisor (Burgess, 2000a) even while retaining the whole accounting function in-house. Technology has simplified many processes, but the operation and management of the majority of these has remained on-site. This increased importance has led the controller to perform a 'lead role' in the hotel, using more effective systems and reports, similar to those found in more technically-advanced industries such as retail. The finance function – and controller – must provide 'financial leadership to the business' that will contribute to the strategic direction of the organization.

Is there a need for professional qualifications?

The role of the accountant or controller is clearly going through major changes, whether in hotels or the wider business environment and, within hotels, generally there are mixed views, from the 'experience is more important' view to those who believe the maintenance of professional competence is crucial (Kafetzi and Hemmington, 2003). The limited findings available show that hotel controllers may well not hold professional qualifications (Burgess, 1999) and tend to have developed their skills through experience rather than professional training. The relationship between this and the shortage of trained staff has not been explored.

Within the USA, Damitio and Schmidgall (2001) showed that professional certification and qualifications are essential in order to raise and maintain standards, but in UK hotels (Burgess, 1999) there seems to be limited real commitment from organizations.

The research

In summary, outsourcing or centralizing the accounting function has become increasingly prevalent in the generic accounting areas in recent years, allowing organizations to concentrate on their core functions, for reasons of cost-savings and increased expertise. Within hotels, however, there has been only limited usage of this and indeed, in recent years, the trend has been for more of the accounting function to be performed in-house, rather than less.

Technological changes, and increasing pressure on costs, have meant that hotel companies are increasingly looking at other industries for examples in how to manage their functions and so are also considering the 'concentrate on core activities' approach. Hotels have been used to outsource some functions, but accounting, other than payroll, is somewhat new. An alternative approach, common some years ago, is to centralize many accounting functions and this may allow a greater degree of internal control.

When considering management of the accounting area, generic sources suggest that the role of the controller may change considerably, although there is still a need for financial management when only the processing is outsourced or centralized. There has been only limited objective research considering the impact of outsourcing or centralization on the role the hotel financial controller plays in the management of the business as a whole. This in turn raises questions as to the future education and development of financial managers.

As little objective research exists in this area, industry financial leaders, via BAHA, wished for further research to be performed to see what was happening in the hotel accounting area. Accordingly, three small research projects have been performed which, together with an open discussion at an industry forum on some of the results, allowed some general trends to be identified. The rationale and design for these projects has been discussed in other papers. The projects consisted of:

- an e-mail survey (243 questionnaires, 17.3 per cent response rate) to BAHA members, with questions regarding the extent of outsourcing and centralization, and opinions of members as to their future role

- a focus group discussion based on findings from the survey, that explored the issues in more depth

- the findings from this were then presented at an industry forum and the open discussion that followed added further opinions

- a mailed survey to a much wider range of hospitality accounting personnel to ascertain the level of professional qualifications and attitudes towards professional development. This was performed at the beginning of 2005 when the uncertainty of hotel revenues in the UK had stabilized and profitability had improved.

The findings from the research projects presented below utilize only the elements related to the finance function within the operation and the impact on the controller's role and their need for qualifications and development. These are compared to the findings from the secondary sources, within the individual section headings.

Issues facing hotels

The major issue for hotels (at the time of the initial research) was control of costs to help deliver the required net profit. Although latterly the situation has eased, hotels continue to be in a period of greater volatility than ever experienced before, with 'uncertainty as the norm'. This presents challenges as accurate cost control requires accurate forecasting of volumes and, with variations in occupancy levels, this is almost impossible to do with any real precision. However, systems have improved as a result of technological advances and so the quality of management information has also become more reliable, with a consequent improvement in decision-making.

At the same time, changes in the marketing areas have meant that branding of hotels has become much more prevalent, with standardization of both the product and services. This appears, say respondents, to have filtered into 'back-of-house' aspects and this, together with the improvement in systems and information, has also resulted in more standardization of reports. Companies now seek to have standard formats in reporting of all types and this has enabled streamlining of systems and management.

The extent of outsourcing and centralization

The initial results from the questionnaire survey showed that almost two thirds claimed to be fully self-accounting with only a very small number having totally centralized accounting and over half definitely expected this situation to continue. The most common function to be outsourced was payroll, although this still accounted for only just over a quarter of respondents. Centralization, however, was far more popular, with two thirds centralizing tax compliance and over half internal audit and insurance management and almost as many for procurement. Systems management, traditionally a part of the controller's role, is also now far more likely to be centralized, possibly due to increased reliance on sophisticated technology. Also, although the literature suggests a high level of automation from investment in technology, there was still evidence from controllers that many manual processes remain where there are 'huge gaps' in the design of integrated systems.

When considering the benefits of outsourcing, the literature suggests that cost should be seen as the main benefit, but this was not as widely accepted as might have been expected. Almost as many respondents as those that saw it as a benefit felt that cost was a risk, contradicting findings from other sources. However, other benefits were quoted such as 'focus on core services' and 'external expertise' as well as 'standardized products and reports', whereas 'loss of in-house expertise' was the main concern of a large majority of respondents.

Subsequent research and analysis showed a clear divide between hotels relating to ownership and style, with those that are independently managed (though they still may form part of group) and those that are part of a large branded chain. The style of organization, and the impact of this on outsourcing, is somewhat ignored in the literature, but in hotels seems to have a major impact on the approach.

The large hotel chains are experiencing increased corporate control and the reasons for this was given as cost, the quality of staff and managers at unit level. Whereas branding in the past was regarded as a marketing issue, it is now recognized as applying to all functions, including finance, with strong corporate processes becoming the norm in brand-driven hotels. This may well mean centralizing many of the accounting processes with a consequent reduction at unit level – and in some brands (particularly at the budget-hotel level) on-site accounting is minimal. It was felt also that developments in IT, together with economic changes, are driving a strategic change towards standardization of systems, again supporting the findings from other research. Even guest accounting can be run from a central computer based many miles away.

For the future in these hotels, there appeared very little impetus to consider outsourcing various functions to an external provider, with concerns regarding lack of control (security) and cost being paramount. It is far more likely that more functions will be centralized, with over a third of the survey respondents, for instance, expecting to centralize the purchase ledger function (payables) and sales ledger (receivables), a substantial growth on previous results. This allows the benefits of economies of scale while retaining the security and control issues within the organization.

Independently managed hotels, by comparison, have a variety of characteristics and may well be more complex and individual in design and systems, and hence have individual needs. Here there is a need for detailed technical support that may not be available from the on-site controller and so there is some incentive to outsource some of the more complex accounting functions, such as tax and pensions management. Additionally, traditional tasks that also require advanced skills and systems such as payroll and stock control can be outsourced, but all other tasks are normally retained on-site. It is unlikely that this will see much change as, with the complexities of the business (whatever the size), it may well be cheaper to maintain the tasks on site. Improvements in technology mean that the systems to support even very small hotels are now affordable and available for on-site use. This then allows the accounting function to serve directly the guest-service areas, for instance by accurate resolution of guest-account queries and hence act as a service provider to operational management.

A further outcome from the research was the opinion, from controllers in all types of hotel, that the concept of performing certain functions off-site is not new, and that some functions, such as payroll, have been outsourced for many years. Additionally, many controllers have past experience of companies who have previously centralized some of their accounting functions, albeit with a greater proportion of paperwork and labour cost than is now required, and then reversed this policy later when they found that standards of control within the hotel unit were suffering, and hence negating the cost savings gained previously. Comments such as 'we've seen this all before' were frequent.

Despite evidence from more generic sources, it appears that the potential for outsourcing in hotels is limited. For standardized, branded hotels the use of centralized functions (where much of the accounting is 'outsourced' from the unit to a central, but in-company, office) may be appropriate, but for others this approach is too regimented. Many hotels are too diverse in their characteristics for standard systems to be designed to suit their needs, even with the advances in technology that have taken place over recent years. For these individual, often independent, hotels an in-house self-accounting system remains the favoured option. The opinions of controllers show a lack of support for centralized functions, but also a feeling of these ideas being not new, just recycled.

The future of the controller

Given the separation of types of hotel, as shown above, a divide is also emerging as to the role of controllers that are based in independently-managed hotels and those that are part of a branded chain. There were very few respondents who thought that the role would be largely unchanged, whatever the type of hotel.

For independent hotels a financial controller is needed on-site, who is likely to be highly skilled and may well have the title of 'finance director', being responsible for all aspects of the accounting process, up to and including submission of tax returns. Even if these 'high level' tasks are performed externally, then it was felt that there is still a need for a controller as 'business advisor' to support other managers. Here the controller is very much a member of the management team who solves problems, advises the business on issues and future directions, and so offers a support service to management in other areas of the hotel. Their skills are likely to be strongly managerial, but also strongly technical in order to complete all accounts in house.

Branded hotels often operate a cluster approach, whereby several hotels (usually in a geographical region) are managed together from a regional office. This system is used not just for accounting but also for human resources and marketing. A senior financial controller oversees several units, reducing the need for high calibre financial staff based within each unit. This person is likely to be highly skilled and experienced, and probably professionally qualified. There may be a more junior financial manager based in each unit who has a lower level of skills and qualifications but who can act as an advisor to the business by interpreting results, identifying areas for concern and taking action. If there is no on-site financial manager at all then there is a danger that controls will be neglected and hence costs and revenues will not be optimized. The centralized controller is likely to have specialist accountants available to complete the final accounting processes.

Within the unit there is even more reliance on operational managers having strong control skills, which in practice may not always be the case. There was concern as to the lack of financial skills of operational and general managers and comments were made as to the need for controllers (whatever their level) to support the operation. There should be a partnership between the general manager and controller, as well as the controller forming part of the management team, in order to ensure optimum controls and maintain profitability. In particular, the quality of the general manager's skills can dominate the approach to financial control in the unit and, if there is a perceived lack of a commercial partnership between the general manager and financial controller, can cause major issues. In many cases, it was felt the finance function has overcompensated for weaknesses in management in other parts of the business. Again, this lack of skills of operational management is not found in the literature and may be a major issue for companies, which needs to be addressed elsewhere.

Wherever they are based, controllers should play a lead role in developing financial skills and processes. The level of this may vary with the type of hotel ownership, but the increased use of technology to improve systems has resulted in a change in role for all managers, not just controllers. The investment in systems means that the skill needs of the regionally-based controller may be different from one who is based within a unit and managing self-accounting systems. Hence three main types of controller have emerged – the experienced unit-based self-accounting person and the regionally-based high-level manager, plus the more junior controller based in a unit who has only limited experience and skills.

The future need for professional qualifications

The final survey was designed specifically to ascertain attitudes towards professional qualifications, particularly for the future. The literature appeared to show a single view – that qualifications were crucial for all – but the research showed a range of opinions as to the need for professional qualifications to support the job of the controller or accountant. There were many respondents who were very committed to their personal development of skills and qualifications, but there were others – often with extensive experience but a lack of professional qualifications – feeling that 'experience is far more valuable'. Less than half of the respondents said that they were 'professionally qualified', although several were in the process of gaining professional qualifications. There was also a distinct gender bias – men were far more likely to be studying at present, but more women wanted to do so. This supports findings from earlier studies by the author (Burgess, 2000b) and will be explored further in subsequent papers.

Are qualifications important for career progression? There were some widely differing views – less than half thought that they were relevant but, when the comments are reviewed more closely, many of the negative respondents have many years hotel accounting experience and, if commencing in their careers again, would need professional qualifications to progress. This then relates more closely to the findings from other sources. The implication is that, for the future, qualifications will become more and more relevant in order to demonstrate skills and professionalism when applying for positions, although the strong perception of respondents is that accounting and hospitality experience will remain the more dominant factor in their ability to do the job, supporting findings from previous research.

Conclusions

Evidence from generic industry suggests that companies can improve their processes and cost management by focusing on their core products or services and by outsourcing non-core aspects such as accounting. The success of this has resulted in hotel groups also considering this approach, resulting in the accounting function, despite being traditionally based in the unit, now being more likely to have some or most of the processes performed externally.

However, different approaches are found dependent on the type of hotel ownership. Within the larger hotel groups, concerns about loss of control and security issues have resulted in internal rather than external outsourcing becoming the preferred option, with functions being centralized at a regional or head office that then allows corporate control. The decision to centralize is also driven by the increase in branding that has resulted in standardization of systems as well as products and services. From an operational perspective, this has resulted in units being clustered into regions, often with a senior financial controller to manage the financial aspects of several hotels, perhaps with a junior financial manager based in the unit.

Independently managed hotels, which may still be part of a group but retain their individuality, still often retain a full or partial self-accounting function. They may be able to outsource some financial aspects, such as tax management, where specific expertise is required, but the majority of functions are still performed on-site. Here the controller is likely to be a financial director, with a high level of skills, experience and qualifications.

As to whether this will continue, opinions from on-site controllers have generally been very sceptical. In terms of the concept of centralizing or outsourcing, they have 'seen it all before' with companies moving from self-accounting to centralized, and back again. The reasons have always been linked to the amount of on-site control and financial management that is required in order to optimize profitability. Removing much of the finance function may well save accounting costs, but has implications for losses elsewhere. There is a need for very strong management if the impact of this is to be minimized and there are concerns as to the lack of finance skills from operational managers within the units, possibly negating some of the benefits of centralization.

Current controllers are inevitably concerned with their own future careers, and so would be expected to be a little sceptical about outsourcing or centralization, but the research showed stronger antipathy than anticipated, based on evidence from the literature. Even those controllers with experience of centralized systems did not demonstrate strong support for it, either now or in the future, although the expectation is that some processes will continue to be performed externally where specific expertise (such as tax) is needed.

For the future, companies do need to consider the skill needs of the different types of controller, and consequently their education, training and professional development needs. From the majority of sources it appears that, as well as gaining experience, controllers need to achieve and maintain a high level of qualification and/or certification, acquisition of these being deemed important in evidencing commitment as well as intellect. Although some controllers were less supportive, it appears advisable from the research that they should seriously consider improving their qualification and skill levels if they are to remain competitive in the current career market-place.

References

Ahrens, T. and Chapman, C. (2004) Accounting for flexibility and efficiency: a field study of management control systems in a restaurant chain. *Contemporary Accounting Research*, **21** (2), 271–301.

Allott, A., Weymouth, P. and Claret, J. (2001) *Transforming the profession: management accounting is changing*, pp. 137–140. International Federation of Accountants/CIMA, London.

Andersen Hospitality and Leisure Executive Report (2001) Spring/Summer, Arthur Andersen, London.

Beasley, M., Bradford, M. and Pagach, D. (2004) Outsourcing? – at your own risk. *Strategic Finance*, **86** (1), 23–29.

Burgess, C. (1999) *Continuing Professional Education: Financial educational needs of controllers, consultants and general managers*. Research report. British Association of Hospitality Accountants/Oxford Brookes University.

Burgess, C. (2000a) The hotel financial manager – challenges for the future. *International Journal of Contemporary Hospitality Management*, **12** (1), 6–12.

Burgess, C. (2000b) Gender and salaries in hotel financial management: it's still a man's world. *Women in Management Review*, **18** (2/33), 50–59.

Burgess, C. (2004) Planning for the future of centralisation of chain hotels. *Tourism and Hospitality Planning and Development Journal*, **1** (2), 145–156.

Chaston, I. and Mangles, T. (2001) *The role of accountants in the provision of e-commerce support to small UK firms.* ACCA Research Report No. 70. Retrieved on 22 July 2003 from www.acca-global.com/research/summaries/23876

CIMA Technical Briefing (2001) *Contracting out the finance function.* Chartered Institute of Management Accountants, London.

CIMA (2004) *CPD Policy.* Retrieved on 02.02.04 from http://www.cimaglobal.com/members/professional/cpd/CPDpolicy.

CIMA/ICAEW (2004) *Better Budgeting.* Report. July. CIMA/ICAEW, London.

Cline, R. and Warner, M. (1999) Hospitality 2000: The Technology. *Bottomline,* **14** (4), 17–23.

Cline, R. and Warner, M. (2001) Hospitality e-business: the future. *Bottomline,* **16** (4), 26–33.

Clott, C. (2004) Perspectives on global outsourcing and the changing nature of work. *Business and Society Review,* **109** (2), 153–170.

Damitio, J. and Schmidgall, R. (2001) The value of professional certification for hospitality financial experts. *Cornell Hotel and Restaurant Administration Quarterly,* **42** (1), 66–70.

Davis, S. and Albright, J. (2000) The changing organisational structure and individual responsibilities of managerial accountants: a case study. *Journal of Managerial Issues,* **12** (4), 446–464.

Espino-Rodriguez, T. and Gil-Padilla, A. (2005) Determinants of information systems outsourcing in hotels from the resource-based view: an empirical study. *International Journal of Tourism Research,* **7** (1), 35–47.

Gallagher, D. and Kelly, S. (2003) The future of hospitality applications. *Hospitality Upgrade,* Spring, 116–117.

Graham, I. (2001) *The dinosaurs face up to the future.* Internal paper, Arthur Andersen in-house journal.

Herbert, I., Wilson, R. and Murphy, W. (2003) *The evolving role of the finance function: an interactive, web-based research project.* Research paper retrieved on 22 July 2003 from www.accaglobal.com/research/180914

ICAEW (2004) *CPE policy.* Retrieved on 02.02.04 from http://www.icaew.co.uk/members/index.cfm?AUB = TB2I_1531,MNXI_11549.

Jackson, C. (2004) *The future of the finance director.* ICAEW Finance and Management special report ST2. March. ICAEW, London.

Kafetzi, V. and Hemmington, N. (2003) HCIMA proposes a new approach to CPD. *Hospitality,* October, 3.

Kakabadse, N. and Kakabadse, A. (2000) Critical review – outsourcing: a paradigm shift. *Journal of Management Development,* **19** (8), 668–669.

Kakabadse, N. and Kakabadse, A. (2002) Trends in outsourcing: contrasting USA and Europe. *European Management Journal*, **20** (2), 189–198.

Matejka, M. and De Waegenaere, A. (2000) *Organizational design and management accounting change*. Center for Economic Research, no 2000-61, July.

McIver, R. and McHugh, M. (2002) The organizational change implications of outsourcing. *Journal of General Management*, **27** (4), 41–52.

Mirchandani, K. and Liggett, J. (2002) Using outsourcing to stay on top. *CPA Journal*, **72** (6), 18.

Paraskevas, A. and Buhalis, D. (2002) Outsourcing IT for small hotels. *Cornell Hotel and Restaurant Administration Quarterly*, **43** (2), 27–39.

Peacock, M. and Kubler, M. (2001) The failure of 'control' in the hospitality industry. *International Journal of Hospitality Management*, **20**, 353–365.

Pierce, B. and O'Dea, T. (2003) Management accounting information and the needs of managers: perceptions of managers and accountants compared. *British Accounting Review*, **35** (3), 257–290.

PricewaterhouseCoopers (2002) *UK Middle Market companies attitudes towards outsourcing of Finance and Accounting*. PwC report, London.

Robertson, P. (2003) The future of management: does business history have anything to tell us? *Australian Economic History Review*, **43** (1), 1–21.

Scapens, R. and Jayazeri, M. (2003) ERP systems and management accounting change: opportunities or impacts? *European Accounting Review*, **12** (1), 201–233.

Tri Hospitality Consulting (2005) *Market Review*. February.

Weldon, C. (1999) *Centralization, wish or need*. Presentation at BAHA regional meeting, Birmingham, June.

Asset Management

This part of the book starts with US and European general perspectives on asset management in the context of the hospitality industry, where some definitions are provided and practices across the two sides of the Atlantic, respectively in chapter 15 and chapter 16, can be compared. Then, the sequence of chapters first focuses on managerial accounting implications of asset management practices, such as outsourcing in chapter 17 and sale and leaseback transactions in chapter 18; secondly presents reflections on hotel asset valuation using risk-return analysis, in chapter 19, and considering the case of management contracts, in chapter 20; thirdly the dimensions of autonomy and control are considered in the management of international hotel companies as network organizations, in chapter 21. The book closes giving career directions for financial directors in the hospitality industry, in chapter 22.

Hotel asset management: will a North American phenomenon expand internationally?

Paul Beals

Introduction

The present chapter is dedicated to exploring hotel asset management and its likely future evolution in the international arena. Because the term 'asset management' may suggest different functions to various participants in today's global lodging industry, a definition of asset management will be promulgated before the definition is further expanded through a review of asset management's component parts. Next, the origins of asset management will be explored, because the history of the function's development informs its present role, then an analysis of the parallels between the structures of the North American and international lodging industries concludes the chapter. Throughout the discussion to follow, a review of some of the asset manager's critical tasks and responsibilities will be offered, culminating in an evaluation of asset management's costs and benefits. Finally, the author will attempt to sketch the future of asset management in the international arena.

Asset management: a definition

Over the last ten plus years, as asset management has become an established feature of the North American lodging industry, various practitioners (among the earliest were Johnstone and Duni (1995:109) with: 'Asset management for hotels is the fiduciary responsibility of managing a hotel investment to accomplish stated financial objectives on behalf of ownership' and Raleigh and McCarthy (2003:52) with: 'Asset management is the managing of a hotel investment from the investor or ownership perspective') have offered similar definitions, but none that corresponds precisely to this writer's preferred version: *Asset management is the fiduciary responsibility of optimizing the value of ownership's lodging holdings*. At least four words of the fourteen comprising the preceding definition deserve elaboration if our straightforward statement is to launch the reader adequately along the path to a full understanding of a function as wide-ranging as asset management.

Fiduciary

There are some participants in the lodging industry – including especially representatives of management companies – who would argue heatedly that when ownership is well served by its operator, there is no need for an asset manager to protect ownership's interests. Although it is true that the typical management contract establishes an agency relationship, obliging the operator to act in the best interests of its principal (ownership), it would be naïve to regard this fiduciary bond as adequate to protect ownership fully. Notwithstanding the evolution in management contracts since the early agreements that egregiously favoured operators, a fundamental misalignment exists. Management companies – including especially branded operators – are intent on driving revenues, gaining market penetration and increasing the number of rooms managed, while ownership seeks to maximize the cash flow derived from individual properties. In the face of this fundamental conflict of interest between investors and operators, ownership needs a full fiduciary – the asset manager – to protect its interests, just as all firms must incur agency costs to motivate managers to act in shareholders' interests.

Optimizing

It would be simplistic to describe the asset manager's task as maximizing value. Often the route to maximizing value is patent, but it is not necessarily available to the asset manager. The asset manager constantly works within constraints – mutating ownership objectives, lodging-industry market shifts, the changing dynamics within a property-management team, conditions in the capital markets, etc. – to achieve not the maximum value but the optimal value for an asset, given its unique situation.

Ownership

Although there are some persons – usually designated by the clumsy descriptor 'high-net-worth individuals' – who own hotels, the complexity of today's equity vehicles is not adequately captured by the simple term 'owner'. Perhaps more important, the breadth and intensity of the asset manager's task varies significantly, depending on the structure of the entity holding the hotel. Thus the use of 'ownership' suggests not only the complexity of today's equity sources and deal structures but also the variegated nature of asset managers' relationships with ownership.

Holdings

Use of the plural holdings is prescriptive, not descriptive. Currently, too many asset managers analyse risk at the asset level rather than the portfolio level, seeking to optimize value asset-by-asset instead of across their portfolios. However, as the asset management profession evolves, and as more study of the function develops in academe, it is likely that the principles of Modern Portfolio Theory (MPT) will be more widely practised in the lodging real estate sector.

As the above discussion suggests, asset management is a concept that has evolved, altering its emphasis and expanding its scope to keep abreast of the changing structure of the North American lodging industry. Before turning to a discussion of the origins of the asset management function, however, let us expand our definition of asset management by reviewing the components comprising the function as it is practised currently.

Asset management: a taxonomy

The earliest academic inquiry into the asset management function in the lodging industry emanated from the Cornell University School of Hotel Administration, where two separate studies were conducted in the 1990s. For her 1995 study (Feldman, 1995a,b) Feldman surveyed owners, operators and asset managers, asking each category of respondents to define the appropriate scope of the asset management function and evaluate its effectiveness. With asset management for the lodging industry less than a decade old, it is not surprising that the 55 participants in Feldman's study reported quite disparate views of the function and its efficacy. In his 1999 study (Denton, 1999), Denton promulgated a definition of asset management and described the asset management process. This formulation was further refined and published as a chapter (Denton, 2004) of the 2004 book, *Hotel Asset Management: Principles and Practices*.

The schematic appearing as Figure 15.1 summarizes Denton's contribution and provides an outline for the expanded definition to follow.

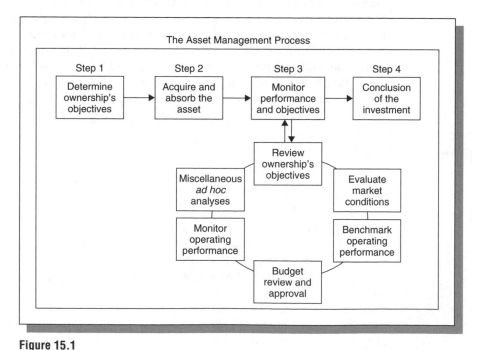

Figure 15.1
The asset management process.
Source: Beals, P. and Denton, G. (eds), *Hotel Asset Management: Principles and Practices*, p. 19. The Educational Institute of the American Hotel and Lodging Association and the University of Denver, East Lansing.

Determine ownership's objectives

Because ownership's objectives may span a range of nuanced options, effective communication between investors and asset managers is essential. Full comprehension of ownership's intent is probably most readily achieved when the asset manager participates in the setting of ownership's objectives for an asset or portfolio, but this ideal circumstance may not obtain if the asset manager is engaged after an asset is acquired or a portfolio assembled. Regardless of when the asset manager enters the process, communication must be continuous because ownership's objectives may, and frequently do, change. Perhaps even more important, an asset or portfolio's capacity to meet ownership's objectives may be altered by shifts in one or more of the three markets impacting hotel property values: lodging market, capital market, and the lodging transactions market. When such shifts occur, it is the asset manager's fiduciary duty to communicate these to ownership – whether the information has positive or negative implications for ownership and its ability to achieve its objectives.

Interpreting ownership's objectives requires a sophisticated understanding of the possible strategies available to hotel investors. To illustrate this wide range of possible strategies, consider two quite different types of owners: private equity funds and publicly traded real estate investment trusts (REITs). Private equity participants – typically including pension funds, insurance companies, high-net-worth individuals, foundations, and university endowments – join forces by forming limited liability partnerships whose general partners are investment advisory firms with long experience in lodging real estate. Private equity funds have finite lives (typically from five to eight years), permitting the partners to recoup and recycle their capital when the partnership is unwound. REITs are creations of the Internal Revenue Code (IRC). Under the IRC, a corporation, trust, or association, duly organized and registered in a state, qualifies as a tax-free entity if it derives substantially all of its income from real estate assets held as passive investments and if it pays out at least 90 per cent of its taxable income to shareholders as dividends. Effectively, a REIT avoids the double taxation of standard corporations and, all other factors held equal, thus enjoys a lower cost of capital.

North American private equity investors in hotel real estate recognize the risks inherent in lodging assets, but they embrace these risks, employing aggressive strategies to enhance their returns. For example, while the high fixed costs of hotels contribute to the risk of lodging investments, they also create opportunities to benefit from operating leverage. Thus, to take the greatest advantage of positive operating leverage, acquirers of hotels seek properties that 'need fixing'. The upside private equity investors seek might be realized through various exercises, including renovation, repositioning, re-branding, the installation of new management, or cost containment. Regardless of the tactic or combination of tactics used, the owner's objective is to create value, and this implies an active role for the asset manager.

The cyclicity of the lodging industry is a risk attacked by aggressive market timing; thus, private equity is perpetually posing the question: 'Should [we] be a buyer or a seller?' The perfect acquisition for private equity is a hotel property or portfolio that provides a robust opportunity to improve operating cash flows and whose performance is stabilized just as the lodging transactions market reaches its peak.

Finally, private equity purposely adds to its risk, using high levels of financial leverage to enhance returns to ownership. Thus, hotels that produce unlevered or 'coupon' returns in the range of 10 to 14 per cent can produce hedge-fund-like total annual returns to ownership ranging from 20+ to 30+ per cent (including gains from asset appreciation).

In contrast to private equity, publicly traded North American hotel REITs typically employ a buy-and-hold strategy, attempting to provide shareholders with current dividend income and capital appreciation through increases in share price rather than the frequent trading of assets. Although the occasional REIT will hold itself out as a 'hotel doctor', acquiring underperforming assets and realizing outsized returns through improved operating performance, most eschew this opportunistic tactic because such acquisitions are dilutive to earnings for multiple reporting periods until the asset's turnaround is accomplished. Thus, unlike private equity, REITs tend to have larger, relatively stable portfolios of assets. Further, these assets tend to be comparable in type, since REIT managers tend to seek the ownership of assets corresponding to their firm's 'sweet spot', i.e. the lodging product whose value enhancement management is confident it can achieve. The most common reason preferred by REIT managers when they sell assets is that the assets no longer provide a strategic fit with the REIT's portfolio – an explanation variously interpreted by analysts as accurate or a confession that the asset was either an inappropriate allocation of capital or has so declined in value that it is best excised from the portfolio.

As the preceding discussion of just two types of entities demonstrates, comprehending ownership's objectives is an all-important first step in the asset management process. Ownership's objectives will determine the assets appropriate to the entity's holdings, as well as informing branding decisions, the selection of property managers and the duration of their contracts. Above all, the investors' intent will determine how assets are managed, the amount of capital reinvested and the appropriate exit strategy.

Acquire and absorb the asset

The process of evaluating an asset for eventual acquisition is a painstaking one, requiring a detailed investigation of the subject property's competitors, the current status and likely evolution of the local lodging market, and the subject's positioning vis-à-vis its competitive set. The condition of the subject's physical plant must be assessed and various contractual relationships – leases, franchises, management contracts, mortgages, investor agreements, service contracts, employment contracts, etc. – explored to determine the property's potential to meet ownership's objectives. Assuming the property is deemed a suitable potential acquisition and an offer is made, ownership's various representatives and consultants repeat the evaluation in earnest – and of course with significantly greater access to information – during the due diligence phase.

Notwithstanding the demands of the acquisition process, most asset managers would prefer to be intimately involved in acquisition decision-making rather than inheriting assets whose potential was evaluated by others. This preference – described by one asset manager as 'I cook what I book' – derives from the sometimes conflicting objectives of asset managers and acquisition executives. Those charged with acquiring assets are motivated to 'get the deal done' and often will have little or no involvement with the asset once it is absorbed into ownership's portfolio. In contrast, asset managers are inclined to be far more attentive not only to the terms of the deal but to the asset's longer term potential, since they are charged with ensuring the investment meets ownership's objectives. Despite this potential for conflicting decision-making criteria within a firm, some ownership entities maintain separate acquisition and asset management functions.

Once the asset is acquired, the asset manager must collect, review and organize all the data relating to a property. Effectively, the asset manager becomes the archivist for all the information collected during the pre-offer evaluation of the property and the due diligence phase. In addition, the asset manager generates and verifies much additional information on the property, developing a comprehensive understanding of the property's market, management team and operating performance, physical plant, capital structure and contractual relationships. The encyclopaedic knowledge of the property developed by the asset manager serves as the basis for the hotel's asset management plan – a strategic road map detailing how the asset manager intends to achieve ownership's objectives. A well-crafted asset management plan will be a concise statement of how the asset manager will enhance the property's value, including: positioning and operating performance objectives, capital-investment opportunities, financial engineering opportunities and an exit strategy.

Monitor performance and objectives

As the expanded description of Step 3 of the asset management suggests, and as most practitioners confirm, asset managers spend at least 50 per cent of their time monitoring the performance of the properties in their portfolios. Asset managers report that this attention is necessary because property-management teams, despite – or perhaps because of – their proximity to their markets, are not sufficiently attuned to changes taking place, necessitating monitoring and intervention on the part of asset managers. Similarly, asset managers must monitor and benchmark operating performance to ensure that operators are driving revenues while controlling costs to maximize the 'flow through' so important to ownership.

The most contentious aspect of the owner-operator relationship surfaces during the annual negotiation of operating and capital expenditure (Cap Ex) budgets. Most asset managers report reasonable success gaining the trust and cooperation of the property-management team to arrive at realistic, attainable operating budgets. Achieving the same result in negotiating Cap Ex budgets, however, is more challenging. Asset managers express particular frustration with property management's 'use it or lose it' approach to the hotel's replacement reserves. While ownership seeks to build up a property's reserves against the eventual need for major capital expenditures, the operator prefers immediate, often low priority, investments that enhance the brand but typically provide inadequate returns to ownership. Thus asset managers are constantly urging property managers to make a business, i.e. return on investment, case for their wish list of capital investments, while operators adduce 'competitive pressures' and brand standards to justify their capital allocation choices.

Asset managers must accomplish the important tasks sketched above without creating a confrontational, 'we-versus-them' environment. In fact, an important role played by the asset manager is that of advocate for the property-management team, communicating to ownership the problems and challenges confronting the operator in achieving ownership's objectives. Further, the asset manager must often act as a coach, guiding the property-management team to resolve anomalous or one-off issues ranging from lawsuits to weather events and personnel conflicts. Finally, the asset manager also acts as a consultant, sharing with property management teams expertise that operators cannot readily or efficiently develop. For example, asset managers typically monitor brand initiatives, evaluating their impact on the guest and the bottom line. If the initiative is deemed unproductive, the asset manager, as ownership's representative, is better placed to negotiate exceptions or modifications with the brand than is the property's general manager, especially if the manager is an employee of the brand, as is typically the case under management contracts with branded operators. Similarly, asset managers develop expertise in various areas, for example, compliance, labour law, property tax appeals, that is spread across multiple properties, reducing the cost of implementing effective policies and procedures for each property in the asset manager's portfolio.

As suggested by the central position occupied by the task 'Review ownership's objectives' in Figure 15.1, throughout the process of monitoring property-level performance, the asset manager must constantly refer to ownership's objectives. Above all, the asset manager must continuously evaluate how well the property is meeting ownership's objectives. Are there, for example, alternative investment opportunities that meet ownership's criteria better? Effective asset managers must also gauge if ownership's objectives have changed or are likely to change, evaluating how well the assets under their control fit with ownership's altered strategy.

Conclusion of the investment

Most North American hotel owners operate under the premise that garnering the best price for lodging assets requires putting them out for bid. Thus, most hotel dispositions are managed by brokerage and advisory services firms or investment bankers in cases where the conveyance, usually of a portfolio, is accomplished by selling the ownership entity's shares or partnership units. Although asset managers may be involved in the selection of the firm brokering the transaction, they are rarely responsible for consummating the sale.

The asset manager's input, however, is key to the decision to put assets up for sale. The asset manager's chief role in the sale process is to help ownership decide when to 'pull the trigger'. Often the disposition decision will coincide with turning points in the life of the asset that are the province of the asset manager, such as franchise renewal, management contract expiry, or debt maturity(ies). Asset managers also participate in the capital-recycling decision, advising ownership on the most productive reinvestment options for the sale proceeds.

As the preceding discussion demonstrates, the asset manager has wide-ranging responsibilities. These responsibilities fall into four broad categories:

1 The asset manager serves as a strategic investment advisor, counselling ownership on the management of its investments and the appropriate acquisition and exit timing.

2 The asset manager is a financier, monitoring the capital markets to determine the most efficient financial structure and capital sources available to finance ownership's assets.

3 The asset manager oversees the execution of the applicable business model for ownership's individual assets, interfacing with property-level management to communicate ownership's objectives and guide the operator to their achievement.

4 The asset manager is the trustee of ownership's assets, husbanding them to protect against loss and ensuring their underlying value by deploying capital for appropriate reinvestment.

A sample of the component tasks comprising the first two broad categories of the asset manager's duties appears in the left-hand panel ('Role: Managing the investment') of Figure 15.2. A sample of the component tasks comprising categories 3 and 4 appears in the right-hand panel ('Role: Oversight of operations and the physical asset') of the same figure.

While the four broad categories are readily stated, the breadth of the pertinent tasks in each category and the knowledge required for their execution can be daunting.

The North American origins of asset management

It is sometimes asserted that the advent of lodging asset management in North America was the result of the shakeout that occurred in the domestic hotel industry in the early 1990s (Arora, 1996). Although the financial debacle of the early 1990s played a role in the development of asset management for the lodging industry, it was not a single tumultuous event that fostered asset management, but a confluence of factors. In addition to the lodging industry shakeout, the factors influencing the development of asset management included the changing nature of hotel ownership, the divergence of interest between owners and hotel management companies and the increasing complexity of the North American lodging industry.

The Hotel Asset Manager's Roles and Responsibilities

Role: Managing the investment

Advise ownership as to optimum investment strategies:
- Perform annual strategic review, comparing properties' expected performance to ownership's investment objectives
- Determine market value of properties and project future increments in market value from holding, renovating, expansion, or other strategic alternatives

Monitor the investment community:
- Track sales prices for comparable properties
- Track capitalization rates for hotel purchases
- Remain apprised of financing terms available

Select and oversee operators, franchise affiliations, and consultants:
- Determine appropriate franchise affiliation for property
- Determine appropriate management for property
- Retain appraisers, environmental consultants, engineering consultants as appropriate

Negotiate and administer contracts:
- Ensure franchise services are provided and billed properly
- Ensure management contract compliance
- Negotiate outside contracts (vendors, retail leases, service contracts) for optimal returns to ownership

Approve/monitor capital expenditures:
- Create long-term capital expenditure plan
- Review annual budget proposals for consistency with capital plan
- Evaluate impact on profitability/value from discretionary expenditures
- Approve capital budgets for presentation to ownership
- Review spending requests for compliance with capital budget

Role: Oversight of operations and the physical asset

Monitor ongoing financial performance:
- Review actual performance compared to budget and prior years
- Compare performance to comparable properties

Monitor the competitive market:
- Track occupancy and average rate trends
- Track new properties being considered for development
- Monitor demand generators for significant increases/decreases

Monitor the asset:
- Evaluate physical condition and anticipated capital requirements
- Evaluate major systems (HVAC, phone, PMS, etc.) for appropriateness and competitiveness
- Ensure legal compliance (health codes, life-safety, access for disabled)

Support and review the budgeting processes:
- Benchmark operations against comparable properties
- Communicate ownership expectations to property management
- Review proposed budgets, marketing plans, and operating plans for compliance with ownership's expectations
- Facilitate approval of budgets, marketing plans, and operating plans by ownership

Advise ownership as to management issues:
- Evaluate operator strengths and weaknesses
- Review industry trends that may impact property

Figure 15.2

The hotel assets manager's roles and responsibilities.
Source: Beals, P. and Denton, G. (eds), *Hotel Asset Management: Principles and Practices*, p. 8. The Educational Institute of the American Hotel and Lodging Association and the University of Denver, East Lansing.

Changing ownership

From the 1970s through the 1980s and into the 1990s, the nature of hotel ownership evolved, moving away from models that had served since the 1920s. The personal, idiosyncratic model of individual or family ownership, the closely held community financed hotel, the tax driven limited partnerships holding the local hotel – these and other forms of artisanal ownership gave way to a consolidation of hotel ownership in the hands of larger, more sophisticated owners. In the early to mid-1990s, the general tendency toward consolidation was facilitated by the increased use of several financing vehicles. REIT's, rehabilitated from the tainted image they earned in the 1970s, became the darlings of Wall Street, permitting real estate owners to recapitalize their holdings in an otherwise difficult financing environment. The rapid expansion of the commercial-mortgage-backed securities (CMBS) market paralleled the securitization of residential mortgage debt that had grown exponentially since the 1950s, providing the same liquidity and diversification to investors in commercial real estate that investors in residential real estate had long enjoyed. Private equity funds – variously described in the 1990s as 'opportunity' or 'vulture' funds – offered sophisticated individual and institutional investors the possibility of placing large sums of cash in leveraged bets on various real estate asset classes, including hotels. From approximately 1993 onward, the lodging industry was a favoured investment of private equity as it acquired hotel assets at far below replacement costs, turned around operations and rode the real estate cycle upward.

Investing through the use of the preceding vehicles – sometimes termed programmatic investing – allows the ultimate refinement of the sophisticated investor's objectives. For example, an institutional investor, such as a pension fund, can channel its monies into a private equity fund with a geographically dispersed portfolio of assets, achieving a diversification unavailable to the pension fund if it invested the same equity dollars in a handful of wholly owned hotels. Similarly, an insurance company buying various *tranches* of a CMBS offering can achieve a range of risk-return trade-offs and diversify its collateral far more efficiently than it could through syndicating a whole loan it originates or participating in loans syndicated by other entities. Regardless of the specific financing vehicle, there are two salient features of all programmatic investing: the entities formed to channel investors' funds to lodging assets are managed by individuals who are knowledgeable about the hotel industry; and the investors are pitting lodging investments against alternative investments, demanding a return commensurate with their higher risk. In this environment, the view of lodging real estate as a buy-and-hold, bond-like investment was supplanted by a far more aggressive approach. The asset manager's stock in trade – active management of the asset coupled with strategic planning of acquisition, financing and disposition – became talents sought by investors who, despite their distance from the individual assets of debt and equity portfolio, are demanding, sophisticated owners.

The lodging industry shakeout

The early 1990s found the North American lodging industry in the most distressed financial circumstances it had encountered since the Great Depression. Falling demand resulting from the Gulf War and a general economic slowdown coincided with an increased supply of rooms, causing a dramatic decline in operating results. As cash flow shrank, the aggressive lending practices of the 1980s left hotel owners with over-leveraged properties, exacerbating their distress and leading to a record number of hotel-loan foreclosures (Rushmore et al., 2001). As hotel property values sank, a creation of the federal government, the Resolution Trust Corporation (RTC), accelerated the process. The RTC was effectively the federal government's lender in possession, charged with liquidating the properties taken back by various federally chartered lending institutions. The RTC accomplished its task with dispatch, conducting, as one commentator observed, a 'fire sale' of assets, including of course hotels – an asset class that inexperienced or rogue lenders at the federally guaranteed lending institutions had found particularly enticing.

As hotel property values plummeted further after the RTC's intervention in the market, owners and lenders in foreclosure were forced to hunker down, continuing to hold their properties and seeking tactics to improve value to avoid selling into a drastically depressed market. In this environment, the asset management function gained significant credibility and grew. Asset managers were engaged to develop and implement turnaround strategies; many were successful, helping ownership to regain at least a portion of the value lost. During this period, the increase in the number of practising asset managers was facilitated because the lodging real estate industry was otherwise moribund. With new development at a virtual standstill, some operations shuttered, and the transactions markets stalled, there were numerous hotel consultants, lenders, owner's representatives and operators ready to take on roles as asset managers, assisting in the turnaround of distressed properties.

Since the asset manager's role in the early to mid-1990s was heavily concentrated on deriving value by improving operations, this has often led to the perception of the asset management function as a redundant system to be activated when property management falters. This misunderstanding is not alleviated by the firms representing themselves as asset management specialists but providing only property oversight. As the discussion earlier in the chapter suggests, although property oversight is an important component of the asset management function, it is hardly the *only* function. A true asset manager is above all a strategist who leverages knowledge of real estate principles, capital markets and the lodging transactions market to guide ownership to timely decisions affecting the make-up of its holdings.

Owner-operator misalignment

The lodging industry shakeout of the early 1990s also exposed the fundamental conflict of interest between ownership and hotel operating companies. During the late 1970s and through the 1980s, branded management companies used their superior knowledge of the lodging industry and their greater experience negotiating operating agreements to forge contracts that heavily favoured them. Operators almost always succeeded in gaining advantage by securing from ownership long-term (20 to 50 years) contracts that provided for rich base fees calculated as a percentage of gross revenues, while avoiding the imposition of performance measures that would ensure profits for ownership.

As long as lodging demand and the industry were growing, ownership was not attentive to this disproportionate sharing of risks and returns. But, when the developments of the early 1990s revealed the operator's impact on value and the relatively risk free income stream management companies enjoyed at the expense of ownership, the tide turned in owner-operator relationships. Owners (and, to a lesser extent, lenders) realized the need to 'push back', resisting operators' attempts to control the relationship and garner outsized returns.

Asset managers led the charge in this effort to rein in hotel operators and franchisers. In fact, one of the principal objectives announced for the formation of the Hospitality Asset Managers Association (HAMA) (Beals, 2004) was to present 'a united front to both operators and brands'. Moreover, as the fiduciary charged with advancing ownership's interests, the asset manager was the logical champion of the cause and this role helped confirm the importance of asset management in a changing industry.

Increasing complexity of the lodging industry

As demand for lodging increased through the 1980s, hotel management and franchising companies responded, creating new hotel concepts. One force driving this evolution was an ever more discriminating consumer devoted to collecting awards through a brand's loyalty programme. Such a consumer welcomed the opportunity to collect loyalty points from a chain across a variety of lodging products – a modest limited service hotel when travelling with family, an extended stay facility when conducting or participating in a training programme, or an upscale full-service property when travelling to meet with and entertain clients.

Branded lodging companies were eager to respond, not only to the needs of consumers, but also to the objectives of investors, who found individual segments across the newly expanded spectrum of lodging products suitable to varying investment objectives. In this more complex environment, asset managers provided added value because they understood the operational and return characteristics of the various products and, above all, because their strategic orientation helped ownership understand how 'the pieces fit together', enabling ownership to develop appropriately diversified or homogeneous portfolios, according to its objectives.

Measuring the performance of asset managers

As suggested in the preceding discussion of its origins, formal asset management for the lodging industry is less than 20 years old. As with any new way of doing business, the measurement of asset management's effectiveness is diverse and inconclusive. There are some common yardsticks employed to measure the asset manager's performance, but none is universally accepted as the most appropriate. The following review will describe some of the more common measures (Feldman, 1995b) of the asset manager's effectiveness. However, as will be demonstrated at the conclusion of the present section, no measure provides an absolute determination of the asset manager's performance because variables other than the asset manager's efforts may affect the outcomes measured.

Ability to understand ownership's investment criteria

As suggested by the examples provided in the discussion of various ownership objectives, owners' investment criteria are often complex and subtle. Obviously, ownership counts the asset manager's comprehension of its objectives as one of the most important measures of the effectiveness of their relationship, since it will guide all the asset manager's choices, both larger scale strategic decisions and those made in the conduct of day-to-day duties.

Changes in cash flow

The use of cash flow as a measure of the asset manager's success is eminently logical, given that the values of lodging assets are ultimately determined by the cash flow they generate (although these values are also affected by conditions in the capital and transactions markets). Moreover, the asset manager is charged not only with generating house profit through supervision of property level management, he or she is also charged with monitoring occupation costs, such as property taxes and insurance, as well as managing the reserve for replacements. Thus it is appropriate that the asset manager be measured at the net operating income (NOI) level, i.e. by the magnitude of the cash available after all cash expenditures but before debt service. Finally, if the asset manager is also responsible, as is often the case, for the property's capital structure, the appropriate measure is one level further down in the cash flow 'cascade', or the change in cash flow available to equity.

Appraised value

For some institutional investors, who must periodically commission appraisals to estimate the market value of their holdings, using changes in appraised value as a measure of the asset manager's effectiveness is appropriate.

Return on assets

Other institutional investors may use a measure of unlevered returns, as follows:

$$Return\ on\ Investment\ (ROI) = \frac{NOI - Capital\ Expenditures}{Average\ Book\ Value}$$

As the above formula demonstrates, the measure is a hybrid of accounting and cash flow figures. The ROI is in fact a return-on-assets (ROA) calculation using accounting values in the denominator and cash flow estimates in the numerator. It can be an appropriate measure of the performance of an asset manager employed by a public company, since the public markets are likely to evaluate management's operating effectiveness by focusing on asset utilization, while the asset manager is of course responsible for the components of the numerator.

Return on investment

Although owners frequently appear tight-fisted, often rejecting property-level management's requests for investment, this is typically because ownership is not convinced the expenditures will add value. In fact, many hotels are acquired because they represent opportunities to achieve a return on investment by investing, often significant sums, to realize marketing or operational advantages. For example, purchasing a hotel that has too little meeting space for its room count and adding meeting rooms can often prove a very profitable investment. Similarly, cost reductions achieved by the installation of more efficient equipment can provide substantial returns on investment. Measuring the asset manager's acumen in selecting such opportunities is usually a relatively straightforward process of comparing the costs to the present value of future benefits. It should be noted, however, that asset managers and ownership regularly perform such analyses *ex ante*, but not all firms rigorously perform the same analyses *ex post*.

Payback measures

Many asset managers, including especially those employed by private equity funds and other entrepreneurial real estate owners, measure their effectiveness in terms of value realized through trading assets. Such an asset manager might report for example that, '[we] bought the hotel for $30 million, invested $20 million, and sold it four years later for $80 million'. In a variant of this type of payback approach to measuring returns, an asset manager for a private equity fund might point with pride to the short period, say, 18 months to three years, between the acquisition of a property and the return of the equity partners' original investment.

Changes in RevPAR

Changes in revenue per available room (RevPAR) are often measured to gauge the asset manager's effectiveness in reorienting a property's marketing. The modifications achieved may be modest, changing the market segmentation, for example, to include 10 per cent more corporate guests at the expense of the group market. Or the modifications may represent a complete repositioning of the hotel, including re-branding and the implementation of a new marketing plan, yielding dramatic shifts in the segments served. In evaluating such efforts, both asset managers and ownership prefer top-line measures of the asset manager's performance, although the asset manager remains responsible of course for ensuring that improved revenues translate into greater profit or flow-through.

Asset management's cost

As the lodging asset management developed and expanded in the 1990s, in general two different fee structures were employed. Perhaps taking their inspiration from the practice of the original asset managers, i.e. investment managers, typically in the employ of banks or brokerage firms, who counselled clients on the appropriate composition of their assets, some North American lodging asset managers based their fees on the value of the assets managed. Under this structure, asset managers' annual compensation might range from 10 basis points (0.10 per cent) to 100 basis points (1 per cent) of the value of an individual property, with the fee for a more valuable property set at the lower end of the range and the fee for smaller property approaching 100 basis points. Under the second scheme, asset managers established a monthly fee for their services, basing their charges on an estimate of the complexity of the assignment as well as the reporting and communications requirements of different ownership entities.

Currently, scope determined fees are the widespread norm. Third-party asset managers will seek to be retained for a minimum of one year at monthly fees ranging from $8000 to $15 000, depending on the asset manager's estimate of the time and attention required by the individual property. Similarly, the budget for in-house asset management services is determined annually based on the asset management team's anticipated workload. If, for example, a number of acquisitions or renovations are expected, the asset management budget and headcount will be increased accordingly.

What is the value of asset management?

Although most of the performance measures enumerated above are quantitative, the use of any one or set of them to link pay to performance is problematic. For example, if a public company were to evaluate an asset manager solely on the basis of the return-on-assets formulation described above, the measure would act as a disincentive to reinvestment. If the asset manager avoids capital expenditures, he or she simultaneously increases the numerator of the ratio and decreases the denominator, apparently improving performance while, in fact, defaulting on two of the asset manager's most important responsibilities – protecting the value of the asset and profitably recycling capital.

A similar disincentive to optimizing value for ownership would develop if an asset manager for a private equity fund were rewarded solely on the basis of payback. Although most private equity partnership agreements set a finite target for the return of investors' funds, there is typically a degree of flexibility built in to avoid having to sell into a moribund market merely to meet the requirements of a partnership agreement. But the prudence that allows the asset manager to hold a property beyond its intended investment horizon might not apply to the sell decision if the asset manager were motivated to sell too *soon*, i.e. before the lodging transactions market reaches its apparent peak, to meet a payback objective.

Consider also the likely outcome if ownership sets both a top-line test and bottom-line test for the asset manager, using improved RevPAR and improved NOI as the measure of an asset manager's success. The asset manager will be motivated to make low-cost, cosmetic changes in the property rather than implementing meaningful long-term improvements yielding sustained increases in RevPAR. Similarly, in meeting the 'flow-through' objective, the asset manager will be pushed toward reducing operating costs, undoubtedly improving cash flow in the short term but, ultimately, leading to customer disaffection as service levels and the price-value relationship erode.

Finally, all the performance measures are necessarily relative. How, for example, is an owner to evaluate an asset manager's report that an investment in technology yielded a 20 per cent return? Twenty per cent may seem impressive if the ownership's equity hurdle rate is 18 per cent, but can the investor be sure that a different investment in technology might not have yielded 30 per cent? Consider also the example in the preceding paragraph. When lodging markets are improving, ownership cannot discern what proportion of an increase in RevPAR (and the asset manager's compensation) is attributable to the asset manager's actions and how much is simply the result of the property's performance being lifted by a rising tide.

As the discussion above suggests, although the performance measures used to evaluate asset managers are concrete and relatively easily applied, they are not used to determine compensation or the cost-benefit trade-off of employing asset managers. Instead, investors in the various North American entities employing asset managers seem to have accepted the proposition that achieving the returns required to compensate for the risk of a hybrid operating and real estate business requires the guidance of a specialist.

Asset management in the international arena: prospects

The spread of hotel asset management to the international arena will not be swift – just as its acceptance in North America is not universal – but it is inevitable. There are two general forces at work to ensure the eventual acceptance of asset management.

First and foremost, as real estate markets become more transparent, investors will comprehend the yield potential of hotels and will inevitably seek ways to participate in hotel ownership. Second, the trend of separating hotel ownership from operations, already a prominent feature in Europe, will accelerate. As illustrated in the discussion below, there are multiple factors (Brock and Foster, 2005) at work to foster the continuation of these developments across the world.

The transformation of publicly traded hotel companies

Although the various difficulties confronting the hotel industry over the last five years – the downturn in North American travel resulting from the bursting of the stock-market bubble and the events of 9/11, the outbreak of mad cow disease in the UK, and the SARS epidemic in Asia – had a disastrous impact on hotels' operations and profitability, the industry's travail was instructive for the financial markets. The management of publicly traded hotel companies, as well as their investors, learned that the markets penalized fee-driven enterprises far less severely than it did those owning hotels. The same participants also learned a corollary dictum well known to private equity investors: in a recovering market, the hotel industry's operating leverage can provide a significant upside. Thus, just as the managements of hotel operating companies were being pushed to shed assets, they found investors rotating into real estate as seemingly the last asset class providing appealing returns. Although there has been tremendous liquidity in the markets for all classes of real estate, since lodging is perceived as having the highest return potential, its multiples rose to record highs in 2004 and 2005. Countless hotel companies, large and small, including Intercontinental Hotel Group, Starwood Hotels and Resorts, Hilton Hotels Corporation and Whitbread, have chosen to deliver shareholder value by selling their owned hotels at premium prices and typically to return driven private investors.

For some hotel companies, including especially France's Groupe Accor, developing hotels and executing sale-leaseback agreements with large institutional investors has proven an effective means to recycle capital. Moreover, if the lease terms negotiated with the lessor-owner were accommodative, say, because Accor underwrote the investor's risk by providing corporate guarantees, Accor might enjoy a significant portion of the property's upside return. Until recently, a final benefit of sale-leaseback agreements was that the device effectively provided off-balance-sheet financing. However, analysts and credit-rating agencies now capitalize the operating lease payments, adding approximately eight times the annual amount of each lease to the operator's debt. In addition, the International Accounting Standards Board (IASB) is likely to follow the lead of the United States Financial Accounting Standards Board (FASB), which is increasingly turning its attention to lease accounting issues with the objective of tightening standards. In the face of these pressures, over the long term it is very likely that Accor and other companies will either take minority interests in new properties developed with joint venture partners, as Accor currently does in China, or sell properties it has developed to owners, taking back market-based management contracts.

Perhaps the most important reason publicly traded hotel companies will eschew ownership of lodging assets is that their brands have grown so strong that they no longer need ownership as a means to add rooms to their system. A company that can grow without the encumbrance of debt and without the drag on earnings of depreciation charges will always enjoy a superior multiple to an ownership entity. To the extent that publicly traded hotel companies can improve the reach of their brands, both within individual hotel categories through market penetration and across multiple categories by extending its range of brands, it will make itself indispensable to a wide range of owners.

Like lenders, who have always eschewed the ownership of hotels, the managements of strong hotel brands will increasingly reason that it is imprudent to compete with their customers by owning hotels.

Programmatic investing supplants direct investment in hotels

In Asia, aggressive real estate investment is a well known phenomenon, with closely held property companies and idiosyncratic individual owners managing their holdings attentively and earning returns appropriate to the risk of real estate. In many European countries, however, a system of government regulations and tax rules penalizes entrepreneurial real estate investing, concentrating ownership in the hands of institutions that contentedly view real estate as a commodity to be held for its bond-like returns. It is unlikely, however, that investors, whether large or small, will continue to accept the paltry returns offered by these institutions when they are confronted with alternative investment choices offering more competitive returns. The trend toward greater transparency and higher yields in property markets is already evident in numerous developments occurring over the last five years.

North American private equity funds have expanded to Europe and Asia. Goldman Sachs, Blackstone and Colony Capital, for example, have both acted independently and partnered with local investors to acquire hotels in the UK, France and Japan. Perhaps more important, international counterparts to North American private equity funds have become active acquirers of hotel real estate and this trend promises to continue. In 2004, for example, 27 per cent of European hotel-portfolio acquisitions were completed by private equity, which also demonstrated an increasing appetite for single-asset acquisitions and an interest in acquiring high yielding assets in emerging markets. Private equity funds are also being made available to the smaller investor, as witnessed by the formation in the UK of The Hotel Corporation, plc, a publicly traded entity christened a PEPSE, for 'public equity in private structured enterprise'.

The most common vehicle for investing in commercial real estate through the public markets, however, is likely to be international equivalents of North America's REITs. France, for example, has authorized a publicly traded investment entity known as a Société d'Investissements Immobiliers Cotée (SIIC), and multiple French property companies and funds have converted to SIICs. The government of Great Britain has committed to the eventual creation of property investment funds, or PIFs, modelled closely on American REITs. Although the hotel property class is not included in the current conception of PIFs, it is likely that a concerted lobbying effort by the lodging industry will convince government officials and the general public of the appropriateness of allowing investors an opportunity to invest in an important real estate asset class. Eventual acceptance is made more likely because the formulation of hotel PIFs, as proposed by the UK lodging industry, mimics the current structure of the American hotel REIT, which is a refinement of the basic REIT structure that developed over the years to resolve many of the same conflicts that concern British authorities (Beals and Arabia, 2003).

The debate in the UK is being watched with great interest by real estate professionals in numerous nations because they, too, are seeking to create parallel structures in their home countries. For the real estate entrepreneur, tax-advantaged REITs offer access to low-cost capital, liquidity and an opportunity to retain a degree of control over their assets. For the investor, whether large or small, REITs offer an opportunity to invest in professionally managed, diversified real estate that trades in a liquid market. As international markets modernize and the movement towards greater transparency increases, it is difficult to imagine that REIT-like structures will not emerge as a viable means of investing in all classes of real estate.

The increasing participation of high-net-worth individuals in hotel ownership also suggests that asset management will grow in importance. Kingdom Hotels International, the investment entity of Prince Alwaleed Bin Talal of Saudi Arabia, is adding to its holdings by developing and acquiring hotels in the Middle East, while also joining forces with the Bank of Scotland and Fairmont Hotels to form FHR European Ventures to acquire continental properties. Like many other high-net-worth individuals, Prince Alwaleed's approach to hotel investing is entrepreneurial and he employs a significant number of asset managers charged with driving superior returns from Kingdom's holdings. The recent trend toward the syndication of lodging investments among several high-net-worth individuals also signals an aggressive approach to hotel investing. Syndications permit wealthy investors to diversify their holdings, but they also interpose a syndicator that must justify its cost by driving superior returns and actively protecting the partners' interests.

The evolution of international property markets limned above will be characterized by the presence of an intermediary – the operating partner in a private equity fund, the managers of a REIT, or the syndicator – who communicates the return potential of lodging assets to investors. More important, these intermediaries will realize the superior returns available from hotel investments through sophisticated management, financing and trading strategies. As direct investment by institutions gives way to the superior returns available through programmatic investing, the need for asset managers will grow and the profession will gain greater acceptance worldwide.

Conclusion

Hotel asset management is a wide-ranging function, encompassing many duties from the setting of strategic objectives to the mundane collection and organization of data. In part because it is so diverse, it is difficult to put a precise value on the asset management function. Perhaps the strongest justification for asset management is that it meets needs that have developed in the lodging-investment market. As investors have come to understand the potential yields to be realized from lodging investments and increasingly demanded to share in the sector's returns, active asset management has become the means to respond to investors' needs. When operators abused the owner-operator relationship, exerting undue control over operations and damaging ownership's returns, asset management rebalanced the relationship. As the lodging industry's investor base increased in size and sophistication through the use of programmatic investment vehicles, asset managers have assisted the intermediaries managing these entities to assure their fiduciary responsibility to their investors. Numerous trends already apparent in the international arena augur developments in lodging real estate markets parallel to North America's, suggesting that the use of hotel asset managers will increase, becoming an accepted feature of lodging investment management across the world.

Acknowledgements

I am indebted to Professor Allen Toman of the Ecole Hôtelière de Lausanne, who provided background information and shared his views of the likely evolution of hotel asset management. The arguments and conclusions of the section on Asset management in the international arena are, however, my own.

References

Arora, S. (1996) The high cost of asset management. *HVS Journal*, June, 10.

Beals, P. (2004) A history of hotel asset management. In Beals, P. and Denton, G. (eds), *Hotel Asset Management: Principles and Practices*, pp. 11–12. The Educational Institute of the American Hotel and Lodging Association and the University of Denver, East Lansing.

Beals, P. and Arabia, J.V. (2003) Lodging REITs. In Raleigh, L.E. and Roginsky, R.J. (eds), *Hotel Investments: Issues and Perspectives*, 3rd edn, pp. 167–181. The Educational Institute of the American Hotel and Lodging Association, East Lansing.

Brock, P. and Foster, B. (2005) *European Hotel Transactions 2004.* Available at: http://www.hvsinternational.com/StaticContent/Library/040605

Denton, G.A. (1999) *Hotel Asset Management at a Crossroads: Identifying Challenges and Developing New Methodologies to Improve the Effectiveness of Hotel Asset Managers.* Unpublished master's thesis. Cornell University, Ithaca.

Denton, G.A. (2004) The asset management process. In Beals, P. and Denton, G. (eds), *Hotel Asset Management: Principles and Practices.* The Educational Institute of the American Hotel and Lodging Association and the University of Denver, East Lansing.

Feldman, D.S. (1995a) *The Roles and Responsibilities of the Asset Manager, the Operator, and the Owner in the Asset Management Function: A Descriptive Analysis.* Unpublished master's thesis. Cornell University, Ithaca.

Feldman, D.S. (1995b) Asset management: here to stay. *Cornell Hotel and Restaurant Administration Quarterly*, **36** (5), 36–51.

Johnstone, D.T. and Duni, J.A. (1995) Asset management issues. In Raleigh, L.E. and Roginsky, R.J. (eds), *Hotel Investments: Issues and Perspectives*. The Educational Institute of the American Hotel and Motel Association, East Lansing.

Raleigh, L.E. and McCarthy, J. (2003) Managing the investment: an introduction to hospitality asset management. In Raleigh, L.E. and Roginsky, R.J. (eds), *Hotel Investments: Issues and Perspectives*, 3rd edn. The Educational Institute of the American Hotel and Lodging Association, East Lansing.

Rushmore, S. et al. (2001) *Hotel Investments Handbook – 2001*. West Group, New York.

CHAPTER 16

Hotel asset management: European principles and practice

Geoff Parkinson

Introduction

Hotel asset management is a service relatively new and as yet not fully recognized in the European hotel sector but is well established as both necessary and appropriate in North America.

However, the number and range of definitions are as diverse as the individuals and companies providing the service. No one single definition currently encompasses the whole of the service provision. For the purposes of this chapter, the definition in use will be *'the commitment of resources for the purposes of enhancing value and maximizing owner's returns'*.

The definition and indeed hotel asset management, generally, presupposes that ownership and operations are vested in different parties. This is commonly referred to us as 'the split of the bricks from the brains' – a memorable catch phrase, which perhaps prompts yet a further definition of hotel asset management as 'putting brains back into the bricks'. This is the essence of hotel asset management – providing the owner (the bricks) with the detailed hotel operational and property market knowledge to ensure operational management activity (the brains) is focused into maximizing value and maximizing the owner's returns.

The requirement for active hotel asset management occurs, therefore, when there is a division of responsibilities between ownership of the hotel property and operation of the hotel business. Generally, this is effected through an agreement between the owner, who has invested in the property, and the operator who has the experience of hotel business operations. The operator also usually has a recognized brand name under which the hotel trades. Generally, such agreements between owner and operator take the form of either a management agreement or a lease.

There seems to be much confusion in the market place over the differences between a management agreement and a lease. Simplistically, the difference lies in whose profit and loss account it is. Under a management agreement, the profit and loss account is that of the owner. In a management agreement, the operator is employed by the owner, as an agent, with responsibility for day-to-day management and operation of the hotel business. For this service the operator will receive payment in the form of fees. In a lease, the profit and loss account is that of the operator to whom the owner grants a right of occupation to carry on the operator's business in exchange for a payment (of rent) to the owner.

However, as with many aspects of hotel ownership and operations, such simplistic arrangements are rarely the reality. Under a management agreement the operator will insist on a 'no interference' clause, which effectively precludes the owner from any but the most general involvement in day-to-day operations, even though it is the owner's business. Under a lease, the rent payable is often directly linked to the performance of the business (perhaps calculated as a percentage of net revenues or as a percentage of earnings before interest, taxation, depreciation and amortization, EBITDA), even though the owner has no other involvement in the business. It is in these circumstances that the role of the hotel asset manager becomes critical in ensuring that the owner's interest in the value of the property and the business is maximized, as is the owner's on-going annual return on the investment made.

With both management agreements and leases, the interests of the owner and those of the operator are never fully aligned. The owner will always seek to maximize annual returns through business profits (management agreement) or rent received (lease).

The operator, while sharing the same ambition to maximize profit and so operator's income in the form of fees (management agreement) or profit after rent (lease), will also have the ambition to maximize the overall value of the operator's brand rather than the value of the individual hotel property. This brand value may well be reflected in the quality and style of physical plant and equipment. Maximizing the operator's brand value across the operator's whole estate (not just individual hotels) may suggest the purchase and installation of, for example, signature beds in every bedroom. This would be at the cost of the owner but with what return to the owner? Similarly, as a sales and marketing tool to boost branded occupancy, the operator may determine that standardized tariffs are appropriate across the whole of the operator's branded estate – good for the operator but perhaps not appropriate for individual hotels.

The potential for such conflicts of interest is endless.

Why invest in a hotel?

With the potential for conflict of interest between owner and operator clear whatever form of agreement is entered into, why should a potential hotel owner invest in a hotel and become an actual owner? The answer is simply profit.

As trading businesses with a substantial property element, hotels have the potential to generate significant annual profits which, in turn, have the potential to provide large upside returns and rarely provide returns significantly lower than those available through other forms of pure property investment (offices, residential, retail).

Historic statistics also demonstrate that hotel transaction values consistently outstrip general inflation (Retail Price Index (RPI) or similar). Statistics gathered over the last 20 years by one of the UK's leading hotel business exchange agencies, Christie and Co, show this clearly (Figure 16.1).

These statistics, produced as an annual index from base 100 in 1975, show the UK hotel transaction value index outstripping RPI consistently over the last 20 years – provided of course the timing of acquisition avoided the peak of the boom period of the late 1980s!

It is every investor's objective to make their investment at or near the bottom of the trading cycle when the future potential is for an upswing. This objective has a dual purpose. Clearly, when the upswing occurs, trading and profits increase and so annual returns improve. But hotels are valued on the basis of their trading performance and so investing at a time when trading and profits are at a cyclical low suggests values will also

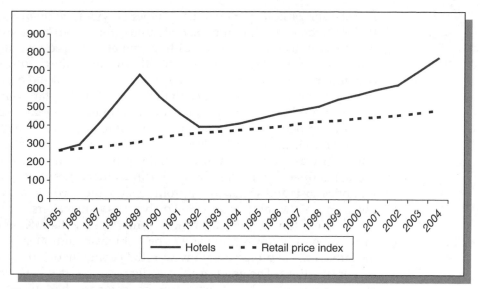

Figure 16.1
Hotel sales price index.
Source: Christie & Co (2005).

be at a cyclical low. With an upswing in trading and profits, not only do annual returns improve but value also increases. The objective is to invest at the bottom of the cycle and divest at the top of the cycle in order to capture improving annual returns and then benefit from the consequent additional capital value on realization.

Predicting these cyclical movements in hotel trading is difficult and the science (or is it art?) is imperfect. In Figure 16.1, the investor acquiring in 1989 at the top of the cycle would either require a hold period until 2002/2003 to recover the original capital value or, if disposal occurred before then, suffer a capital loss.

However, most investors are acutely aware that hotels are unlike most other property based investments. In the office market, property is let often to a single tenant at a fully agreed fixed annual rental which generally escalates in line with the retail index price over a period of many years. Few if any other services are provided to that tenant. The property owner does not get involved in the business of the tenant and indeed cares little as to whether that tenant is an accountant, a lawyer, a marketing organization, a public body or any other reasonable occupier, provided they can pay the agreed rent. In the hotel market with the owner's income dependent upon the trading performance of the business, the owner must take an active interest in the business. Space (bedrooms or meeting rooms) are let to multiple occupiers (guests) for 24-hour periods, many other services are offered to the occupier, even in limited service units (reception, breakfast, business services and the like), 24-hour rental rates (room tariffs) can vary day by day, month by month and are subject to discounting policies. The business and financial status of the occupier (guest) is of little relevance to the owner, but the status and brand of the business manager is of paramount importance in gaining competitive advantage and so maximizing revenues. The status and efficiency of the business manager is also of critical importance as the owner's income (be it profits or rent based on profits) is directly impacted by the business managers' ability to minimize costs and so maximize profits. Hence the need for 'active ownership' – the services provided by hotel asset managers.

Currently, the commercial property markets in the UK, and many other areas of Europe, are at best sluggish and offer little incentive for the professional investor to become involved as an owner/landlord. The hotel sector has therefore become 'fashionable' and the ownership structures of the sector are changing rapidly. Many of the major brand owners (Intercontinental, Marriott, Hilton, Ramada to name just four of the more well known brands) have all sold properties to institutional and private equity investors. These investors have then simultaneously entered into arrangements for the brand representation and management to remain. These new investor/owners see the potential upside benefits of hotel ownership through enhanced values and strong annual returns, but have little or no experience of hotel business management. Their need for active hotel asset management is clear.

As trading businesses, hotels are susceptible to the impact of economic cycles and to the effects of unconnected events. The hotel sector in Europe is generally recognized as tracking an approximate eight-year cycle. For the UK, and with hindsight, the peak of the last cycle occurred in 2000. The subsequent downturn which, if unaffected by external events, may have bottomed out in 2003 or 2004 was exacerbated by the events of September 2001 in New York, by the countrywide outbreak of foot and mouth disease, the SARS epidemic curtailing travel, the threat of war with Iraq and then by actual conflict. The downturn in 2002 was, as a result, much more severe and immediate than anyone could have anticipated. The consequence was immediate distress for many trading units with the most spectacular being the demise of Meridien hotels as a viable business. The company had been acquired in 2000 by an institutional investor with a number of the units being immediately sold and leased back on revenue based rental terms. The downturn in business activity following the world events of 2001 and 2002 was such that rental guarantees were not met and Meridien defaulted.

While the sequence of events in 2001 and 2002 had an unusually strong impact on demand for hotel facilities, it cannot be seen as a unique sequence which would never again occur. Investors into the hotel sector can anticipate substantial increases in value and good annual returns but also need to focus on the deal that is struck with their operator or, more particularly, their tenant. In recent years a number of sale and leaseback transactions have been completed. Most are on commercial and financial terms which, given normalized trading cycles, are sustainable. However, a small number have been struck on commercial and financial terms which, in even the most buoyant of trading conditions, must inevitably lead to conflict between owner and tenant operator.

By way of example, a sale and leaseback transaction between an institutional investor and a branded operator struck on the basis of rent being calculated as say 30 per cent of revenues must at some point lead to conflict. Many items of hotel revenues do not achieve a net profit contribution of 30 per cent of revenue – most food transactions do not make a 30 per cent profit. From the owner's perspective every additional £1 of revenue generates an additional 30p in rent. From the tenant operator's perspective every £1 of revenue which does not make a 30 per cent profit costs that tenant money – the tenant pays 30 per cent of revenue as rent regardless of the profit margin. It is therefore in the interest of the tenant not to transact when a 30 per cent profit margin is not assured. There is therefore clearly a conflict of interest between the owner and the operator tenant.

But why might such a deal have been conceived? The answer is probably arithmetic. For most Stock Exchange quoted hotel companies, as a result of the various world events, the City downgraded their share prices often to the extent of the value, as reflected in share price, being lower than the anticipated realization value of the individual business enterprises (the break-up value). Some companies reverted to private ownership and de-listed. Others took the view that returning funds to the shareholder through transactions such as sale and leaseback could redress this imbalance. If the quantum of funds to be returned to shareholders was, for example, £85 million, this would require a cash input into the company of say £150 million to cover the costs of the transactions and to maintain balance sheet ratios at acceptable levels. To achieve a cash input of £150 million would require the disposal of hotels independently valued at that amount. The new investor would be prepared to acquire these hotels provided the deal was struck on terms that resulted in the investor receiving say a minimum 9 per cent return on the investment, i.e. £13.5 million annually, with a 9 per cent return being attractive against other property sector investment. Having identified the hotels which in aggregate are valued at the required £150 million, the calculation is then what percentage of revenues of these hotels does the investor need as rent to achieve the 9 per cent annual return – the arithmetic results in 30 per cent of annual revenues of £45 million. Hence the rent is struck at 30 per cent of revenues. To cross check this sequence of calculations, these hotels generating £45 million revenues would achieve during the down-cycle an EBITDA before rent of say 33 to 35 per cent of revenues – £14.9 to £15.8 million. At that level of EBITDA the valuation based on a 10 times multiple of EBITDA would be £150 million. These arithmetic calculations are individually quite plausible and do reflect market norms in terms of return to investors, EBITDA margins and valuations. However, they do not reflect the reality of the critical element in the structure of the deal – the way in which future rents are calculated and the conflict of interest that can result.

The role of the hotel asset manager is to ensure that such anomalies do not occur. How then are such anomalous elements of these deals avoided? The professional hotel asset manager will say one word, 'process', and then qualify that word with 'hotel sector knowledge and experience'. The process begins with understanding and then defining the objectives of the owner/investor – setting the strategy for the investment. In this there are five key areas to consider.

Process's five key areas

Understanding what

What is the investor intending to acquire or develop? And then defining:

- How much capital expenditure will the asset require?

- How much additional investment will be necessary to maintain/change the brand?

- Does potential future performance support the purchase price and the additional investment required or the turn-key development costs?

Understanding how

How is the deal structured? And then defining:

- Is this an equitable deal?

- Is there sufficient 'breathing room' to accommodate market/economic fluctuations?

Understanding when

Is this the right time to acquire? And then defining:

- When is asset disposal proposed?
- Does the investment horizon match with the hotel sector economic cycle?

Understanding where

Where does this asset fit within the overall investment strategy? And then defining:

- How does this asset enhance the portfolio?

Understanding why

Why this investment? And then defining:

- Does this investment meet the criteria for required returns?
- Does this investment reflect a good blend of assets/locations/ product type?

Any business strategy should include these five key components and while this element of the process will not guarantee positive results, it does start to guide the investment, providing a roadmap towards achieving the desired and intended results. Of course, the route may be altered as the environment changes, but a good strategic plan should provide guidance for all interim tactical decisions so that they are directly and philosophically aligned with the original objectives.

If there are negative answers arising from the understanding and defining process, then the hotel asset manager needs to address the issues identified and assist the investor in perhaps renegotiating the structure of the deal, renegotiating elements of the commercial terms proposed, reviewing the proposed branding or, in the extreme, advising that this deal will not meet the investor's own objectives and so should not proceed. However, with positive answers to the questions posed, the deal can proceed and the process continues.

The next stage in the process focuses upon the pre-opening activities.

Pre-opening activities

Pre-opening activities set the stage for the relationship between the owner through the hotel asset manager and hotel operator.

During this period, it is important to have a thorough understanding of the history of the project, the owner's objectives and the owner's reporting requirements. At this time it is also useful to review again the key elements of the management agreement or lease and begin to prepare the information request for the hotel operator. The process then continues with the hotel asset manager:

- Serving as the owner's representative at all meetings with the operator.

- Developing a detailed monitoring process with the aim of ensuring that realistic budgets, which challenge management and meet owner's financial objectives, are established. On an on-going basis the hotel asset manager will then implement the budget review process, variance analysis, monthly forecasting and accuracy reports to monitor achieved results and ensure operator accountability.

- Establishing reporting routines and expectations between the hotel asset manager and owner. Normally this would include summarized weekly and monthly written memorandum/report for the owner giving brief headline results and commentary thereon. On a quarterly and annual basis reporting will be more detailed and exhaustive.

With the reporting expectations of the owner established and agreed, the next steps are:

- Establish reporting requirements and expectations between the hotel operator and hotel asset manager, with the hotel asset manager detailing the expectation and ensuring that the schedule and detail of communications is clearly established and agreed.

- Review and recommend to the owner, the hotel operator's initial operating and capital expenditure plan and the levels of initial and operating inventories. This is a vitally important element of the pre-opening hotel asset management function. The operating and capital expenditure plans set the foundation for the hotel's operation for the following years. It is therefore most important to ensure that the plans are reasonable and appropriate, given the size of the hotel, its age and the markets in which the hotel will operate. It is equally important that the hotel asset manager works with the operator to establish appropriate initial and operating inventories based on the size of the hotel and its anticipated business volume.

- Review, monitor and make recommendations regarding the hotel operator's pre-opening sales, marketing and public relations efforts. One of the critical items for new hotels, and in particular for conference/convention and resort properties, is the hotel operational management's marketing strategy and planned sales activity, and the corporate support provided, to ensure that advance bookings are achieved in volumes matching budget anticipation. Marketing and sales activity must be a prominent agenda item discussed with management on a weekly/monthly basis to ensure that goals are clearly defined, action steps are focused, and funds are available to support the effort. These regular discussions with the operator will evaluate the number of people directed to the effort and their individual objectives and successes. It is important to ensure that sufficient incentives are in place to motivate the staff and that not only are room-nights booked important, but that the food, beverage and ancillary revenue generated by those room-nights is considered.

- Review the hotel operator's proposed staffing plan. Given that payroll costs comprises approximately 60 per cent of hotel's expenses, careful evaluation of the staffing plan is needed, including numbers of people and the established productivity benchmarks.

- Review and make recommendations to the owner regarding the hiring of key hotel executives (general manager, director of sales, financial controller etc.). Typically, the operator would provide résumés of qualified candidates who are proposed for each position. The hotel asset manager would assist the owner in reviewing each candidate's qualifications and conduct personal interviews for those recommended by the operator.

- Assist in determining opening inventory levels of food, beverage and operating supplies and equipment. This task would reflect the operating inventories review which will have established inventory levels appropriate for the size of the hotel and its anticipated business volume.

- Work with the owner to establish working capital requirements which are often established within the management agreement. The hotel asset manager should test those requirements to ensure that they are sufficient for property operations on a month-to-month basis but are not in excess of reasonable requirements.

- Monitor the hotel operator's compliance with the pre-opening and technical services agreements between the owner and hotel operator. Part of the role of a hotel asset manager is to have a comprehensive understanding of the agreements under which the hotel is developed and operated to ensure that all parties are in compliance.

- Assist in the preparation of the proforma operating results and in reviewing the hotel operator's projections. Typically, the hotel asset manager will prepare a comparative financial analysis using data from similar hotels (size, location, anticipated ADR, market orientation, etc.) as well as from the initial market feasibility or other projections of future trading prepared during the analysis of the initial investment decision. The hotel operator would also be expected to prepare the operating budget for the hotel, which the hotel asset manager will incorporate into the comparative financial model to evaluate and assess the budget for reasonableness. It is important that the budget does include 'stretch' goals for hotel management. In management agreements it is common that performance standards for the operator that relate to incentive management fees (and perhaps early termination through non-performance) are typically based upon anticipated proforma results. The benchmarks established must therefore meet the financial objectives of the owner.

- Assist in reviewing the actual versus budget for both capital and operational expenditure. If the hotel is new or has undertaken major refurbishment, little expenditure on capital improvements would be anticipated during the initial operating year. For an existing hotel the hotel asset manager would ensure that the work required to meet the incoming operator brand standards (often called 'the punch list') is necessary, comprehensive and complete.

Operations

With the foundation of the relationship established during the pre-opening phase, the hotel asset manager's role is clearly established. It is then appropriate to develop an on-going strategic plan for the asset, which would merge together the owner/investment's strategy with a competitive market overview, the proposed market positioning of the hotel and the performance expectations, the operating strategy and any proposed capital expenditure. This strategic asset plan becomes the referral point against which all the tactical decisions required during the operation of the hotel can be assessed. The hotel asset manager will then:

- Serve as the owner's representative at meetings with the operator and when appropriate attend the owner's Board meetings to provide current inputs to the owner's decision-making.

- Provide on-going monitoring and oversight of the hotel operator's management and operations and report to the owner on a periodic basis (determined by the owner but usually monthly).

This monitoring process begins at the time the budget is presented, reviewed and approved. With an approved budget, the monitoring process would generally involve a weekly meeting with the general manager of the hotel to discuss the past week's performance and forecasts for the coming periods, the pace and volume of advance bookings, the detailed financial performance and variances from budget/forecast with particular emphasis given to unanticipated expenses, opportunities for reducing future period costs and enhancements to revenue.

- Evaluate the hotel operator's management team performance and their ability to adhere to budget, effectively explain variances and have standard operating and financial controls in place. It is generally accepted that the hotel general manager should be accountable to the owner for the current performance of the hotel. Performance should be benchmarked against an agreed competitive set of hotels, the performance of comparable same brand hotels system-wide as well as against budget and forecast.

- Early in the fourth quarter, the hotel asset manager will begin the next year's budget process. The process is the same as described earlier for the review of the first year proforma. Once reviewed, the hotel asset manager will prepare a summary of questions and comments for the hotel operator and, where appropriate (and with the benefit of operator responses), request such modifications to the budget as appear reasonable and appropriate. This element of the process again needs to focus on pushing management to perform to higher levels ('stretch budget').

- As an adjunct to the strategic asset plan that focuses on longer-term objectives, the hotel asset manager can assist the hotel operator in developing the tactics required to enhance operational and financial performance. This is best presented as an annual strategic plan, which again can then be utilized as a tool to guide tactical operational changes throughout the year. Progress within this annual strategic plan then becomes a major part of the agenda for the monthly owner's meeting.

- Ensure timely and accurate decision-making reporting and cash distribution as set out in the management agreement or lease. While most agreements require hotel accounting to follow the principles of the *Uniform System of Accounts*, this manual is not totally prescriptive and does allow for variations in accounting treatment of some revenue and expense items which need to be reviewed in the context of the provisions within the management agreement or lease.

- Monitor capital expenditures, ensuring projects are completed satisfactorily, within budget and as approved by the annual CAPEX budget. It is also important for the hotel asset manager to ensure that reserve funds are not released without appropriate operator and owner approvals.

- Evaluate operator's central cost allocations and any policy changes relating to them. If significant policy changes do occur, the impact on the hotel needs to be assessed and, if warranted, appealed either directly to the operator's central office or via the owner's association.

- Ensure that the hotel is receiving appropriate support from the hotel operator's regional and corporate resources as well as its worldwide sales and marketing resources. National and international hotel companies have extensive marketing and distribution resources but the amount and breadth of resource directed at an individual hotel will be a direct result of the combined efforts of that hotel's management team and the hotel asset manager in ensuring the hotel receives appropriate levels of corporate attention. Some aspects of this are easy, such as ensuring the hotel is properly identified and categorized in the brand reservations and marketing systems. Other activities are less obvious, and it is important that they are monitored to confirm that the benefit of the activities out-weigh the associated costs. In this respect brand loyalty and frequent stay programmes have received much recent attention.

- Perform routine inspections of the physical facilities, at minimum on a quarterly basis, to assess issues such as health and safety compliance, liability and risk assessment (particularly if an increase in guest and/or staff accidents is noted), investigate guest complaints associated with physical plant issues, and assess overall physical condition and upkeep.

- Monitor fixed cost issues such as capital reserves, insurance and property taxes. Capital reserves require careful monitoring and perhaps re-forecasting during the cyclical periods of declining revenues. If capital expenditures require proportionate readjustment, this would feature during discussion with the hotel operator in the following budget season.

- Assist the owner in evaluating those parts of the hotel operated by third parties under subleases or concession arrangements, such as car parking, health and beauty salons, retail units, travel agency and similar activities. Is the decision to outsource these services financially beneficial to the owner?

This outline of the role of the hotel asset manager in the pre-opening and operation of the hotel is only one part of the task. This role is effectively 'asset monitoring'. To be truly effective a hotel asset manager must also be continuously aware of and actively seek out opportunities for revenue and profit improvement. The day-to-day operational management of the hotel rarely have the time (or perhaps the skill sets) needed to identify those areas of the operation which, while not necessarily under-performing against expectations, do occupy time or physical space which can be more profitably utilized by other activities. Noting that lobby gift shop revenues have declined over time but meet budget expectations is asset monitoring, identifying an alternative use as a new profit centre is asset management. Ensuring capital expenditure programmes are delivered in accordance with plan, on time and within budget is asset monitoring, reprioritizing capital expenditure to address projects which yield the greatest financial returns and so add to asset value is asset management.

Equally, the hotel asset manager must constantly be aware of the strategy of the investor/owner and ensure that all decisions made with respect to the operation contribute to the achievement of the investor/owner strategic objectives. At any given time the effective hotel asset manager must be able to advise the investor/owner of what stage in the life cycle the asset is now in, where that asset sits in the roadmap set out in the strategic asset plan and what the timeframes are for the achievement of the ultimate investment goals.

The effective hotel asset manager must be able to assess current asset value and have the skill sets available to identify and advise the owner on ways in which to enhance that existing asset value, perhaps through converting under-utilized space, redevelopment, outsourcing, adjacent property sale or through further acquisition.

In time and in accordance with the strategic asset plan, the hotel asset manager must consider the timeframe for disposal and redeployment of the investment. It is important that, in the decision to dispose and liquidate an investment, the envisaged timeframe allows for predisposal preparation of the asset and its operation. The implications of disposal under the terms of the management agreement or lease need consideration. Proposed capital expenditure generally is viewed in the context of the longer-term maintenance or enhancement of asset value and in the pre-disposal period projects not yet underway need review to ensure they add to value within the shorter timeframe available prior to disposal.

If disposal is contemplated on the basis of the hotel business cycle, consideration must be given to whether economies made during the downturn need to be reversed prior to disposal or whether that should be the prerogative of the new investor.

And finally with regard to disposal, experience has shown that it is important to leave some small asset value enhancements unrealized thus providing the incoming investor with at least the theoretical opportunity to realize their own short-term enhancement to their incoming investment value.

In this short chapter it is not possible to detail all the tasks an experienced professional hotel asset manager will undertake. Each hotel has its own unique opportunities for value enhancement – the hotel asset manager will identify these and establish the activities required for their realization.

A management accounting perspective on hotel outsourcing

Dawne Lamminmaki

Introduction

Outsourcing carries significant implications for a hotel's cost structure and control procedures. In light of this, it is important that hotel accountants are appropriately equipped to play an active role in outsourcing decision-making and control. The objective of this chapter is to provide a management accounting perspective on issues surrounding hotel outsourcing management. This objective is pursued by initially overviewing accounting and managerial outsourcing commentaries. Following this, the chapter outlines the many costs and benefits that should be considered when deciding whether to outsource and a discussion of the desirability of applying a long-term oriented financial analysis when appraising outsourcing proposals.

The chapter is informed extensively by a review of pertinent literature together with findings emanating from the conduct of interviews with 15 managers representing 11 large hotels in Queensland, Australia. The interviewees comprised three general managers, nine financial controllers, two food and beverage managers and one project engineer.

In this chapter, outsourcing will be viewed as '... the process whereby activities traditionally carried out internally are contracted out to external providers' (Domberger, 1998:12). Outsourcing can assume various forms of inter-firm relationships such as joint ventures, alliances, partnerships, shared service arrangements (Kakabadse and Kakabadse, 2000), franchising (Roh and Kwag, 1997) and the establishment of virtual organizations involving a core of executives and workers supported by outside contractors and part-time help (Handy, 1989). It should be noted that outsourcing is not the same as downsizing.

Accounting and outsourcing management commentaries

Outsourcing has become a significant facet of modern hotel management. Hospitality accounting consultants, Hottman and Adams (1996:23), note that outsourcing has: '... become a common facet of the business operations for lodging properties and clubs. As the market for outsourcing grows, it will have a dramatic impact on how businesses are structured, managed and viewed by owners, employees, and customers'. Despite this view and fairly extensive coverage given to hotel outsourcing management issues in professional-oriented periodicals (e.g. *Hotel and Motel Management*, *Lodging Hospitality*), there has been limited academic research in this area (Goldman and Eyster, 1992; Hallam and Baum, 1996; Hemmington and King, 2000; Paraskevas and Buhalis, 2002; Espino-Rodríguez and Padrón-Robaina, 2004, 2005; Lam and Han, 2005), and no specific accounting focused studies concerned with hotel outsourcing have been found in the literature.

There is also a paucity of outsourcing focused commentary in many management accounting texts. These texts generally afford outsourcing little more than a cursory consideration (see, for example, Barfield et al., 1998; Horngren et al., 2000, 2005; Langfield-Smith et al., 2003; Drury, 2004; Hansen and Mowen, 2005). In these texts the outsourcing decision is typically characterized as an overly-simplified short-term choice between conducting an activity in-house or contracting it out, with most texts discussing the decision from a relevant costing or make/buy perspective. Shank and Govindarajan (1988) criticize this approach to decision-making as does Gietzmann (1996) who notes that this dichotomous and short-termist view fails to capture the breadth of governance structures that may be employed to manage an outsourced activity and also the potentially highly significant role that trust can play in sub-contracting relationships.

The traditional make/buy scenario can also be criticized on the grounds that the product or activity considered is treated as stand-ard and unchanging. The only variable of interest appears to be price. If businesses want to motivate service and product sup-pliers, incentives other than short-term prices need to be considered. Gietzmann claims that the practice of subcontracting to the lowest cost provider can result in suboptimal outcomes, as it provides sub-contractors with little inducement to view the relationship as long-term and little incentive to improve product/service quality.

Despite the limited attention given to outsourcing in manage-ment accounting texts, it is notable that some recent editions of established texts have broadened their coverage by recogniz-ing strategic and qualitative issues associated with outsourcing. Langfield-Smith et al. (2003), for example, emphasize the import-ance of a long-term focus and the consideration of product and service quality. They note that outsourcing is often easier when the functions are relatively simple and the benefits readily identi-fiable. In connection with this, they compare the outsourcing of housekeeping in hotels with the complexity of information tech-nology outsourcing in a large bank.

Surprisingly, none of the management accounting texts reviewed considers outsourcing in the context of capital budget decision-making. The discounting principles of capital budgeting appear relevant to outsourcing given the long-term nature of many out-sourcing decisions and the uneven nature of cash flows over the long-term. Equally surprising, little discussion is given to issues of control and performance measurement of subcontractors. While the traditional management accounting focus has been intra-firm, the shifting boundaries of the firm heightens the need to establish inter-firm focused control and performance measurement proced-ures. A potential for change in this literature is evident from comments provided by Langfield-Smith et al. (2000:5), who note that: 'Outsourcing situations may create a new set of control issues for the firm; the design of traditional management control sys-tems is based on the assumption that all activities are within the direct control of the firm'.

Recently, there has been increased attention directed to out-sourcing in the academic management accounting literature (e.g. Seal et al., 1999; Widener and Selto, 1999; Van der Meer-Kooistra and Vosselman, 2000; Mouritsen et al., 2001; Tomkins, 2001; Langfield-Smith and Smith, 2003). (It is also noteworthy that a forthcoming issue of the journal *Management Accounting Research* is being devoted to the topic of management control of inter-firm transactional relationships). Several outsourcing monographs have also been written (e.g. Domberger, 1998; Langfield-Smith et al., 2000). The extent to which many academic studies consider outsourcing from a strategic perspective is also notable (e.g. Shank and Govindarajan, 1988; Teresko, 1990; Quinn and Hilmer, 1994; DiRomulado and Gurbaxani, 1998; Stacey, 1998a; Kakabadse and Kakabadse, 2000; Park et al., 2000; Simke, 2000). Of particular pertinence are the Johns and Lee-Ross (1996) and Lam and Han (2005) studies that provide strategically informed studies of hospitality industry outsourcing.

The costs and benefits of outsourcing

The important role the accountant can play in the outsourcing management process becomes particularly apparent when one considers the decision-making and control issues. Stacey (1998c:44) notes that 'the role of the accountant is key . . . in providing the relevant analysis, decision-making support and pricing and control mechanisms for the contract. The skill sets for the accountant are also enhanced by developing new skills in service and relationship management'. From a management accounting perspective, a strong appreciation of the nature of the costs and benefits of outsourcing is obviously key to formulating a thorough analysis in outsourcing decision-making. This section of the chapter provides an overview of these costs and benefits. It should be noted that not all of these costs and benefits lend themselves to easy quantification. Accountants should take care not to allow this factor to cloud their judgement, however. Cost and benefit issues that do not lend themselves to quantification can be highly significant and therefore merit detailed consideration!

Benefits of outsourcing
Competitive advantage and a focus on core activities

There are many examples of companies outsourcing to sharpen their quest for competitive advantage (Domberger, 1998). Hayward (2002:26) cites a managing director of a consultancy firm who stated: 'There are only two things that give enterprises sustainable competitive advantage: their brands and their people. Everything else can be copied'. This comment appears particularly pertinent here, given the significance of hotel branding and the labour intensive nature of hotel operations. Significant competition barriers can be constructed by organizations focusing on what they do best and outsourcing to suppliers who can develop their own specializations. This enables each activity to be conducted in a 'state of the art' manner.

Related to the idea of competitive advantage is the issue of core activities. It is widely suggested that core activities should be insourced and non-core outsourced, as non-core activities are peripheral to a company's competitive advantage. Hottman and Adams (1996) and Guerrier and Lockwood (1989) note how hotel outsourcing should pertain to non-core activities. Hotel outsourcing is '… useful when dealing with ancillary activities or activities which are not at all firm-specific' (Guerrier and Lockwood, 1989:10). The need to consider whether an activity is core when approaching an outsourcing decision is also underlined by Hemmington and King (2000:256) who alert us to the dangers of outsourcing a core hotel activity: 'The delivery of a core dimension of the hotel product in association with a partner is likely to be more complex and potentially threatening to the hotel's image and brand.'

Understanding and serving the customer should be regarded by organizations as a core competency (Quinn and Hilmer, 1994). The chief executive of a budget airline comments: 'We wouldn't consider outsourcing areas where we spend time with our customers. For example, we would always employ our own cabin crews' (Hayward, 2002:26). This perspective appears particularly pertinent to the context of hotel service delivery. Despite this, from the hotel literature and interviews conducted, it is evident that many hotels appear to be successfully outsourcing functions that involve relatively high degrees of interaction between the customer and the service provider. These functions include: concierge (Seal, 1995), security (*Hotel/Motel Security and Safety Management*, 1995), reservations and call centres (Selwitz, 2002; Adams, 2003), food and beverage (Chaudhry, 1993; Rowe, 1993; Wexler, 1994; Hottman and Adams, 1996; Hemmington and King, 2000; Ruggless, 2004; Espino-Rodríguez and Padrón-Robaina, 2005) and housekeeping (interview findings).

This discussion of core activities beckons the question: what activities qualify as 'core' in the context of hotel management? Johns and Lee-Ross (1996:15) note: 'Restaurants may produce and serve, produce or serve, or do neither'. What is core depends on a hotel's star rating, strategy and market segment. There appears to be no magic formula for determining what constitutes a core activity. It was interesting to note that in one hotel where two interviews were conducted, the financial controller and general manager held very conflicting views on what they saw to be the core activities of the same hotel.

Specialization

A major benefit of outsourcing is the specialization that it facilitates (Ansley, 2000; Langfield-Smith and Smith, 2003). Specialist outside suppliers are able to achieve greater volumes than that possible if activities are spread across a number of companies performing them in-house. This signifies that the specialist supplier can reap the benefits of economies of scale that may be unattainable by an in-house provider. Domberger (1998:91) notes: 'The benefits of specialization come from the economies of scale and the investment intensity of functional specialists...' Larger volumes also enable outside suppliers to make more sophisticated investments in assets, labour and technology thus enhancing efficiency and productivity. This is one of the main reasons cited for hotels outsourcing the reservation function to large call centres (Selwitz, 2002; Adams, 2003). As a result of the large number of operators employed, large call centres can provide a specialized service that includes the provision of a range of language options (Selwitz, 2002).

The importance of the specialization benefit was especially apparent to one of the general managers interviewed. He preferred to outsource where there was specialized work or specialized equipment: 'Where we want to shy away is where you have to constantly upgrade your equipment, constantly retrain the people. We would rather give it to you as a 3 year contract, we know the costs we are up against, and we know we get it done'. Other interviewees highlighted many functions that had been outsourced in connection with a quest for heightened specialization. These functions included carpet and window cleaning, food and beverage, gardening, housekeeping, laundry, pastry production, payroll and public area cleaning.

Information technology (IT) is an example of a particular function where in-house providers have difficulty competing with specialists (Domberger, 1998). IT activity has now become so specialized, even IT suppliers are outsourcing it (Domberger, 1998; Kakabadse and Kakabadse, 2000; Adams, 2003) and, in the UK, 70 per cent of outsourcing contracts relate to IT (Hayward, 2002). In connection with this, it is notable that Kakabadse and Kakabadse (2000) suggest that a large proportion of the hospitality market is served by Holiday Inn's hotel reservation system software design business.

The hotel literature provides a strong case for food and beverage outsourcing based on the specialization rationale. Many practitioners and consultants feel hotels are not expert food service operators and that the hotel manager is trying to wear 'too many hats' (Rowe, 1993). Hemmington and King (2000) note that problems with poor performing hotel restaurants frequently stem from the breadth of specializations that are required to run a hotel and restaurant. One of the interviewees in Hemmington and King's study (2000:258) commented: 'Hoteliers know room sales but there is always something wrong with food and beverage; they should not pretend to know how to operate food and beverage'. Also, Rowe (1993:57) comments: 'Despite the best efforts of some of the finest chefs over the years, "the hotel restaurant" still carries a certain stigma. But slap a brand name on it and let somebody else run it, and your problems are over'.

Market induced competition

A third outsourcing benefit concerns the market induced competitive environment introduced. Domberger (1998:81 and 91) comments: 'Competition adds powerful incentives to raise productivity, to improve quality, and to innovate. ... The combination of specialisation and market competition is particularly powerful: it ensures that every latent opportunity for efficiency gain is vigorously pursued'. Domberger reports survey findings indicating that significant cost savings (around 20 per cent) ensue from exposing in-house services to competitive tendering from outside and a comparison of competitively tendered cleaning contracts to a monopoly supplier found the contracts cost less (48.2 per cent per square metre cleaned) and provided better quality (12.5 per cent more).

In addition to instilling a sense of competition, maintaining several suppliers facilitates the collection of benchmark data (Domberger, 1998; Ansley, 2000). Organizations have successfully developed world class competencies in non-core functional areas by exposing their in-house service providers to external competition (Kakabadse and Kakabadse, 2000). An additional outsourcing benefit is that suppliers may place greater efforts on innovative solutions. Downsides include the additional complexity of having to manage more suppliers and that prices may be driven down at the expense of quality.

In a hotel environment, maintaining several suppliers could be beneficial for some activities, such as laundry, food and beverage, or housekeeping. The general managers and financial controllers interviewed did not generally concur with this view, however. One general manager felt it would be inappropriate to outsource to multiple suppliers any activities that involve contact with customers, as each supplier needs to be trained on appropriate guest interaction. Another interviewee felt it more important to foster a good relationship with one supplier in a manner that aligns with Gietzmann's (1996) emphasis on the need to build trust.

Flexibility

Large vertically integrated and diversified organizations tend to be bureaucratic, slow to react and senior management are limited in their ability to obtain and process relevant information. Ansley (2000:35) notes that a supplier: '… can readjust manufacturing capacity … far more quickly and effectively than a vertically integrated manufacturing facility'. Outsourcing can also assist with meeting seasonal demand (Bromage, 2000). Outsourcing also affords flexibility as it can facilitate access to rapidly developing new technologies or complex systems (Kakabadse and Kakabadse, 2000).

By spreading operations over a variety of suppliers, risk can be reduced and shared as the more focused organizations are better able to react to changes in the market. Using a network of suppliers also enables an organization rapidly to change the scale and scope of production as demand changes (Kakabadse and Kakabadse, 2000).

Hotel activities that can be outsourced as a result of pursuing the flexibility motive include laundry and housekeeping. One interviewee described how his hotel conducted laundry in-house, but also maintained the services of an outside supplier. When demand exceeded the capacity of the hotel's laundry facilities, outside providers were called upon. This reduced the need for the hotel to invest in large facilities which would only be periodically required. Hotels that are subject to volatile occupancy levels may also benefit by outsourcing housekeeping. One financial controller explained that room occupancy volatility resulted in additional costs due to the management and training of casual labour which has a high turnover rate. He felt that where a hotel experiences high occupancy level volatility and unpredictability, it makes sense to outsource occupancy related activities such as housekeeping. In effect, the hotel was outsourcing the problem of volatility management to the supplier. Due to its size, a speciality supplier is more capable of managing this volatility problem, i.e. it has greater scope to smooth peak demand across a larger work force. The supplier of housekeeping is also able to offer better employment to those wanting more hours, as they can spread their services across several customers.

Cost savings

Cost savings derive from all of the factors described above (outsourcing non-core activities can provide structural cost savings, specialization leads to economies of scale, market induced competition drives efficiencies and flexibility means businesses can react in more efficient ways). Outsourcing driven cost savings have been realized by many businesses (Domberger, 1998; Ansley, 2000; Simke, 2000; Deans, 2001; Syvret, 2001; Hayward, 2002) and improving mediocre hotel restaurant profits by outsourcing is noted by many commentators (e.g. Chaudhry, 1993; Rowe, 1993; Wexler, 1994; Hottman and Adams, 1996; Hemmington and King, 2000). Enhanced revenues and decreased costs were found to be the 'overwhelming reason for outsourcing' hotel food and beverage (Hemmington and King, 2000:257). Outsourcing reservations to large call centres can result in savings as high as 50 per cent of what it would cost to provide the reservation function in-house (Selwitz, 2002). It is noteworthy that the second highest performing Australian company in 2001 (ranked on return on net assets) was an outsourcing provider of security, cleaning, catering and courier services (Deans, 2001).

In addition to the outsourcing benefits described above, other benefits include:

- replacement of unsatisfactory in-house services (Teresko, 1990)

- a way to facilitate change (Domberger, 1998; Mise, 2001)

- reduced staff and modified employment terms (Kakabadse and Kakabadse, 2000)

- improved balance sheet by freeing up cash for more lucrative investments (Hayward, 2002:27)

- ability to set up quickly and expand a business (Hayward, 2002)

- enhanced customer satisfaction and loyalty (Ansley, 2000)

- decreased time taken to introduce new services and products, through collaboration with suppliers specializing in prototyping, design change, testing, etc. (Ansley, 2000).

The costs of outsourcing

The general managers and financial controllers interviewed noted the importance of appraising a range of costs arising from a decision to outsource. As will be evident from the discussion presented below, these costs extend well beyond the direct cost of a negotiated fee with a subcontractor.

Transaction costs

Coase (1937) was the first to coin the term 'transaction costs'. He recognized that, in addition to production costs, a cost arises in connection with how transactions are organized within markets or organizations (hierarchies). Transaction costs are 'those costs associated with an economic exchange that vary independent of the competitive market price of the goods or services exchanged' (Robins, 1987:69). More specifically, transaction costs include costs associated with searching for suppliers, securing information on potential suppliers, the cost of setting up contracts, monitoring and enforcing contractual performance (Robins, 1987), the costs of coordinating and the costs of motivating (Milgrom and Roberts, 1992), switching costs (i.e. the cost of moving from in-house to external provision), loss of in-house skills, loss of innovation and loss of control (Domberger, 1998). Domberger (1998) notes the importance of implicit, as well as explicit, costs. Implicit costs relate to the incompleteness of contracts which can trigger expensive renegotiation costs and opportunistic behaviour. Opportunistic behaviour can arise when a contract has scope for one party to act outside the spirit of the contract in a way that damages the other party. It is difficult to foresee every event and contract renegotiation time can be significant. As unexpected events unfold, 'contractual hazards' can emerge in which opportunistic behaviour can result.

It is also important that internal and external transaction costs are considered (Quinn and Hilmer, 1994). Internal transaction costs such as head office costs, support costs relating to staff development and investment in infrastructure required to control the provision of a service, need to be assessed. These costs can be significant, yet they are often overlooked (Chalos, 1995). In connection with housekeeping, three interviewed financial controllers commented on the ease of conducting an outsourcing analysis when the activity is conducted in-house, because costs are easily identifiable. Only one acknowledged that some costs are relatively hidden. Another financial controller noted that managers affected by an outsourcing proposal may be economical with the truth. He commented:

> My background is operations. For the last number of years I have been in finance. Before that, I worked as … front office manager, … F&B, and all over the place. So I know roughly what the requirements are in the operation and what you would need in terms of payroll and miscellaneous costs … no one can feed you bull.

Domberger (1998) notes that some theorists feel transaction costs between or within firms are not that different, as a firm is just 'a nexus of contracts' between the organization and its employees. Stigler (1951) comments: '… too numerous people … believe that transactions between firms are expensive and those within firms are free…' (cited by Domberger,1998:53). In this vein, Domberger feels that the significance of incomplete contracting and opportunism has been exaggerated in the literature and that transaction cost economics (TCE) does not explain why transaction costs should be less in vertically organized businesses. Outsourcing IT, for example, is said to result in reduced transaction costs through outsourcing (Kakabadse and Kakabadse (2000) cite Clemons et al. (1993) and Mahe and Perras (1994)). Despite this, Kakabadse and Kakabadse (2000) note that outsourcing can also increase costs. A survey of 1000 managers worldwide revealed only 5 per cent achieved high levels of outsourcing benefits, and 39 per cent only mediocre results (Kakabadse and Kakabadse, 2000). This may be however, because of the difficulty in assessing all costs.

Social costs

The emerging wisdom is that outsourcing has a negative impact on people (Kakabadse and Kakabadse, 2000:695). Social costs relating to retraining, redeployment and redundancy can be considerable (Kakabadse and Kakabadse (2000) refer to Hall and Domberger (1995) and Domberger (1998)). Employees who remain within the organization following a round of outsourcing can suffer from job insecurity, decreased employee morale, distrust, reduced productivity, increased absenteeism and an increased level of staff turnover can result (Kakabadse and Kakabadse (2000) refer to Brockner et al. (1987, 1988), Labib and Abbelbaum (1993), Appelbaum et al. (1997, 1999)). This is known as the 'survivor syndrome' and is said to be a significant reason affecting organizations' inability to realize anticipated downsizing benefits (Kakabadse and Kakabadse (2000) refer to Labib and Appelbaum (1993)). As individuals seek new employment due to a fear of job loss in a subsequent outsourcing round, an organization's key people can disappear. A consequence of outsourcing can thus be diminished organization loyalty (Korac-Kakabadse et al., 1999).

Social costs can thus be seen as another important outsourcing cost to consider, yet social costs are not explicitly addressed in the TCE literature. Given the intensity of labour, the issue of worker loyalty is obviously a key consideration in the hotel industry. In light of the nature of these social costs, they are bound to be difficult to quantify. From interviewee comments, it was evident that one way social costs can be mitigated was by outsourcing activities only when key individuals resigned. One financial controller noted that when implementing a decision to outsource the housekeeping function in his hotel, the housekeeping executive was seconded to an overseas hotel that was part of the same hotel group. Another social cost minimization strategy involves transferring all affected staff to the supplier (Kakabadse and Kakabadse, 2000). Although this may be more costly in the short-term, it may be a long-term cost saving relative to the negative goodwill that may otherwise ensue.

Loss of control

It is widely held that outsourcing may lead to a loss of control (Domberger, 1998; Kakabadse and Kakabadse, 2000). However, maintaining control can be difficult regardless of whether an activity is outsourced. As Domberger (1998:68) notes: 'Control of employment is not synonymous with control of outcomes'. Connected with this, Langfield-Smith and Smith (2001:6) described differing cultures as a potential barrier to control. An advantage of having an in-house provider is that it is more likely to be in tune with an organization's culture, thereby resulting in enhanced control: 'within a firm shared cultural values are an important source of control'.

Loss of control and differing cultures are both addressed in the hotel literature in relation to food and beverage outsourcing. Outsourcing restaurants, for example, may mean losing pricing and promotional flexibility. This can be a significant factor, as many hotels' room pricing strategy includes breakfast provision (Hemmington and King, 2000). Despite this, it is important that contractors are given the control needed to perform their task (Harmer, 1994). Harmer (1994:60) cites the general manager of one hotel as commenting: 'It is important . . . that the general manager understands the philosophy of the outside company running the restaurant and is quite prepared to stand back and hand over its control'. The mismatching of organizational cultures can be a problem, as hotels are often rigid and slow to adapt, whereas restaurant companies, especially celebrity chefs, operate in a flexible and autonomous style (Hemmington and King, 2000). Hemmington and King (2000:259) cite one restaurateur who commented: 'It is difficult to change an existing restaurant or food and beverage department to reflect your style. Hoteliers are set in their ways, comfortable and even complacent. We disturbed this environment and their lack of support created more problems'.

Another contentious issue can be the division of responsibilities. Most hotels do not want to outsource F&B entirely and wish to maintain control of those areas that are profitable. Hemmington and King (2000:257) cite the following restaurateur comment: 'Hotels want to have their cake and eat it' (Hemmington and King, 2000:257). Sharing F&B activities is likely to result in operational tensions in relation to receiving, storing and food production.

Many of the general managers and financial controllers interviewed cited fear over loss of control as a significant factor constraining outsourcing. Obtaining reliable suppliers that could provide acceptable quality in a timely and trustworthy manner was problematic for some hotels. Quality is obviously a key factor for many hotels given the emphasis on star ratings, and those with a higher quality standing were often resistant to outsourcing because of the potential negative implications for their brand image. One financial controller commented:

> We can save x amount of money by doing this, but what potential problems are there for us in making that decision?...The savings alone will not do it...Hotels like to keep control because we are providing a service...Will the service be sacrificed by saving money. If it will, then it will not happen, and that is always the case in our industry.

Coordination costs

The importance of a cooperative relationship is noted by Langfield-Smith et al. (2000:3) who emphasize that: 'a mismanaged relationship between a firm and its outsourcer may have serious implications for the firm's long term strategy, continued competitiveness and profitability, even when the initial outsourcing decision was well conceived'. Successful coordination can be hampered by self-interest (Domberger, 1998). To enhance cooperation, control mechanisms such as financial penalties, longer contracts, legal enforcement, or trust, can be used.

In relation to trust and hotel subcontractor selection, Sieburgh (1992) feels that the three most important aspects to appraise are the subcontractor's integrity, independence and accessibility. Although a contractor's expertise and experience is important, if these three criteria are not met, the service is bound to be compromised. Domberger (1998:58) sees cooperation and trust as key for a successful supplier-buyer relationship and comments: 'The role of trust goes beyond individual economic relationship; ... it is a pre-condition for successful economic adjustment and prosperity ... Since trust is essential to successful economic transactions, where it lies in abundance, business will also flourish'.

Domberger (1998:208) warns that: 'It may take a long time to build up trust, but very little to destroy it'. The financial controller of one high quality hotel described how loss of control was not of great concern for one of the hotel's outsourced restaurants. The subcontractor engaged to manage the hotel restaurant had a strong brand reputation. The subcontractor thus had much to lose if the quality of service were to diminish. From this it can be seen that control can be achieved by engaging a reputable supplier.

Costs of monitoring and evaluating performance

Outsourcing is seen as a trade-off between lower production costs (assuming economies of scale and specialization can be achieved by suppliers) and higher monitoring costs (Kakabadse and Kakabadse,

2000 refer to Lewis and Sappington, 1991). Stacey (1998c) warns that failure to make adequate investment in an effective supply management team can result in higher costs combined with increased business risk. Although control costs are widely cited as a negative aspect of outsourcing, it should be noted that activities managed in-house also have to be monitored and controlled (Domberger, 1998; Langfield-Smith and Smith, 2003).

Attempts to create remuneration packages that mimic the driving force of market incentives have proven to be difficult to design (Domberger, 1998). Langfield-Smith and Smith (2003) noted problems of 'funny' transfer prices of an in-house IT provider. A senior manager commented:

> A business would ask … [the in-house provider] for something to be done, but they were not being charged the true cost. There was no discipline in the management of costs. One of the drivers … to outsource … was to introduce that discipline, so that if you do ask for something … someone comes back to you and says 'You know it's going to cost you $20 000' (Langfield-Smith and Smith, 2003:291).

Increased control costs often result because in-house service providers typically are not monitored to the same degree as outsiders. This is frequently because clearly defined specifications have not been drawn up (Domberger, 1998). Consistent with this view, Stacey (1998b) notes that outsourcing usually results in organizations moving to more formal reporting mechanisms. Stacey (1998b) also notes that costs may increase because new skills are required to deal with the new and sophisticated relationships that outsourcing brings.

Loss of in-house skills

It is widely acknowledged that outsourcing is risky because if a supplier's performance is unacceptable, it can be problematical bringing the activity in-house due to the lost skill base. Domberger (1998) believes this concern to be overstated and feels that a more pertinent issue is whether the expertise can be effectively acquired in the marketplace. He feels rather than fearing a loss of skills, potential outsourcers should focus on the improved skill set that can result from outsourcing.

Increased risks

Two dimensions of risk appear pertinent: the risk of outsourcing and the risk of the activity itself (Domberger, 1998). The hotel can control outsourcing risk during the selection process with careful screening, contracting and monitoring. Bidders should be asked to prepare risk management plans that identify risks and how they would be managed (Domberger, 1998; Mise, 2001). Risk sharing can be achieved using a combination of fixed and variable pricing, so that neither party feels unduly exposed, and with 'gainsharing contracts' so that the benefits of advancement are shared. The party with greatest control should bear the greater portion of risk and if control is equal, the greatest risk should be borne by the partner most able to absorb it (Domberger, 1998). To reduce risk, the provider should be required to use current best practice (Stacey, 1998b; Mise, 2001). Incentives and penalties for good and bad performance are other control measures that can be used to reduce risk to the buyer (Domberger, 1998).

Outsourcing, however, can be viewed as a mechanism for sharing risks and benefits (Quinn, 1999; Bromage, 2000; Kakabadse and Kakabadse, 2000), or as a way to remove risk. With respect to activity risk it was evident that liability management associated with injuries sustained at work was a key factor for outsourcing housekeeping in one of the hotels where an interview was conducted. The responsibility for workplace health and safety was moved outside the hotel by the outsourcing of this function.

Application of long-term oriented financial analyses

When describing approaches to appraising outsourcing proposals, few interviewees referred to long-term oriented techniques such as those prescribed in the capital budgeting literature (e.g. Pike, 1988; Lamminmaki et al., 1996). In only one case was a long-term perspective commentary initiated by an interviewee. The interviewees tended to view outsourcing costs as repetitive annual costs and not warranting a discounted cash flow analysis. Some of the analyses conducted in the place of discounted cash flow based approaches appeared questionable, e.g. earning multiples used to value investments. One general manager commented:

> There really would be a fairly thorough analysis … As far as the capital expenditure arm of [owner named], they really do look very closely at what value it will add to this building and to the operations. Generally it is very easy, if you add 17 million in the revenue and add 1–1.5 m on the bottom line and then multiply by 10, then they figure you have added 10 million dollars of value on the building. So it is quite thorough.

The failure to apply discounted cash flow approaches to appraise the long-term implications of outsourcing decisions may result from the fact that many outsourcing decisions involve no capital outlay. The absence of a capital outlay signifies that the outsourcing decision is insulated from the discipline associated with the capital budgeting cycle. Absence of a capital outlay does not signify, however, that the cash flows associated with an outsourcing decision will be the same every year. Although the decision to outsource may require no immediate outlay, it can signify an initial cash saving (e.g. expenditure saved as a result of not having to overhaul existing equipment), or an initial cash inflow due to the sale of surplus assets (e.g. sale of housekeeping uniforms and equipment, or laundry equipment and linen). Further examples of irregular cash flows that can result from a decision to outsource include:

- initial costs associated with retraining, redeploying, or redundancy

- future costs due to job insecurity resulting in increased absenteeism and increased employee turnover

- future cash flows resulting from outsourcing failure (e.g. costs of finding a new supplier, or bringing the activity in-house).

With respect to failure costs, a decision to outsource will result in one of three outcomes: a successful and enduring relationship, a failed relationship and a switch to another supplier, or a failed relationship and moving in-house. The cash flows and probabilities associated with each of these three outcomes could be factored into an analysis.

Relative to the capital budgeting decision-making cycle, outsourcing decision-making may be less sophisticated due to the *ad hoc* manner in which outsourcing decisions frequently appear to be taken. The capital budgeting process is conducted in a routine and therefore relatively systematic manner. It appears that a more formalized approach to outsourcing might result in the application of more sophisticated analytical procedures.

Summary

In light of the significant growth of outsourcing in the last decade, it is striking how little management accounting issues relating to this contemporary phenomenon have been considered in the academic hotel literature. This chapter can be seen as an attempt to ameliorate this literary shortcoming.

The main benefits of outsourcing noted in this chapter concern heightened competitive advantage by focusing on core competencies, specialization, a market induced discipline, greater flexibility and cost savings. Costs of outsourcing discussed included transaction costs, social costs, loss of control, coordination costs, costs of monitoring, failure costs and increased risk. Transaction costs are complex and include the problem of subcontractor opportunism resulting from incomplete contracting, coordination costs, and monitoring costs. An attempt to identify all costs is bound to be difficult as many are hidden and therefore frequently overlooked. It has also been noted that despite the long-term implications associated with an outsourcing decision, sophisticated financial analytical techniques that recognize the long term appear to be rarely used in hotel outsourcing management.

References

Adams, B. (2003) Outsourcing call centers is a growing trend. *Hotel and Motel Management*, **218** (14), 128.

Anonymous (1995) Hotel finds contract security officers can fit in a lodging environment. *Hotel/Motel Security & Safety Management*, **13** (10), 12.

Ansley, M. (2000) Virtual manufacturing. *CMA Management for Strategic Business Ideas*, February, 31–35.

Appelbaum, S., Delage, C., Labib, N. and Gault, G. (1997) The survivor syndrome: aftermath of downsizing. *Career Development International*, **2** (6), 278–286.

Appelbaum, S., Everard, A. and Hung, L. (1999) Strategic downsizing: critical success factors. *Management Decision*, **37** (7), 84–97.

Barfield, J., Raiborn, C. and Kinney, M. (1998) *Cost Accounting: Traditions and Innovations*, 3rd edn. South-Western College, Cincinnati.

Brockner, J., Davy, J. and Carter, C. (1988) Layoffs, self-esteem, and survivor guilt: motivational, affective, and attitudinal consequences. In Cameron, K.S., Sutton, R.I. and Whetten, D.Q.A. (eds), *Readings in Organizational Decline*, pp. 279–290. Ballinger Publishing, Cambridge.

Brockner, J., Grover, S., Reed, T., DeWitt, T. and O'Malley, M. (1987) 'Survivors' reactions to layoffs: we get by with a little help from our friends. *Administrative Science Quarterly*, **32** (4), 526–541.

Bromage, N. (2000) Outsourcing: To do or not to do, that is the question. *Management Accounting* (UK), January, 22–23.

Chalos, P. (1995) Costing, control, and strategic analysis in outsourcing decisions. *Cost Management*, Winter, 31–37.

Chaudhry, R. (1993) Casual dining checks. In, *Restaurants and Institutions*, November, 18–32.

Clemons, E., Reddi, S. and Row, M. (1993) The impact of information technology on the organisation of economic activity: the 'move to the middle' hypothesis. *Journal of Management Information Systems*, **10** (2), 9–35.

Coase, R. (1937) The nature of the firm. *Economica*, **4**, 386–405.

Deans, A. (2001) The best CEOs: Cream of the crop. *The Bulletin*, 27 November, 72–76.

DiRomualdo, A. and Gurbaxani, V. (1998) Strategic intent for IT outsourcing. *Sloan Management Review*, **39** (4), 67–80.

Domberger, S. (1998) *The Contracting Organization: A Strategic Guide to Outsourcing*. Oxford University Press, Oxford.

Drury, C. (2004) *Management and Cost Accounting*, 6th edn. Thomson, London.

Espino-Rodríguez, T. and Padrón-Robaina, V. (2004) Outsourcing and its impact on operational objectives and performance: a study of hotels in the Canary Islands. *International Journal of Hospitality Management*, **23** (3), 287–306.

Espino-Rodríguez, T. and Padrón-Robaina, V. (2005). A resource based view of outsourcing and its implications for organizational performance in the hotel sector. *Tourism Management*, **26** (5), 707–721.

Gietzmann, M. (1996) Incomplete contracts and the make or buy decision: governance design and attainable flexibility. *Accounting, Organizations and Society*, **21** (6), 611–626.

Goldman, K.L. and Eyster, J.J. (1992) Hotel F&B Leases: the view from the restaurant. *The Cornell HRA Quarterly*, **32**, 72–83.

Guerrier, Y. and Lockwood, A. (1989) Core and peripheral employees in hotel operations. *Personnel Review*, **18** (1), 9–15.

Hall, C. and Domberger, S. (1995) Competitive tendering for domestic services: a competitive study of three hospitals in New South Wales. In Domberger, S. and Hall, C. (eds), *The Contracting Casebook: Competitive Tendering in Action*, pp. 99–126. AGPS, Canberra.

Hallam, G. and Baum, T. (1996) Contracting out food and beverage operations in hotels: a comparative study of practice in North America and the United Kingdom. *International Journal of Hospitality Management*, **15** (1), 41–50.

Handy, C. (1989). *The Age of Unreason*. Harvard Business School Press, Boston.

Hansen, D. and Mowen, M. (2005) *Management Accounting*, 7th edn. Thomson South-Western, Cincinnati, Ohio.

Harmer, J. (1994) Calling in the experts. *Caterer & Hotelkeeper*, July, 60–62.

Hayward, C. (2002) Out of site. *Financial Management*, **16**, 26–27.

Hemmington, N. and King, C. (2002) Key dimensions of outsourcing hotel food and beverage services. *International Journal of Contemporary Hospitality Management*, **12** (4), 256–261.

Horngren, C., Bhimani, A., Datar, S. and Foster, G. (2005) *Management and Cost Accounting*, 3rd edn. Prentice-Hall, Upper Saddle River.

Horngren, C., Foster, G. and Datar, S. (2000) *Cost Accounting: a Managerial Emphasis*, 10th edn. Prentice-Hall, Upper Saddle River.

Hottman, R. and Adams, J. (1996) Go with what you know: outsourcing – reality or myth? *Bottomline*, **11** (7), 22–23.

Johns, N. and Lee-Ross, D. (1996) Strategy, risk and decentralization in hospitality operations. *International Journal of Contemporary Hospitality Management*, **8** (2), 14–16.

Kakabadse, N. and Kakabadse, A. (2000) Critical review – outsourcing: a paradigm shift. *Journal of Management Development*, **19** (8), 670–728.

Korac-Kakabadse, A., Korac-Kakabadse, N. and Kouzmin, A. (1999) The changing nature of the social contract and the consequences. In Mazain, A. (ed.), *Public Service Management: Achieving Quality Performance in the 21st century*, pp. 450–472. Eastern Regional Organisational for Public Administration (EROPA) and Public Service Department, Manila.

Labib, N. and Abbelbaum, S. (1993) Strategic downsizing: a human resources perspective. *Human Resource Planning*, **16** (4), 69–91.

Lam, T. and Han, M. (2005) A study of outsourcing strategy: a case involving the hotel industry in Shanghai, China. *International Journal of Hospitality Management*, **24**, 41–56.

Lamminmaki, D., Guilding, C. and Pike, R. (1996) A comparison of British and New Zealand capital budgeting practices. *Pacific Accounting Review*, **8** (1), 1–12.

Langfield-Smith, K. and Smith, D. (2001) Management and control of outsourcing relationships: evidence from the electricity industry. Paper presented at the *University of New South Wales Biennial Management Accounting Conference*, Sydney, Australia (February).

Langfield-Smith, K. and Smith, D. (2003) Management control systems and trust in outsourcing relationships. *Management Accounting Research*, **14** (3), 281–307.

Langfield-Smith, K., Smith, D. and Stringer, C. (2000) *Managing the Outsourcing Relationship*. University of New South Wales Press, Sydney.

Langfield-Smith, K., Thorne, H. and Hilton, R. (2003) *Management Accounting: An Australian Perspective*, 3rd edn. McGraw-Hill, Macquarie Park.

Lewis, T. and Sappington, D. (1991) Technological change and the boundaries of the firm. *American Economic Review*, September, 887–900.

Mahe, H. and Perras, C. (1994) Successful global strategies for service companies. *Long Range Planning*, **27** (1), 36–49.

Milgrom, P. and Roberts, J. (1992) *Economics, Organization and Management*. Prentice Hall, Englewood Cliffs.

Mise, I.J. (2001) Payroll and HR outsourcing: Is it a viable solution for your organisation? *CMA Management*, March, 30–32.

Mouritsen, J., Hansen, A. and Hansen, C.O. (2001) Inter-organizational controls and organizational competencies: episodes around target cost management/functional analysis and open book accounting. *Management Accounting Research*, **12** (2), 221–244.

Paraskevas, A. and Buhalis, D. (2002) Outsourcing IT for small hotels. *Cornell Hotel and Restaurant Administration Quarterly*, April, 27–39.

Park, H.Y., Reddy, C.S. and Sarkar, S. (2000) Make or buy strategy of firms in the US. *Multinational Business Review*, **8** (2), 89–97.

Pike, R. (1988) An empirical study of the adoption of sophisticated capital budgeting practices and decision-making effectiveness. *Accounting and Business Research*, **18** (72), 341–351.

Quinn, J.B. (1999) Strategic outsourcing: leverage knowledge capabilities. *Sloan Management Review*, **40** (4), 9–22.

Quinn, J.B. and Hilmer, F.G. (1994) Strategic outsourcing. *Sloan Management Review*, **35**, 43–55.

Robins, J.A. (1987) Organizational economics: notes on the use of transaction cost theory in the study of organizations. *Administrative Science Quarterly*, **32**, 68–86.

Roh, J.S. and Kwag, H.M. (1997) The ownership structure of property rights: theory and empirical evidence of restaurant franchising. *Journal of Hospitality and Tourism Research*, **21** (2), 75–85.

Rowe, M. (1993) If you can't beat 'em, join 'em. *Lodging Hospitality*, **49** (13), 57–59.

Ruggless, R. (2004) Hotels keep outsourcing as industry recovers from 3-year slump. *Nation's Restaurant News*, **38** (30), 110.

Seal, K. (1995) Hotels contracting out concierge. *Hotel and Motel Management*, April, 3, 36.

Seal, W., Cullen, J., Dunlop, A., Berry, T. and Ahmen, M. (1999) Enacting a European supply chain: a case study on the role of management accounting. *Management Accounting Research*, **10** (3), 303–322.

Selwitz, R. (2002) Hotel companies weigh pros, cons of using call centers for reservations. *Hotel and Motel Management*, **16** (217), 48.

Shank, J.K. and Govindarajan, V. (1988) Making strategy explicit in cost analysis: a case study. *Sloan Management Review*, **29**, 19–29.

Sieburgh, J. (1992) The time is right for outsourcing. *Lodging Hospitality*, **48** (6), 57.

Simke, J. (2000) Emerging trends in outsourcing. *CMA Management for strategic business ideas*, February, 26–27.

Stacey, M. (1998a) Outsourcing: how organisations need to pre-pare in order to realise the full potential benefits. *Management Accounting*, May, 14–16.

Stacey, M. (1998b) Outsourcing: how to differentiate supplier offer-ings in order to realise the full potential benefits. *Management Accounting*, June, 24–26.

Stacey, M. (1998c) Outsourcing: how to deliver the full benefits through expert supply management teams. *Management Accounting*, July/August, 42–44.

Stigler, G.J. (1951) The division of labor is limited by the extent of the market. *Journal of Political Economy*, **59** (3), 185–193.

Syvret, P. (2001) Steady as she grows. *The Bulletin*, November 27, 82–83.

Teresko, J. (1990) Make or buy? Now it's a data processing ques-tion too. *Industry Week*, **239** (14), 54–55.

Tomkins, C. (2001) Interdependencies, trust and information in relationships, alliances and networks. *Accounting, Organizations and Society*, **26** (2), 161–191.

Van der Meer-Kooistra, J. and Vosselman, E.J. (2000) Management control of interfirm transactional relationships: the case of indus-trial renovation and maintenance. *Accounting, Organizations and Society*, **25**, 51–77.

Wexler, M. (1994) Name chefs, food chains team up with hotels. *Hotels*, May, 67–70.

Widener, S.K. and Selto, F.H. (1999) Management control systems and boundaries of the firm: why do firms outsource internal auditing activities. *Journal of Management Accounting Research*, **11**, 48–73.

Sale and leaseback transactions in the hospitality industry

Charles Whittaker

Introduction

The term 'sale and leaseback' refers to the practice of selling long-term assets that have been purchased for use in a business to a third party investor (generally a financial institution or property company) but retaining use of them by taking back a lease. This type of transaction has been used in a variety of industries and for different assets. Airlines, for instance, have frequently used the technique for funding aircraft (Anon, 2004a) while others have used it for operating equipment (Bergsman, 2004) and even complete manufacturing plants (Koza and Sibayan, 2001). However, this chapter is concerned with real estate, land and buildings, in the UK hotel industry, an area that throws up specific issues so far subject to little academic research. It views the transactions partly in terms of the contractual relationship between landlord and tenant, but starts from the more strategic view that they are essentially a funding mechanism, providing an alternative to borrowing funds and investing them in owned property or to development strategies, such as management contracts and franchising that have been traditional routes in the industry.

Sale and leaseback transactions (SLBT) of portfolios of hotels have become a prominent part of financing and property ownership arrangements in the industry only in the last 10 years. Prior to this, as Hopper and van Marken (2001) note, institutional investment in hotels had been limited. Typically, there were low levels of overall value of properties in any year involving individual properties. The hotel industry is not unique nor at the forefront in adopting this form of financing. Researchers have written generally on SLBT and have identified certain industries as major users of this approach. They report a range of industries that have used them, particularly retail, telecoms, financial services and energy (Dixon et al., 2000; Barris, 2002), as well as its use as part of the Private Funding Initiative (PFI) under which government departments and government owned operations, such as hospitals, finance property needs. No academic research has been done in the UK on the advent of this approach to hotels, though some consultants to the industry, real estate agents and accountants mainly, have published reports on the subject in the UK (Jones et al., 2002) and in the USA (Hess et al., 2001).

The hotel industry has certain peculiarities that affect both the needs of the lessee, the hotel operator, and the lessor, the lending institution. Not least of these is the integral part of the property in the basic transaction of the industry, the sale of space on a, normally, short-term basis. Arguably in many other industries property is peripheral to their core business. It has been noted that SLBT work best when applied to what are referred to as 'non-generic' properties, those which can be used for other purposes or by a range of industries. A hotel property clearly does not fit into this category and this has, historically, been cited as a reason why institutions did not favour investments in the industry. As a third and final example of a non-exhaustive list, there has historically been a concern on the part of lenders that they did not understand the industry, a factor made more important by the first point above. It is important therefore that not only the financing approach itself, but also the change in apparent sentiment, are understood more fully.

At the same time, the adoption of SLBT by companies in the industry has been far from universal. While Hilton, Jarvis Hotels and Choice (then Friendly Hotels plc) hotels set the lead, followed by the venture buy-out of Le Meridien from Granada

(Table 18.1), others have been noticeable by their reticence to adopt the new methods, despite carrying large freehold property portfolios. Whitbread owned a large proportion of their hotels, but have been reluctant to enter the fray, while Paul Dermody, as Managing Director of De Vere hotels, was vociferous in his opposition to SLBT as a funding option. At a forum of industry managers and experts in September 2002, only 20 per cent voted that SLBT were 'in the long-term interest of their business' (Pannell Kerr Forster, 2002). Speakers suggested that it was 'selling the family silver', reflecting the centrality of hotel assets commented on later, and that it was no more than a fashion. Contrary to the latter view, transactions have, if anything, accelerated since then, especially in value terms. These opposing views need to be examined, coming as they do from leaders in the industry.

Table 18.1
UK sale and leaseback transactions 1999–2004

Date	Operator	Lessor	Value (£m)
1997	Friendly (single hotel)	Scottish American Investment Co	5
1998	CHE (formerly Friendly)	Norwich Union/Farnsworth	N/A
1999	Jarvis	Norwich Union/Farnsworth	69
2000	Premier Hotels	Accor/London & Regional	70
2001	Accor	London & Regional Properties	64
	Hilton	Royal Bank of Scotland	312
	Le Meridien	Royal Bank of Scotland	1000
2002	Thistle*	Orb Estates	600
	Hilton	Rotch/Farnsworth	336
	Jarvis	Trefick/Lioncourt	150
2003	Hanover	Trefick	36
	Swallow Hotels	REIT Asset Management	49
	Accor (UK & Holland)	Goldman Sachs	400
2004	Accor	Heron/AXA Sun Life	40
2005	IHG	Lehmann Bros Consortium	1000
	Thistle	Topland	185

Sources: HVS European Hotel Transactions 2002–4, various newspapers and company annual reports.
* Sale and management back. Thistle managed assets sold to Atlantic Hotels in 2003.

The significance of property to the industry is reflected in their financial statements, the major vehicle by which investors evaluate a company in terms of equity investment. Property is usually by far the largest asset on a balance sheet and the costs of funding and maintaining it is a major cost in the income statement. The impact of how that asset is funded and the way it is reported therefore becomes of more importance to hotel companies than it might to companies in other industries. The typical measures of corporate performance include profitability ratios, return on assets calculations and gearing. A number of researchers have demonstrated that the way SLBT are reported is likely to affect the attractiveness of companies competing for stock market funding (Beattie et al., 1998; Goodacre, 2001).

Accounting rules for leases have a long-history. At the time of writing, the rules in the UK, as in the USA, are that a distinction is made between finance leases, under which the assets and liabilities are reported in the balance sheet, and operating leases where the rent is reported as a cost in the income statement and the future rent obligations are reported as a note to the accounts. Long-term property leases have generally fallen into the second category. This results in some hotel companies potentially having better gearing ratios than others purely because they lease their property rather than own it, even though both have similar long-term assets and liabilities. There are also distortions in the income statement whereby under an operating lease the rent is reported as an operating expense while a company owning a property will report depreciation as an operating cost, but interest costs on the loans used to fund the assets are reported below the operating earnings line. In addition to being used to compare hotel companies through the use of accounting ratios, a comparison is also made with other industries. Thus the way that the industry finances its high level of assets could determine the flow of equity funds to the industry as a whole.

There is currently a proposal being considered by the UK, US and international accounting standards bodies, to eliminate the distinction between finance and operating leases (ASB, 1999a) requiring all leases to be reported as assets and liabilities on the balance sheet. This would change the way that hotel companies are reported and is likely to impact the choices made by company executives on property financing and hence on funding strategies generally, both in the industry and elsewhere (Goodacre, 2001). This, too, is a reason to focus on SLBT and to ensure that those decisions are made on an informed basis. A comprehensive treatment of the accounting aspects of SLBT are beyond the scope of this chapter and the reader is referred to articles by Beattie et al. (1998, 2000a,b) and to the discussions of the Accounting Standards Board (ASB, 1999a,b).

Beyond these issues, there is a question of how the interests of institutional investors and those of hotel companies can be reconciled through the structuring of leases. This has been a stumbling point in the past, hoteliers being fearful of ever increasing rents under inflation proofed traditional full repairing and insuring leases in an industry where profit levels are notoriously vulnerable to economic cycles and political instability. Some parts of the industry have long experience of dealing with third-party hotel owners through the use of management contracts that separate the ownership from the operating aspects of the industry. The challenge has always been to achieve the same flexibility of structure with institutional lessors whose principal aims are long-term stability and income growth combined with risk-avoidance.

The aim of this chapter then is to evaluate certain key aspects of the use of SLBT in the hotel industry, particularly the scope of its use, the drivers of the two parties and the mechanisms for reconciling their respective concerns. As can be seen from the above, this is only part of a potentially wide-ranging and complex study. It will involve a number of objectives. First, it will try to analyse the number, value and types of SLBT in the hotel industry and the parties involved. It will analyse the apparent economic drivers of hotel companies and investors identified in academic research and reported transactions and identify the features of the industry that influence the former. There is not always a congruence of motivations between lenders and lessees and the chapter will analyse the key features of the leasing structures that attempt to reconcile the interests and needs of hotel industry lessees and investors to identify mechanisms that seek to bridge the gap. This examination of the scope, drivers and contractual hurdles should provide the basis for an understanding of the SLBT phenomenon. There are a number of areas that are not given the depth of treatment they deserve, partly due to their specialist natures, partly availability of information in the public domain and partly the space available in this chapter. These are the accounting treatment touched on above, the valuation of hotels both in the transactions and in financial reporting should recent proposals be adopted, detailed arrangements regarding property upkeep and upgrading and, finally, taxation that tends to vary according to the circumstances of the parties in each deal. It is hoped that these limitations will be addressed in other research at a later date.

The scope of sale and leaseback transactions

Sale and leaseback transactions in the UK began in a relatively small way with the purchase of portfolios by Norwich Union in 1997/8 from Friendly Hotels plc and Jarvis Hotels plc consisting of around 10 mid-range hotels in each case. This was followed by larger players and larger deals through Accor, Hilton and Thistle.

The facts contradicted the PKF conference vote. Hilton, having already raised over £300 m from a transaction with Royal Bank of

Scotland, raised a similar sum in 2002 through Rotch. In 2001 the same bank had joined with Nomura in funding the ill-fated, acquisition of the Le Meridien chain, largely through sale and leaseback in a transaction totalling a reported £1.0 billion.

Nor did the story end there. Bock and Forster (2004) predicted that 'the representation of non-specialist buyers is likely to strengthen in 2004, due to their continued desire to build increasingly diversified portfolios, geared towards higher yielding investments'. This acceleration certainly came to fruition as IHG found Lehman Brothers in their quest for a £1 billion SLBT (Walsh, 2005a), while Marriott is now, in 2005, seeking a similar sum for a UK portfolio being acquired from Whitbread, after the latter decided to exit the brand for strategic reasons rather than adopt the sale and leaseback route (Whitbread, 2005). On the investor side there is clear evidence of a wider range of interest with new players Trefick and Heron/AXA, while Topland is a company previously known for investing in retail.

A pattern worthy of note is that it is the larger companies and larger transactions that seem to be increasingly adopting SLBT while medium-sized companies are finding them less attractive or more difficult to obtain. Hilton, IHG, the FTSE 100 representatives of the industry, and now Whitbread/Marriott are coming to the forefront in the UK, just as Accor has dominated in continental Europe. This is perhaps not surprising in that these companies have larger portfolios to sell, as well as providing stronger covenants to investors. Also of note is the fact that the failure of the RBS/Le Meridien transaction does not seem to have deterred progress, suggesting that it was the poor operating performance or the pricing or structure of the leases that were causal factors rather than the nature of the funding method.

Differences between the hotel industry and other users of SLBT

It is worth, at this stage, examining certain differences between the hotel industry and others that are likely to influence the way in which both hoteliers and investors view the industry.

Location

It is a widely recognized dictum in the industry that the three most important factors for the success of a hotel are 'location, location and location', allegedly coined by Conrad Hilton. Location may have some importance for, say, a factory or an office in terms of having a suitable workforce or access to transportation routes, but this is of a different magnitude to the location of a hotel where its customers stay largely because it is where they want to go, whether that be near to a town that they visit on business or it be a prestigious location such as Park Lane in London, Central Park in New York or a beach front in Thailand. Perhaps the closest comparison would be retail where the customer preference can dictate location, though even here the example of out-of-town malls suggests that the customer can be persuaded to previously unfashionable areas by shopping malls such as Sheffield's Meadowhall, or superstores like Ikea on London's north circular road.

If location is that important then hoteliers might be reluctant to cede control of key sites that might be lost at the end of a lease term if the owner chooses to lease to a competitor. There is evidence that this is the case. Intercontinental Hotel Group plc (IHG) are reported to have withheld only their Hyde Park Corner property in central London and two others, considered as 'strategic' locations, from the UK owned portfolio of 76 hotels offered for sale and leaseback in early 2005 (Walsh, 2005b). At the same time hotel companies have successfully secured longer leases on key properties, sometimes with options to extend.

Core business

Gibson (2000) (quoted in Dixon et al., 2000) defines core facilities as those:

- viewed as necessary in the longer term, because they are strategically located, embody cultural values of the organization and/or are central to competitive advantage

- in which the organization is willing to invest, and over which it requires a high degree of control to adapt to change

- likely to be held freehold or long leasehold and,

- for which functional flexibility is key and, by implication, physical flexibility is important, but where financial flexibility, in terms of easy exit, is less important.

Hotels would appear to meet all of these criteria. Certainly, many hoteliers view the prospect of exit, easy or otherwise, as an unpleasant option from an operational and marketing point of view.

In this context the building can also be seen as financially central to a hotel operation. In a typical hotel company, the tangible fixed assets, the land, buildings and equipment, represent the major part of the assets of the business. To take a pertinent example, we might look at the balance sheet and operating figures of Intercontinental Hotels Group (IHG) as of December 31, 2004

(Table 18.2), particularly as it had already sold property to the tune of £750 m and announced its intention to seek a sale and management back transaction of over £1 billion, a deal which was completed in 2005.

Table 18.2
IHG plc balance sheet at December 31, 2004

	£m
Tangible fixed assets	3776
Other long-term assets	241
Short-term assets	757
Total assets	4774
Short-term liabilities	1013
Borrowings	1252
Provisions	532
Shareholders funds	1977
Total liabilities and shareholders funds	4774
Total turnover	2204
Operating profit	331

Source: IHG (2005a) Annual Report 2004.

The land, buildings and equipment represent almost 80 per cent of the total assets and are equivalent to over 170 per cent of turnover. The return on assets is around 6.9 per cent of total assets. Given that a majority of the company's hotels are already franchised under the Holiday Inn brand, the relationship of tangible fixed assets to turnover is probably lower than a company largely based on ownership. To remove £1 billion of assets from this balance sheet would enable the company to repay virtually all its borrowings, or, as happened, return funds to shareholders.

Specificity

A hotel, because of its function and design, is difficult to convert to other uses. The small rooms, extensive plumbing, heating and wiring and the ancillary areas such as restaurants, kitchens, storerooms, leisure facilities make conversion, even to residential use, almost impossible. Barris (2002) suggests that the non-generic nature of assets is the greatest deterrent to institutional investors seeking the maximum flexibility for re-letting or conversion to other uses. The level of hotel transactions indicates that this perception may be being overcome. Hotels are being viewed simply as sources of income that can be switched to other operators, even if the use is specific.

High level of fixed costs

The hotel industry is generally considered to have a high level of fixed costs (Graham and Harris, 1999:200) compared to manufacturing or retail where the variable cost of sales element is more dominant. Not only is the property itself a fixed cost, but to a large extent, so are the workforce and operating costs such as keeping the heating and lighting at set levels. The result of this is that a hotel earns very high percentage profits on earnings above the break even point. Thus, providing the hotelier is able to negotiate a fixed rent that is affordable, the hotel company is in a situation where there is very low investment in assets and high profits resulting in a much higher return on investment.

Volatility of earnings

Largely as a result of the above factor, the industry has been seen to have more volatile earnings than other industries. In times of recession operating profits have fallen below fixed costs to provide negative percentage returns on investment of a high order. This has been exacerbated by the sensitivity of revenues to other factors, such as political instability and terrorism. Clearly this is of concern to the hotelier in that a fixed rent commitment would result in losses, in a downturn. The high levels of revenue supporting rents in the region of 25–35 per cent might, in a downturn, prove expensive, particularly when insurance, property taxes and renovation costs place a further fixed cost burden on operating profits. Hotel companies bear the risk of losses under a lease, hence their preference for management contracts where this risk passes to the owner, except insofar as there are guarantees of income from the operator.

Duality

It could be argued that the hotel industry has a dual nature and that the hotel ownership can be seen as an activity quite separate from the operation. Certainly the skill sets are different and the vast majority of staff in a hotel are engaged in looking after guests. Only a few finance and property specialists are directly concerned with the funding and long-term property management aspects.

They too are seen as 'support' staff and decisions that might be made on the basis of good financial and property management reasons, such as the timing of major repairs or the quality of upgrades, are strongly influenced by a senior management perception that is often operationally oriented. This has led to arguments that hotel companies should stick to what they are good at, i.e. attracting and looking after guests. The motivation for such a separation of 'bricks from brains' also comes from market forces that consider that by removing debt and assets from the balance sheet, the remaining operation-only hotel entity will produce better returns and make investment in property clearer. Teerapittayapaisan et al. (2002) note the pressure on the major hotel operating companies to release capital tied up in real estate to pay down debt and concentrate on brand development to drive share value. This, however, can, in the author's view, be argued to be true of other real estate carried by retailers or even the occupants of offices and is perhaps a key driver of SLBT across a range of industries.

Market valuation

Like many property owning companies, the stock market capitalization of the company tends to under-reflect the current market value of the underlying assets. This has been a source of some frustration to hoteliers given the dominance of land and buildings in their balance sheets. Peter Eyles, as managing director of Hanover Hotels plc, expressed it clearly, being quoted as saying: 'Where else can you buy 100p for 50p?' (Blackwell, 2001). From the market's perspective, one analyst observed that '... for Jarvis [a SLBT] will narrow the discount between net asset value and market cap[italization]' (quoted by Jolliffe, 2002).

Drivers – hotel companies

What then is leading hoteliers down this funding route rather than the ownership/debt previously adopted? Barris (2002) dealt with this question without addressing the specifics of the industry and proves, in the absence of specific research, a useful place to start. Based on a range of non-industry examples he suggests the motives of sellers of property are to:

- raise funding (off-balance sheet, off-budget) for other purposes, e.g. international expansion or debt reduction

- diversify funding sources

- improve efficiency in managing and use of property (forced by paying market rates for it). Outsourcing property management

- improve occupational flexibility, can leave premises when they want

- disposal of low returning assets.

Outsourcing in the form of asset management has not been a major factor in the hotel industry. Although lessors might employ asset managers to ensure the proper upkeep of hotels and advise on capital expenditure, this is an essentially monitoring role that leaves the day-to-day operation with the operator. Nor is the desire to leave premises at short notice an issue. Hotel companies are keen to maintain competitive advantage from location and typically seek long leases of 20 to 30 years in the case of Hilton and even 35 years for two Travelodge hotels in London (Anon, 2004b). In the limited reported details of industry transactions diversifying funding resources has not been mentioned as a major motivation. Thus off-balance sheet funding for other purposes and disposal of low returning assets remain from Barris's list. The role of off-balance sheet was mentioned earlier. The last point begs the question 'low returning in relation to what?' and seems to lead back to the question of what hotel companies do with the funds raised by SLBT. The argument would only hold if more profitable uses of the funds can be found. In a number of cases companies have returned, or proposed to return, funds to shareholders (who might have more profitable places to invest), pay off pension fund deficits or to invest in new properties that will take time to mature into the same level of profits as the ones sold. So even this 'motive' might benefit from closer examination.

In the absence of academic research within the industry, reports by real estate and accounting consultancies provide a more focused view of the motivations of hoteliers. Jones Lang Lasalle published two papers on SLBT in 2002, reflecting the level of interest following the initial portfolio deals. The first, by Elgonemy et al. (2002) suggests the following drivers from the hoteliers' side:

- the opportunity to release funds for brand expansion

- the off-balance sheet treatment of operating leases leading to the improvement of financial investment ratios such as liquidity, gearing and return on investment (ROI) and hence of credit ratings and stock market perception

- securing long-term presence without up front investment

- rent is fully tax deductible against current earnings (while depreciation on the current value is not and no amortization of the land element is deductible)

- there is an opportunity to negotiate flexible rent patterns
- the availability of a new funding source.

The second article by Teerapittayapaisan et al. (2002) adds to the range of motivations, *inter alia*:

- increasing mergers and acquisition activity in the industry
- improved awareness of the industry through consultants and institutions setting up in-house specialists
- difficulties in obtaining management contracts, an alternative off-balance sheet form of funding hotel property.

It is notable that Barris's point about the disposal of low yielding assets is not mentioned, though it is implicit in Elgonemy et al.'s second point. These points can be demonstrated in practice. Hilton, having raised a net £300 m from a sale and leaseback transaction in 2002, showed reduced net borrowings in that year of £309 m (Hilton, 2002). In the previous year a sale and leaseback of 11 hotels raised £311 m. This provided a substantial contribution to the £455 m cash portion of the acquisition cost of Scandic hotels. These are two standard strategies in SLBT, the reduction of debt and the improvement of the strategic operating position of the company in an industry, in this case an increase in market presence through the 132 hotels in Scandanavia, a region previously difficult to penetrate. In terms of profit improvement, the 2001 transactions brought a guaranteed rent commitment of 4 per cent (£12.5 m) of the consideration received. The total rent payable, the basis for a comparison with the costs of ownership, is not disclosed. The information is presented alongside to Scandic's reported profits of £34 m for a period of less than 7 months, implying a more profitable use of the funds. While these are details from the company's statements and thus designed to present a favourable picture, they are significant in showing examples of the strategic intent behind the SLBT. In 2002, the company was keen to point out that the minimum rent commitment was only 5.2 per cent of the consideration, somewhat lower than the borrowing rates on much of the debt, though it is difficult to determine from the accounts what the exact rate was on the debt replaced. The overall effect of the two transactions on the group gearing as of the end of 2002 was 57 per cent compared to in excess of 80 per cent had they not taken place, all other things remaining equal.

A consideration not highlighted in the literature is the opportunity to return funds to shareholders, generally to the extent that funds are not required for expansion. Thus IHG announced a proposed repayment of £1 billion, out of a total of transactions totalling £1.75 billion since April 2003, to shareholders based on a stated strategy of concentrating on hotel management, following the £1 billion SLBT in March 2005 (IHG, 2005b).

Drivers – investors

Elgonemy et al. (2002) cite a number of key drivers for investors. The following list draws on their work and includes commentary based on the author's experience and discussions with industry representatives:

- the need to diversify their investment portfolio as funds increase in relation to traditional property areas

- increased prospects of capital appreciation, especially on variable rent leases

- stronger credit ratings of hotel companies due to increasing size and financial stability.

While Teerapittayapaisan et al. (2002:2) point out that the growth of branding has made the industry more attractive: 'It is the quality branded hotels (operated by national or international hotel chains) that are of interest to, and have become the target of the wider investment market.'

'Institutional investors have a strong preference to own only those properties which are let on standard leases. In this way the UK has developed in a unique way, with long leases, typically 20 to 25 years' duration, and with the lessee accepting full responsibility for all repairs and outgoings' (Sayce, 2002:48).

The above describes the lease generally available prior to 1998 and an underlying philosophy of institutions of conservatism, seeking safe and stable but growing returns (index linked to inflation or to property values) over a long period. They were generally linked to strong covenants for the upkeep of the property, typically involving regular maintenance and the property's return to its original state at the end of the lease.

The question of strong credit ratings and brand appears to have been crucial in the case of the hotel industry. The very large publicly quoted players appear to dominate the reported transactions, Hilton, Accor, IHG and the like. Although early players were medium sized, Jarvis Hotels plc and Friendly plc, there does not appear to have been much more activity at this level. The notable exception turned out to be the Le Meridien deal where the track record of the chain as an independent operation was not well established and the brand was, arguably, not as strong as other large chains, despite its size.

Another aspect to note is the range of investors that have, and have not, been attracted to the hotel industry. The Royal Bank of Scotland is by far the largest institutional investor in the UK and has invested in hotels operated by a number of groups. It also showed a new level of skill in replacing its Meridien portfolio with other operators. The IHG deal went to an American finance company, Lehmann Brothers, reflecting a surplus of funds in the USA where hotel investments are more common through specific investment vehicles (REITS) (Beard, 2002). Other deals have been set up by firms, such as Rotch, that put together complex funding and tax based schemes. Norwich Union, on the other hand, have not followed up on their early investments. What is noticeable is the absence of most of the major UK funding institutions and of property companies that have been prominent in other sectors, notably British Land, London and Regional or Topland in retail. Further research would be helpful to understand why some investors do not select hotel industry assets as part of their portfolio.

The forms of transactions

Although not discussed by the authors, SLBT can be seen, along with franchises and management contracts as non-equity strategic alliances under the definition of Prakash and Olsen (2003): 'an agreement between two or more firms to co-operate in some way that does not involve either the creation of a new firm or one firm purchasing equity in the other(s).'

They speak of complementary assets of the two parties creating a stronger source of value generation and competitive advantage. In the case of portfolio transactions there is a need for a strong lender, as the size of some transactions has shown, on the one hand and an operator of hotels that is capable of providing a strong covenant based on its financial and operational capabilities over the long term.

Given the perspectives of the parties and the nature of the industry, clearly any transaction must represent a compromise between the often opposing interests and drivers. The contracts developed show some interesting ways of achieving such a compromise.

Stability of income for investors

The lessors are typically long-term investors seeking stable and growing investments. The primary method of achieving this is to set a 'base' or minimum rent which is set as a percentage of the value of the property in the transaction. This base rent is normally subject to inflation provisions based on the retail price index (RPI) or property indices. The initial rate is often attractive compared to borrowing rates for equivalent sums.

Variable rents

In an attempt to recognize the volatility of revenues and profits in the industry, leases have adopted two basic methods of achieving variable rent formulae. The first is a rent based on revenues, such as the Hilton leases in 2001 and 2002, which provided for rents at 25 and 28.8 per cent respectively. It is important to note, however, that in both cases a guaranteed minimum was provided of 4 and 5.2 per cent of the consideration (Hilton Group, 2002, 2003). Thus the lessor is able to share in any upside in terms of enhanced earnings while retaining a base return on the investment that is subject to uplift in line with RPI. The second option is to provide an additional rent in the form of a percentage of profit, which would then be defined in the contract. The early Jarvis and Friendly deals had such provisions. From the hotel company's perspective this has the advantage of being linked to its earnings. With a turnover based uplift the operator is taking on the risk of ensuring that costs are kept in line in order to ensure that a profit remains after the base and turnover rents are paid.

Upgrade investments

Hotels need not only day-to-day maintenance but also refurbishment and upgrade expenditure to compensate for inevitable wear and tear and to maintain competitiveness in a fast changing market. The lessor is owner of the building and fixed equipment but the question arises as to who should bear these costs and how they should be determined. Traditional leases had typically, but not always, required the lessee to pay. The lessee, however, argued that upgrade expenditure, at least, represented a benefit to the owner in the form of an enhanced asset and therefore greater market value. Details of these terms in the contracts are not often revealed in public documents. However, in the recent sale and leaseback deals two patterns can be identified. In the simplest arrangement the operator bears the cost of refurbishment against a detailed requirement set out in the lease. This has reportedly in one case resulted in the hotel company having to meet unexpectedly high costs that of course must be paid out of its own profits. In other cases the owner pays the costs of upgrades, but not refurbishment, but is able to increase the base rent on the basis of the current percentage, uplifted by indexation, of the cost of the upgrade. Clearly the question of ongoing capital expenditure is key to the parties and needs to be negotiated with care. It is as crucial to the future earnings of the parties as is the rent formula itself.

Shared ownership

In the Hilton transaction of 2002, the operator retained a 25 per cent interest in the ownership of the hotels sold through a limited partnership, as well as taking a lease back from that entity. This was a complex deal and not typical. However, it can be seen to have benefits for both parties. The owner can see that the operator is encouraged to share the risks and benefits of ownership, the two parties thus being aligned. For the operator it has the added benefit of maintaining a greater element of control, particularly in the choice of operator at the end of the lease period.

Management contracts

While this chapter is about sale and leaseback transactions, it is worth noting that there appears to be a move towards sale and management back. In particular, the IHG deal with Lehman Brothers for £1 billion worth of hotels in the UK and elsewhere takes this form with a term of 20 years. Management contracts generally leave the owner with a greater responsibility for the upkeep of the building and equipment and the operational risk, thus being less attractive than leases. The press release from the operator does not report any details of this nor of any guarantees of earnings to the owner. This represents a significant move in the attitude of property investors. IHG reports that its earnings from management fees are expected to be £12 billion though again the basis is not provided. Such contracts also resolve the issue of accounting for leases and the possibility of a change requiring lessees to report the value of leases on their balance sheets.

Selling the family silver

The concern over loss of control over key assets is to some extent met by the longer lease terms. As noted earlier, hotel groups will retain ownership of what they consider to be key properties or seek much longer lease terms. Shared ownership can provide further protection as can contract terms that provide for options to extend those terms. However, there appears to be a further issue that results from the consolidation of the industry. Hotel groups now typically operate many more hotels than in, say, 1990 and the loss of one or two at the end of a lease period is clearly of less concern to a group with 300 hotels than to one with only 15, which was the size of the fifth largest hotel group in the UK at that time.

Single use assets

That same consolidation also gives the investors more confidence in larger groups and their stability and credit worthiness. However, what has become apparent to investors is that, if a hotel company does not meet its obligations under a lease there are other reputable companies that will take over the property and the lease. Royal Bank of Scotland had no difficulty in finding other operators when its leases with Le Meridien fell in through non-compliance of rental payments (John, 2003). The point does, however, highlight the need to be careful in the selection of hotels to be purchased in the first place and to ensure their proper upkeep.

Full value sales

Historically, lenders would provide loans to a certain percentage, usually 75–80 per cent, of the current market value of the hotel(s). It appears that SLBT have been done at figures close to the full market value. This is odd in one key respect. The valuation methods used for hotels are based upon a multiple of the earnings. A lease arrangement would only make sense from the hotel company's point of view if the rental payments (and other costs under the lease) were less than the total earnings, i.e. the lease represents a sharing of the earnings between the lessor and the lessee. In this case the value of the transaction should, theoretically, be less than the value shown on the books. This apparent anomaly needs to be the subject of further research.

Spread of risk

Just as lending to a major company with a wide spread of assets provides a greater assurance of earnings, so acquiring a portfolio of hotels can provide greater safety. It is noticeable that most reported deals have been with large operators, IHG, Hilton, Accor, etc. If there is a shortfall of earnings within the portfolio acquired, the size of the company, its asset base and overall earnings minimize the risk of being unable to pay the rent or meet other obligations under the lease. Yet the Le Meridien case shows that this might not always be the solution. It is still important to ensure that the economics of the deal are worked out with prudence. The purchase of a portfolio of hotels also means that the owner is not at risk from a sudden downfall in a single location, as sometimes occurs, though it would appear that the security provided by the size of company remains more important. For the operator, too, having a portfolio of hotels under a single deal means that if one or two hotels have earnings that do not meet the rent payments then it is likely that there will be others to offset the shortfalls. For both parties it is important to ensure that the portfolio is sustainable. An operator must accept that it is unwise to put all its poorly performing properties into a deal and retain the best under ownership, however tempting that might be. The strategic alliance aspect comes into play again here.

Conclusion

The analysis above points to a number of issues of importance for hotel companies and for potential investors in the properties they operate. The interest of the hotel company centres around releasing funds and, under current accounting rules, improving the gearing on their balance sheets. There is also the pressure, both internally and from the investment community to focus on the core business of looking after guests, leaving property ownership, funding and management to experts in that field. At the same time the hotel operator does look for security of tenure in the properties and hence longer lease periods. While some change in the operator's portfolio is manageable in marketing terms, major shifts in the locations and properties are still perceived as potentially damaging to customer perception of a brand and thus a threat to earnings.

From the investors' side there is clearly a greater willingness to invest in hotels through leasing on flexible terms that are more acceptable to hotel operators. They too seek long-term investments, though there are terms in contracts that allow for early termination for non-compliance. It appears that investors do have a need to diversify their portfolio and that the hotel industry has been recognized as a suitable place for investment, having built up a track record for security of earnings, particularly through consolidation and branding, and for capital appreciation. It has become apparent that the large operators with strong brands have become the borrowers/lessees of choice. It will be interesting to see to what extent such contracts might move into the smaller and less well-known hotel companies where much of the hotel stock in the UK remains owned. Perhaps a more significant trend is the willingness to adopt management contracts that might prove more attractive to hoteliers, both in the transfer of risk and the impact of changes in accounting treatment.

The key message is that SLBT is neither a panacea for either party nor something to be rejected out of hand based on a simplistic view, such as 'selling the family silver'. It is, however, a complex route that needs careful financial analysis to consider the various aspects of such transactions, some of which, like taxation and legal questions, are beyond the scope of this chapter. The interests of the two parties are not aligned, *per se* and it is necessary to work out a schema that is both sustainable and equitable to the parties. SLBT should therefore be seen as strategic alliances.

Finally, it should be acknowledged that this area is in need of further academic research to update prior work for the significant activity in the area in the last five years and to explore aspects that have hardly been touched. While it must be acknowledged that there is much proprietary knowledge that investors, hotel companies and their advisors might be reluctant to divulge, since it is perceived as providing competitive edge in achieving better investment returns, funding structures and knowledge, there is much to learn from each other to avoid mistakes in such major transactions. This chapter is based almost solely on secondary research of publicly available material, informal discussions with involved parties and the experience of the author as a finance director in hotel groups. First-hand input from participants in SLBT would, clearly, provide a more reliable basis for establishing some first principles in this field specifically for the industry.

References

Anon (2004a) RBS Aviation keeps busy. *Airfinance Journal*, **267**, 13.

Anon (2004b) Travelodge books into Thistle beds. *Estates Gazette*, **425**, 38.

ASB (1999a) *Leases: Implementation of a New Approach, Discussion Paper*. Accounting Standards Board, London.

ASB (1999b) *Statement of Principles for Financial Reporting*. Accounting Standards Board, London.

Barris, R. (2002) Sale-leasebacks move to the forefront: What is motivating buyers and sellers and what are their preferred methods? *Briefings in Real Estate Finance*, **2** (2), 103–112.

Beard, A. (2002) New hotel leaseback plans offer a vacation from risk. *Financial Times*, (USA edition), London, June 4, p. 23.

Beattie, V.A., Edwards, K. and Goodacre, A. (1998) The impact of constructive operating lease capitalisation on key accounting ratios. *Accounting and Business Research*, **28** (4), 233–254.

Beattie, V.A., Goodacre, A. and Thomson, S. (2000a) Operating leases and the assessment of lease-debt substitutability. *Journal of Banking and Finance*, **24** (3), 427–470.

Beattie, V.A., Goodacre, A. and Thomson, S. (2000b) Recognition versus disclosure: an investigation of the impact on equity risk using UK operating lease disclosures. *Journal of Business Finance and Accounting*, **27** (9&10), 1185–1224.

Bergsman, S. (2004) Hewlett-Packard gets its dollars in S. Korea. *Treasury and Risk Management*, **9** (2), 15.

Blackwell, D. (2001) Hotelier finds key to expansion plans. *Financial Times*, April 21.

Bock, P. and Forster, B. (2004) *HVS Transaction survey 2003*. Hotel Valuation Services, London.

Dixon, T., Pottinger, G., Marston, A. and Beard, M. (2000) *Occupational Futures? Real Estate Refinancing and Restructuring*. College of Estate Management paper, Reading University.

Elgonemy, A., Craig, T. and Gibson, D. (2002) Overview of hotel sale-leaseback transactions, London. *Jones Lang Lasalle Hotels*, 11, June, 1–3.

Gibson, V. (2000) Evaluating office space needs & choices. The University of Reading, quoted in Dixon et al. (2000).

Goodacre, A. (2001) Assessing the impact of lease accounting reform: a review of the empirical evidence, paper to the RICS Cutting Edge Conference, Nottingham, University of Sterling.

Graham, I.C. and Harris, P. J. (1999) Development of a profit planning framework in an international hotel chain: a case study. *International Journal of Contemporary Hospitality Management*, **11** (5), 198–204.

Hess, Liang and McAllister (2001) An institutional perspective on hotel investing. *Real Estate Finance*, **18** (2), 51.

Hilton (2002) *Hilton Group plc. Annual Report and Accounts 2001*.

Hilton (2003) *Hilton Group plc. Annual Report and Accounts 2002*.

Hopper, A. and van Marken, N. (2001) The long-term view: an extended investment in hotels can produce above-average returns. *Andersen Hospitality and Leisure Executive Report*, **8** (1).

IHG (2005a) *Intercontinental Hotels Group plc. Annual Report and Financial Statements 2004*.

IHG (2005) Sale of 73 Hotels in UK for £1 billion; Further Return of Funds, Press Release, March 10, 2005 retrieved May 20, 2005 11:29am from http://www.ihgplc.com/media/index.asp?PageID=6&Year=2005&NewsID=1192.

John, P. (2003) Meridien misses deadline on crucial rental payment. *Financial Times*, July 1.

Jolliffe, A. (2002) Jarvis in sale and leaseback. *Financial Times*, October 12.

Jones Lang LaSalle (2002) Hotel sale-leaseback transactions. *Hotel Topics*, 11, June.

Koza, H. and Sibayan, K. (2001) Canada's CMBS pipeline flows. *Asset Securitization Report*, **1** (19), 14.

Pannell Kerr Forster (2002) PKF reveals surprise hotel industry vote on sale and leaseback deals http://www.pkf.co.uk/

web/pkfweb.nsf/pagesByID/IDC5E59D71AB97D9D480256C
4500560FC3?OpenDocument retrieved May 13, 2005 at 11:28
am. Press release Sept 27, 2002.

Prakash, K.C. and Olsen, M.D. (2003) Strategic alliances: a hospitality industry perspective. *International Journal of Hospitality Management*, **22**, 419–434.

Sayce, S. (2002) The new leisure leases: Do they measure up to institutional requirements? *Journal of Leisure Property*, **1** (1), 42–65.

Teerapittayapaisan, S., Astbury, K. and Clack, V. (2002) Changing ownership structures – Europe, London. *Jones Lang Lasalle Hotels*, 12, December, 1–3.

Walsh D. (2005a) Lehman looks to buy IHG hotels, London. *The Times*, March 8.

Walsh, D. (2005b) IHG to hand back £1bn after asset sale, London. *The Times*, March 11.

Whitbread (2005) Official Company Statement on Sale of Marriott Chain in UK, retrieved from http://miranda.hemscott.com/servlet/HsPublic?context=ir.access&ir_option=RNS_NEWS&item=26265872543065&ir_client_id=43 on March 15, 2005 at 14:35pm.

Hospitality firm risk determinants and value enhancement

Zheng Gu

Introduction

The goal of a firm is to maximize the value of the firm because this goal justifies the existence of a business entity and considers the complexities of the operating environment (Keown et al., 2002:5). For a publicly traded firm, the firm value is reflected in its stock price. Therefore, the goal of a publicly traded firm is to maximize the shareholders' wealth as represented by the firm's stock price. Just like businesses in any other industries, hospitality firms should also take value maximization as their ultimate goal.

A hospitality firm's value is affected by a potential investor's investment decision that is determined by the investor's required rate of return (RRR) and his or her perceived risk associated with the investment in the hospitality firm. This chapter will discuss the relationship between the RRR and risk and show how the risk may affect hospitality firm value through its impact on the RRR. Furthermore, determinants of hospitality firms' systematic risk, the relevant risk that affects the RRR and firm value, will be examined. In the meantime, ways to lower the systematic risk and enhance hospitality firm value will be proposed.

Risk-return trade-off and firm value

The stock price of a hospitality firm is affected by prospective investors' interest in the firm. When investors like a firm, the firm's stock price will go up and the existing shareholders will benefit. When investors dislike the firm, the stock price will go down and existing shareholders' wealth will decline. For existing shareholders of a hospitality firm, their wealth in the firm depends on the decisions of potential investors. Then, how do investors make their decisions on whether or not to invest in a hospitality firm? According to the finance theory (Keown et al., 2002:5), an investor makes an investment decision based on his or her RRR and the risk associated with the investment. A rationale investor is risk-averse. He or she will always require additional return for bearing additional investment risk. Therefore, higher risk is associated with higher RRR and vice versa.

This risk-return trade-off should affect hospitality investors' decision-making and hence the value of a hospitality firm. When the firm risk as perceived by the capital market rises, investors will raise their RRR to compensate for bearing additional risk. Demanding a higher RRR, hospitality investors will not buy the stock unless the stock price drops to a very low level so as to achieve a higher expected return or to realize their higher RRR. On the other hand, when the perceived risk of investing in a hospitality firm declines, investors will lower their risk premium and hence the RRR from investing in the firm. Demanding a lower RRR from investing in the firm, investors will be willing to purchase the stock even when the stock price is high because they do not expect to achieve a high return from a safe investment. In the final analysis, the risk associated with the investment in a hospitality firm affects the investor's RRR and eventually affects the stock price or the value of the firm.

Relevant risk for firm valuation

Financial researchers commonly use the capital asset pricing model (CAPM) to describe the risk-return trade-off relationship in stock investment. The CAPM theory (Sharpe, 1963:277, 1964:425; Lintner, 1965:587) holds that the expected return or the RRR on a risky asset, such as a stock, has two components: the risk-free rate of return, which is to compensate for delaying consumption, and the risk premium to compensate for bearing the risk. According to the CAPM, the risk premium must be measured in a portfolio sense and is the excess market return over the risk-free rate multiplied by the level of the market-related risk or systematic risk for the specific asset or stock. Mathematically, the CAPM can be described in the following equation:

$$R_i = R_f + (R_m - R_f) * \beta_i \qquad (1)$$

where:

R_i is the expected rate of return or RRR on the ith security;

R_f is the risk-free rate of return;

R_m is the return on the market portfolio including all stocks in the market; and

β_i is the systematic risk of the ith stock.

According to the CAPM theory, there are two types of risks of a firm or its stock. The first is the market-related systematic risk, commonly denoted as beta. It is a stock's volatility resulting from the market's volatility or simply the covariance of a stock's return with that of the entire market. The second is the unsystematic risk, i.e. the stocks volatility caused by firm-specific events, such as lawsuits, strikes, unexpected good or bad earnings announcements. The total risk of a firm, measured by the variance or standard deviation of the stock return, is a combination of the two types of risk.

For shareholders, the volatility or unsystematic risk due to firm-specific events can be reduced or eliminated by holding a well-diversified portfolio of different stocks. If the shareholder holds a large portfolio consisting of many different stocks, stock price movements caused by firm-specific events may offset each other, thus neutralizing the effect of those events. This type of stock volatility or unsystematic risk can be completely diversified away if the investor holds a sufficiently large portfolio of stocks. According to the CAPM, investors should not be rewarded for bearing the unsystematic risk because, in the final analysis, it can be diversified away. Consequently, unsystematic risk should not be a relevant factor in determining the investor's RRR and capital assets pricing.

On the other hand, the market-related volatility or systematic risk of a stock is its covariance with the market. This type of volatility or risk cannot be diversified away because the volatility is caused by events that affect all stocks across the capital market. Even if a shareholder owns a portfolio including all stocks in the market, such as an index fund, he or she will still face the market risk caused by market events, such as presidential elections, rising oil prices and major terrorist attacks. The systematic risk cannot be diversified away and investors have to deal with it. Therefore, investors must be rewarded for bearing it and thus the systematic risk is the relevant risk that affects the investor's RRR. In other words, the systematic risk of a firm must be considered when determining the price of a stock on the capital market. High systematic risk needs to be compensated by high return. In contrast, because the unsystematic risk can be completely diversified away, investors need not to be compensated for bearing it.

Sharpe (1963:277) developed a single-index model that relates the rate of return of a stock to a common market index in a linear equation. The model, often referred to as characteristic line, is commonly used for estimating the systematic risk. Based on the model, the sensitivity of a security's return to the return on the capital market (market portfolio), or beta, can be estimated by the characteristic line with historical data as in the following equation:

$$R_i = \alpha_i + \beta_i R_m + e_i \tag{2}$$

where:

R_i is the rate of return on the ith security;

α_i is the estimated vertical intercept.

β_i is the estimated beta or systematic risk of the ith stock;

R_m is the rate of return on the market portfolio;

e_i is the error around the regression line that represents the relationship of the two;

Variables affecting the systematic risk

A firm's operating, investing, financing and dividend policies affect its business and financial risk and eventually its systematic risk. Business risk is the volatility of a firm's earnings before interests and taxes (EBIT). Financial risk is the additional variability in return on equity or earnings per share (EPS) due to the use of debt leverage. The management of a firm can control financial and business risk variables that will eventually affect the company's systematic risk. Breen and Lerner (1973:339) suggest that changes in a firm's financing, investing and operating decisions can alter its stock return and risk features. In particular, the systematic risk or beta of the firm is likely to change. As the systematic risk affects investors' RRR in a framework as described by the CAPM model (see Equation **1**), an increase in the systematic risk will raise the investor's RRR and decrease the firm value and vice versa. Therefore, beta, the systematic risk of a firm's common stock, links corporate decisions and behaviours with the market value of the firm's stock. The importance of beta to firm value has prompted many financial researchers to explore the relationship between beta and financial variables in an attempt to identify beta determinants.

To investigate beta determinants, research studies have focused on the relationship between beta and liquidity, debt leverage, efficiency, profitability, dividend payout, firm size and growth variables. Most empirical studies have used the multiple regression method with beta as the dependent variable and firm-wise financial variables as independent variables.

Liquidity

Competing theories exist regarding how a firm's liquidity may affect its systematic risk. Jensen (1984:323) proposes a positive relationship between a firm's liquidity and its systematic risk, arguing that overly high liquidity may increase a firm's agency cost of free cash flow, thus raising its systematic risk. Nevertheless, Logue and Merville (1972:37) and Moyer and Chatfield (1983:123) assume a negative relationship between the two and hold that high liquidity is an indicator of low level of short-term liabilities and low systematic risk. An investigation of the correlation between current ratio and beta by Beaver et al. (1970:654) found current ratio negatively correlated with beta. However, the empirical studies by Borde (1998:64), Rosenberg and McKibeen (1973:317), and Pettit and Westerfield (1972:1649) found liquidity ratios positively associated with the systematic risk. On the other hand, the study by Logue and Merville (1972:37) failed to find a significant relationship between liquidity ratios and beta.

Debt leverage

Financial theory suggests that higher debt leverage exposes shareholders to greater financial risk and hence higher systematic risk (Bowman, 1979:617; Moyer and Chatfield, 1983:123; Chu, 1986:48; Amit and Livnat, 1988:19). Previous research studies in this field have employed a variety of ratios to measure financial leverage and the most commonly used ratio is total liabilities to total assets or debt ratio. Empirical findings unanimously report a positive relationship between leverage and beta (Beaver et al., 1970:654;

Hamada, 1972:435; Logue and Merville, 1972:37; Rosenberg and McKibeen, 1973:317; Mandelker and Rhee, 1984:45; Amit and Livnat, 1988:19; Borde et al., 1994:177). Melicher's (1974:231) results showed that the beta and debt leverage relationship might be positive but non-linear. In his study, when leverage increased, beta increased at an increasing rather than at a constant rate.

Operating efficiency

Logue and Merville (1972:37) assert that operating efficiency, or the efficiency in using assets to generate revenues, should have a negative influence on the systematic risk. Firms with higher operating efficiency may produce greater profits and are thus associated with lower probability of failure and smaller systematic risk. The empirical results of Logue and Merville (1972:37) confirmed their assertion by showing beta's negative correlation with assets turnover ratio, a ratio measuring the efficiency in using total assets to generate revenues, in a linear pattern.

Profitability

According to Logue and Merville (1972:37), high profitability lowers the probability of business failure, thus helping lower a firm's systematic risk. Scherrer and Mathison (1996:5) also argue for a negative relationship between profitability and systematic risk. They propose that the stability of the cash flow from operation, which reduces the systematic risk, is determined by the ability to manage the property profitably. Using profit margin and return on assets as profitability ratios, Logue and Merville (1972:37) empirically proved that beta was negatively correlated with both ratios. Melicher's (1974:231) regression analysis, however, found beta positively related to return on equity. It is possible that some firms generating high profits over time may implement aggressive business strategies, subjecting themselves to a higher level of risk.

Dividend payout

Financial theory holds that high dividend payout ratio should have a negative impact on systematic risk, either because returns from dividends are perceived by investors to be more certain than returns through higher stock prices (Logue and Merville, 1972:37) or because high dividend payout implies low agency cost (Ang et al., 1985:3). According to Jahankhani and Lynge (1980:169), firms with greater earnings variability tend to distribute fewer dividends than more stable companies. Therefore, dividend payout should be inversely associated with systematic risk. Numerous empirical studies confirmed the negative relationship between dividend payout and beta (Beaver et al., 1970:654; Pettit and Westerfield, 1972:1649; Breen and Lerner, 1973:339; Rosenberg and McKibeen, 1973:317; Melicher, 1974:231; Fabozzi and Francis, 1979:61; Ang et al., 1985; Borde, 1998:64).

Firm size

Theoretically, large firms tend to have low systematic risk because of their better ability to minimize the impact of economic, social and political changes (Sullivan, 1978:209) or their market power that enables them to achieve superior profits unattainable in a more competitive environment (Moyer and Chatfield, 1983:123; Ang et al., 1985:3). The negative impact of size on systematic risk has been confirmed in a number of empirical studies, including those by Ang et al. (1985:3), Patel and Olsen (1984:481), Lev and Kunitzky (1974:259), Breen and Lerner (1973:339) and Logue and Merville (1972:37).

Growth

Fast growth is assumed to increase the systematic risk of a firm. Logue and Merville (1972:37) contend that fast-growth firms may face great competition and are more sensitive to economic fluctuations. Idol (1978:55) points out that firms experiencing high growth are perceived by investors as possessing substantial risk. His hypothesis was first supported by Logue and Merville (1972:37) who found a positive association between annual growth in total assets and beta. Borde (1998:64) showed that growth in EBIT was positively related to beta, providing further support to the hypothesized relationship between growth and the systematic risk.

Beta-affecting variables differ across industries

The link between financial variables and beta may differ greatly across industries. Logue and Merville (1972:37) examined the relationship between beta and financial variables using data from four different industries (autos and auto parts, building and building supplies, electronic and electrical supplies, and machinery). They found that debt leverage was the only variable demonstrating a positive impact on beta across the four industries. Moreover, the signs and significance levels of other financial variables differed among the industries. Melicher (1974:231) provided further evidence for the claim that the relationship between financial variables and beta varies across industries.

In summary, previous empirical studies on the relationship between beta and financial variables indicate that debt leverage and growth tend to increase the systematic risk, whereas operating efficiency, dividend pay out and firm size are likely to have a negative impact on the risk. On the other hand, the findings of the impact of liquidity and profitability on beta are inconclusive.

As the relationship between financial variables and beta may differ widely across industries, findings based on non-hospitality firm data may not be applicable to the hospitality industry. To enhance the value of hospitality firms, hospitality researchers need to find the particular financial variables that exert an impact on hospitality systematic risk, thus finding ways to reduce the systematic risk for hospitality firms. Presented below are three empirical studies investigating beta determinants for different sectors in the hospitality industry. They may shed light on how hospitality firms can reduce their systematic risk and strengthen firm value.

Case one: beta determinants in the casino industry

In an attempt to identify variables that determine casino firms' systematic risk, Gu and Kim (1998:357) conducted an empirical investigation using a sample of 35 US casino firms for the period of 1992–1994 when the US casino industry experienced the fastest growth. Using weekly firm stock return and the New York Stock Exchange (NYSE) index weekly change as the market return, the study first estimated the beta or systematic risk of each casino firm based on the characteristic line model (see Equation **2**). The slope of the characteristic line of each firm, estimated by regressing the firm's weekly stock return against the NYSE weekly return, represented the sensitivity of the stock's return to the market return and was the estimated beta.

Four financial ratios were tested as potential determinants of casino beta. They were current ratio, which was current assets divided by current liabilities; leverage ratio, a ratio of total liabilities to total assets; assets turnover ratio, which was total revenue divided by total assets; and profit margin, a ratio of net income to total revenue. The four ratios represent liquidity, leverage, efficiency and profitability, respectively. With the estimated beta as the dependent variable and the three-year averages of the financial ratios as the independent variables in a cross-firm multiple regression analysis, the relationship between those financial variables and beta were examined.

The results of the multiple regression are presented in Table 19.1. Only one variable, total assets turnover, was found negatively correlated with beta at a statistically significant level, suggesting

Table 19.1
Casino firm beta determinants

Independent variable	Coefficient	t-statistic
Intercept	2.378	7.385**
Current ratio	−0.029	−0.630
Leverage ratio	−0.344	−0.802
Assets turnover	−0.493	−1.838*
Profit margin	−0.043	−0.166

Note: ** and * indicate significance at the 0.05 and 0.1 levels, respectively.

that a casino firm efficiently using its existing assets to generate revenue tends to have a low beta. Current ratio and profit margin were negatively associated with beta, suggesting that higher liquidity and profitability lead to lower beta. Both of them, however, were statistically insignificant. The impact of debt leverage on beta was also found statistically insignificant.

The significant negative correlation between assets turnover ratio and beta implies that efficient assets management can lead to lower systematic risk for casino firms. In the mid-1990s, the US casino market was becoming saturated as a result of gaming proliferation and the industry was experiencing sluggish revenue growth (Gu, 1997:30). Gu and Kim's (1998:357) findings suggest that making existing gaming capacity more productive, rather than further expanding the capacity, during a market saturation may help reduce a casino firm's systematic risk and enhance the firm value. Continuous expansion of gaming capacity in a saturated market would further increase the total assets of casinos and deteriorate the assets turnover ratio. Lower assets efficiency would eventually increase casino firms' systematic risk and negatively affect their value.

Case two: beta determinants of hotel REITs

As a unique property sector in the hotel industry, hotel real estate investment trust (REIT) companies have grown at a remarkable pace since their introduction to the public in 1993. By the end of 1999, the number of publicly traded US hotel REITs increased to 19 firms and their total market capitalization reached $8.8 billion (Grupe and DiRocco, 1999:21). Based on the data of 19 publicly traded hotel REIT companies during 1993–1999, Kim et al. (2002:138) examined the relationship between hotel REITs' beta and financial variables. In this study, monthly, rather than weekly, stock return and market return were used to estimate the betas of the hotel REIT firms based on the characteristic line (see Equation 2). Monthly stock return was regressed against the monthly NYSE return to obtain the beta coefficient for each hotel REIT firm.

Seven variables commonly used in empirical studies on beta determinants were tested as potential determinants of beta. They were quick ratio, debt ratio, return on equity, assets turnover, dividend payout, capitalization and assets growth. Quick ratio, representing liquidity, was defined as cash, marketable securities and accounts receivables divided by current liabilities. Debt ratio, a measure of leverage, was a ratio of total liabilities to total assets. Assets turnover ratio was total revenue divided by total assets, indicating the efficiency of using assets to generate revenue. Return on equity, a ratio of net income to total equity, was a measure of profitability relevant to the owner's investment. Dividend payout was the average annual dividend paid to shareholders. Capitalization, which was the number of outstanding shares multiplied by the closing stock price at the end of the year, was as a measure of firm size. Finally, assets growth was the annual percentage change in total assets, a measure of firm growth.

With the estimated beta as the dependent variable and the seven-year averages of the seven financial variables as the independent variables in cross-firm multiple regression, the relationship between selected financial variables and beta was examined. The findings are presented in Table 19.2.

Table 19.2
Determinants of systematic risk of hotel REITs

Independent variable	Coefficient	t-statistic
Intercept	0.1819	0.69
QR	0.0359	1.42
TD/TA	0.0115	2.38*
ROE	0.0098	1.72
AT	0.4646	0.55
DIV	0.0008	0.58
CAP	−0.0004	−2.87*
GrTA	0.1263	3.66**

Note:*, ** indicate significance at the 0.05 and 0.01 levels, respectively; QR = the average quick ratio over the study period; TD/TA = the average total debt to total assets over the study period; ROE = the average return on equity over the study period; AT = the average assets turnover ratio over the study period; DIV = the average total dividend payout over the study period; CAP = the average total capitalization over the study period; GrTA = the average annual growth rate in total assets over the study period.

The three statistically significant variables in the regression model deserve more attention. Consistent with beta determinants theory, debt ratio was positively correlated with beta. Evidently, higher leverage contributes to higher systematic risk for hotel REITs. Capitalization, as expected, had a negative and significant relationship with beta, suggesting that large hotel REITs are less risky in terms of their covariance with the market. The most influencing variable in the regression model was asset growth, as indicated by its coefficient size and significance level. The positive coefficient shows that high growth tends to increase the systematic risk of a hotel REIT firm.

The positive and significant correlation between debt ratio and beta found in this study suggests that using less debt can help reduce the systematic risk of a hotel REIT. Debt financing creates financial risk, thus augmenting the systematic risk of a firm. Furthermore, according to Howe and Shilling (1988:983), the tax gain from corporate borrowing is negative for firms whose effective marginal tax rate is zero. Consequently, non-tax-paying firms, such as hotel REITs, are forced to pay high interest on their external loans. This relative disadvantage of using debt for tax-exempt firms may further magnify systematic risk of hotel REITs. When formulating their financing policy, hotel REITs must be cautious about the financial risk associated with leverage. Hotel REITs should carefully weigh the advantages of high leverage against its risk.

The significant and positive regression coefficient for asset growth in the model suggests that hotel REITs pursuing conservative growth may carry lower systematic risk. Fast-growing hotel REITs need large amounts of external capital to support their expansion and growth. While raising additional debt will certainly augment the firm's financial risk, issuing new stocks carries the risk of diluting future earnings and increases uncertainty. Moreover, as hotels were increasingly faced with less favourable operating conditions in the late 1990s, aggressive expansion may be even riskier. According to Rushmore (1998:10), most hotel industry analysts believed that the US lodging market was heading into another cycle of overbuilding in the late 1990s. Bloomberg (1998) reported that after eight years of growth since 1991, profits were slowing down for US hotels and expansion was likely to take a toll on room prices and occupancy levels. With an imbalance between room supply and demand, occupancy would fall, room rates would turn flat and profits would decline. In such a market environment, growth via new expansion might not be a wise pursuance, because such a strategy can greatly increase the systematic risk. A conservative growth was thus a more appropriate approach for hotel REITs during the late 1990s.

The negative relationship between capitalization and beta suggests that large hotel REITs have lower systematic risk. While synergy may enable large hotel REITs to benefit from low operating and capital costs, large hotel REITs are better positioned for geographical diversification to achieve revenue stability. These advantages combined, as indicated by Scherrer and Mathison (1996:5), may help improve the stability of operating income, which is the dividend base, and lower systematic risk for large hotel REITs. However, increasing firm size by developing more hotel properties may be unwise in a saturated hotel market. To achieve synergy and geographical diversification, hotel REITs may consider consolidation within the industry's existing capacity through mergers and acquisitions.

Based on the above empirical results, two basic conclusions with policy implications can be drawn for hotel REITs. First, when the lodging industry is heading for a slow down in its business cycle, growth should be pursued via consolidation, or mergers and acquisitions, rather than via new capacity expansion. Consolidation may bring about synergy and geographical diversification, thus lowering systematic risk and strengthening the firm value. Aggressive expansion with new property development is risky in a relatively saturated market. Second, to reduce the financial risk associated with debt and hence to lower systematic risk, debt-burdened hotel REITs need to adjust their financing more toward equity. In particular, if new financing is needed for supporting growth, internal financing should be preferred to external financing. The REIT Modernization Act, which went into effect in January 2001, enables hotel REITs to obtain more funds needed for growth through internal financing. The 2001 Act reduces the required annual dividend distribution from 95 to 90 per cent, thereby increasing the level of internal funding available for hotel REITs. Hotel REITs should take full advantage of this new opportunity to support their growth via internally generated funds.

Case three: restaurant firms' beta determinants

To investigate the beta determinants in the restaurant industry, Gu and Kim (2002:1) used a sample of 75 publicly traded restaurant firms for the period of 1996–1999. Monthly stock return was regressed against monthly market return, represented by NYSE index percentage change, to estimate the beta of each restaurant firm in the same manner as discussed in previous sections. This study also employed seven variables as candidates of beta determinants. Like the study by Kim et al. (2002:138), this study used quick ratio, dividend payout and total assets as liquidity, dividend and size variables. Unlike the study by Kim et al. (2002:138), this study used equity ratio, which is total equity to total assets, return on assets, total assets growth rate and total assets as proxies for debt leverage, profitability, growth and firm size. Each of the seven variables was quantified by its four-year average value of the data period.

With estimated restaurant beta as the dependent variable and the seven financial variables as the independent variables in a cross-firm multiple regression analysis, the relationship between the seven variables and beta was investigated. Different from previous beta determinants studies that typically used ordinary least square (OLS) regression, Gu and Kim (2002:1) made two methodological changes. First, the weighted least-squares (WLS) regression procedure, as suggested by Kleinbaum et al. (1988:219) was used to avoid the heteroscedasticity problem commonly encountered in regression using cross-firm data. The weights were the reciprocals of the absolute values of the residuals from an initial ordinary least-squares regression. Second, a forward selection procedure was employed in establishing the final WLS regression model. In a forward selection procedure, the first variable to enter the model is the one that has the largest correlation with the dependent variable. If the variable is statistically significant, then the second variable with the largest semi-partial correlation with the dependent is considered. If the second variable is significant, then a third variable with the next largest semi-partial correlation is considered, etc. At some stage a given variable will not make a significant contribution to the prediction of the dependent variable and the procedure is terminated (Kleinbaum et al., 1988:326).

The final WLS model has only assets turnover and quick ratio as remaining variables (Table 19.3). The other five candidates were excluded by the forward selection procedure because of their insignificant partial correlation with beta. Like the study of Gu and Kim (1998:357), this study found assets turnover significantly and negatively associated with the firm's systematic risk.

Table 19.3
Restaurant beta determinants

Independent variable	Coefficient	t-statistic
Intercept	0.882	9.973*
Quick ratio	0.125	2.046**
Assets turnover	−0.242	−5.186*

Note: * Significant at the 0.01 level; ** significant at the 0.05 level.

High efficiency in using assets to generate revenue helps lower the restaurant risk. Unlike the Gu and Kim (1998:357) study, which found the systematic risk not significantly affected by firm liquidity, this study shows that liquidity tends to increase restaurant systematic risk. The inconsistency in the findings of the two studies is understandable. Beta determinants may vary not only across industries, but also across different sectors within the same industry.

The positive association between liquidity and beta identified in this study indicates that investors dislike excess liquidity of restaurant firms. Too much liquidity implies that available sources are not being invested in operating assets that may create higher return than cash or near-cash assets (Borde, 1998:64), thus increasing the risk of losing high-return opportunities. Therefore, to lower the beta and increase the firm value for shareholders, restaurant firms should avoid holding too much cash and near-cash assets not needed for covering their short-term liabilities. If high-return opportunities are available, excess cash and near-cash assets should be invested. Otherwise, they should be distributed to shareholders as dividends.

The results also revealed the dominant impact of assets turnover on restaurant beta. The highly significant and negative relationship between assets turnover and beta found in this study strongly suggests that using existing restaurant assets to generate more sales revenue is critical to lowering systematic risk of a restaurant firm. According to Schwartz (1999:203), many restaurant chains simply expanded too quickly and consequently went bankrupt. The restaurant industry is typically of low profit margin. In markets that are approaching saturation and where the competition is intensifying, restaurants' operating costs will increase dramatically, especially for new properties. Expansion by establishing more restaurant properties may subject firms to lower profit margins and higher default risk. Therefore, relying on existing properties to generate more sales revenue may reduce the risk as perceived by potential restaurant investors, thus lowering the beta and enhancing the firm value for existing shareholders.

Summary

Maximizing the firm value or the shareholder's wealth should be the goal of a hospitality firm. Like in any other industry, the firm value in the hospitality industry is affected by the risk-return trade-off of investors. In the theoretical framework of the CAPM, the unsystematic risk caused by firm-specific events can be diversified away and is thus not compensated for bearing it. The relevant risk affecting the investor's RRR and hospitality firm value is the non-diversifiable and market-related systematic risk.

The higher the systematic risk of a hospitality firm, the higher will be the investor's RRR and the lower the firm value, and vice versa.

A hospitality firm's operating, investing, financing and dividend policies affect the business and financial risks of the firm and eventually its systematic risk. Those policies are reflected in the firm's various financial variables. Identifying the financial variables that may affect the systematic risk will help hospitality executives make right decisions and control those variables for risk reduction and value enhancement.

The three empirical case studies presented in this chapter found that the beta determinants for the casino firms, hotel REITs and restaurant companies were not all the same. The inconsistency is mainly due to two reasons. First, the firms under investigation belong to three different sectors in the hospitality industry and are facing quite different operating and financing environments. As beta determinants are likely to differ across industries (Melicher, 1974:231), they may also differ across sectors within the same industry. Second, the data periods covered by the three studies were different. This also may have caused differences in their beta determinants due to different stages in the economic cycle. However, among the three investigated hospitality sectors, two sectors, namely the casino and restaurant sectors, had assets turnover negatively and significantly correlated with beta, suggesting that firms that use existing assets to generate more revenues have lower systematic risk. Therefore, with regard to how hospitality firms should lower the systematic risk and enhance firm value, our recommendation based on the case studies would lean toward raising the efficiency of existing assets.

Of course, more research on hospitality beta determinants needs to be conducted before we can reach final conclusions regarding lowering risk and strengthening firm value in the hospitality industry. Especially, the beta determinants of non-REIT hotels firms, which represent a significant part of the lodging industry, have never been examined. A more comprehensive and thorough study is needed for an in-depth understanding of beta determinants and ways to enhance firm value in the hospitality industry.

References

Amit, R. and Livnat, J. (1988) Diversification, capital structure, and systematic risk: An empirical investigation. *Journal of Accounting, Auditing & Finance*, **3** (1), 19–43.

Ang, J., Peterson, P. and Peterson, D. (1985) Investigations into the determinants of risk: A new look. *Quarterly Journal of Business and Economics*, **24** (1), 3–20.

Beaver, H., Kettler, P. and Scholes, M. (1970) The association between market determined and accounting determined risk measures. *The Accounting Review*, **45** (3), 654–682.

Bloomberg (1998) After eight years of growth, profits slow for US hotels. *Las Vegas Review Journal*, Business Section, http://www.lvrj.com

Borde, S. (1998) Risk diversity across restaurants. *Cornell Hotel Quarterly and Restaurant Administration Quarterly*, **39** (6), 64–69.

Borde, S., Chambliss, K. and Madura, J. (1994) Explaining variation in risk across insurances companies. *Journal of Financial Services Research*, **8** (3), 177–191.

Bowman, R.G. (1979) The theoretical relationship between systematic risk and financial (accounting) variables. *The Journal of Finance*, **34** (3), 617–630.

Breen, J. and Lerner, M. (1973) Corporate financial strategies and market measures of risk and return. *The Journal of Finance*, **28** (2), 339–351.

Chu, J. (1986) Toward a flexible capital structure. *The Bankers Magazine*, **169** (2), 48–54.

Fabozzi, F. and Francis, J. (1979) Industry effects and the determinants of beta. *The Quarterly Review of Economics and Business*, **19** (3), 61–74.

Grupe, M. and DiRocco, C. (1999) The NAREIT index of REIT industry performance. *Real Estate Finance*, **16** (1), 21–50.

Gu, Z. (1997) Saturation surfaces on Strip. *Casino Journal*, **10** (8), 30.

Gu, Z. and Kim, H. (1998) Casino firm's risk features and their beta determinants. *Progress in Tourism and Hospitality Research*, **4** (4), 357–365.

Gu, Z. and Kim, H. (2002) Determinants of restaurant systematic risk: A reexamination. *Journal of Hospitality Financial Management*, **10** (1), 1–14.

Hamada, R. (1972) The effects of the firm's capital structure on systematic risk of Common stocks. *Journal of Finance*, **27** (2), 435–452.

Howe, J. and Shilling, J. (1988) Capital structure theory and REIT security offerings. *The Journal of Finance*, **43** (4), 983–993.

Idol, C. (1978) The financial determinants of systematic risk. *Baylor Business Studies*, **9** (3), 55–69.

Jahankhani, A. and Lynge, M. (1980) Commercial bank financial policies and their impact on market-determined measures of risk. *Journal of Bank Research*, **11** (3), 169–178.

Jensen, M. (1984) Agency costs of free cash flow, corporate finance, and takeovers. *American Economic Review*, **76**, 323–329.

Keown, A., Martin, J., Petty, W. and Scott, D. (2002) *Foundations of Finance*. Prentice Hall, Englewood Cliffs.

Kim, H., Gu, Z. and Mattila, A. (2002) Hotel real estate investment trusts' risk features and beta determinants. *Journal of Hospitality and Tourism Research*, **20** (2), 138–154.

Kleinbaum, D.G., Kupper, L.L. and Muller, K.E. (1988) *Applied Regression Analysis and Other Multivariable Method*. PWS-KENT Publishing Company, Boston.

Lev, B. and Kunitzky, S. (1974) On the association between smoothing measures and the risk of common stocks. *The Accounting Review*, **49**, 259–270.

Lintner, J. (1965) Security prices, risk and maximal gains from diversification. *Journal of Finance*, **20** (4), 587–615.

Logue, L. and Merville, J. (1972) Financial policy and market expectations. *Financial Management*, **1** (3), 37–44.

Mandelker, N. and Rhee, S. (1984) The impact of the degree of operating and financial leverage on systematic risk of common stock. *Journal of Financial and Quantitative Analysis*, **19** (1), 45–57.

Melicher, W. (1974) Financial factors which influence beta variations within an homogeneous industry environment. *Journal of Financial Quantitative Analysis*, **9** (2), 231–241.

Moyer, R. and Chatfield, R. (1983) Market power and systematic risk. *Journal of Economics and Business*, **35** (1), 123–130.

Patel, R. and Olsen, R. (1984) Financial determinants of systematic risk in real estate investment trusts. *Journal of Business Research*, **12** (4), 481–491.

Pettit, R. and Westerfield, R. (1972) A model of capital asset risk. *Journal of Financial and Quantitative Analysis*, **7** (4), 1649–1668.

Rosenberg, B. and McKibeen, W. (1973) The prediction of systematic and specific risk in common stocks. *Journal of Business and Quantitative Analysis*, **8** (3), 317–334.

Rushmore, S. (1998) Get ready for another round of overbuilding. *Lodging Hospitality*, **54** (2), 10.

Scherrer, P. and Mathison, T. (1996) Investment strategies for REIT investors. *Real Estate Review*, **26** (1), 5–10.

Schwartz, N. (1999) Still perking after these years. *Fortune*, **139**, 203–207.

Sharpe, W. (1963) A simplified model of portfolio analysis, *Management Science*, **9** (2), 277–293.

Sharpe, W. (1964) Capital asset prices: A theory of market equilibrium under conditions of risk. *Journal of Finance*, **19** (3), 425–442.

Sullivan, T. (1978) The cost of capital and market power of firms. *Review of Economics and Statistics*, **60**, 209–217.

Investment appraisal issues arising in hotels governed by a management contract

Chris Guilding

Introduction

The way that organizations manage their investment appraisal activities is perhaps one of the most extensively researched facets of organizational behaviour. This is probably because the investment decision is highly significant, representing the commitment of substantial organizational resources for an extended period of time. Few, if any, organizational decisions carry more profound implications for organizational success than the investment decision.

The breadth and depth of prior studies that have investigated the nature and context of investment appraisal activity is evident from Dempsey's (2003) review of the evolution of investment appraisal research. Dempsey classifies investment appraisal research according to three disciplinary perspectives: finance, management accounting and strategic management. He sees the finance research tradition as exhibiting an economic theoretical orientation. Examples of research conducted within this tradition tend to have a highly mathematical orientation and include work based on the capital asset pricing model (Ross, 1978) and real options theory (Cortazar and Casassus, 1998; Pinches, 1998). Investment appraisal research conducted within the management accounting tradition frequently involves qualitative case analysis in an attempt to shed light on the context and procedures of capital budget allocation (e.g. Slagmulder, 1997; Carr and Tomkins, 1998). The strategic management oriented investment appraisal research is characterized by a focus on strategy development and application (e.g. Porter, 1985; Seal, 2001). The study reported herein explores how organizational issues specific to the hotel industry can affect investment appraisal procedures. In light of this, it can be best characterized as falling within the management accounting investment appraisal research tradition.

Further, the study's focus on hotels' investment appraisal procedures signifies that it should be viewed as extending the prior work of Collier and Gregory (1995) and Guilding (2003). In this regard it is particularly pertinent to recognize the three reasons that Collier and Gregory (1995:38) cite as motivating further research into hotels' investment appraisal practices:

> (i) hotel groups have certain unusual characteristics as a business due to the dual nature of their activities involving property and management. These characteristics give rise to some interesting implications for investment appraisal; (ii) hotel groups are capital intensive businesses where the assets are long-lived and not subject to obsolescence, provided they are adequately maintained. This gives rise to the interesting problem of the estimation of the residual value of such assets; and (iii) the hotel industry is a key component of the important (and expanding) tourist industry.

There is, however, a further factor that underscores the significance of investment appraisal research in the hotel industry. Two separate contracting parties are involved in investment appraisal in many hotels, as many hotels are owned by one company and managed by another. The existence of the hotel management contract that mediates the relationship between a hotel owner and operator signifies that an investment proposal must cross an organizational divide in satisfying the investment appraisal criteria of both contracting parties. Recognition of this factor calls into play the nature of the relationship between these two contracting parties. This was the primary factor motivating the investigation of hotel investment appraisal practices reported herein.

The ubiquity of the hotel management contract in Western economies can be viewed as a highly significant and differentiating aspect of the hotel industry. In light of this significance, the paucity of research focusing on the managerial implications resulting from this distinguishing commercial facet is somewhat surprising. Field (1995:261) comments:

> For an area which has provided the basis of such a great part of the development of the hotel industry over the past 30 years, and is performing an even more important role in the 1990s, there has been remarkably little published research into the impact of management contracting within the hotel sector.

When one turns to consider investment appraisal ramifications arising in the presence of the management contract, it is particularly surprising that this issue has not been subjected to investigation by financially oriented hotel management researchers. In connection with hotel investment appraisal procedures, Beals (1995:281) believes the management contract raises profound issues. He states: 'The distinctly different outlooks of the two entities all but ensure a clash between investors and hoteliers.'

The remainder of this chapter is organized in the following manner. In the next section an elaboration of the nature of the typical hotel management contract is provided. Subsequent sections describe the research design and field study findings. The final section considers the significance of the study, its shortcomings as well as opportunities to expand on the research initiative reported.

The nature of the hotel management contract

Under a typical management contract, the hotel operator assumes control for managing the operational matters of the property while the owner retains legal title of all assets, i.e. the land, building and operating assets, and assumes responsibility for the project. Eyster (1988:4) describes a hotel management contract as:

> A written agreement between the owner and the operator of a hotel or motor inn by which the owner employs the operator as an agent (employee) to assume full responsibility for operating and managing the property. As an agent, the operator pays, in the name of the owner, all operating expenses from the cash flow generated from the property, retains management fees and remits the remaining cash flow, if any, to the owner.

Under most arrangements, all hotel staff, with the exception of the general manager and in some cases the financial controller, are employees of the owner. This arrangement limits the legal obligations of the operator and appears to result from the need to facilitate easy transition when one operator is replaced by another. The fact that general managers and financial controllers are generally employees of the operating company highlights their key placement with respect to mediating the relationship between hotel owner and operator.

The hotel operator's fee is generally computed as an algorithm based on the hotel's gross revenue and profitability (Field, 1995). It appears this basis of remuneration still predominates, although Field has noted the development of other bases, such as the payment of no fees until a specific level of cash flow or profit is achieved. As will be noted in subsequent discussion, it is surprising that algorithms recognizing profit as a return on assets do not serve as a basis for calculating the operator's fee.

To facilitate a classification of the hotels that served as subject companies in this study, a typology of owner/operators structures has been developed (Figure 20.1). The fundamental dimension captured in this typology is the distinction between divorced owner/operator structures (archetypal structures within this category are presented in the left hand panel and are numbered with the prefix '1') and unified owner/operator structures (archetypal structures within this category are presented in the right hand panel and are numbered with '2' as the prefix). Other key factors in the owner/operator structure that are captured through this typology include size of the owning company, size of the operating company and whether the operating company is a subsidiary of the owning company.

This typology is offered not only to support the description of this study's empirical observations, it may also serve as a useful working model for others pursuing research in hotel management or management in other industrial sectors where similar

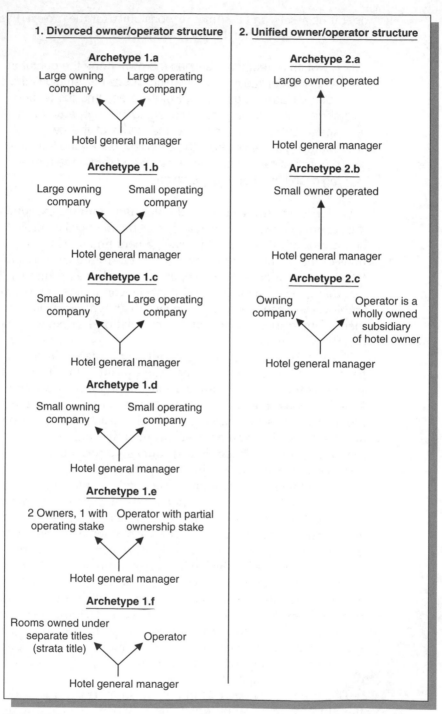

Figure 20.1
Typology of hotel owner/operator structures.

owner/operator structures prevail. In the interests of parsimony, the model presented does not represent an attempt to capture all permutations of hotel owner/operator structures. For example, one archetypal management structure not recognized in the typology presented concerns hotels managed by two or more operating companies, none of which is the owning company. This owner/operator configuration has not been included in Figure 20.1 as it was not encountered in the field study described herein. Field (1995), however, has observed such operating configurations and notes that they provide scope for specialization, i.e. one operator might manage a complex's accommodation as well as food and beverage activities, while another operator might manage sport and health related activities.

The research design

Qualitative data have been collected by interviewing five general managers and nine financial controllers (financial controllers) in a sample of South East Queensland (Australia) hotels. One of the hotels selected had a three star rating, two had a five star rating and the remainder were rated at the four or four and a half star level. Selection of this sample frame was strongly influenced by casual observations and informal discussions with hotel managers suggesting that higher star rating complexes have a greater propensity to be internationally branded and governed by a management contract.

General managers and financial controllers were identified as holding a highly appropriate job designation for subjects to be interviewed. As already noted, in hotels governed by a management contract, general managers and financial controllers are generally employees of the operating company. This signifies that they are in a highly significant position in terms of exposure to potential investment appraisal tensions arising between the two contracting parties. As they work for the operator, the general managers and financial controllers can be expected to hold goals that may have some inconsistency with the hotel owner's goals. As it is the owner who finances the purchase of any hotel asset and assumes the ultimate risk associated with ownership (i.e. potential decline in the asset's value), it is the owner who represents the party with ultimate sanctioning authority in any asset purchase decision. For this reason, the general manager and financial controller can be seen to be well placed to observe any 'cross-fire' between a hotel owner and operator.

Table 20.1 provides an overview of the sample of subjects interviewed. An alphabetical reference for each hotel in the sample frame and also an abbreviated reference to each interviewee's job

Table 20.1

Overview of the subject companies

Hotel reference/ interviewee function[a]	Size: 1 Revenue p.a. ($m) 2 Number of rooms	Main activities	Owner/ operator structure (see Figure 20.1)	Operating company	Owning company	Comments on the investment appraisal system
A/G.M.	1 $15 m 2 298	Accommod'n, F&B[b], banqueting, gaming	1.a	Publicly traded, large international hotel management company	Publicly traded, overseas-based owning company	Highly formalized, slow and sometimes problems securing repeat quotes from potential sub-contractors/suppliers experienced
B/G.M. & F.C.	1 $12 m 2 403	Accommod'n, F&B, hosting functions	1.e	Small overseas company (also has ownership stake)	Jointly owned by 2 companies: a) the operating company, b) a small, high-growth, domestic company	Relatively 'liberal' approach. Close involvement of owner resulted in controls akin to 'personnel' controls
C/F.C.	1 $20 m 2 296	Accommod'n, F&B, hosting functions	2.a	Same as owning company, although most of the company's hotels are managed by separate operating companies	Publicly-traded overseas company	Thorough and formalized. Room refurbishment expenditure includes preparation of a 'mock up' room for inspection by owners
D/G.M.	1 $2.5 m 2 150	Accommod'n, F&B	2.b	Same as owning company	Small sole trader, owns three properties	Simplistic. Minimal use of formal appraisal models

Case		Activities	Code			Investment process
E/F.C.	1 N.A. 2 609	Accommod'n, F&B, conferences, gaming	1.a	Overseas publicly traded company	Domestic publicly traded company	Highly formalized. Investments classified according to $ size and nature (e.g. workplace health and safety, operational replacement, etc.)
F/G.M.	1 N.A. 2 329	Accommod'n, F&B, golf, residential, conferences	2.c	Wholly owned subsidiary of owning company	Large overseas publicly traded company	Relatively formalized. Conducted in context of well-defined long-term strategic plan. High use of financial modelling (NPV, payback, etc.). Minimal bureaucracy or politicality evident
G/F.C.	1 $16 m 2 405	Accommod'n, F&B	1.a	Large overseas publicly traded company	Large overseas publicly traded company	Highly formalized. Investment proposals considered at divisional and head office of operating company prior to submission to owners
H/F.C.	1 N.A. 2 205 hotel rooms + 72 condos	Hotel accommod'n, residential accommod'n, F&B	2.c	Subsidiary of the owning company	Small domestic company	Formalized aspects, however very close owner involvement results in some impulsive investment decision-making
I/F.C.	1 $30 m 2 330	Accommod'n, F&B, conferences	2.a	Large overseas publicly traded company	Same as operating company	Highly formalized procedure
J/F.C.	1 N.A. 2 317	Accommod'n, F&B, functions, gaming	1.a	Large overseas company	Large overseas company	Formalized procedure. General manager puts forward more projects than actually required, due to the expectations of a bargaining process

(Continued)

Table 20.1
(*Continued*)

Hotel reference/ interviewee function[a]	Size: 1 Revenue p.a. ($m) 2 Number of rooms	Main activities	Owner/ operator structure (see Figure 20.1)	Operating company	Owning company	Comments on the investment appraisal system
K/F.C.	1 $40 m 2 300	Accommod'n, F&B, recreation, conferences	1.a	Large overseas company	Medium/large overseas-based consortium	Formalized. Some politicality, although 'not overwhelming and not degrading the owner/ operator relationship'. Financial modelling used with particular importance attached to payback period
L/F.C.	1 $15 m 2 380	Accommod'n, F&B, conferences	1.f	Rooms individually owned under separate titles; owners represented through a body corporate	Large overseas company	Formalized process. Good working relations with owners in evidence
M/G.M.	1 $12 m 2 302	Accommod'n, F&B	1.c	Large overseas company	Small overseas investment company	Relatively formalized process with emphasis attached to financial modelling. Can become political

[a] F.C.: Financial controller; G.M. general manager; [b] F&B: Food and beverage.

designation is provided in the table's first column. The remaining columns provide information on each hotel's size (measured by annual revenue and number of rooms), main activities, the owner/operator structure (cross-referenced to the archetypes presented in Figure 20.1), the nature of the operating and owning companies and a very brief commentary that sketches some key facets of each hotel's investment appraisal system. Two interviewees represented Hotel B. Following the conduct of the interview with the financial controller in this hotel, the general manager expressed a desire also to be involved in the study.

All interviews were tape recorded and then transcribed. The initial eight interviews were attended by two researchers (the lead researcher and a research assistant with hotel management experience). This approach enhanced reflection on the qualitative data collected, as considerable importance was attached to the completion of an extended post interview discussion between the researchers. The first question posed in each interview was open-ended. It asked the subjects to elaborate on any organizational problems and shortcomings associated with their hotel's investment appraisal procedure. This proved to be a useful approach as many interviewees provided unprompted commentary on investment appraisal issues that are particular to hotels operating in the context of a management contract. Data analysis was conducted by examining the transcribed interview data for common themes and latent variable relationships.

The field study findings

In this section, the study findings are ordered in accordance with the following four subheadings:

1 ranking of factors significant in the investment decision-making process

2 investment project initiation

3 ego-trip ownership

4 political factors.

Ranking of factors significant in the investment decision-making process

While considerable research interest has focused on the relative usage rates of different financial investment appraisal techniques (Lamminmaki et al., 1996; Pike, 1996; Kester et al., 1999), an issue that has also commanded some research attention is the relative importance of non-financial factors (Butler et al., 1993; Van Cauwenbergh et al., 1996). Due to the additional dynamics posed by the divorced owner/operator structure, there appears to be considerable potential for a range of perspectives being implicated in hotel investment appraisal. Interviewees were asked to rank and comment on the importance of four perspectives in the investment decision-making process. These perspectives were drawn from the literature and are presented in the first column of Table 20.2. Due to the large literature concerned with financial

Table 20.2
Ranking of the thematic factors affecting the investment decision-making process

	Ranking			
	1st	**2nd**	**3rd**	**4th**
Financial analysis	A, B^2, J, K	B^1, C, E, F, H, I, L, M	D, G	
Strategic analysis	B^1, C, E, F, G, H, I, M	A, B^2, D, J, K	L	
Internal political factors			H, K	A, B^1, B^2, C, D, E, F, G, I, J, L, M
Managerial intuition	D, L	G	A, B^1, B^2, C, E, F, I, J, M	H, K

The letters appearing in the final four columns denote the ranking provided by each interviewee. B^1: Financial controller in hotel B; B^2: General manager in hotel B.

appraisal techniques used in investment appraisal, little justification for this study's inclusion of the first perspective, 'financial analysis', is warranted. The second perspective, 'strategic analysis', has also been subjected to extensive consideration in the context of investment appraisal (e.g. Marsh et al., 1988; Carr and Tomkins, 1996; Shank, 1996). The third perspective, 'internal political factors', was explored in the context of investment appraisal by Butler et al. (1993). Political models of decision-making view organizations as a coalescence of potentially competing, self-interested individuals employing guile and strategies, such as coalition building, in the pursuit of their own personal ends (Pfeffer, 1981; Hickson et al., 1986). The importance of the fourth perspective, 'managerial intuition', has been considered in the context of investment appraisal by Butler et al. (1993) and Van Cauwenbergh et al. (1996).

The letters appearing in the final four columns of Table 20.2 are based on the hotel referencing system established in Table 20.1 and indicate each interviewees' perception of the relative importance of the four factors. A striking finding emanating from this exercise is the degree of consensus apparent across the interviewees. Most of the interviewees ranked strategic analysis and financial analysis as the two most important factors and all but two of the interviewees ranked internal political factors as least important. It is particularly pertinent to note that, despite the fact that the majority of the interviewees were financial controllers, the sample's consensus view is that strategic analysis is more important than financial analysis in investment decision-making. The financial controller in Hotel I commented: 'I would like to think that financial analysis ranks up there, but I really believe strategic analysis is ranked one, followed by financial, and followed then by managerial intuition and lastly politics.'

The rankings recorded by this financial controller can be seen as typifying views held by most of the hotel executives interviewed. Contrasting with this view, however, the financial controller in Hotel K noted: 'I think financial analysis is primary because that's what drives the owner to decide whether to spend the money. Strategic position, which is critically important, is second.'

With respect to relationships between different hotel owner/operator structures and the views expressed through this ranking exercise, it is pertinent to note that Hotel D appears as a relative outlier in Table 20.2. The general manager in this hotel attached little importance to financial analysis, he was one of only two interviewees to rank it outside the two most important factors. In addition, he was one of only two interviewees to rank managerial intuition as the most important factor. From the owner/operator structure standpoint, this was the only interviewee working in a hotel that had a small owner in a unified owner/operated management structure. Hotel L also appears as a relative outlier (the financial controller placed managerial intuition first), however, the interviewee in this hotel appeared to misinterpret the intent of the ranking exercise. From the interview's transcript it appears that he viewed the exercise primarily in terms of the chronology of investment appraisal events and he felt that exercise of managerial intuition was the initial step in investment proposal development.

An insightful commentary with respect to the conduct of this ranking exercise was provided by the general manager in Hotel A, who saw the relative importance of the four factors as dependent on the project's stage within the investment decision-making cycle. He felt that at the project initiation stage, strategic factors and also managerial intuition tend to be important. At the stage of seeking owner ratification for the project, however, he felt financial factors to be most important. Variations in the importance attached to the four factors at different stages in the investment appraisal process has also been noted by Butler et al. (1993).

A further commentary on the exercise was provided by the financial controller in Hotel H. She felt that the factors can come into play in combination in the course of investment decision-making. When elaborating on internal political factors, she commented:

> For me, when I decide on anything, part of the decision I will make is what approach I will take because of the people I am dealing with. So that will influence the outcome, there is no question. If I hadn't done these two (points to financial analysis and strategic analysis), it will never influence the outcome. That alone (points to internal political factors) will not get me anywhere ... Managerial intuition, that's the same, it's an integral part of achieving your outcome. I have had a lot of success of capital approval in the properties I've been at, and it's because of all of those factors that I have had it. I think if you sacrifice one, you reduce your chances of getting it.

A related reflection was also in evidence in commentary provided by the financial controller of Hotel K. He observed:

> Sometimes in doing that preliminary analysis the political issues become number one, and then financial and strategic third and the reason for that is that there are some issues that owners are hot on, some issues that owners are cold on. ... Some of the political issues are paramount to deciding which project you'll tackle. But, to be honest with you, I'm not interested in fighting unwinnable battles. I want to focus on the things that we can drive to a conclusion.

As a final comment with respect to the data reported in Table 20.2, it is interesting to note the slight difference in the responses provided by the two interviewees in Hotel B. While they both placed financial analysis and strategic analysis in the top two, the general manager saw financial analysis as ranking first, while the financial controller saw strategic analysis ranking first. This is perhaps surprising as one might have anticipated that the financial controller would have attached the greater significance to financial analysis. This observation highlights that different perspectives and backgrounds can result in different managerial perceptions. Further, following the rationale offered by the general manager in Hotel A, it may have been the case that the two managers were envisaging different stages of the investment decision-making process when conducting this ranking exercise.

Investment project initiation

Butler et al. (1993) claim that one of the most significant capital budgeting roles for top management concerns the development of a culture that encourages managers to seek, identify and promote investment ideas. Such a culture needs to promote a willingness to collect information that is externally-oriented and frequently non-financial (Gordon and Pinches, 1984). Butler et al. (1993:53) comment: 'Any manager who has experienced the hurt and frustrations of having an investment proposal dismissed or an accepted proposal fail is likely to develop an in-built resistance to creating further proposals unless the organization culture rewards are conducive to such activity.'

The issue of a supportive corporate culture can be seen to be complicated somewhat in those hotels operating under a divorced owner/operator structure. The involvement of two contracting parties raises the spectre of an organizational fracture in the 'culture setting' and 'incentive providing' senior management roles which are normally conducted within the confines of a single organization. In the hotel industry, the owning company's position as the party funding capital expenditure highlights its fundamentally significant role in capital budgeting 'culture setting'. Incentives for the general manager (whose position can be seen as pivotal to the dissemination of a capital expenditure initiation culture), however, are set by the operating company, as the operating company employs the general manager.

In most of the hotels investigated, investment projects were initiated by the operating company. This was especially the case in those hotels characterized by low owner involvement. A benefit deriving from the involvement of two contracting parties in the delivery of hotel services was evident in Hotel A, which was characterized by relatively close owner involvement. Hotel A had recently installed gaming machines. The operating company and the general manager had negligible experience in the gaming industry and they were able to benefit substantially from the hotel owning company's extensive experience with running gaming facilities. In this instance, the investment was initiated by the owning company and the owning company provided expertise that was critical to an activity that, at the time of data collection, was providing a significant contribution to the hotel's profit.

A distinguishing feature of hotel investment appraisal systems may well be the degree to which customers can play an active role in initiating capital expenditure proposals. This was particularly apparent in Hotel E. Citing the example of the replacement of coin phones with card phones, the financial controller in Hotel E commented: 'We really operate from a business perspective in collecting our capital requirements in response to guest demands – something the guests are asking for.'

In Hotel E's capital budgeting system, a customer request is forwarded to the operations manager whose position is most closely related to the proposed investment. If the manager believes the request to be worthy of further examination, the suggestion will have to be operationalized using specifications that will facilitate collection of data in a manner compatible with the hotel's relatively formalized investment approval process. While this signifies investment initiation at the operating company level, Hotel E's financial controller did note that the owner's position was significant at an early stage in the investment review process:

> We prepare a wish list in January/February each year and that gets pulled together and assessed throughout the complex. We then try to establish from the owner of the company what sort of capital is going to be available to us. There's no point asking for $25 million if there's only $15 million.

Ego-trip ownership

Field (1995) sees 'an image of glamorous properties in glamorous locations' as a factor that can appeal to some prospective owners. This phenomenon was noted to be significant by the financial controller in Hotel I who used the term 'ego-trip ownership'. He felt this was much more apparent in some overseas' cultures relative to others. These views are similar to those of the general manager in Hotel A, who felt that he had witnessed high ego-trip ownership in some of the hotels where he had previously worked, but that it was relatively absent in his current employ. He commented:

> The culture of the owner entity is very, very, very important, it drives everything. You may have owners who are totally cash driven; empty the lake to get the fish. You may have an owner who is more environmentally aware. So that's why, from a management point of view, you've got to find the middle ground. ... Most are give me cash, give me cash, because they have other agendas. Some want to build up a portfolio because they have a twenty year plan. Getting to know that owner is just like getting to know that customer. ... (Commenting on a hotel owner where the general manager had previously worked) the

guy had more money than you could poke a stick at. (My current hotel's owners) bought this for $60 million, whereas that one was built for $3 million and $1 million was spent a year on whatever toys they required, so it's a totally different situation. … (My previous owner would say) 'I want to go fishing, buy a boat, a big boat like that. Well, get two, one with a mast and one without'. Really it was quite amazing.

The term 'ego ownership' appears to be fairly widespread in the industry. It was also used by the financial controller in Hotel K. The financial controller in Hotel B perceived a degree of ego-trip ownership in his current employ. He referred to the owners having a 'showpiece philosophy' and he felt this was manifested by:

No problems getting approval for in-house refurbishment, upgrades, things like that. I speak specifically about this hotel. I have worked in others where it was virtually impossible. Something literally had to fall down or 'can't you do it next month'.

The ego-trip issue was also apparent to the financial controller in Hotel H who noted that:

'So many people get into hotels for ego, I think. Why do they do this? There is so much money to be made out there, and it's not in this industry.

The issue of ego-trip ownership would appear to be a significant mediating variable in the capital budgeting processes of hotels. Where it is present, it is likely to be easier for the operating company to gain the owner's support for proposed capital expenditure. The potential for ego-trip ownership mediating in this manner would appear greatest with respect to front-of-house expenditure (i.e. expenditure where the resultant asset is readily observable to the hotel's patrons), as the incentive for ostentation is more apparent. In these situations, less formalized capital budgeting procedures can be expected to result. This expectation appears to be borne out by the case of Hotel B, and also by the previous hotel experience recounted by the general manager in Hotel A. These situations can be contrasted with the current experience of Hotel A's general manager, whose comments cited above suggest that when ego-trip ownership is absent, gaining owner support for capital expenditure proposals can be challenging as it places an onus on the general manager developing an understanding of the owner's business philosophy. Such an understanding appears important for the general manager seeking to secure capital expenditure funding.

Political factors

In connection with the ranking exercise of factors significant in the investment decision-making process, it has already been noted that the sample of interviewees accorded relatively low importance to internal political factors. Despite this, political factors appear worthy of further comment due to the extent to which they signify a perspective that is distinct from financial and formalized models of investment decision-making. Further, relative to the single company context of the conventional investment decision, there would appear to be greater scope for politicality in investment decision-making in hotels operating under a divorced owner/operator structure. It is expected that more politics will be invoked in divorced owner/operator structures, as in this context the capital budgeting process must transcend the boundary between two organizations.

Political models of decision-making view organizations as comprising a number of potentially competing, self-interested parties. Butler et al. (1993) note that activities such as bargaining (i.e. individuals competing for resources in a manner designed to gain the best outcome for themselves), use of guile, (Pfeffer, 1981; Hickson et al., 1986), coalition building (i.e. forming groups of individuals in order to increase bargaining strength) and biasing (attempting to influence the manner in which decisions are made) are all closely related to the notion of politicality. In light of the multidimensionality of the politicality construct, the approach taken here has been to interpret 'politicality' in a manner sensitive to the way that the interviewees responded to the question: 'How political is the capital budgeting process in your organization?'

Several of the interviewees' comments support the expectation of a greater incidence of politicality in the capital budgeting process of divorced owner/operator hotels. The general manager in Hotel F felt that investment decision-making in his hotel (which operated with a unified owner/operator structure) was not at all political, however, he claimed that investment decision-making politics were more prevalent in divorced owner/operator structures due to the contrasting agendas of the two contracting parties. In a similar vein, Hotel E's financial controller commented:

> I guess the budgeting process in any organization is going to be fairly political. Where we've got this division, if you like, between the owner's corporate office and the management structure, there's always going to be a certain challenge in there, so that makes it slightly more political.

The manner in which the owner/operator division presents an additional raft of investment authorization giving greater scope for internal politics was also noted by this financial controller:

> The time when it gets most political is when we have a certain amount of needs in the operation and the owning company decides that you can't have all of that, and I'm not talking insignificant dollars. If we've asked for $15 million and they say 'No, you've only got $10 million', cutting out a third of your capital requests is quite a challenge. So that's where it gets difficult, and I guess you could call it political.

The financial controller in Hotel H also believed she had experienced significant political problems when dealing with the owning company of a hotel she had previously worked in. She commented:

> In most hotels, when there is an owning and a management company, it is definitely more the owner that you are answering to. ... The politics are awful at [names the owning company], quite awful. [Names the CEO] is in charge of the hotel side and he had three men underneath him that looked after different regions in hotels and they were the political problem. ... Now these people would very comfortably blame us if something went wrong, and that was the dilemma, and trying to actually get through all of that without discrediting anybody and all that type of thing was very, very difficult at times. The bureaucracy on a day-to-day basis was very difficult. Politics were just terrible because they all were so ambitious and they all wanted to be top dog.

With respect to an earlier experience in another hotel the same financial controller commented:

> [Commenting on a computer system installation] it took four years up in [names a resort]. That was learning to understand the owners and playing a game that was necessary to be played with them to achieve it, and not lose sight, not give up was basically what it was. ... The political side, I've had a lot of success with the political side and I'm not a political person.

It should be noted that not all of the interviewees in hotels with a divorced owner/operator structure felt that their capital budgeting system was particularly political, however. The financial controller in Hotel J which operated with a divorced owner/operator structure commented:

> Within the hotel the investment decision-making process is not political. Dealing with the owners is fantastic. At the end of the day, it's the owner's asset. They sometimes spend money on something that we don't think is worthwhile.

The financial controller in Hotel K observed:

> There are always politics. You'll never get away from it, but I wouldn't call the politics strong or overwhelming and I wouldn't say that they're at the point where they degrade the relationship between the management company and the owner.

A fairly enduring finding of capital budgeting research concerns the view that company size is positively related to capital budgeting sophistication (e.g. Lamminmaki et al., 1996). The size of the owning and operating companies may also be a significant determinant of the incidence of politicality in the investment appraisal process. From the interview data, it appears that internal politics tend to be more of an issue in those hotels where the owning and operating companies are large. (It should be noted that Hotel J again appears as an exception in this regard.) This view is particularly apparent from the following comments made by Hotel B's financial controller: 'Well luckily again, with this company being quite small, everyone pretty much knows everyone. This means there is not much politics involved.'

It might well be the case that ego-ownership not only affects the ease with which a hotel operator can convert capital budget requisitions into capital budgeting expenditure, but also the degree to which politics are evident in the owner/operator capital budgeting negotiation process. In the presence of high ego-ownership, it is to be expected the owner would have a higher propensity to maintain the property in good working order, thereby lessening tension that may arise in the capital budgeting process.

Conclusion

This chapter reports the findings emanating from a qualitative investigation into the nature of hotel investment appraisal processes applied in hotels. The study was directed particularly towards examining investment appraisal implications arising in the presence of a hotel management contract. Several implications, largely consistent with expectations, have been noted. In the discussion below, it will be noted that all of these investment appraisal implications suggest a degree of dysfunctionalism for the divorced owner/operator structure.

Building on prior research, the relative importance of four perspectives applying to the capital budgeting process have been investigated. A broad consensus among the hotel executives that strategic factors are highly important was noted. Financial factors rank as a relatively close second, and managerial intuition and internal political factors ranked third and fourth respectively. The noted importance attached to the strategic perspective supports one of the findings of Collier and Gregory (1995:48) who commented:

> In the hotel industry issues such as branding, location and package style (e.g. tour versus business hotel, star ratings, fitness and leisure facilities, etc.) are of fundamental importance. All of our sample companies were well aware of this, and appeared to assign more importance to these strategic areas than to the pure numerical analysis.

This investigation has also highlighted the extent to which researchers should view the investment appraisal exercise as comprising a series of phases and not as a discrete one-off activity. From comments made by one interviewee, it appears that while managerial intuition and strategic considerations might be prominent during the initial formulation of an investment idea, a financial analytic perspective may well dominate when a hotel operator is attempting to justify a proposed investment outlay to a hotel owner. Recognition that different perspectives might be prominent at different stages of the investment appraisal cycle should be borne in mind when designing survey instruments concerned with eliciting the nature of investment appraisal practice. It is also noteworthy that one interviewee saw the different perspectives as a portfolio of approaches and that a manager who is successful in securing capital budget requisitions will need to ensure adequate consideration has been given to all elements of the portfolio.

With respect to investment appraisal initiation, it appears that in most hotels operating under a divorced owner/operator structure, it is the operator that initiates most investment proposals. This is to be expected as, in most cases (particularly when the owner is based overseas), the operator is better-placed to be aware of those parts of the hotel's physical infrastructure that are in need of overhaul or replacement. Identification of the hotel operator as the main instigator of investment expenditures appears as a particularly significant observation. Butler et al. (1993) noted the importance of developing an organizational culture consistent with motivating staff to initiate investment proposals. The party with the prime onus for this motivational role is the hotel owning company, as it is the owner that bears the greatest risk if an investment turns out to be a failure and it is the owner who will enjoy the bulk of equity related residual benefits resulting if an investment outlay turns out to be a major success. Yet a paradox appears here as the key hotel player that oversees investment proposal initiation is the general manager, and the general manager is not an employee of the owning company. So the party to a hotel management contract that stands to gain the most from instilling a culture supportive of the formulation of high quality investment proposals has muted influence in affecting the organizational culture of the manager with greatest scope to affect investment proposal initiations.

An unanticipated finding of the study concerned the role of a construct referred to by several interviewees as 'ego-trip ownership'. This appears to be closely related to an ostentatious desire to own a lavish hotel decorated with expensive furniture and fittings. The number of early interviewees that referred to 'ego-trip ownership' resulted in its inclusion in the study's interview schedule. Ego-trip ownership would appear to be a significant factor affecting the investment appraisal culture of hotels because its presence signifies that asset improvement proposals (particularly front of house assets) are likely to be subjected to less exacting owner scrutiny.

Although it was noted that internal political factors do not rank highly as a perspective affecting investment appraisal decisions, the presence of the divorced owner/operator structure motivated further investigation into the nature and potential of politicality in hotel investment appraisal decision-making. Comments made by several of the interviewees suggest that greater politicality exists when hotels are mediated by a management contract. One manager specifically referred to more politics resulting from the 'division' between owner and operator.

It should be borne in mind that this study suffers from the normal shortcomings of qualitative research. The findings are based on a sample that is too small to permit generalized claims to be made. The compensating strength of the research approach adopted is that it has facilitated an exploratory consideration of investment appraisal issues arising when hotels are mediated by a management contract. A further study could build on this research initiative by collecting survey data and comparing facets of investment appraisal systems in hotels owned by the operator with those of hotels operating a divorced owner/operator structure. Further examination of the significance of 'ego-trip ownership', in particular, could prove to be a fruitful line of enquiry.

As a concluding comment, it is noteworthy that no operator was found to be remunerated on a basis that recognized profit as a function of investment. All operators were remunerated based on a percentage of profit and percentage of sales basis (this finding is consistent with Beals' (1995) commentary pertaining to owner/operator contractual arrangements in the USA). To use a remuneration basis that recognizes the value of assets involved (e.g. ROI) would appear to lessen the potential for owner/operator goal incongruency that can become particularly evident in the context of investment appraisal. When ranking two mutually exclusive projects where project A has a higher NPV than project B, the operators of the hotel will have an incentive to promote project B if it is the option that generates higher levels of absolute sales and profit. This issue had not been anticipated in advance of conducting the interviews. It does appear, however, to be another issue worthy of further research enquiry.

References

Beals, P. (1995) The hotel management contract: lessons from the North American experience. In Harris, P. (ed.), *Accounting and Finance for the International Hospitality Industry*, pp. 278–294. Butterworth-Heinemann, London.

Butler, R.J., Davies, L., Pike, R. and Sharp, J. (1993) *Strategic Investment Decisions*. Routledge, London.

Carr, C. and Tomkins, C. (1996) Strategic investment decisions: the importance of SCM. A comparative analysis of 51 case studies in UK, US and German companies. *Management Accounting Research*, **7** (2), 199–217.

Carr, C. and Tomkins, C. (1998) Context, culture and the role of the finance function in strategic decisions: a comparative analysis of Britain, Germany, the USA and Japan. *Management Accounting Research*, **9** (1), 213–239.

Collier, P. and Gregory, A. (1995) Investment appraisal in service industries: a field study analysis of the UK hotels sector. *Management Accounting Research*, **6**, 33–57.

Cortazar, G. and Casassus, J. (1998) Optimal timing of a mine expansion: implementing a real options model. *The Quarterly Review of Economics and Finance*, **38** (Special Issue), 755–769.

Dempsey, M. (2003) A multidisciplinary perspective on the evolution of corporate investment decision making. *Accounting, Accountability & Performance*, **9** (1), 1–33.

Eyster, J.J. (1988) *The Negotiation and Administration of Hotel and Restaurant Management Contracts*, 3rd edn. School of Hotel Administration, Cornell University, Ithaca.

Field, H.M. (1995) Financial management implications of hotel management contracts: a UK perspective. In Harris, P. (ed.), *Accounting and Finance for the International Hospitality Industry*, pp. 261–277. Butterworth-Heinemann, London.

Gordon, L.A. and Pinches, G.E. (1984) *Improving Capital Budgeting: A Decision Support System Approach*. Addison-Wesley, Reading.

Guilding, C. (2003) Hotel owner/operator structures: implications for capital budgeting process. *Management Accounting Research*, **14**, 179–199.

Hickson, D.J., Butler, R.J., Cray, D., Mallory, G.R. and Wilson, D.C. (1986) *Top Decisions: Strategic Decision-Making in Organizations*. Basil Blackwell, Oxford and Jossey-Bass, San Francisco.

Kester, G.W., Chang, R.P., Echanis, E.S. et al. (1999) Capital budgeting practices in the Asia-Pacific Region: Australia, Hong Kong, Indonesia, Malaysia, Philippines, and Singapore. *Financial Practice and Education*, Spring/Summer, 25–33.

Lamminmaki, D., Guilding, C. and Pike, R. (1996) A comparison of British and New Zealand capital budgeting practices. *Pacific Accounting Review*, **8**, 1–29.

Marsh, P., Barwise, P., Thomas, K. and Wensley, R. (1988) *Strategic Investment Decisions in Large Diversities Companies*. Centre for Business Strategy Report Series, London Business School, London.

Pfeffer, J. (1981) *Power in Organizations*. Pitman & Co., Marshfield.

Pike, R. (1996) A longitudinal survey of capital budgeting practices. *Journal of Business Finance and Accounting*, **23** (1), 79–92.

Pinches, G.E. (1998) Real options: developments and applications. *The Quarterly Review of Economics and Finance*, **38** (Special Issue), 533–536.

Porter, M.E. (1985) *Competitive Advantage: Creating and Sustaining Superior Performance*. Free Press, New York.

Ross, S.A. (1978) The current status of the capital asset pricing model. *Journal of Finance*, **III** (3), 885–901.

Seal, W. (2001) Management accounting and the challenge of strategic focus. *Management Accounting Research*, **12** (4), 487–506.

Shank, J. (1996) Analysing technology investments – from NPV to strategic cost management. *Management Accounting Research*, **7** (2), 185–197.

Slagmulder, R. (1997) Using management control systems to achieve alignment between strategic investment decisions and strategy. *Management Accounting Research*, **8** (1), 103–139.

Van Cauwenbergh, A., Durinck, E., Martens, R., Laveren, E. and Bogaert, I. (1996) On the role and function of formal analysis in strategic investment decision processes: results from an empirical study in Belgium. *Management Accounting Research*, **7** (2), 169–184.

Autonomy and control in managing network organizations: the case of multinational hotel companies

Marco Mongiello and Peter Harris

Introduction

Beyond the traditional definition of remote units in network organizations, which classifies them as 'subsidiaries' or 'associates', depending on the level of control exercised by the headquarters, there is a more substantial manifestation; goals and objectives are accomplished at varying levels of the organizations in order to facilitate the needs of different stakeholders. This chapter analyses the interaction between the needs of autonomy and control in network organizations and how these are reflected in the use of innovative control mechanisms, whereby the corporate office controls unit management in terms of the balance between local environments and corporate requirements. This has implications on the design of the managerial accounting systems, which are expected to convey relevant information in both directions from the corporate office (centre of the network organization) to the units (periphery) and vice versa. Centre-to-unit communication conveys information related to goals, guidelines, targets; unit-to-centre conveys feedback, achievements, results. However, it is apparent that there is more to the information system than surfaces from the formal corporate reports; corporate managers expect a *broader scope* of decisions from the unit managers than that strictly required in the reports and unit managers produce *more specific* information for managing their units than those required to be submitted to the corporate office.

On the one hand, existing classifications of organizational control do not yet provide a satisfactorily established explanation of how unit managers are expected to take decisions in the context of network organizations; on the other hand, the works on 'trust in organizations' and 'agency theory', 'control of strategic business units', 'management by objectives' and 'work related values', and 'construct of selves in power/knowledge organizational contexts', already provide elements for new insights in the figure of unit managers, which should contribute to more extensive understanding of their role in the organizations and should support more effective choices of management control at corporate level. With the aim of investigating unit managers' decision processes in international network organizations, this chapter presents a review of relevant literature on strategic managerial accounting and organizational science and corroborates its results with the findings of a qualitative field research.

Literature review

The term 'heterarchy or network' has been proposed for multinational companies 'where multiple centres of excellence exist'

(Delany, 2000), also different types of subsidiary mandate have been identified, nominally 'advanced', 'intermediate' and 'basic' on a scale of increasing independency which corresponds to the stages of development of a multinational company.

In network organizations, where headquarters report to the shareholders and units report to headquarters, the centre-to-units and units-to-centre communication channels bring direction and coordination (centre-to-units) and crucial information (units-to-centre) in order to implement a global strategy (Hibbert, 1997). However, in terms of management control '... the network avoids the problems of duplication of effort, inefficiency and resistance to ideas developed elsewhere by giving subsidiaries latitude, encouragement and tools to pursue local business development within the framework of global strategy' (Hibbert, 1997:266). As a consequence, a balance must be struck between external (or environmental) forces and internal (or corporate) forces, in order to maximize the final corporate goals laid down by the top management. A managerial solution has been proposed with the name of 'structured network' where 'the default position is decentralisation, yet there is just enough structure to promote the right kind of self-managed behaviour and there are just enough processes, rules and controls to ensure success' (Goold and Campbell, 2003).

Knowledge developed at unit level can make the use of resources more effective, as each unit faces different challenges. The decentralized approach allows organizations to benefit from 'entrepreneurial instincts' (Shapiro and Balber, 2000:362), echoing, in a managerial context, Adam Smith's theory of the 'selfish passion' (Smith, 1976:I.ii.5.2.) of individuals 'led by an invisible hand to promote an end which was not part of [their] intention' (Smith, 1993: IV, ii). This leads to the conceptualization of 'trust as an organizing principle' where 'trust makes organizations more organic in the sense that members do not need to rely exclusively on mechanistic co-ordination devices and impersonal rules to manage interdependence in the face of uncertainty' (McEvily et al., 2003).

A decentralized network remains one company, has its corporate strategy and continues to report to the same shareholders, but makes a trade-off between coordination and autonomy. 'The overall coordination in a relationship [...] based on a rather complicated structure involving hierarchies, relationships between sub-units and even market characteristics' (Hakansson and Lind, 2004) is more evident in a network than in any other type of organization as per Ouchi's classical classification of Market, Hierarchy and Clan (Ouchi, 1979, 1980); the units, which belong to the network, may even be regarded as quasi-independent organizations whereby interorganizational mechanisms of control apply. We recognize this typology of networks in those organizations that operate in a wide variety of environments with the consequence of having to respond to different challenges, such as multinational consulting firms and multinational hotel companies, which show features of virtual organizations in respect of their unit's weak dependency on headquarters and the relatively high turnover of ownership in contrast with the effort to deliver a consistent worldwide image and to 'convey the requisite firm-specific skills [and corporate standards] to personnel in the new outlets' (Winter and Szulanski, 2001). A variety of forms of governance have been identified in virtual organizations, according to criteria such as 'goal incongruence' and 'performance ambiguity' resulting in some extreme organizational configurations, e.g. the 'minimal network' (Pina et al., 2004) but also in the widely recognized common denominator that 'the performance potential of virtual organizations is undoubtedly rooted in their capacity to develop and maintain trust-based relationships between their members' (Clases et al., 2003). High levels of autonomy run the risk of a 'principal/agent' problem arising, in terms of corporate and unit management as well as between shareholders and corporate management, e.g. trust. The key issue arising is, therefore, related to the trade-off between the maximum level of autonomy balanced with the need of centralized direction and coordination, given that 'on the one hand, it [the accountability process] is a necessary part of senior managers' due diligence in checking how well managers with decentralized responsibilities are performing. On the other, it provides motivation for unit managers to be strongly committed to delivering good results' (Goold and Campbell, 2003).

The reporting system adopted is an essential part of the accountability process – in a microversion of Foucault's intuition of how knowledge is related to power in any social context (Foucault, 1980, 1982) – in that it enables the flow of information upon which the senior managers monitor units' performance and consequently will evaluate their managers. The reporting system, therefore, is assumed to feature a coherent orientation with the autonomy-versus-control choice of the organization. However, where corporate reports stick to a traditional mainly financial orientation (Hartman, 2000; Otley and Fakiolas, 2000; Vagneur and Peiperl, 2000), the unit managers are required to submit to the corporate level only some aspects of performance. In particular, they often focus on past results and short-term objectives, which does little to monitor the consistency of medium- and long-term goals at different levels within network organizations. As a result the gap between the general target of shareholders' wealth and the goals actually pursued within organizations becomes wider (Jensen and Meckling, 1976; Fama, 1980; Fama and Jensen, 1983; Douglas, 1992; Jensen, 1993; Watson and Head, 1998), as indicated in Figure 21.1, where the two 'tiers' of shareholders to corporate (Pratt and Storrar, 1997; Frankforter et al., 2000) and corporate to unit principal/agent problem (Rindova, 1999; Young et al., 2000) are also shown, because 'the broad scope of knowledge transfer and the role of central organization' (Winter and Szulanski, 2001) are not effectively addressed with this type of performance management system, while in a network organization, and particularly when adopting to any degree a 'replication strategy', they are key aspects of the corporate strategy.

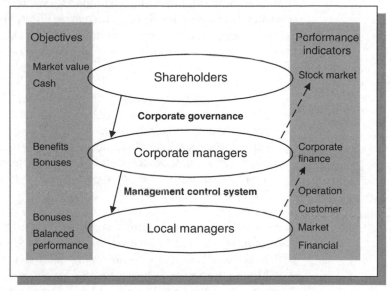

Figure 21.1
The two tiers of the principal/agent problem as reflected in the use of performance indicators.

Coherence between the three levels is the result of a sequence of causes and effects; multidimensional indicators at unit level should support continuous and consistent performance, which is then reflected in unit level finance results. Unit level results are aggregated in corporate results. Corporate results and perception of continuity of good financial results bring market confidence and positive market response. The vehicles through this chain are the incentive schemes based on different types of indicators, which lead managers at each level towards their goals. Consistency is not guaranteed and, in fact, clashes occur between short-term and long-term approaches as well as between broader and narrower visions of the business. A comprehensive review of literature on the topic is reported and analysed by Veliyath (1999), where mechanisms of controlling the relationship between corporate management and shareholders are presented; by Kren and Kerr (1997), where the debate on independence of corporate management is addressed; and by Scott and Tissen (1999), where it is discussed and recognized why management accounting systems are 'an integral part of the information base necessary for decision-making and reward performance' (Scott and Tissen, 1999). The issue has been recently addressed as a consequence of the Enron and other major managerial misconduct events, which demonstrated that a revision of financial and managerial accounting practices should accompany the evolution of managerial techniques, seeking consistency between levels of governance (Elliott and Elliott, 2004).

Building upon the work of Hillman et al. (2000), who maintain that much of the extant literature 'has focused on the agency role of the board of directors', where:

> directors act as fiduciaries of shareholders, serving to alleviate or reduce the problems associated with the separation of ownership and control [...] For example, when the strategies of incumbent managers are ineffective, directors are expected to take action, replacing managers if necessary to improve performance' (Hillman et al., 2000).

The research presented in this chapter focuses on a particular type of organizational control called 'management by values' (MBV), which is based on individuals' work-related-values and trustworthiness; the research enters the debate about the contradiction that 'agency theory works on the basis of trust – both parties trust that the other party will *not* trust them. Both parties, however, do trust accounting information for monitoring the contract. What gets left out of the theory is that if the agent is actually trustworthy, does not exploit hidden information, and does tell the truth' (Jonsson and Macintosh, 1997).

Literature concerning work-related-values (WRV) focuses on the 'congruence between individuals' WRV, and an entity's strategic goals and organisational design' as 'vital for enhancing performance' (Subramaniam and Lokman, 2003) and, by giving evidence that the accounting systems themselves must be designed coherently with the WRV, entails that WRV is not a control system in its own right, but serves to support control mechanisms based on personal values. In literature, management by values seems to spurn as an evolution of 'management by objectives' (MBO); managers at unit level are expected to manage their units according to their own set of 'values'; however, reportedly 'not all writers [...] share the view that decentralisation is synonymous with devolution of decision making' (Hales, 1999). As a consequence, specific financial targets represent the minimal requirements, which enable top management to monitor the short-term effects of unit managers' activities, while the actual (real) control is effected by delegating a high level of autonomy to the unit managers and 'putting to work' their own knowledge and experience; 'control, in short, is exerted through the complex interplay of formal and informal power and authority relations' (Ferner, 2000). The evolution from a more hierarchical control to MBV, through management by objectives (MBO), is a 'culture change' that occurs gradually and implies sophisticated plans, where top management commitment, communication processes and training are required and also audit and measurement of effectiveness must be put in place (Driscoll and Hoffman, 1999). Critically, though, there is the evidence that tacit knowledge is valued, acquired and shared within organizations by means of strategic management recruitment policies and managerial mobility, aiming at exploiting their experience with no harm to the coherence of corporate goals (Madsen et al., 2003). It has to do with establishing a form of socio-ideological control, based on 'how motives and selves are constructed in organizations. [...] What motivates people is partly a matter of how they construct themselves' (Alvesson and Karreman, 2004) – strictly related to their individual work-related-values – and partly a matter of how interpersonal trust is enabled within the organization by applying control mechanisms and rewarding systems (Ferrin and Dirks, 2003).

An important dimension arising from the above discussion relates to the communication systems between corporate management and unit management and highlights their limitations as control tools. The two directions of the communication systems in network organizations, namely centre-to-units and units-to-centre communication, originate from different decision-makers: respectively corporate managers and local managers, but they are consistent because they both result from the unique control system adopted at corporate level. In the centre-to-units communication system, the communication channels aim to bring directives – in the form of strategic guidance and operative instructions – from the headquarters to the edges of the organization which, in network organizations, may often be a challenge. Although the directives are often classified in financial, marketing, human resources and operations terms (Lynch, 2000), the headquarters require mostly financial feedback reports, to match budget requirements, as a way to reduce ambiguity of communication and managers' uncertainty. This view has been reinforced in recent literature (Marginson and Ogden, 2005) where the 'positive effects of budgetary targets on managers' budgeting behaviours' are addressed.

Notwithstanding the kind of organization, the level of detail of the directives transmitted depends on the degree of standardization of operations processes and products and is related to the external environment in which the units are operating. Organizations choose different approaches to competence-sharing depending '… on a company's own culture and also on its commercial imperatives' (Campbell and Sommers-Luchs, 1997); 'imposing best practise from the centre' is, therefore, an appropriate approach where 'standardisation of routines is critical', while 'stimulating the network' is seen as an appropriate approach 'where business unit independence is highly valued'. For example, a business organized with employees spread around the world, but connected in real time by electronic means – such as a call centre – is more consistent than a network organization – such as a multinational consulting firm – where each office faces different markets and local environments. The first should be operated on the basis of a strict procedure control system. An example of such an organization is Best Western (Johnson and Scholes, 1999), which is an international network that provides worldwide marketing and reservation systems. Customers expect to receive the same kind of service, wherever they are willing to go and from wherever they are making contact. The procedures followed by the employees must describe, in every detail, how to react to the possible requests of the customers. On the other hand, multinational consulting firms serve as an example of highly independent network organizations, where although there is a requirement for a list of quality standards to be similar in each office, local managers must be allowed to exercise a degree of autonomy when facing unique contingent challenges and using local resources.

In the latter example the corporate directives should give more emphasis on 'targets', i.e. adopting MBO, and 'goals', i.e. adopting MBV, rather than procedures; and these targets are often suitable for a financial representation. In contrast to this, in the former example, the call centre, procedures will have the priority over strategic goals, and targets may be represented as operational indicators, e.g. time per call, number of successful bookings per 100 calls. In the highly independent network organizations, corporate directives are more effectively transmitted via gathering together regional and local managers, e.g. in conferences, meetings and seminars, which encourage greater motivation and strengthen organizational commitment; the aim of the centre-to-units communication being to transmit the company's 'values' and match them with the individuals' work-related-values.

The principal/agent problem is addressed, though not necessarily solved, through monitoring periodical financial reports and by performance related payment schemes (Rappaport, 1999) in enhanced strategic performance management systems (SPMS). These are traditional SPMS (Shank and Govindarajan, 1993; Kaplan, 1994) to which the characteristic of *'integrativeness'* is added, aiming at bringing together centre and subunits by sharing not only documents, but also 'informal mental models' (Chenhall, 2005), which are naturally influenced by the individuals' work-related-values, and formal reward schemes that increase the level of trust (Ferrin and Dirks, 2003) and commitment (Marginson and Ogden, 2005). Bearing in mind, though, that in any event 'performance measures (upon which reward may be based) provide the opportunity for employees to "game the system" by emphasising actual, rather than intended, and short-term, rather than long-term, performance' (Ezzamel and Willmott, 1998), quality audits are conducted, with the aim of checking if procedures are applied.

The two dimensions alongside which the SPMS seem to take form in the network organizations are represented in Figure 21.2, where predominant SPMS forms are related to the level of autonomy of the unit managers and the level complexity of the corporate targets.

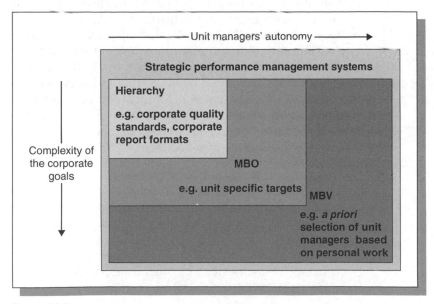

Figure 21.2
Two dimensions of the strategic performance management systems in network organizations.

Reports containing results of the local business units are used to communicate in a units-to-centre direction. They usually comprise a core financial component because the presentation of results in financial terms is a universal language and allows the local management to communicate consistently with headquarters. Financial indicators also allow a comprehensive and standardized picture of performance and position of the units represented; they respond to the corporate managers' need for tangible economic measures to monitor unit level results.

An apparent consequence arising from this review seems to be that where a network organization significantly benefits from the advantages of decentralization, the reports of local managers to corporate managers should include less detailed information. Hence, at unit level the set of data used by local managers to control and monitor their day-to-day activities is broader and should therefore be included in *ad hoc* reports. The question arising is, therefore: 'how do unit managers make and implement decisions within network organizations?'

Research
Methodology

For this research the hospitality industry has been chosen, given its favourable features, i.e. the industry consists of network organizations, which mostly (i) are significantly decentralized and (ii) face remarkably different environments, but still (iii) show the need to guarantee a consistency of their image throughout all of their units and over time. The hospitality industry also provides insights into different types of product/output, i.e. from pure *service* of room letting to *retailing* in bars, and *manufacturing* in restaurants. Furthermore, the service component of this industry enables the researchers' approach to:

> treat organizations as 'people gathering' or cultures rather than as depicted by economic theory as atomistic collections of information processing decision makers neatly arranged in the organizational hierarchy [...] [in order to] produce a much richer and more informative theory of the way management accounting systems are used and trusted (or mistrusted) in organizations (Jonsson and Macintosh, 1997).

Previous research (Harris and Mongiello, 2001), where a survey that included 402 European hotels was conducted – with a 43.5% response rate – showed that unit managers of hotels (general managers) use sets of indicators which enable them to monitor and control their business through a number of perspectives, in addition to finance. The concept of 'company performance indicators' profile' was introduced, suggesting that general managers in each hotel chain surveyed indicated, to a greater or lesser extent, a particular pattern of performance measures, within the framework of finance, human resources, operations and customer perspectives.

The current study builds upon the previous findings by conducting in-depth interviews. A pilot interview was carried out, before thirteen in-depth interviews took place, in order to obtain the most out of the subsequent main in-depth interviews conducted with general managers belonging to four companies in four European countries (Belgium, Germany, Italy and the UK).

The in-depth semi-structured interview was chosen as the research method, because in accordance with predominant literature on methodology (Saunders et al., 2003:250) personal contact with the general managers was necessary to gain an insight to the respondents' approach and managerial style; particularly in terms of context and rationale and that 'trust seems to be a concept that can only be described in terms of examples of discourse' (Jonsson and Macintosh, 1997). The interviews would also enable follow up, reflection on responses and, in particular, use face-to-face discussions to make respondents comfortable with the confidentiality aspect of the topic, where the types of data and the decision process that led to their choice – rather than the actual figures – were relevant.

A qualitative method was seen as appropriate, to match the suggested phenomenographical framework (Wisker, 2001) that is observation of social phenomena. This corresponds with the nature of the phenomenon being studied in terms of how decision processes are carried out, what role trust plays within the organization and how the underpinning knowledge is used (van der Bent et al., 1999) to construct the social discourse that results in the interpretation of the context of the unit managers' decisions in network organizations. The self-report element of interviews was considered appropriate because the 'participants have the language and experience to describe their own actions and reactions' (Rosenthal and Rosnow, 1991:178). They represent 'pipelines for transmitting knowledge' (Weston and Copeland, 1986) from respondents to researchers and are particularly able to ease the discussion of specific topics 'rarely to be effectively captured in their natural habitat' (Holstein and Gubrium, 1997:126); in subsequent investigation stages the research may cross the border of the interpretative approach (Prasad and Prasad, 2002) and enter the grounded theory approach (Glaser and Strauss, 1967; Glaser, 1992, 1996, 1998) when the results could support the formulation of theory or organization models (Seale, 1999).

The line of questioning pursued the goals the interviewees set in their role as unit managers and what their perception was of the context variables – current strengths and weaknesses of their unit – and their approach to the strategy to achieve the goals. Once the scenario was set, the next question was about what indicators managers would use for their daily decision-making activity. The interviews then explored how the indicators were evaluated and if they were chosen in-house or were corporate led. Finally, the discussion would probe the actions that managers would normally take as consequence of the use of the chosen indicators.

All interviews comprised between one and one-and-a-half hour's duration and were conducted *in situ*, but in different parts of the properties, i.e. managers' office, lounge, meeting room, bar; interestingly partly reflecting the interviewees' managerial style.

Data and data analysis

A systematic comparison of the data gathered from the thirteen interviewees was conducted with the aim to find patterns that would start to answer the research question. A purposive grouping of interviewees was then adopted, whereby four relevant scenarios were identified in order to address the research question. Eight interviews matched the grouping dimensions, which refer to 'corporate' and 'local environment' and have been classified as follows:

(i) three interviewees belonging to the same company, but facing different competitive environments

(ii) two interviewees operating in the same competitive environment – of which they showed similar perceptions – but belonging to different companies

(iii) two interviewees belonging to the same company and operating in a similar competitive environment

(iv) an interviewee playing a 'special' role in recurring situations.

This classification is represented in the matrix of Figure 21.3, where the interviewee groups (i), (ii) and (iii) find position according to two dimensions: 'contingent external variables', i.e. managers' perception of the environment, and 'company contingent variable', i.e. belonging or not to the same company. The interviewee of group (iv) refers to contingent internal variables being similar every time a special situation recurs in a company.

(i) Interviewees belonging to the same company but facing different environments

From these interviews it was found out that the corporate management of the company had started a few years before a

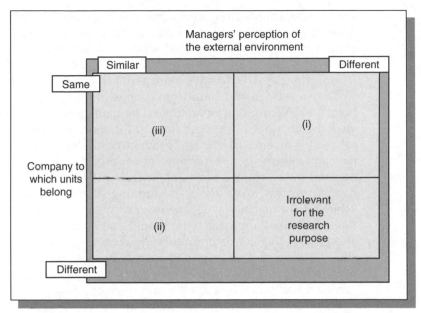

Figure 21.3
External and internal contingent variables for the classification of eight interviewees.

transformation of its approach to the market, in order to compete more effectively. Their mission statement included the aim to be more proactive, causing a marketing re-style and operations revision in all the owned units. Therefore, corporate management put in place a monitoring system based on a number of financial and operations indicators, such as daily average room rate and daily occupancy compared to budgeted figures. In fact, the real control system applied by the corporate office is delegating to the unit managers; they are autonomous decision-makers who must deal with specific environment challenges.

In this service restructuring – equivalent to the manufacturing business process re-engineering – one of the units manifested the need to create a pleasant and safe environment to contrast the rather unwelcoming features of the location. During the interview the manager showed a rank of work-related-values, which would value the care of the smallest details in furniture items, the choice of flower decoration or even the types of music played at the piano bar. His way to communicate directly with the guests and with the customers confirmed he used his personal skills for inter-personal relationship as a key managerial tool, which had previously been recognized in other units within the company.

Another unit was seen by the corporate level as in need of pursuing an aggressive strategy of market penetration in its specific area, where competitors were consolidating their fair share in a growing business segment market. In order to address this situation a manager was appointed who could use entrepreneurial creativity – proven by having led numerous unit openings in different countries. His decisive managerial style would enable him to drive a sudden and significant change in many aspects of the hotel's marketing and operations. His managerial style permeated and energized the entire unit. In the short term this seemed to result in an enthusiastic and productive implementation of the new and more proactive management approach, but was also recognized to be creating a level of stress in the unit. As part of the routine process, once the re-positioning of the unit had been achieved, the manager would transfer responsibility to another of more measured approach, who would embed the new configuration, providing consistent quality to customers and security to staff. In effect, this strategy had already been applied to another unit, which is the subject of the next paragraph, where this manager had previously led the unit re-positioning.

The third manager interviewed had taken over a unit from the second interviewee, which had just completed a process of restructuring and re-positioning similar to that described in the previous paragraph. He was charged with the responsibility to maintain the quality standard required by the newly achieved status, but expressed concern that the stress caused by the recent restructuring would undermine the ability of the unit staff to provide customers with quality service. Consequently, his main task was to create a stable working environment where employees were enabled to provide a service that would maintain and improve customers' recognition of the unit's new standards. The manager's approach was reflecting his own management philosophy, which was reportedly based on the 'close control of the matching between customers' expectations and human resource's needs'.

Although the reports and information for corporate management were organized in the same format for the three hotels, the indicators actually used by the three managers to manage their units were significantly different. Thus, the corporate office had the role of selecting the 'right' manager to match the needs of a unit at a given point in time. In effect, the interviewees created sets of performance indicators consistent with their individual managerial approach. Examples, among others, are the 'customer satisfaction gathered face-to-face' by the first interviewee as opposed to the 'detailed and systematic analysis of competitive environment' of the second interviewee and the 'booking performance measured in terms of courtesy and effectiveness' referred to by the third interviewee.

(ii) Interviewees operating in the same competitive environment, but belonging to different companies

This case consists of two managers who shared a similar perception of opportunities and threats in their common competitive environment, where the market was expected to grow suddenly and significantly in relation to a foreseen political event and where a cultural gap had to be filled in order for the staff to reach the quality standards that the corporate office required. The two managers, though, belonged to two different companies.

In both the units, standard reports for the companies were perceived as a routine activity unrelated to the indicators used by the managers to monitor their daily performance. Therefore, the corporate management would not receive reports about daily activity. Instead, the managers were charged with achieving medium- and long-term goals, which they had been selected to match. For example, one of the managers would monitor guests' demand and competitors' strategies through direct research on the Internet, with the objective of picking any signal of a changing market trend – this was an admission of his interest in the use of IT and his personal skills of analysing the market. The other manager focused his attention on monitoring and managing 'real time' customer and employee satisfaction. The corporate requirement for both managers was the readiness to face the anticipated tourist demand in the medium term.

(iii) Interviewees belonging to the same company and operating in a similar competitive environment

In this case two unit managers were driven by similar goals. Both the units were experiencing a period of good performance in terms of revenues and occupancy and it was perceived that there was no need for dramatic changes in strategic approach. No particular external environment challenges were apparent. Therefore, strategic goals seemed to be related to a natural increase of financial performance with slight and constant improvements as opposed to sudden revolutions.

Despite belonging to the same company and operating in the same environment, their managerial approaches were markedly distinct. Of particular interest is that a sophisticated tool provided by the corporate office, in the form of a comprehensive balanced scorecard, was extensively used by one of the two managers and virtually ignored by the other. One manager demonstrated that he was integrating his personal knowledge and experience with balanced scorecard results elaborated by the corporate office on units' data. In contrast, the balance scorecard was disregarded by the other manager, who emphasized interpersonal relationships as she felt she could use her personal attribute of being a woman, remarking, 'it eases contact with people; I mean … staff and guests'.

In this example corporate management was satisfied with both the units and just aimed to pursue a limited increase of the financial results through a broad improvement of the overall performance represented by the corporate balanced scorecard. Both the managers were reflective and 'peace-keepers' and their main target was to stimulate their respective units, in order not to let routine activities lose the momentum of constant quality improvement; both cognizant of the danger of their stable position drifting due to the lack of direction. They used a range of indicators for them to take actions, which were heavily influenced by the corporate office, but in part different and unrelated to what the corporate office required. Examples of different indicators are the 'customer satisfaction revealed via balanced score card' in one case and the 'customer (and employee) satisfaction gathered by walking about' in the other case.

(iv) One interviewee with a specific role within the company

This case shows a manager whose 'special' skills, developed through years in the job, were related to dealing with the issues of closing down units. As in several previous situations, the interviewee was once again managing a unit which would close in a few months from his appointment. The manager's specific skills enabled him to deal with customers and to cope with employees in the related critical matters, such as employee redundancy, job interruption, customer disappointment. His targets were expressed as short-term performance 'to get the best out of the remaining period in business' and, when conditions allow, he also has the long-term target of creating the conditions for customers to be engaged again and for the best workforce to be employed again, on recommencement of the business.

This manager is routinely appointed to this specific task wherever a closure occurs in the company. He has a great degree of autonomy in the choice of actions and also in the creation of specific indicators, given that the corporate reports and related indicators are suitable for on-going business, rather than for closing programmes. His priorities include the need to manage the overall quality on a 'holding' basis when no substantial additional resources are available and monitoring and motivating employees by constant personal presence, as inevitably the lag time of corporate reports would render them obsolete.

Discussion

An interesting theme emerged from the data; all the interviewed managers were concerned with the indicators, mainly financial, requested by the corporate management in order to show the results of their activity, but they described a significantly broader range of indicators as the ones they choose to manage their units. This is reflected in the responses of managers across the cases analysed: (i) where managers operating in the same company face different external contingent variables; (ii) where managers operating in different companies face the same external contingent variables; (iii) where managers operating in the same company face similar external contingent variables; and (iv) where managers face a recurrent scenario of contingent internal variables.

It is suggested, therefore, that the 'company performance indicators' profile' (Harris and Mongiello, 2001) of network companies is shaped out of the choices of managers, more than by schemes provided by the headquarters. Unit managers appear to be influenced by the guidelines and the statements produced for corporate level, but they decide independently how to run their units towards specific objectives; 'the subsidiaries' power derives from their position in the local market and their role as interpreter of the profusion of data emanating from the local environment' (Ferner, 2000:537). The indicators chosen, often created on an *ad hoc* basis, are used by the unit managers to underpin their decisions towards unit objectives, which prove to be functional to the corporate goals.

As the variety of the environment challenges requires companies to respond with a similar variety of approaches, it emerged from this research that any form of control, where instructions or even objectives were strictly set in network organizations, would fail to control the units. Such systems, in fact, would keep track of indicators, ignoring that they have different meanings and interpretation in different situations. For instance, repeat business indicators are less significant in a unit undergoing product re-positioning than in a unit operating with a well established clientele; or, in terms of business orientation, cost indicators are more critical in product oriented units than in market oriented units. Thus, it is apparent that unit managers' decisions, such as cost structure, customer mix or product mix, which are influenced by managers' interpretation of their unit environment, directly impact on their choice of performance measures. Therefore, a key skill expected from unit managers is their interpretation of local environments, which enables them to steer each unit towards appropriate objectives. Consistently, from this research it emerged that wide delegation of decision-making is used to maintain control in network organizations.

In addition to this, it becomes apparent that the selection and allocation of managers to the units is a tool for corporate management to give initial strategic direction to the units; unit managers' previous experience and accumulated knowledge imply what course of action will be taken and how actions will be pursued. This chapter gives evidence from a specific industry – hospitality – which supports that in network organizations attention is 'paid to the invisible and informal support structures that make formal systems work, particularly where cultural and geographical distance dilute the intended impact of such systems' (Ferner, 2000).

As a corollary to the above point, evidence is also given that individual background and personal values are significant characteristics which corporate management seek in unit managers, because corporate management works in an *a priori* perspective, namely management by values (MBV), based on the expectation that unit managers will act according to pre-selected visions and insights, i.e. work-related-values.

The findings concur with the widely documented (Turnbull, 2001) studies about relationship between middle managers and corporate ideologies, where an element of 'managerial schizophrenia' (Anthony and Peter, 1994) appeared, for example, in the interviewees of case (ii), who were reconciling their respective corporate international standards with a local workforce culturally distant from quality service expectations; similarly, in case (i), the third interviewee was pulled in two directions, namely satisfying the demand of corporate office in terms of continual improvement of services and reducing the stress levels following the product re-positioning. Also, this research drives the debate on 'roles of individual directors [unit managers] as environmental links' (Hillman et al., 2000:239) into the context of strategy implementation in network organizations, and concludes showing that, in the context analysed, there is a wide awareness of 'the complexity and dangers of organisations engaging in programmes which seek to control managerial behaviours for economic purpose, without addressing the emotions and perceptions of those to whom these messages are directed' addressed by Turnbull (2001:241). Nevertheless, in a management accounting approach, further research can also be encouraged, with the aim of finding methods and techniques able to formalize uniform sets of results (financial and non-financial), which better match the type of industry-specific information needed for control.

Conclusions

Although a definitive conclusion as to whether MBV is the best control mechanism in network organizations cannot be drawn, this research revealed evidence that MBV is deliberately used in network organizations, in combination with other control mechanisms. This was found where unit managers belonging to the same company were facing different local environments, as well as where unit managers belonging to the same company were challenged by the same local environment and also in situations where unit managers belonging to different companies were facing similar local environments; proving that it is not the dichotomy belonging/not belonging to the same company nor is it the dichotomy similar/different local environments – in any combination between them – that determines the adoption of MBV. This leaves the researchers with the conclusion that MBV is seemingly effective in addressing the features of certain network organizations, by not only recognizing the diversity of the units' microenvironments but also – and independently – by valuing the variety of the units' possible responses. Therefore, it seems possible to suggest that in those network organizations where the flexibility of MBV is not present, the corporate managerial approach should be critically revisited and some consideration given to the introduction of MBV. In such cases, corporate management might consider adopting a flexible approach of delegation of decision power, by encouraging unit managers to follow their own knowledge and experience within the broad guidance of corporate, as 'quasi-entrepreneurs' who share similar firm-specific work-related-values.

Furthermore, this chapter contributes to the literature on network organizations' control systems by showing that previous conclusions are proved valid in a specific service industry context. Elaborating on the classical Ouchi's organizational categories and more recent literature on 'trust in organizations', this research found that unit managers of network organizations can see themselves – and indeed construct themselves – as 'entrepreneurs' operating within the boundaries of bigger systems; where the tension between autonomous initiative and corporate control, as two contradicting features of their role, is far from creating a destructive schizophrenia and turns into a powerful combination of motives with great benefit for the organizations.

However, the interesting nature of the MBV phenomenon observed carries an inherent limitation as the work-related-values were constructed in a series of unique discourse situations involving researchers and participants 'there and then' that cannot be replicated. In this context, management by values emerged as a fundamental underpinning of centre-to-unit/unit-to-centre organizational relationships, but more evidence for the development of an MBV formal framework should be sought.

References

Alvesson, M. and Karreman, D. (2004) Interface of control. Technocratic and socio-ideological control in a global management consultancy firm. *Accounting, Organization and Society*, **29**, 423–444.

Anthony, P.D. and Peter, D. (1994) *Managing culture*, p. 79. Open University Press, Buckingham.

Campbell, A. and Sommers-Luchs, K. (1997) *Core Competency-Based Strategy*. International Thomson Business Press, London.

Chenhall, R.H. (2005) Integrative strategic performance measurement systems, strategic alignment of manufacturing, learning and strategic outcomes: an exploratory study. *Accounting Organizations and Society*, **30**, 395–422.

Clases, C., Bachmann, R. and Wehner, T. (2003) Studying trust in virtual organizations. *International Studies of Management & Organizations*, **33** (3), 7–27.

Delany, E. (2000) Strategic development of the multinational subsidiary through subsidiary initiative-taking. *Long Range Planning*, **33**, 220–244.

Douglas, E.J. (1992) *Managerial economics. Analysis and strategy*. Prentice-Hall International, New Jersey.

Driscoll, D.M. and Hoffman, W.M. (1999) Gaining the ethical edge: procedures for delivering values-driven management. *Long Range Planning*, **32** (2), 179–189.

Elliott, B. and Elliott, J. (2004) *Financial Accounting and Reporting*, 8th edn. Prentice Hall, Harlow.

Ezzamel, M. and Willmott, H. (1998) Accounting, remuneration and employee motivation in the new organisation. *Accounting and Business Research*, **28** (2), 97–110.

Fama, E.F. (1980) Agency problems and the theory of the firm. *Journal of Political Economy*, **88**, 288–307.

Fama, E.F. and Jensen, M.C. (1983) Separation of ownership and control. *Journal of Law and Economics*, **26**, 301–324.

Ferner, A. (2000) The underpinning of 'bureaucratic' control systems: HRM in European multinationals. *Journal of Management Studies*, **37** (4), 521–539.

Ferrin, D.L. and Dirks, K.T. (2003) The use of rewards to increase and decrease trust: mediating processes and differential effects. *Organization Science*, **14** (1), 18–31.

Foucault, M. (1980) *Power/Knowledge*. Harvester Publishing, Brighton.

Foucault, M. (1982) The subject and power. In Dreyfus, H. and Rabinow, P. (eds), *Beyond Structuralism and Hermeneutics*. Harvester Publishing, Brighton.

Frankforter, S.A., Berman, S.L. and Jones, T.M. (2000) Boards of directors and shark repellents: assessing the value of an agency theory perspective. *Journal of Management Studies*, **37** (3), 321–348.

Glaser, B.G. (1992) *Basics of Grounded Theory Analysis*. Sociology Press, California.

Glaser, B.G. (1996) *Gerund Grounded Theory: The Basic Social Process Dissertation*. Sociology Press, California.

Glaser, B.G. (1998) *Doing Grounded Theory*. Sociology Press, California.

Glaser, B.G. and Strauss, A.L. (1967) *The Discovery of Grounded Theory: Strategies for Qualitative Research*. Aldine-Transaction, New Jersey.

Goold, M. and Campbell, A. (2003) Structured networks. *Long Range Planning*, **36**, 427–439.

Hakansson, H. and Lind, J. (2004) Accounting and network coordination. *Accounting, Organizations and Society*, **29**, 51–72.

Hales, C. (1999) Leading horses to water? The impact of decentralisation on managerial behaviour. *Journal of Management Studies*, **36** (6), 831–851.

Harris, P.J. and Mongiello, M. (2001) Key performance indicators in European hotel properties: general managers' choices and company profiles. *International Journal of Contemporary Hospitality Management*, **13** (3), 120–127.

Hartman, F.G.H. (2000) The appropriateness of RAPM: towards the further development of theory. *Accounting, Organisations and Society*, **25**, 451–482.

Hibbert, E.P. (1997) *International Business. Strategy and Operations*. MacMillan Press, London.

Hillman, A.J., Cannella, A.A. Jr and Paetzold, R.L. (2000) The resource dependant role of corporate directors: strategic adaptation of board composition in response to environmental change. *Journal of Management Studies*, **37** (2), 235–255.

Holstein, J.A. and Gubrium, J.F. (1997) Active interviewing. In Silverman, D. (ed.), *Qualitative Research: theory, method and practice*. Sage Publications, London.

Jensen, M.C. and Meckling, W.H. (1976) Theory of the firm: management behavior, agency costs, and ownership structure. *Journal of Financial Economics*, **3**, 305–360.

Jensen, M.C. (1993) The modern industrial revolution: exit and failure of internal control. *Journal of Finance*, **48**, 831–880.

Johnson, G. and Scholes, K. (1999) *Exploring Corporate Strategy*. Prentice Hall, Harlow.

Jonsson, S. and Macintosh, N.B. (1997) CATS, RATS, and EARS: making the case for ethnographic accounting research. *Accounting, Organizations and Society*, **22** (3/4), 367–386.

Kaplan, R.S. (1994) Management accounting (1984–1994): development of new practices and trends of development. *Management Accounting Research*, **5**, 247–260.

Kren, L. and Kerr, J.L. (1997) The effect of outside directors and board of shareholdings on the relation between chief executive compensation and firm performance. *Accounting and Business Research*, **27** (4), 297–309.

Lynch, R. (2000) *Corporate Strategy*. Prentice Hall, Harlow.

Madsen, T., Mosakowski, E. and Zaheer, S. (2003) Knowledge retention and personal mobility: the nondisruptive effects of inflows of experience. *Organization Science*, **14** (2), 173–191.

Marginson, D. and Ogden, S. (2005) Coping with ambiguity through the budget: the positive effects of budgetary targets on managers' budgeting behaviours. *Accounting, Organization and Society*, **30**, 435–456.

McEvily, B., Perrone, V. and Zaheer, A. (2003) Trust as an organizing principle. *Organization Science*, **14** (1), 91–103.

Otley, D. and Fakiolas, A. (2000) Reliance on accounting performance measure: dead end or new beginning? *Accounting, Organisations and Society*, **25**, 497–510.

Ouchi, W.G. (1979) A conceptual framework for the design of organizational control mechanisms. *Management Science*, **29** (9), 833–848.

Ouchi, W.G. (1980) Markets, bureaucracies and clans. *Administrative Science Quarterly*, **25**, 129–141.

Pina, M., Kamoche, K., Mariziliano, N. and da Chuna, V.J.V. (2004) Minimal network. A contribution to the understanding of control in trust-based organizations. *International Studies of Management & Organizations*, **33** (4), 94–120.

Prasad, A. and Prasad, P. (2002) The coming age of interpretive organizational research. *Organizational Research Methods*, **5** (1), 4–11.

Pratt, K.C. and Storrar, A.C. (1997) UK shareholders' lost access to management information. *Accounting and Business Research*, **27** (3), 205–218.

Rappaport, A. (1999) New pay on how to link executive pay with performance. *Harvard Business Review*, March–April, 91–101.

Rindova, V.P. (1999) What corporate boards have to do with strategy: a cognitive perspective. *Journal of Management Studies*, **36** (7), 953–975.

Rosenthal, R. and Rosnow, R.L. (1991) *Essentials of behavioral research: methods and data analysis*, p. 178. McGraw Hill, New York.

Saunders, M., Lewis, P. and Thornhill, A. (2003) *Research Methods for Business Students*, p. 250. Prentice Hall, New Jersey.

Scott, T.W. and Tissen, P. (1999) Performance measurement and managerial teams. *Accounting, Organisations and Society*, **24**, 263–285.

Seale, C. (1999) *The Quality of Qualitative Research*. SAGE, London.

Shank, J.K. and Govindarajan, V. (1993) *Strategic Cost Management*. The Free Press, New York.

Shapiro, A.C. and Balber, S.D. (2000) *Modern Corporate Finance. A Multidisciplinary Approach to Value Creation*. Prentice Hall, New Jersey.

Smith, A. (1976) *The Theory of Moral Sentiments*, Raphael, D.D. and Macfie, A.L. (eds). Clarendon Press, Oxford.

Smith, A. (1993) *An Inquiry into the Nature and Causes of the Wealth of Nations*, a selected edition. Oxford University Press, Oxford.

Subramaniam, N. and Lokman, M. (2003) A note on work-related values, budget emphasis and managers' organisational commitment. *Management Accounting Research*, **14**, 389–408.

Turnbull, S. (2001) Corporate ideology – meaning and contradictions for middle managers. *British Journal of Management*, **12**, 231–241.

Vagneur, K. and Peiperl, M. (2000) Reconsidering performance evaluation style. *Accounting, Organisations and Society*, **25**, 511–525.

van der Bent, J., Paauwe, J. and Williams, R. (1999) Organizational learning: an exploration of organizational memory and its role in organizational change processes. *Journal of Organizational Change Management*, **12** (5), 377–404.

Veliyath, R. (1999) Top management compensation and shareholder return: unravelling different models of the relationship. *Journal of Management Studies*, **36** (1), 123–143.

Watson, D. and Head, T. (1998) *Corporate Finance. Principles & Practice*. Financial Times Management, London.

Weston, J.F. and Copeland, T.E. (1986) *Managerial Finance*. CBS College Publishing, New York.

Winter, S.G. and Szulanski, G. (2001) Replication as strategy. *Organization Science*, **12** (6), 730–743.

Wisker, G. (2001) *The Postgraduate Research Handbook*. Palgrave, London.

Young, G.J., Stedham, Y. and Rafik, I.B. (2000) Boards of directors and the adoption of a CEO performance evaluation process: agency – and institutional – theory perspectives. *Journal of Management Studies*, **37** (2), 277–295.

Career directions in financial management in the hospitality industry

Howard Field

Introduction

Until the mid to late 1960s, there were few hotels that were large enough to warrant the employment of a qualified accountant in the management team. Most hotels in the UK were locally or nationally owned. Where they were businesses within larger groups, much of the administration was centralized in head offices, often under the 'company secretary' – a role that generally concentrates more on corporate administration and compliance than with dynamic commercial issues.

By the early 1970s, many new or extended hotels – some developments having been encouraged by government grants, loans and tax incentives – had appeared on the scene. The UK public owning companies (at that time the major names were Forte and Grand Metropolitan) were starting to embrace techniques of management accounting and reporting, which had their origins in the USA.

A UK version of an industry management accounting system, called 'A Standard System of Accounts for Hotels', was proposed and published by the NEDC (National Economic Development Council – an early 'quango') working with the industry. This was not fully adopted and used and has been out of print for many years. United States based hotel groups – such as InterContinental, Hilton, Sheraton, Holiday Inn, Ramada – were expanding into Europe. These companies were far more unit focused and implemented comprehensive management accounting at the hotel property level. They were almost 100 per cent users of the US-developed Uniform System of Accounts. This originated in New York as long ago as 1926 and has been updated periodically since then; its current full title is *Uniform System of Accounts for the Lodging Industry* (1996).

The internationally branded hotels referred to were (and are) not always owned by the operating company. For financial accounting to comply with local requirements and to reflect the resulting corporate structures meant there was a need for management accounting and financial accounting to be addressed as separate issues. In general, the larger international hotels have been fully self-accounting from the outset, i.e. the unit accounting function carries out the whole financial and management accounting and reporting for the business in-house. This often includes handling statutory accounts and taxation matters.

Other major factors affecting the evolution of the role of the financial manager have included the advances in data processing and software tools, either tailored for the hotel industry or available for general business use. 'Scorekeeping' and historical bookkeeping take second place to dynamic business information production to support management planning and control on an on-going basis. The degree of autonomous accounting and reporting at unit level remains the prime factor which impacts on the level of skills and experience required by hotel unit financial managers.

In more recent times, there has been a trend towards greater distinction being made between ownership and operation of hotel businesses. The owners are often financial institutions or private investors, some of these being pooled funds managed aggressively on behalf of high net worth individuals by teams of 'asset managers'. This can result in pressures on unit managers and their teams to perform to a variety of measures imposed by the owners' representatives, the management companies, the brand standards and their own internal targets. The net effect is a major increase in demand for management information and analysis. A side effect is that the 'owner's books' are often dealt with externally.

Financial management in the hospitality industry therefore encompasses a wide range of functions and responsibilities. This chapter aims to identify the role of the finance manager, outline its nature, indicate the education and technical requirements and show potential career paths available within this dynamic service sector. The focus is principally on UK located or based hotel businesses, but what follows can be seen to be applicable to a large extent to restaurant, bar, catering and allied businesses, and to international locations.

The hospitality industry financial management context

An almost unique feature of the hotel industry is that the operations of the business are twenty-four hours, seven days a week, year-round (with of course some exceptions for seasonal-only operations). Once a hotel property has opened its doors, it is for all practical purposes a perpetual motion economic unit.

A further feature is that the business comprises a mix of manufacturing and service elements. The manufacturing element, catering, involves the input of raw materials, and a process to turn these for onward retail sale. Varying inputs of labour are needed to provide the production and service elements of the catering operations and the hotel's other outputs of accommodation, bars, leisure and so on. As a whole, the product is highly perishable. The major revenue producer for most hotels, rooms, on offer on one-day cannot, if unsold, be held in stock and sold twice the next day.

Pricing has to be flexible to optimize revenue, creating the need for systems enabling differential pricing for every element of the product to reflect supply and demand, and market sector issues. The customers, the guests, are transient – coming and going as they please, which in itself is somewhat of a unique feature from a business standpoint. While there, they give rise to numerous transactions varying from small values to large, some for credit and some for cash – creating a further variety of unique control challenges. The nearest equivalent is a retail department store but, as yet, customers in such businesses do not have the option of staying overnight or being given access to a range of other services such as laundry or indeed holding major functions, conferences, meetings and banquets on the premises.

A wide range of IT systems underpins the operations of a modern hotel business. These play a part at the front end in business generation, reservations and revenue management, sales, customer relations and marketing and in accounting for guest and other point of sale transactions. Behind the scenes, purchasing, storing, issuing and production, accounts payable and receivable, cashiering, payroll, management and financial reporting are all now carried out by integrated or interfaced systems. Further specialist systems support such aspects as telecommunications, Internet access, entertainment, security and maintenance functions.

The hotel business is initially highly capital intensive. To build or acquire a hotel, and prepare it for trading is costly and it requires significant additional investment to maintain its standard and market position. In operations, hotels generate significant cash flow, with a major ongoing cost being for labour, a substantial part of which is often 'fixed' to ensure it can meet its service standards. Covering the cost of its capital, which will be dependent on its financing structure, may also be one of the largest fixed costs. Leasehold hotels will have rent, sometimes fixed and sometimes with a link to turnover. Owned hotel properties may have loan capital to service.

The nature of the business entity itself will also play a part in defining the scope of the financial manager's role. The following section examines typical structures in the hospitality industry.

Hotel ownership and operating structures

- The most common format for mainly privately owned hotel businesses is that of the owner operated unit, where the property and the business are one entity. This structure might also apply to larger organizations including major companies but, as has already been mentioned, ownership is fast becoming the exception for the latter category of operator.

- The next level is where the property is leased (i.e. it is owned by a landlord) by the operator. This is found with private hotels, but implies a level of financial obligation that limits the number of individuals who would qualify for a lease. It is becoming far more prominent for multi-unit operators and major groups. It removes a substantial capital investment burden from the operator and replaces it with a cost that can be more directly related to the operating revenues. In some recent examples, the rents fluctuate based on the actual sales of the hotel.

- A further separation of ownership and operation involves the hotel company in entering into a management contract to run the hotel on behalf of the owner. In this latter case, the property and the business are those of the owner. The operator runs the business as the owner's agent and earns fees that are generally based partly on the level of sales revenue and partly on a defined level of profit.

- Joint ventures, performance guarantees, franchise licences – these are all factors which can complicate the structures outlined above and which will have an impact on the hotel's financial management requirements. Joint ventures imply that there is more than one party interested in the performance of the business. Performance guarantees may involve financial penalties if the management of the hotel under-performs against certain criteria. Franchise licences impose standards with which the hotel must comply in order to maintain the brand identity of the hotel.

Hotel management structures

To reflect the ownership and operating needs of these different business arrangements requires a management structure to mirror the owning and operating elements. A business that is both owner and operator might have only one financial manager. A large-scale business might need to separate its corporate requirements from the day-to-day operation. Multi-unit businesses could also require separation of corporate and operational financial management. In major companies, this might mean area, regional, national and international financial managers. If the operations (properties) are large enough economic units, they will often have individual financial managers on-site.

Owners have management structures that differ from those of the operators. Landlords are interested in collecting rents and ensuring compliance with the lease terms. Owners whose hotels are operated under management agreements have an interest in every aspect of the operation. The extent of the reports each of these types of owner or their asset managers require will be governed by the terms of the leases or management contracts. The roles of financial managers for landlords and for owners of managed hotels will vary accordingly. Often these individuals do not have detailed hotel industry knowledge. They will therefore rely more heavily on the quality of the financial reporting from the hotel being of a standard on which they can rely. This might be supported by independent audit or monitoring by appropriately experienced external advisors.

With these factors in mind, the next section looks at the scope of accounting, control and reporting needs that form the foundation of the hospitality financial manager's role.

Scope of the hospitality financial management role

Probably the best way to illustrate the responsibilities of a typical financial manager in a hotel business is to set out a job description. A detailed example for a senior unit financial controller is shown in Appendix A. There will be variations between companies in areas such as procurement and IT but, in this example, these functions are within the scope of responsibilities.

The aspects noted in the example as 'areas which remain the responsibility of the corporate finance director' will depend on whether the operation is independent, part of a group or a fully self-accounting entity. In a larger business, and in public companies, a company secretary may also be involved in certain of the functions.

Being a senior executive in a hotel, the financial manager will be expected to play a full part in the management team. This can include being the financial advisor to the business and the individuals, participating in guest and employee relations activities, performing 'duty management' responsibilities.

The financial manager is often expected to be the most independent voice in the operation, but also to be a full team member. The role in a major hotel is commonly second only in seniority to the general manager. There is some variation in the policies of different hotel groups as to whether the primary reporting relationship is to the unit general manager or to the corporate office.

Skills and qualifications for the future hospitality financial manager

Educational qualifications will need to be complemented by experience which demonstrates appropriate technical and professional knowledge, skills and aptitude. An accountancy qualification is generally preferred. Examples of those most relevant follow. Chartered Accountants are commonly found in the largest hotels and at Board level. Qualifications such as those awarded by the Chartered Institute of Management Accountants (CIMA) and the Chartered Association of Certified Accountants (CACA) are equally recognized. At unit level, Association of Accounting Technicians (AAT) and accounting degrees are often sufficient. A summary of the various entry and study requirements is set out as Appendix B.

Within the hotel sector, membership of and qualifications gained via the British Association of Hospitality Accountants (BAHA) are now widely accepted. The latter enable more junior accounting staff to secure a recognized qualification within their specialized field – or more senior financial managers to underpin their on-the-job training with more structured learning. Indeed, the core BAHA qualification also provides certain exemptions for subjects within the CIMA syllabus, and recent developments of the BAHA courses will lead to further recognition by other professional bodies.

The professional qualifications mentioned are those most appropriate for and recognized within the hospitality industry. For senior positions greater emphasis is given to formal educational and professional qualifications, exposure to sophisticated operations, international standards and current operating systems.

The following is a schedule of skill and experience attributes which will facilitate entry into employment at the most senior levels of financial management in the hospitality industry:

- a sound academic record

- professional standard training in finance, accountancy, control systems and business techniques

- commercial experience gained in an international standard hospitality business, preferably in the hotel sector

- strong numeracy skills, including both analytical and spreadsheet competency

- ability to produce relevant, incisive and informative reports

- knowledge of financial appraisal techniques, including familiarity with discounted cash flow and investment return appraisals

- sector experience involving analytical aspects of development, corporate finance or similar roles

- knowledge of and familiarity with industry specific operational controls and IT systems, and of Uniform System style financial reporting

- knowledge of real estate aspects, such as leases and rent terms, and of management contracts, franchises and similar arrangements

- a high standard of English – articulate in both written and spoken forms.

Appropriate tests to assess skills levels and psychometric analysis to support personality aspects can be expected when candidates are being selected. Demonstrating lateral thinking ability will score highly, as will determination and drive. Good personal presence or gravitas and being able to create a positive impression of professionalism and credibility will be important when selecting a senior financial manager, who will often have to represent the business unit as the most senior finance executive to external sources, such as directors, owner representatives, bankers, investors and the like.

Anyone with aspirations towards a career in finance in the hospitality sector would be well advised to explore all the avenues to entry at as early a stage as possible. Career advice can often be obtained by contact with recruitment consultants. Sources of unbiased advice for finance positions are accounting and financial management recruitment specialists. Some operating companies have development programmes for entry-level employees, but many rely on some prior directly relevant experience when hiring new staff. Students and graduates should ensure that their study and work programmes provide demonstrable evidence of relevant aptitude, skills and exposure to the function.

A key to future success in the role will depend on the ability to manage the basics of the function in the dynamic operating environment of the hospitality sector without losing the overall perspective of the longer-term profit and value building objectives of the business.

Appendix A

Job description for a hotel financial controller

Department	Finance & Accounting
Reports to	General Manager
Indirectly to	Corporate Finance Director
Subordinates	Accounts Department, IT Manager, Food & Beverage Cost Controller, Purchasing & Stores

Overall objectives

To be responsible for the hotel's accounting and financial management requirements. Managing the accounting department, procurement function and electronic data processing systems. To provide the general manager and unit management team with meaningful and timely information on the status of the hotel's performance. To assist proactively with cost containment, revenue enhancement, profit improvement opportunities and safeguarding of the company's assets.

Main duties

Records

To maintain proper and complete accounting records of the hotel. To ensure that the accounts, records and transactions of the hotel are accurate and correct at all times.

Safeguarding of assets

To implement all necessary controls to safeguard the assets of the hotel.

Financial reports

To prepare and interpret the financial statements and reports of the hotel.

Management information

To provide financial information to management as tools for maximizing profits and planning for the future. Reports which should stimulate management action.

Budgets and forecasts

To compile, together with the other executives, budgets and forecasts covering all activities of the hotel.
To compile treasury/cash flow forecasts for the business.

Controls and procedures

To ensure that the established controls and procedures in respect of the controller's areas of responsibility are being complied with at all times.

Electronic data processing systems

To ensure that the hotel's computer systems and their software are fully utilized, well safeguarded and properly maintained.
To implement future changes/additions to the electronic data processing systems of the hotel.

Cashiers

To ensure that there are, at all times, proper procedures and controls for the guest cashiers and other cashiers in the hotel, notwithstanding the fact that these areas are not the direct responsibility of the controller.
To ensure proper controls for F&B cashiers.

Purchasing, receiving and stores

To ensure that there are, at all times, proper procedures and controls for purchasing, receiving, stores and requisitioning.

Stocktakes

To ensure that physical inventories of all supplies are being taken on a monthly basis and of all operating equipment on a quarterly basis.

Credit and collection

To ensure that the hotel complies with the established credit and collection procedures, with particular attention to front office, group and meetings/banqueting processes.

Expenditures

To check and approve expenditures (via purchase requests, expenditure approval forms and purchase orders) in accordance with established procedures.

Payments

To approve and sign payments in accordance with established procedures.

Bank accounts

To ensure that bank account statements are checked on a daily basis.

To ensure that bank accounts are reconciled each month.

Income audit

To ensure that all revenue due to the hotel is properly accounted for and reconciled.

Receivables

To ensure that all receivables are collected within the hotel's credit periods.

Accounts payable

To ensure that payments are made for all goods and services on a timely basis.

To ensure that all payments are adequately supported by documentation, properly coded and properly authorized.

To ensure that suppliers' accounts are reconciled to the hotel's records on a regular basis.

Payroll

To ensure that payments are properly calculated, authorized and paid on a timely basis to employees.

To ensure returns, declarations and administration are properly handled concerning Inland Revenue, Pension Trustees and other relevant bodies.

To ensure that proper deductions are made at all times for PAYE, NI, pensions and other relevant items.

Inventories

To ensure that proper records are kept for all inventory items.

VAT

To ensure that payments and returns are made accurately and on a timely basis to Customs and Excise in respect of value added tax.

To ensure that compliance is continuous and that refunds are appropriately kept for inspection by external bodies.

General ledger

To ensure that all revenue and expenditure are properly recorded in the general ledger.

To ensure that all balances are reconciled on a regular basis.

General cashier

To ensure that disbursements made by the General Cashier are properly authorized and adequately supported by documentation.

To ensure that the float of the General Cashier is verified daily.

Contracts

To keep and safeguard the hotel's contracts and agreements.

Auditors

To liaise with internal and external auditors in compliance with the company's requirements.

Insurances

To assist in the renewal of insurances.
To administer insurance claims.

Corporation tax

To provide information required for the preparation of corporation tax computation.

Statutory accounts

To assist in the preparation of the year end statutory accounts.

Employee matters

To manage the staffing of the Accounting, Credit, Purchasing and Systems departments, liaising closely with the hotel's Personnel & Training Manager. Staffing management involves the selection, employment, supervision, transfer, review, promotion and dismissal (with due cause) of individuals within the above mentioned departments.

To implement appropriate training programmes in conjunction with the Personnel & Training Manager and to develop Departmental Trainers in these departments.

To maximize productivity and morale by setting goals, providing clear guidelines and by developing team spirit. To assist in other accounting and financial matters as and when required.

Finance director

The following require the approval of the finance director:

Purchase orders over [£5000]
Expenditures (including capital expenditures) not within budget [£500 excess and over]
Payments exceeding [£10 000]
Rebates and write offs over [£500]
Changes to established policies, controls and procedures.

The following areas will remain the responsibility of the corporate finance director

Banks, borrowings and loans
Insurance renewals
Property taxes
Licences
Rental of space
Auditors (external and internal)
Pensions
Corporation tax
Company secretarial matters
Communications with owning company
Communications with sister company.

Appendix B

Professional accounting qualifications

Association of Accounting Technicians www.aat.co.uk

No previous qualifications required. Foundation, intermediate and technician level stages – each of which is certified and represents a qualification in its own right. Involves skill tests and exams. Studies can be undertaken on a full or part-time basis, and at the candidate's own pace.

Some of the advantages of choosing the AAT course include:

- easier entry requirements
- can be undertaken while working
- flexible studying with elements that can be directly related to work experience
- a formal qualification which can also be used to gain exemptions from significant elements of the requirements for the senior institutes
- often supported by the employer in terms of study time and financial subsidy.

Chartered Institute of Management Accountants www.cimaglobal.com

Entry generally requires a higher level of education achievements and exemptions from various levels are available to graduates, AAT members, Open University Accounting Certificate holders and certain other professional qualifications (e.g. BAHA).

The full membership qualification involves exams covering managerial, strategic levels and the test of professional competence in management accounting – a total of 10 exams, each of 3 hours. These must be underpinned by evidence of at least three years of relevant work experience.

The studies are generally undertaken on a full or part-time basis and the whole course can be undertaken while working. Employers often provide study time and financial support. The timescale is flexible and around three years of work and study would be a norm for completion.

Chartered Association of Certified Accountants
www.accaglobal.com

As with the other associations, there is a range of available certificates and intermediate qualifications but, for the Chartered Certified Accountant level, there are initial age and educational level requirements. The latter are similar to those of CIMA.

The full qualification involves a range of exams split into three parts and with up to 14 papers to be completed. At least three years of supervised, relevant work experience is also a requirement. The timescale for completion is flexible within 10 years of registering as a student and three to four years would be a norm. The ACCA qualification is sometimes used for those who wish to follow a public practice career route, which requires a period in a professional firm to achieve certification.

Chartered Accountant www.icaew.co.uk

(The Institute of Chartered Accountants in England & Wales (ICAEW) covers only England & Wales. Scotland and Ireland have their own institutes, with similar standards)

Training for the Associate Chartered Accountant (ACA) qualification can start with A levels, but generally requires any degree. Other professional accounting qualifications (e.g. AAT) can give exemptions and reduce the time needed to qualify.

A training contract is an essential part of ACA work experience requirements. This will be for a minimum of three years and not more than five years. A contract is commonly provided by professional firms, although there are provisions for other types of employer to provide recognized contracts.

Exams are in two stages, professional and advanced. They are designed to test ability to perform as a professional rather than to show how well facts have been learned. They are considered to be the toughest professional exams. Employers are responsible for establishing with the students a programme which balances the work experience with the need for studying and exams.

While ACA is often considered to be the senior of the professional accounting qualifications, it is also one where students may have little or no commercial experience while studying. This can result in some positions in the hospitality industry being difficult or impossible to secure for those who have no prior exposure to the sector. On the other hand, some employers give preference to ACA qualified accountants who then have to deal with the steep learning curve of both entering a commercial environment and the peculiarities of the twenty-four hour, seven-day week service sector.

Hospitality Accountant www.baha-uk.org

The British Association of Hospitality Accountants (BAHA) has an educational programme which is aimed at providing career development for trainees and further development for more experienced managers within the sector.

The BAHA Education & Training Programme is a unique course specifically aimed at developing assistant/financial controllers who wish to further their careers within the hospitality industry. Delivered by the University of Bournemouth, it is designed to enable students to work full time while they study, using a range of resources both on-line and textbook based. Course assessments focus significantly on solving work-based problems. This means the learner has the opportunity to make a real difference in the workplace, dealing with issues relevant to the business. This approach has been well received by employers, many of whom use the course as part of the ongoing development of their finance specialists.

Benefits of the BAHA Education and Training Programme include:

- extensive course materials written by experienced educators specifically to match the needs of hospitality industry finance specialists

- students in the UK and abroad have access to tutor support via e-mail or telephone

- access is available to students to a range of full text management and accounting journals through the university's on-line library services

- successful completion of the course awards Associate membership status of BAHA and eligibility to use the designated letters ABHA (cert)

- outstanding students at each stage are honoured by BAHA

- successful students are awarded exemptions from certain CIMA Foundation level exams.

BAHA's Professional Education Programme (Sharing Excellence in Hospitality Finance) is a course designed for financial controllers and assistants, auditors, consultants, research analysts and senior hospitality managers. It is open to all Associates of BAHA or those eligible for the Associate membership status. Successful completion of the course provides CPD points leading to Fellowship status of BAHA membership and the course can also be used to build CPD points for other professional accounting bodies.

The programme comprises short group workshop sessions held in different UK locations, supported by secure access to a dedicated on-line community with interactive resources, tutors and case studies hosted by arena4finance ltd. Each workshop is focused on a specific theme brought to life by a variety of relevant experienced speakers, facilitators and educationalists. They comprise sessions of presentations, case study activities and project work. Participants are expected to complete a project, with tutor support, based on the needs of the businesses, which will provide direct benefit to employers.

Index